Disfellowshiped

Princeton Theological Monograph Series

K. C. Hanson, Charles M. Collier, D. Christopher Spinks,
and Robin Parry, Series Editors

Recent volumes in the series:

Lisa E. Dahill
*Reading from the Underside of Selfhood:
Bonhoeffer and Spiritual Formation*

Paul Ingram, editor
Constructing a Relational Cosmology

Chris Budden
*Following Jesus in Invaded Space:
Doing Theology on Aboriginal Land*

Philip Ruge-Jones
Cross in Tensions

Christian T. Collins Winn
*"Jesus Is Victor":
The Significance of the Blumhardts for the Theology of Karl Barth*

Charles Bellinger
*The Trinitarian Self:
The Key to the Puzzle of Violence*

Mary Clark Moschella
*Living Devotions:
Reflections on Immigration, Identity, and Religious Imagination*

Caryn D. Riswold
*Coram Deo:
Human Life in the Vision of God*

Guttesen, Poul F.
*Leaning into the Future:
The Kingdom of God in the Theology of Jürgen Moltmann
and the Book of Revelation*

Disfellowshiped

*Pentecostal Responses to Fundamentalism
in the United States, 1906–1943*

GERALD W. KING

With a Foreword by Allan H. Anderson

☙PICKWICK *Publications* · Eugene, Oregon

DISFELLOWSHIPED
Pentecostal Responses to Fundamentalism in the United States, 1906–1943

Princeton Theological Monograph Series 164

Copyright © 2011 Gerald W. King. All rights reserved. Except for brief quotations in critical publications or reviews, no part of this book may be reproduced in any manner without prior written permission from the publisher. Write: Permissions, Wipf and Stock Publishers, 199 W. 8th Ave., Suite 3, Eugene, OR 97401.

Pickwick Publications
A Division of Wipf and Stock Publishers
199 W. 8th Ave., Suite 3
Eugene, OR 97401

www.wipfandstock.com

Permission has been granted to reprint portions of the following articles:

Gerald W. King, "Evolving Paradigms: Creationism as Pentecostal Variation on a Fundamentalist Theme." In *The Spirit Renews the Face of the Earth: Pentecostal Forays in Science and Theology of Creation*, edited by Amos Yong, 93–114. Eugene, OR: Wipf & Stock, 2009.

Gerald W. King, "Mae Eleanor Frey: Pentecostal Evangelist and Novelist." *Assemblies of God Heritage* 29 (2009) 57–62. Permission granted by Gospel Publishing House.

Gerald W. King, "Streams of Convergence: The Pentecostal-Fundamentalist Response to Modernism." *PentecoStudies* 7 (Autumn 2008) 64–84. Permission granted by Equinox Publishing Ltd., 2008.

ISBN 13: 978-1-60899-255-3

Cataloging-in-Publication data:

King, Gerald W.

    Disfellowshiped : Pentecostal responses to Fundamentalism in the United States, 1906–1943 / Gerald W. King ; with a foreword by Allan H. Anderson.

    Princeton Theological Monograph Series 164

    xviii + 262 p. ; 23 cm. Includes bibliographical references and index.

    ISBN 13: 978-1-60899-255-3

    1. Pentecostalism—United States—History. 2. Fundamentalism—United States. 3. Protestantism—United States. I. Title. II. Series.

BR1644.5 K38 2011

Manufactured in the U.S.A.

For Jim

In Memoriam
November 22, 1964—May 4, 2008

A friend sticks closer than a brother; you were both.

Contents

Foreword by Allan H. Anderson • *ix*
Acknowledgments • *xiii*
List of Abbreviations • *xv*

PART ONE: Introduction

1. Defining the Study • 3
2. Historical Background • 19

PART TWO: Genesis

3. Emerging Pentecostalism (1906–1909) • 37

PART THREE: Adaptation

4. Forming Denominations (1910–1919) • 65
5. Emerging Fundamentalism (1920–1924) • 94

PART FOUR: Retention

6. Battling One Another (1925–1929) • 125
7. Adopting a Fundamentalist Rhetoric (1930–1934) • 151
8. Battling a Common Foe (1935–1943) • 177

PART FIVE: Conclusion

9. Conclusion • 207

Appendix A: Articles by A. J. Gordon • 221

Appendix B: Bibliography of Anti-Pentecostal Articles in Holiness Periodicals • 222

Appendix C: Book Advertisements in the *Christian Evangel* in 1915 • 224

Appendix D: Book Advertisements in the *Pentecostal Evangel* in 1920 • 225

Appendix E: A. C. Gaebelein's Anti-Pentecostal and Anti-Healing Articles from *Our Hope* • 228

Appendix F: D. M. Panton's Articles in *Pentecostal Evangel* from 1920–1925 • 230

Appendix G: Book Advertisements in the *Pentecostal Evangel* in 1925 • 231

Contents

    Appendix H: Sermons of J. N. Hoover • 236

    Appendix I: Cartoon from *Pentecostal Evangel* (15 May 1937) • 239

    Appendix J: Cartoon from *Pentecostal Evangel* (8 June 1940) • 240

    Appendix K: Cartoon from *Pentecostal Evangel* (14 August 1937) • 241

    Bibliography • 243

    Index • 253

Foreword

IN THIS STUDY GERALD KING DISCUSSES THE COMPLEX RELATIONSHIP BETWEEN "Fundamentalists" (narrowly defined as those who ascribed to the "Fundamentals" published in reaction to liberal Protestant theology in the U.S.A.) and Pentecostals, and taken from the perspective of the Pentecostals. It is my great pleasure to write a foreword to this significant and fascinating study, one that I have spent many hours reading and discussing with the author while he was doing doctoral research under my supervision at the University of Birmingham. Of course, this is primarily an American historical study, in which the author makes use of an abundance of primary texts in exploring the first four decades of Pentecostalism and its interaction with the Fundamentalists. It is a remarkable study in its breadth and depth, for no stone has been left unturned in its honest appraisal of the historical facts. Some American Pentecostal scholars may feel a tad uncomfortable with its findings, particularly as its main conclusion is that fundamentalism has always been closer to Pentecostalism than is often portrayed in academic literature, and that often Pentecostals and Fundamentalists have been singing from the same hymn sheet, especially when it comes to issues considered essential to their common conservative evangelical faith and in opposition to the liberal Protestantism of the time. As Gerald King shows here, the primary means through which fundamentalism affected Pentecostalism was premillennialism.

But there is also a tension portrayed here, which has been described in the literature in various ways. Pentecostalism throughout the world has absorbed various areas of its cultural context, sometimes with most undesirable results. Often Pentecostals are branded as "fundamentalist" and the "religious right," but this identification with fundamentalism does not always assist us to understand Pentecostalism or place it within its historical context. Harvey Cox's sympathetic yet critical study of Pentecostalism shows some of the traps into which Pentecostalism has fallen, but as this book shows, the perceived dichotomy between Pentecostalism and fundamentalism is more imagined than real. Cox sees Pentecostalism as the fulfilment of the human longing for a direct experience of God and so Pentecostals should not to be preoccupied with what he calls "abstract religious ideas," which is the preoccupation of fundamentalism. He thinks that Pentecostals are (or should be) quite unlike fundamentalists, who are "text-oriented believers." Thus Pentecostal experience is contrasted over against a dogmatic rationalism that thinks it has solutions or biblical texts for every problem. In actual fact, as this study shows, Pentecostals have also been "text-oriented," taking scripture even more literally, though their hermeneutical approach to the text is often quite different in orientation. Cox contrasts the otherworldliness of early Pentecostals with the this-worldliness of modern Pentecostals particularly manifested in the "prosperity gospel." The early rebellion against creeds has given way to

Foreword

dogmatism, and the "techniques of raptures" have replaced the original message of "signs and wonders" as a portent of the coming kingdom of God. He shows the changes from pacifists to "super-patriots" and from a race- and gender-inclusive fellowship to white male-dominated denominationalism, and suggests that Pentecostals might be facing a dilemma they may not be able to solve without betraying their origins.[1]

Some Pentecostal scholars have discussed the relationship between Pentecostalism and fundamentalism and like Cox, mostly accentuate the differences. But these are based on more recent events than this study focuses on. Russell Spittler shows how journalists used the terms "evangelical," "fundamentalist," "charismatic," and "Pentecostal" interchangeably when reporting on the television scandals of 1987–1993.[2] This confusion also affected theological assessments of Pentecostalism. British theologian Martyn Percy, for example, considered the late Vineyard leader John Wimber a "pre-eminent contemporary fundamentalist in the 'revivalist tradition,'" and thinks that Wimber's appeal to "power" to authenticate his message was characteristic of this tradition. Percy's analysis seems to lack an appreciation of the difference between experiential Christianity (the Charismatic emphasis) and the more rational, reactionary Fundamentalism from which it can be distinguished.[3] King's analysis here also shows the interaction between the two in the early history, but that the distinction has to be more carefully nuanced. Spittler observes that fundamentalism was an intellectual, apologetic, "argumentative, logical, rational" reaction while in contrast, Pentecostalism "profoundly distrusted the intellectual enterprise" and focussed on reacting against "withered piety," "collapsed feeling" and "the decay of devotion." Instead of arguing about creeds, Pentecostals give testimonies of their experiences.

As King shows in this study, the nadir of this relationship was reached in 1928 when Fundamentalists condemned Pentecostalism in resolutions by the World's Christian Fundamentals Association stating that the "tongues movement" was "a menace in many churches and a real injury to the sure testimony of Fundamentalist Christians." Because of this, they were "unreservedly opposed to Modern Pentecostalism, including the speaking in unknown tongues, and the fanatical healing known as general healing in the atonement, and the perpetuation of the miraculous sign-healing of Jesus and His disciples."[4] This was clearly and unambiguously anti-Pentecostal, even if it was not unanimous, and from this came the feeling that Pentecostals had been *Disfellowshiped*. Nevertheless, because many of the early American Pentecostals came from churches that later became Fundamentalist, Pentecostalism was profoundly influenced by Fundamentalism. Their reaction to their disfellowshiping was to aver that they were true fundamentalists. This is the particular contribution to scholarship of King's study. Pentecostalism predated Fundamentalism and although different from it, this difference is not as clear as some would hope. Pentecostals were as opposed to theological liberalism as the Fundamentalists were. But Fundamentalism was one of Pentecostalism's harshest critics. In a presidential address to the Society for Pentecostal Studies in 1992, the Episcopalian scholar and historian

1. Cox, *Fire from Heaven*, 5, 15–17.
2. Spittler, "Are Pentecostals Fundamentalists?," 103.
3. Percy, *Words, Wonders and Power*, 13; Spittler, "Are Pentecostals Fundamentalists," 107.
4. Cited in Spittler, "Are Pentecostals Fundamentalists," 108–9.

Foreword

William Faupel pointed out that the early Pentecostal critique was directed at the "emerging fundamentalism." Subsequent American Pentecostal history was to reverse this early critique and through the creation of Pentecostal Bible colleges Fundamentalism began to shape the movement, another aspect of King's study. Faupel prefers to see Pentecostalism as something completely different, and writes that seeing Pentecostalism as a "subgroup of Evangelicalism" was a major concern that would result in the movement becoming "increasingly rationalistic and sterile," more concerned about correct belief than about a deepening relationship with God, and silencing the voices of women.[5]

Harvey Cox points out that although fundamentalists claim to be faithful to the traditions of the past, they are in fact "all modern by-products of the religious crisis of the twentieth century." He writes that fundamentalism leads to inevitable conflict, but that experientialism takes many forms "unified by a common effort to restore 'experience' . . . as the key dimension of faith." He thinks that the struggle between fundamentalists and experientialists is being played out in Pentecostalism.[6] This book is an account of that struggle, and I commend it to you for your serious attention. We will be indebted to its author for this accurate and comprehensive account that explains the relationship so often misunderstood.

Allan Anderson
University of Birmingham, England

---

5. Faupel, "Whither Pentecostalism?" 21, 24, 26–27.
6. Cox, *Fire from Heaven,* 71, 299–300, 302–6, 309–11, 313, 315–17, 320.

Acknowledgments

First and foremost, I want to thank my parents, Jim and Joyce, for their love and support throughout this project. From them I collectively gain my interest in faith and history, and all the benefits of lives well lived.

Second, I wish to thank my supervisor, Prof. Allan Anderson, and my advisor, Dr. Mark Cartledge. Allan has been a great encourager from the beginning stages and helped me avoid pitfalls along the way. Mark has been a wonderful sounding board and has directed me to works that have enriched my study. Nor can I fail to mention their spouses, Olwyn Anderson and Joan Cartledge, for encouragement, friendship, food, and tea.

Third, I wish to thank the Panacea Society in Bedford, England, for their generous grant which helped make this research possible.

Fourth, I would be remiss if I did not mention the friendly staff at the Orchard Learning Resource Center in Selly Oak and the University of Birmingham main library and Special Collections staff on the Edgbaston campus.

Fifth, I have numerous thanks to various archives around the U.S. At the top of the list is the Flower Pentecostal Heritage Center in Springfield, Missouri, whose resources and staff were always helpful. Especially, I'd like to thank Darrin Rodgers for his generous hospitality and taking me on a bookstore tour of Springfield. Glenn Gohr has been an invaluable resource through his detailed knowledge of AG history and by his eagerness to answer my inquiries as they surfaced. Joyce Lee, Sharon Rasnake, and the entire staff were unflappable in their willingness to locate materials and offer assistance if a look of puzzlement even registered on my face.

The staff at Asbury Theological Seminary in Wilmore, Kentucky made my nine-month stay there in 2007 enjoyable and productive. Grace Yoder and her student helpers Tom and Carolyn, who helped sift through materials in the archives, not to mention the library staff. Dorothy James amazed me with her ability at tracking down obscure articles and deserves encomium. The academic and housing staff were very accommodating in providing space to study and sleep, and for that I thank Dr. Bill Arnold, Sandy Martin, Korrie Harper, and Sherry Peyton.

I spent three weeks at the Crowell Library of Moody Bible Institute in Chicago, Illinois, so I have to thank my brother Bill for hosting me and Joe Cataio, Marian Shaw, Roger Van Olsen, and the staff for access to volumes of periodicals, catalogues, and collections of interesting and valuable materials.

Dr. David Roebuck and staff at the Dixon Pentecostal Research Center at Lee University in Cleveland, Tennessee, allowed me access to archive material and reams of microfilm during my stay there. David was ever gracious, as was his assistant, Amy

Acknowledgments

Fletcher, and were not even visibly upset when the microfilm snapped under my care. I'm relieved, and probably they are too, that these materials can now be had on CD-ROM.

For other archives on shorter visits I wish to thank Dora Wagner at Northwestern College in St. Paul, Minnesota, and Wayne Weber at the Billy Graham Center in Wheaton, Illinois, for their assistance in locating materials at their respective institutions. I must also mention Jessica Steytler at the Congregational Library, Boston, Massachusetts, for help in finding Dr. Blosser's obscure pamphlet, and Dr. Lynn Anderson, archivist at Central Bible College in Springfield, Missouri, for access to the collection in the Pearlman Memorial Library.

Sixth, I wish to express thanks to my fellow sojourners at the Centre for Pentecostal and Charismatic Research at the University of Birmingham, too numerous to mention by name without risk of leaving some off.

Last, and far from least, I wish to thank "the church on birch," Celebration Community Church in Denver, Colorado, for their continuous encouragement by incarnating Christ's love in tangible ways. Dale and Mickey Howard have been constant e-mail companions over the years. Others deserving special mention have helped in various ways with encouragement and prayers: Steve and Bonnie Garcia, Russ and Leslie Powell, Brad and Marcie Cornish, John and Karen Schultz, Dan and Karen Hoglund, Jay and Teri Randall, and Bruce and Linda Johnson. To list everyone at the church who have shared their lives is impossible without adding more pages, so I can only add an et al. for everyone else. You are in my heart always.

GWK
Grand Forks, North Dakota

Abbreviations

Archives

ATS Arch	Fisher Library, Asbury Theological Seminary—Wilmore, KY
BGC	Billy Graham Center—Wheaton, IL
Carter-ATS	Steven Carter Collection—Asbury Theological Seminary
CBC Arch	Pearlman Memorial Library, Central Bible College—Springfield, MO
DPRC	Dixon Pentecostal Research Center—Cleveland, TN
FPHC	Flower Pentecostal Heritage Center—Springfield, MO
MBI Arch	Crowell Library, Moody Bible Institute—Chicago, IL
NWC Arch	Bernsten Library, Northwestern College—St. Paul, MN

Books and Bibles

FSRB	*Scofield Reference Bible* ("first" edition—1909)
OSRB	*Scofield Reference Bible* ("old" revised edition—1917)
DPCM	*Dictionary of Pentecostal and Charismatic Movements*, edited by Stanley M. Burgess and Gary B. McGee. Grand Rapids: Zondervan, 1988
JPTSup	Journal of Pentecostal Theology Supplement

Bible Schools

Biola	Bible Institute of Los Angeles, Los Angeles, CA
CBI	Central Bible Institute, Springfield, MO
MBI	Moody Bible Institute, Chicago, IL

Organizations

ACCC	American Council of Christian Churches
AG	Assemblies of God
BBU	Bible Baptist Union

Abbreviations

CIM	China Inland Mission
CG	Church of God (Cleveland, TN)
CMA	Christian and Missionary Alliance
COGIC	Church of God in Christ
FCC	Federal Council of Churches
FFH	First Fruit Harvesters
GPH	Gospel Publishing House
IHA	Iowa Holiness Association
IPC	International Prophecy Conference
ISSL	International Sunday School Lessons
NAE	National Association of Evangelicals
NBC	Northern Baptist Convention
PHC	Pentecostal Holiness Church
VBS	Vacation Bible School
WCFA	World's Christian Fundamentals Association
YMCA	Young Men's Christian Association

Periodicals

AF(LA)	*The Apostolic Faith*	(P*—Los Angeles, CA—Seymour)
BC	*Bridal Call*	(P—Los Angeles, CA—McPherson)
BM	*The Bridegroom's Messenger*	(P—Atlanta, GA—Sexton)
CAH	*The Christ's Ambassadors Herald*	(P—Springfield, MO—AG)
CE	*The Christian Evangel*	(P—Plainfield, IN—Myland)
CFSC	*Christian Fundamentals in School and Church*	(F—Minneapolis, MN—Riley)
Church	*The Churchman*	(M—New York, NY—Episcopal)
COGE	*Church of God Evangel*	(P—Cleveland, TN—CG)
Conf	*Confidence*	(P—Sunderland, UK—Boddy)
CWM	*The Christian Worker's Magazine*	(F—Chicago, IL—MBI)
Dawn	*The Dawn*	(F—UK—Panton)
EF	*Exploits of Faith*	(P—Bosworth)

* F – Fundamentalist   H – Holiness   M – Modernist   P - Pentecostal

Abbreviations

ELCOGE	The Evening Light and Church of God Evangel	(P—Cleveland, TN—CG)
FS	The Faithful Standard	(P—Cleveland, TN—CG)
Fund	The Fundamentalist	(F—Fort Worth, TX; Detroit, MI—Norris)
GGl	Gospel Gleaners	(P—Springfield, MO—AG)
GGr	Golden Grain	(P—Price)
GN	Good News	(F—Chicago, IL—Moody Church)
GR	God's Revivalist	(H—Cincinnati, OH—Knapp)
GTH	Glad Tidings Herald	(P—New York, NY—Brown)
Hope	Our Hope	(F—New York, NY—Gaebelein)
IM	Intercessory Missionary	(P—Fort Wayne, IN—Street)
IT	The Institute Tie	(F—Chicago, IL—MBI)
KB	The King's Business	(F—Los Angeles, CA—Biola)
LF	Life of Faith	(F—London, UK—Hopkins)
LP	The Lighted Pathway	(P—Cleveland, TN—CG)
LRE	Latter Rain Evangel	(P—Chicago, IL—Piper, Reiff)
MBIM	Moody Bible Institute Monthly	(F—Chicago, IL—MBI)
MC	Midnight Cry	(P—New York, NY—Brown)
MRW	Missionary Review of the World	(F—Gordon, Pierson)
NW Pilot	Northwestern Pilot	(F—Minneapolis, MN—Riley)
PE	The Pentecostal Evangel	(P—Springfield, MO—AG)
Pent	The Pentecost	(P—Indianapolis, IN; Kansas City, MO—Flower, Copley)
Petals	Petals from the Rose of Sharon	(P—Utley)
PH	Pentecostal Herald	(H—Louisville and Wilmore, KY—Morrison)
PT	Pentecostal Testimony	(P—Chicago, IL—Durham)
RCW	Record of Christian Work	(F/M—Northfield, MA—Moody)
Rev	Revelation	(F—Philadelphia, PA—Barnhouse)
SC	School and Church	(F—Minneapolis, MN—Riley)
Search	The Searchlight	(F—Fort Worth, TX—Norris)
Shiloh	The Shiloh Scroll	(P—Zion, IL—Dake)
SST	Sunday School Times	(F—Philadelphia, PA—Trumbull)
TF	Triumphs of Faith	(H/P—Buffalo, NY; Oakland, CA—Montgomery)
TRev	The Revivalist	(H—Cincinnati, OH—Knapp)
Way	The Way	(H—Cleveland, TN—CG)

Abbreviations

WE	*The Weekly Evangel*	(P—St. Louis and Springfield, MO—AG)
WF	*Way of Faith*	(H—Columbia, SC—Pike)
W&Wk	*Word and Work*	(P—Framingham, MA—Otis)
W&Wt	*Word and Witness*	(P—Malvern, AR—Bell)

PART ONE

Introduction

1

Defining the Study

Introduction to the Study

IN HIS INTRODUCTORY REMARKS TO HIS NOW CLASSIC STUDY ON PENTECOSTALISM, *VISION of the Disinherited* (1977), social historian Robert Mapes Anderson commented that an analysis of fundamentalism from a pentecostal perspective had been absent but necessary. "When this is done," the author predicted, "the inadequacies of existing historical interpretations of fundamentalism will be readily apparent."[1] As an example, Anderson believed that the perception of fundamentalism as a political entity would be discarded when such an analysis took place. Thirty years on and a detailed description of the relationship between pentecostalism and fundamentalism has yet to be carried out. This study is an attempt to fill that gap. There is much more that needs to be done, and whether inadequacies "will be readily apparent" in politics or any other area remains to be seen.

What is apparent is that the nature of this relationship has been poorly understood and poorly explicated. It is as though the two movements have looked at each other from across a great chasm and found little in common. Is pentecostalism a branch of fundamentalism, or is it a separate expression with its own unique contribution to Christianity? To the first view belongs Anderson himself, although he does subsume pentecostalism under fundamentalism from a distance, likening the relationship to that of the Quakers to Puritanism.[2] The second belongs to D. William Faupel, who juxtaposes the two movements, setting modernism alongside pentecostalism as equally reactionary forces against fundamentalism.[3] Did pentecostals adopt fundamentalist positions and institutions uncritically as Edith Blumhofer hints, or did they develop their positions and institutions independent of the fundamentalist network as Douglas Jacobsen has challenged?[4] In short,

---

1. Anderson, *Vision*, 5.

2. Ibid., 6. This view was endorsed by Marsden, *American Culture*, 256 n. 8, and tacitly endorsed by Bebbington, *Evangelicalism in Modern Britain*, 198.

3. Faupel, "Whither Pentecostalism?" 3–27; see p. 26. Faupel asserts that there are two competing visions for understanding pentecostalism's relationship to the broader evangelical movement. One sees it as a subgroup of evangelicalism and the other as a distinct movement in its own right apart from evangelicalism. Faupel urges the latter while this author opts for the former..

4. See Blumhofer, *Restoring*, 150, and Jacobsen, *Thinking*, 105–6 n. 7. Blumhofer cites Central Bible Institute of the Assemblies of God, founded in 1922, as one school influenced by fundamentalism. As Jacobsen points out, Blumhofer adopts Brereton's assumptions in *Training God's Army* (p. 13), but adds, "Even if this is the case,

were pentecostals "fundamentalists with a difference," or were they just different?[5] The answer to these and related questions await our attention.

Defining a Framework

In reviewing the literature pertaining to the definitions for our two movements, one comes across words like "difficult" and "complex" with enough frequency to cause some trepidation. "Terms lead to generalisations and are therefore often misleading," pentecostal scholar Allan Anderson reminds us.[6] Yet, if we are to make any headway, we must gain some governance over the terminology involved. As Martin Marty cautions, "Historians, reluctant as they are . . . to begin accounts with too many definitions, usually prefer to let fences grow around concepts in the course of a narrative. Yet terms have to be used with some sense of propriety."[7] Thus, with some sense of propriety and much of trepidation, I shall state at the outset that the controlling motif behind this thesis is that of *movement*. And therein lies the problem. By definition, movements *move*, and so do their definitions. Whatever else may be relayed about any movement's characteristics, it must be remembered that they are dynamic and fluid, whose direction can change and whose boundaries are porous and flexible.

In this regard, I find helpful Robert Wuthnow and Matthew Lawson's application of field studies in population ecology to fundamentalism. The authors utilize three stages of species development in a given ecological context and relate this to religious movements: 1) *production*, where movements come into being and thus enlarge the options of various faith systems, 2) *selection*, where movements adapt to the existing religious environment and seek out a distinct niche, and 3) *retention*, where movements gain control of their resources and thus become stabilized organizations.[8] Additionally, as with biological species, such movements "are always in competition with other movements . . . attempting to make claims on individuals' time and energy."[9] In other words, they conflict with other aggregates for available resources in order to survive and expand. In ecology, it is the species that are most *alike* who struggle against one another to gain supremacy over their environment. Because these species share similar requirements for survival, they battle for whatever meager food sources may be available in order to gain dominance. Those species who feed off other resources are not in direct competition with the new species and therefore have little cause for jealousy. In the religious arena, this model helps explain the initial hostility of holiness and fundamentalist leaders to pentecostals, who were most threatened by their

---

there is no reason to assume that the borrowing of an educational form from fundamentalism demanded a similar and uncritical borrowing of fundamentalist theological ideas." Even so, the fundamentalist impulse was strongly felt in the AG from the founding of CBI.

5. Blumhofer, *Restoring*, 5. I do agree with Blumhofer in that pentecostals assumed they were fundamentalists at heart, but it is important to keep in mind that they did not start off so. See also Blumhofer, *Assemblies of God*, 2:15.

6. Anderson, *Zion and Pentecost*, 9.

7. Marty, *Behavers*, 40.

8. Wuthnow and Lawson, "Sources of Christian Fundamentalism," 18–56.

9. Ibid., 35.

existence. My one addendum is that movements are not always as combative as Wuthnow and Lawson suggests because they may also engage in organic symbiosis.[10] Sociologist David Moberg indicates that external conflict can drive adversaries together as happened in the 1920s between fundamentalists and movie theatres to promote prohibition.[11] In short, under the right conditions, movements, like organisms, can survive their environments better in cooperation than in isolation.

This ecological model will also provide the framework from which we will proceed. Implementing the three stages of dynamic growth as historical development, the thesis will be divided into three eras accordingly. The first is designated *genesis*, corresponding to the "production" period above. This initial stage is necessarily short, covering the years 1906–1909 in our study. It is here that pentecostalism emerged from the holiness movement. The second I have labeled *adaptation*, corresponding to "selection." Here religious movements adapt to their given cultural environment. This period witnessed the formation of pentecostal denominations as internal disputes erupted from 1910–1919, and an adjustment to the emerging fundamentalist network from 1920–1924. For the third I have kept Wuthnow and Lawson's term *retention*. As movements mature, retaining the loyalties of succeeding generations becomes paramount. One facet of this program is the Sunday school, which, while ever important at the local level, attains criticality at the national level. In our study, this development took place primarily from 1925–1940.

Methodology and Limitations

While it is recognized that movements, whether religious, cultural or otherwise, do not fit neatly into the time frame historians often assign them, yet such strictures are welcomed in order to place them within their historical context. Undoubtedly considerable overlap exists whenever one period transitions into another. Within the overall expanse of the thesis one question will supersede all others: why did two groups seemingly at odds with one another from the outset in 1906 join forces in 1943 in an umbrella organization, viz. the National Association of Evangelicals (NAE)? Towards this end, I will examine the rift between them and how they reacted to one another. Tracing the influence of fundamentalism upon pentecostalism and the resultant shift in theology will be worthy of interest. I will demonstrate that the two movements were really much closer in temperament than is often given credence. Their underpinning through a common evangelical heritage lay at the heart of their cooperative effort.

I will argue that the process of "leavening" in pentecostalism from holiness to fundamentalist thought transpired through three stages, which I call here the "vocabulary" of fundamentalism, the "content" of fundamentalism, and the "rhetoric" of fundamentalism; and that these stages correspond roughly to the 1910s, the 1920s, and the 1930s respectively. By "vocabulary" I mean that pentecostals adopted the terminology used by fundamentalists without necessarily agreeing with the concepts associated with those terms. By

---

10. Haught has made a similar point, stressing that many scientists now view evolutionary processes as both cooperative and competitive (*God after Darwin*, 45).

11. Moberg, *Social Institution*, 242.

"content" I mean that pentecostals adopted those concepts as part of their own worldview, particularly when it came to eschatological matters. By "rhetoric" I mean that pentecostals adopted the arguments of fundamentalism and its battle against modernism to such an extent that fundamentalist issues became pentecostal ones as well.

This study applies a historical approach to the movements concerned, relying chiefly on an analysis of primary source materials. It is this author's conviction that the changing patterns in the life of a religious movement are best exemplified in its periodicals. A potential danger to this approach is that editors exercise great control over the selection of material, which may reflect their peculiar bias rather than that of the organization. Therefore, books, church records, and personal correspondence will also be consulted. This study will also engage past and current research upon the groups in question for additional insight. From the fundamentalist side I have relied upon tracts written against pentecostalism and on various magazines from the era. As my focus is on the NAE, the pentecostal side will be represented by the two largest participants in its formation, the Assemblies of God and the Church of God (Cleveland, Tennessee).

The scope of this study will be limited phenomenologically to the movements commonly known as fundamentalism and pentecostalism, geographically to the United States, and temporally from 1906 to 1943. British adherents will be introduced only in so far as they interact with the American scene. I will largely ignore the holiness movement's reaction to pentecostalism, except at the initial stage. The fundamentalists will be limited to those who have been labeled by historians as protofundamentalists associated with the prophecy conferences of the late nineteenth and early twentieth centuries, and to those who identified themselves with the more formal fundamentalist network that emerged after World War I. Due to its theological proximity to the fundamentalist cause, pentecostalism will be largely confined to the white, "Reformed" or "Keswick" branch represented by the Assemblies of God (AG). The Church of God (CG), which had greater antecedents in the Wesleyan tradition, consequently had less to say about fundamentalism—particularly in the 1920s—and thus offers a perspective which will help avoid gross generalization. To gain some coherence of the terms, we will now explore some definitions of the movements involved in this study.

Pentecostalism

Pentecostal theologian Simon Chan warns us that a consensus definition of "pentecostalism" is unlikely to appear soon. Meanwhile, scholars will need to construct their own "working definition" to guide their respective studies.[12] Arriving at such a definition is "complex" according to German researcher Michael Bergunder and deemed "untenable" by the Swiss doyen Walter Hollenweger.[13] The need has become even more acute in the past three decades as academia has transferred focus on pentecostalism as a predominantly North American entity to a diffuse, worldwide phenomenon. And even its primacy within the Western world in the early years has been questioned by a number of more

---

12. Chan, "Whither Pentecostalism?" 576.
13. Bergunder, "Constructing Indian Pentecostalism," 177; Hollenweger, *Pentecostalism*, 327.

recent academicians such as Allan Anderson, who contends that pentecostalism had more than one center of origin, such as the revival at Pune, India in 1905–1906, which in turn spurred a pentecostal revival in Chile, and an independent revival in Pyongyang, Korea, in 1907.[14]

However, granting the limits of this study to the North American continent and to the first half of the twentieth century, we may safely focus on what is now known as "classical" pentecostalism with its stress upon *glossolalia* or speaking in tongues as the "initial physical evidence" of Spirit-baptism. This emphasis has long been recognized as the distinguishing mark of the pentecostal movement, particularly from those inside.[15] But even in its incipient days this was not uniformly agreed upon. As Douglas Jacobsen observes, "the question of precisely who was and who was not a pentecostal Christian was at least as difficult to answer in the early years of the twentieth century as it is today."[16] With this in mind, I add four caveats before arriving at a definition.

First, the possibility that other charismata could evidence Spirit-baptism just as well as tongues was contested by both groups and individuals. Most notable among these was F. F. Bosworth, who raised the topic at a pastors' conference of the Assemblies of God in 1918.[17] The matter never came to a vote, and Bosworth graciously withdrew from the fellowship rather than create a row, though he did articulate his position in a pamphlet entitled *Do all Speak with Tongues?*[18] Dissenting groups such as Elim in Rochester, New York, led by the Duncan sisters, never gained widespread appeal. Outside the United States, the "initial evidence" position has been even less uniform, with organizations like the Elim Fellowship in Britain rejecting it.

Based on Bosworth's challenge, Jacobsen doubts that glossolalia should be considered the distinctive feature of pentecostalism and cites Donald Dayton's posture on this as one to which he takes exception.[19] In fairness, however, Dayton himself jettisoned this view in favor of what he calls the pentecostal *gestalt* of the four-fold gospel.[20] Dayton advanced three reasons for repudiating "tongues" as the distinctive mark, namely that other religious movements like the Mormons also advocated tongues, that it reinforces an ahistorical approach to religion, and that it leaves pentecostals open to a reductionist theory concerning tongues as a by-product of psychological deprivation while ignoring their larger theological contribution.[21] Instead, he promotes four components that shaped pentecostal

---

14. Anderson argues for a "multiple Jerusalems" approach in his most recent work, *Spreading Fires* (passim), as well as in "Global Expansion," 175–91, and "Revising Pentecostal History," 147–73. On Pune and Chile, see also McGee, "Minnie Abrams," 87–104. On a broader approach to pentecostal origins similar to Anderson, see Irvin, "Pentecostal Historiography," 35–50.

15. The question of whether "tongues" should be the defining element of pentecostalism has been given positive treatment by the following: Chan, *Pentecostal Theology*, 13; Anderson, *Vision*, 4; Nichol, "Pentecostalism," 460; and Bloch-Hoell, *Pentecostal Movement*, 2.

16. Jacobsen, *Thinking*, 10.

17. Hollenweger, *Pentecostals*, 32.

18. Bosworth, *Do all Speak with Tongues?*

19. Jacobsen, *Thinking*, 288.

20. Dayton, *Theological Roots*, 21–28.

21. Ibid., 15–16.

theology through its nineteenth-century holiness roots: sanctification, Spirit-baptism, healing and premillennialism.[22] This forms the structure of his most significant study on the movement, *Theological Roots of Pentecostalism* (1987). Nichol earlier in his landmark research recognized these same features.[23]

Second, though Spirit-baptism is agreed upon by all pentecostals to take place subsequent to salvation, a major split occurred between those who retained a Wesleyan model wherein tongues also followed an intermediary sanctification experience and those who adopted a Reformed model that regarded sanctification as initiating concurrently with justification; or, in other words, three-stage versus two-stage pentecostals. A further quarrel affected two-stage pentecostals over water baptism, some employing the "Jesus Name" formula as used by the Apostle Peter in Acts 2:38 and others utilizing the trinitarian formula in Matthew 28:19. Black Pentecostals sidled toward the Wesleyan model, but for historical reasons were shunned from the broader culture dominated by whites. Therefore, the influence of fundamentalism among the two-stage pentecostals, comprised largely of the Assemblies of God and the International Church of the Foursquare Gospel, was more readily apparent upon them than others.

Third, it will be acknowledged that defining tongues as the essential feature of pentecostalism as presented here is too restrictive if projected on a worldwide scale. Allan Anderson is correct to state that pentecostalism is better construed in terms of its experience with the Holy Spirit and the practice of charismatic gifts rather than the singular experience of tongues.[24] In this he consciously follows Robert Anderson,[25] who in turn cites Martin Marty.[26] By underscoring the utility of tongues, Marty shifted the foundation of pentecostalism from theory to praxis. Dale Fredrick Bruner offered a similar assessment in *A Theology of the Holy Spirit* (1972): "It is important to notice that it is not the *doctrine*, it is the *experience* of the Holy Spirit which Pentecostals repeatedly assert that they wish to stress."[27] Nichol has averred that it would be more accurate to use the term "pentecostalisms" rather than "Pentecostalism" to absorb the divergent practices found within it.[28]

Fourth, pentecostalism was not the unified spiritual bloc that Steven Land has assumed in *Pentecostal Spirituality* (2001).[29] Rather, as Jacobsen has suggested, pentecostalism "fragmented" not because it was united but because there was no unity to begin with, thus making the appearance of fragmentation illusory.[30] The debate entails the cleft in the

---

22. Ibid., 21.
23. Nichol, "Pentecostalism," 36.
24. Anderson, *Zion and Pentecost*, 24-25.
25. Anderson, *Introduction to Pentecostalism*, 14 and 256.
26. Anderson, *Vision* , 4; Marty, *Behavers*, 106–25.
27. Bruner, *Holy Spirit*, 21.
28. Nichol, "Pentecostalism," 475. A similar approach is used by Harris in *Fundamentalism and Evangelicals*, in which she applauds the US-based Institute for the Study of American Evangelicalism for preferring "evangelicalisms"—denoting its multifaceted institutions—to the more monolithic and misleading term "evangelicalism" (p. 4).
29. Land, *Pentecostal Spirituality*, 13.
30. Jacobsen, *Thinking*, 10.

ranks over the "Finished Work" controversy. Land wishes to return pentecostalism to its supposed pristine state prior to its rupture in 1910, agreeing with Walter Hollenweger that pentecostalism was in its "purest" form up until that moment when William H. Durham introduced schism into the movement.[31] Land's treatise, valuable as it is, reflects the holiness-pentecostal view that a two-stage *ordo baptismus* necessarily divorces sanctification from spiritual power. "Reformed" or "Finished Work" Pentecostals would not agree that holiness has been lost from their experience—only that it has been "bumped up" in the conversion process.

Finally, this study will view pentecostalism in terms of its relationship with fundamentalism. Functionally, pentecostalism like fundamentalism includes a diverse grouping of individuals, denominations, missions organizations, Bible institutes, and periodicals.[32] This functional definition however fails to distinguish it from other movements and therefore we turn to the descriptive. What distinguishes them, at least in their own view, is the *experience of Spirit-baptism as evidenced by speaking in tongues*. Though, as noted above, this is neither universally subscribed to nor universally applicable, in the context of our study it is both significant and determinative.

Fundamentalism

As with pentecostalism, arriving at a definition for fundamentalism is fraught with peril, at least in the judgment of perennial critic James Barr, who refused to supply one in his extended treatment eponymously entitled *Fundamentalism* (1977). "Complex social and religious movements cannot be defined in a few words," said Barr in his opening paragraph, and instead offered the entire 400-plus page tome as a description rather than a definition.[33] In the next paragraph, however, Barr did identify some of the salient features of fundamentalism, viz. its emphasis on inerrancy, its indomitable antipathy towards modernism, and its belligerence towards those who disagreed with it.

Such a characterization is amply displayed in George Dollar's assessment of the movement as a card-carrying member. "Historic Fundamentalism is the literal exposition of all the affirmations and attitudes of the Bible and the militant exposure of all non-Biblical affirmations and attitudes," he printed in bold font preceding his introduction to *A History of Fundamentalism in America* (1973).[34] David Beale, Dollar's successor as historian at Bob Jones University in Greenville, South Carolina, was less pugnacious but no less adamant: "Fundamentalism is not a philosophy of Christianity, nor is it essentially an interpretation of the Scriptures . . . [I]t is the *unqualified acceptance of and obedience to the Scriptures*."[35] Both embody the type of strident sectarianism so often criticized in the movement.

---

31. Land, *Pentecostal Spirituality*, 13, 47. Land cites Hollenweger, "Pentecostals and the Charismatic Movement," 549–53.
32. Cf. Wacker, *Heaven Below*, 3.
33. Barr, *Fundamentalism*, 1.
34. Dollar, *History of Fundamentalism*, insert.
35. Beale, *Purity*, 3.

DISFELLOWSHIPED

Such sentiments give credence to George Marsden's depiction of the movement as *militant*. It comprised for him the one idiosyncrasy that separated its members from other evangelicals.[36] Elsewhere he describes fundamentalists as "conservatives who are willing to take a stand" and as "evangelicals who are angry about something."[37] One drawback to this approach is that the term "fundamentalism" has been applied to so many other religious movements in the past twenty years that "militant" has accrued connotations which have escaped its original confines. The University of Chicago's massive Fundamentalist Project in the 1990s under the editorship of Martin Marty and Scott Appleby testifies to the changing dynamic of its character.[38] The term is now affixed to such diverse creeds as Hinduism and the Amish. Further, the militancy of Christian fundamentalism is different in tactics from that of Islamic fundamentalism though not so much in spirit. Both wish to defend religious belief against the incursions of the modern world, as Bruce Lawrence has outlined,[39] though Christian fundamentalists are less inclined to lob actual grenades at their foes.

Returning to the United States, in the most significant study of the movement since the 1930s, *The Roots of Fundamentalism* (1970), Ernest Sandeen documented its heritage through the prophecy conferences of the late nineteenth century. This millenarian campaign with its propensity to read the Bible literally was coupled with the Princetonian doctrine of inerrancy as espoused by B. B. Warfield and A. A. Hodge.[40] However, several scholars have remarked on the deficiency of Sandeen's approach, among them George Marsden in *Fundamentalism and American Culture* (1980).[41] Marsden additionally registers both fundamentalism's militant stance as mentioned above and its biblicist roots through the philosophy of Scottish Common Sense Realism which prevailed at Princeton throughout the nineteenth century.[42] Ultimately, Marsden attributes the rise of fundamentalism to its roots in nineteenth-century revivalism as opposed to Sandeen's millenarianism.[43]

Joel Carpenter in *Revive Us Again* (1997) has penned an excellent treatment of the "dormant" years of fundamentalism from the Scopes Trial of 1925 to the emergence of neo-evangelicalism in the 1940s. Along with Sandeen, Carpenter protests against assumptions of Cole (1931) and Furniss (1954) among others that fundamentalism was a religious fad of the 1920s.[44] Cole's evaluation essentially came too soon after Scopes and surmised from

---

36. Marsden, *American Culture*, 4.

37. Marsden, *Understanding Fundamentalism*, 1.

38. The five volumes are: Marty and Appleby, editors, *Fundamentalisms Observed* (1991); *Fundamentalisms and Society* (1993); *Fundamentalisms and the State* (1993); *Accounting for Fundamentalisms* (1994); and *Fundamentalisms Comprehended* (1995).

39. Lawrence, *Defenders of God*, passim.

40. Warfield and Hodge worked out their theology in articles appearing in *Presbyterian Review* from April 1881 to April 1883. See Noll, *Between Faith and Criticism*, 15–27.

41. A succinct summary of literature on fundamentalism can also be found in Ingersol, "Strange Bedfellows," 123–41. Ingersol deals with a larger body of literature on fundamentalism than I do here.

42. Marsden, *American Culture*, 4–5, 141.

43. Ibid., 38-39. Marsden summarizes his position effectively on pp. 224–25.

44. Carpenter, *Revive Us Again*, 253 n. 17. Cf. Cole, *History of Fundamentalism*; Furniss, *Fundamentalist Controversy*.

it an early death.⁴⁵ Rather than expiring, Carpenter argues that fundamentalism retreated from mainstream culture into a cocoon of Bible colleges, conferences, periodicals, and missions organizations.⁴⁶ He directs the reader to the more vibrant aspects of the movement's spirituality that eventually spawned the more broad-minded neo-evangelicals. From the 1940s onwards fundamentalists remained separatists while their neo-evangelical children became more irenic, reaching out to both pentecostal and holiness folk.

One element Carpenter accents that often gets overlooked is its adoption of Keswick spirituality. R. Anderson legitimately hyphenates the movement as "Keswick-Fundamentalism" when referring to it, further asserting that the Keswick teaching on the Holy Spirit was crucial to the emergence of pentecostalism.⁴⁷ This distinctive spiritual demeanor also provided fundamentalism with its vitality. As such, fundamentalism was a departure from historic Calvinism, as Warfield was quick to point out when Keswick conferences visited the Princeton campus from 1916 to 1918.⁴⁸ What fundamentalism retained from its Calvinistic roots was an adherence to doctrinal confession, which at the same stroke marked its supporters from the lax confessional attitude of the pentecostals and their holiness forebearers.

Sandeen, then, correctly stresses fundamentalism's rise around premillennialism, though it is not primarily "millenarian." In fairness, Sandeen recognized it as a wider movement than Marsden and others seem to give him credit.⁴⁹ Both Marsden and Carpenter underscore its revivalist roots in American evangelicalism. Fundamentalism originally began in opposition to modernism largely in the Northern Baptist and Northern Presbyterian denominations in the United States until the two movements came into open conflict following World War I. Losing control of these denominations, fundamentalism then retreated into its network of existing institutions. As a complex movement, then, fundamentalism was a broad coalition of premillennialists and inerrantists of largely Reformed stock who sought to defend the historic faith from modernist incursion.

Karen Armstrong has presented a substantive interpretation in *The Battle for God* (2000). In her estimation, fundamentalism confuses *logos*, a rational worldview, with *mythos*, a spiritual one.⁵⁰ Fundamentalism mirrored modernism's cerebral assumptions but lavished its scientific principles upon an agrarian *biblos* that modernism never mistook for science. Armstrong juxtaposes this view with pentecostalism's mystical rebellion against modernism's rationalistic constraints, appropriating the primal concepts described by

---

45. Carpenter fingers H. R. Niebuhr's article on fundamentalism in *Encyclopedia of the Social Sciences* (1931) as a case in point, for it referred to the movement only in the past tense (*Revive Us Again*, 13).

46. See especially chapter 1, "A Thriving Popular Movement," in *Revive Us Again*. Sandeen was the first to separate fundamentalism as a movement from the controversies which embroiled it (*Roots*, xiii).

47. Anderson, *Vision*, 43.

48. Warfield's critiques of Oberlin, Keswick and similar movements were culled from various articles and published posthumously under the title *Perfectionism* (1931).

49. See Sandeen, *Roots*, xiii and xix. Sandeen saw fundamentalism only partly as a millenarian movement (xix), although much of his study focuses on this aspect.

50. Armstrong, *Battle for God*, xiii–xvi.

Harvey Cox.[51] In this scenario, fundamentalism may be conceived of as an *ultra-rational* response to modernism and pentecostalism as a *supra-rational* one, accounting for the basic difference between the two.

Holiness Movement

If, as Russell Spittler perceives, "words mean different things to different people, or different things to the same people at different times,"[52] a view supported by Chan,[53] then the problem becomes especially acute concerning the holiness movement. The difficulty is that there are two wings within it, one which historians designate as the "Wesleyan" or "Methodist" wing and the other as the "Higher Life," "Keswick," or "Reformed" wing. Furthermore, the term "holiness" can refer to either the Wesleyan branch or to both branches at the same time, but rarely to the "Reformed" side alone. Scholars are not always clear or even consistent in how they apply the terms.

Faupel avoids this conundrum in *The Everlasting Gospel* (1996) by encompassing both branches under the appellation "Perfectionism." Though this has its advantages, it is not clear from the term itself in what sense Keswick "perfectionism" should be understood as essentially different from the Wesleyan one. "Perfectionism" has the further disadvantage in that it does not bear this common usage in current scholarship and therefore, though an attractive option, must be rejected in light of academic discourse. The scholar is unfortunately saddled with the ambiguity of the term "holiness" to mean the two wings of the movement as well as just the Wesleyan-wing.

To avoid confusion, one must therefore distinguish these aspects economically. "Wesleyan" is too ambiguous and "Wesleyan-Holiness" too cumbersome. This study will therefore use the hyphenated forms "Wesleyan-wing" and "Reformed-wing" to separate the two and retain "holiness movement" to refer to the entire movement. The Wesleyan-wing will be identified as those adherents hailing largely from a Methodist background with an emphasis on sanctification as a secondary experience to salvation resulting in the eradication of sin and the resultant ability to live in purity. Conversely, the Reformed-wing will be identified with those adherents from a traditionally Reformed church background (i.e., Baptists, Presbyterians and Congregationalists) but with the following clarifications.

First, though those of the Reformed-wing came from historically Reformed denominations, most were not Calvinists in the strict sense of the word. The Reformed-wing had long been "Arminianized" through the doctrine of the Oberlin College perfectionists; evangelist and professor Charles Finney and President Asa Mahan. Finney's theology also infected the "New School Presbyterians," stipulating the role of human agency in salvation rather than God's sovereignty as traditionally imagined by Calvinists.[54] Both wings

---

51. Ibid., 180–82; cf. Cox, *Fire from Heaven*. Cox explores the pentecostal contribution to spirituality in three categories: primal speech, primal piety, and primal hope.

52. Spilttler, "Are Pentecostals and Charismatics Fundamentalists?" 103–4.

53. Chan, "Whither Pentecostalism?" 576.

54. Faupel, *Everlasting Gospel*, 67, citing Dieter, *Holiness Revival*, 19–22. McLoughlin in *Modern Revivalism* argues that Finney's emphasis on the will combined Scottish Common Sense Realism's religious psychology with transcendentalism's reliance on the self (p. 69). The Romantic roots of the Keswick movement are explored by Bebbington in *Holiness in Nineteenth Century England*, 73–90.

emphasized the consecration of oneself to God through Spirit-immersion. The Reformed-wing however disposed of eradicationism, replacing it with the empowering presence of the Spirit to "overcome" fallen human nature.

One could opt for "Keswick" to cover the Reformed-wing, but this also contains deficiencies. Essentially, the Keswick movement began in Britain in the 1870s, though it was influenced by holiness doctrine from the United States. This teaching in turn was replanted on American soil through D. L. Moody's Northfield Conferences beginning in the 1880s and came into its own in New Jersey in the early twentieth century. Prior to that, the movement had been known as "Higher Life," taking its title from Presbyterian layman William E. Boardman's *The Christian Higher Life* (1858). The emphasis on "overcoming" was more conducive to those who were from a Reformed background, but, as noted above, it was not compatible with the views of dyed-in-the-wool Calvinists like Warfield.

One pitfall with "Keswick" is that it did not become identified as such until well after it had been known as the "Higher Life" movement. The advantage is that it does identify a body of teaching that was distinct from the Wesleyan-wing and shows its essential influence on fundamentalism. Several leaders of the premillennialist movement, like R. A. Torrey and A. T. Pierson, were participants in the Keswick movement in Britain and instrumental in its adaptation in America. Historians refer to these leaders, especially those associated with the prophecy conferences at Niagara, as protofundamentalists. The situation is further complicated by the fact that protofundamentalists like Torrey also became founders of fundamentalism. Others such as A. J. Gordon and D. L. Moody died well before a fundamentalist movement could become readily identified. For the purposes of this study, the demarcating line between protofundamentalism and fundamentalism is 1920, when the term was first used. Those who died before that date will be considered protofundamentalist and those after as fundamentalist.

In sum, the holiness movement can be divided into two wings with the following periods. The Wesleyan-wing arose among Methodists through the efforts of Phoebe Palmer beginning in 1835 up to the Civil War. After the Civil War, the Wesleyan-wing took on national prominence through the National Holiness Association, which began in 1867. By 1894, however, the Methodist leadership began to dissociate itself from the excesses of the movement.[55] At this point, independent holiness associations became more radicalized, paving the way for the pentecostal message. The Reformed-wing commenced with the Oberlin perfectionists in the mid-1830s, became more widely disseminated after the Prayer Meeting Revival of 1857–1858, and transferred to England and back again through the Keswick movement after 1875.[56] By World War I, Keswick spirituality had permeated much of the growing fundamentalist network.

---

55. Synan, *Holiness-Pentecostal*, 59.

56. Faupel's *The Everlasting Gospel* is indispensable for understanding the development of Keswick teaching and its contribution to pentecostalism from the Prayer Meeting Revival to Azusa Street.

Modernism

The term modernism is plagued by the same distractions as above. Like other movements, modernism represented a diverse coalition without a consistent center. "Modernism" and "liberalism" are nearly synonymous, but neatly differentiated by Marsden respectively as "an accommodation with the modern world" and as "freedom from tradition."[57] Marty reckons that both terms are misleading as only a few modernists were truly of a militant nature and also because evangelicals populated the mainline churches normally associated with the movement.[58] Harvard church historian William Hutchison insists in *The Modernist Impulse in American Protestantism* (1976) that "Protestant liberalism, even more notoriously than its modernist formulation, has been difficult to capture in any agreed description."[59] Hutchison discerns three paralipses: 1) the immanence of God in society, 2) the redemptive progress of culture as a reflection of the Kingdom of God, and 3) the adaptation of theological inquiry to modern science, such as Darwinism and historical criticism.[60]

In a more recent survey, Gary Dorrien in *The Making of American Liberalism* (2003) attributes modernism's formation to two antecedents: evangelicalism, which emphasized experiential religion and the sovereignty of Christ, and the Enlightenment, which emphasized the primacy of rationalism and the freedom of the individual.[61] Dorrien faults Hutchison and Francis Schüssler Fiorenza for dispensing with the phrases "evangelical liberal" and "modernist liberal" as too indistinct.[62] Many of the early modernists preferred the label "evangelical liberal" as evinced in pastor Harry Emerson Fosdick's autobiography *The Living of these Days* (1957), where he proudly identifies himself with both the liberal and evangelical traditions.[63] Dorrien muses that the transition from "evangelical liberal" to "modernist liberal" transpired in 1924 with the publication of Shailer Mathews' *The Faith of Modernism*.[64] For Dorrien, the evangelical strand accentuated the transcendence of God while the modernist strand accentuated His immanence.[65]

Hutchison regards the division between "liberal" and "modern" as troublesome in that each term represents only a portion of the movement. He additionally rejects "liberalism" as too much maligned. In many ways, modernism was as much a revolt against the constricting forces of Calvinism as fundamentalism was a reaction to modernism.[66] I would also argue that an element of the Romantic is embedded in modernism with its

---

57. Marsden, *Understanding Fundamentalism*, 33.
58. Marty, *Behavers*, 86.
59. Hutchison, *Modernist Impulse*, 3.
60. Ibid., 2.
61. Dorrien, *Liberal Theology*, 10–11.
62. Ibid., 10–11, 532. See also Hutchison, *Modernist Impulse*, 7.
63. Fosdick, *Living*, 173. See also Hutchison, *Modern Impulse*, 8; and Dorrien, *Liberal Theology*, 547.
64. Dorrien, *Liberal Theology*, 532.
65. Ibid., 532. Dorrien admits that though the distinction is not absolute it essentially "names the difference between claiming that God transcends history [evangelical-liberal] and claiming that God is the reality of historical process [modern-liberal]."
66. See for example Fosdick, *Living*, 66–67.

Defining the Study

emphasis on society maturing out of the past just as evolution represented the progression of life from the past. As stated earlier, modernists viewed their task as the melding of the ancient faith with the modern world by incorporating the new science of Darwinism and the new technique of biblical criticism into a progressive theology. It is in this sense that modernism will be used. Historically, it can be traced from the trial of David Swing in 1874 (see chapter 2) to its triumph over fundamentalism in the 1920s. Liberalism is here established along Dorrien's account as a longer succession of movements stretching from Unitarianism to present day liberation theologies. Modernism's demise was hastened by its disillusionment with progress during the Depression and from the neo-orthodox critiques of Reinhold Niebuhr, though it continued to enjoy prestige in American culture well into the 1950s.

Evangelicalism

Broadly speaking, evangelicalism encompasses the three more conservative branches of Protestantism as defined above, for if they could not agree on anything else, they could at least be uniformly opposed to modernism. British historian David Bebbington has identified four traits of evangelicalism, repeated by American church historian Mark Noll: 1) biblicism (a stress on scriptural authority), 2) conversionism (a stress on the new birth), 3) activism (a stress on religious duty), and 4) crucicentrism (a stress on Christ's redeeming work).[67] Susan Rose compiles a nearly identical list of evangelical tenets: 1) Christ as savior, 2) Scripture as inerrant, and 3) conversion as necessary.[68] Marsden is correct however to substitute scriptural authority for inerrancy as a common element.[69] Contra Rose, evangelicals do not uniformly agree on the doctrine of inerrancy as advocated by most fundamentalists.

The term "evangelical" has had a varied history in the United States. Marty submits and Marsden confirms that in the mid-nineteenth century the word had come to denote just about anybody in Protestant Christianity—Methodists, Presbyterians, Baptists, Congregationalists, etc.[70] Marsden figures that "evangelical" fell into disuse by the 1930s,[71] although Boston University sociologist Nancy Ammerman is more accurate in claiming that the terms "fundamentalist" and "evangelical" were virtually interchangeable during that period.[72] By the 1940s however they assimilated distinct meanings while sharing the properties described above. The main difference is that fundamentalists became separatists while evangelicals retained their commitment to the historic churches.

---

67. Noll, "Introduction," in Noll, Bebbington and Rawlyk, editors, *Evangelicalism*, 6; Noll, *Scandal of the Evangelical Mind*, 6. In both instances, Noll cites Bebbington, *Evangelicalism in Modern Britain*, 2–19.

68. Rose, "Christian Fundamentalism," 453.

69. Marsden, *Understanding Fundamentalism*, 4–5. Otherwise Marsden's characteristics are substantially the same as Noll and Rose.

70. Marty, *Behavers*, 85; Marsden, *Understanding Fundamentalism*, 2.

71. Marsden, *Understanding Fundamentalism*, 66.

72. Ammerman, "North American Protestant Fundamentalism," 36.

Elsewhere, Noll defines evangelicalism as "plastic" and as "extraordinarily complex."[73] In his opening remarks to *American Evangelical Christianity* (2001), Noll shies away from providing a theological definition and offers instead a picture of its "interlocking institutions, personal networks, and common traditions."[74] He further identifies evangelicals as "less separatist" and "more educationally ambitious" than the fundamentalists from whom they had sprung. These were in fact the "neo-evangelicals," a term coined by Boston pastor Harold John Ockenga in 1947,[75] who embraced a more expansive vision of Christianity than his fundamentalist forebearers.

Barr rebuffs evangelicals for distancing themselves from fundamentalists when he sees little substantive difference between the two. "I do not say therefore all conservative evangelicals are also fundamentalists, but the overlap is great," he charges.[76] Harriet Harris, in an exposition of the two movements called appropriately enough *Evangelicals and Fundamentalism* (1998), concurs with Barr. She takes British evangelicals to task for drawing a "straw-man" to separate the two, maintaining "that a predominant feature of much contemporary evangelicalism is a fundamentalist mentality."[77] As this illustrates, outsiders to evangelicalism downplay the differences between them and fundamentalists. Like many religious movements of great similarity, the differences are marked for those who are involved and immaterial for those who are not. Evangelicalism then is a complex network of groups sharing the essential ingredients of biblical authority and the necessity of regeneration through faith in the Savior.

Randall Balmer in his survey of contemporary evangelicalism, *Mine Eyes Have Seen the Glory* (1993), compares the evangelical subculture of America to a quilt.[78] It is a patchwork of patterns, assembled by many hands to comprise a whole. And—like the quilt—it is quintessentially American. I think however that Timothy Smith is nearer the truth when he likens American evangelicalism to a kaleidoscope, with ever changing colors and patterns.[79] Here I opine that fundamentalism and pentecostalism both belong under the larger category of evangelicalism though they do not agree on the finer points of doctrine or experience. Thus, I disagree with Matthew Sutton for subsuming "pentecostals, holiness, dispensationalists, and Presbyterians" under the fundamentalist banner.[80] Sutton uses a 1930s definition of fundamentalism which I find to be inappropriate for our post-World War II situation. Though evangelicalism and fundamentalism may have been nearly synonymous at one time in history, they are so no longer.

---

73. Noll, *Between Faith and Criticism*, 1; Noll, *American Evangelical Christianity*, 14.
74. Noll, *American Evangelical Christianity*, 3.
75. Dollar, *History of Fundamentalism*, 203.
76. Barr, *Fundamentalism*, 5.
77. Harris, *Evangelicals and Fundamentalism*, 7.
78. Balmer, *Mine Eyes*, 278–79.
79. Cited in Carpenter, *Revive Us Again*, 64; Smith, "Evangelical Kaleidoscope," 125–40.
80. Sutton, "Wildfire," 162.

Conclusion

Given the broad spectrum within evangelicalism, chapter 2 will briefly outline the nineteenth-century background of both fundamentalism in its internal squabbles with modernism and of the protofundamentalist influence on pentecostalism via the holiness movement. The study will then trace in chapter 3 the genesis of pentecostalism: how pentecostalism arose largely out of its holiness roots and contacted fundamentalist religion, examining in the process how proto-/fundamentalists reacted to tongues and the pentecostal response to their criticisms. It will also detail pentecostal concepts of premillennialism, which became the primary venue through which fundamentalism impacted pentecostalism.

The next two chapters chronicle changes during the adaptation stage. Chapter 4 concerns the formation of pentecostal denominations through theological controversy, influenced by fundamentalist doctrine. It will also examine the fundamentalist criticism during this period and how pentecostals countered their arguments through their publications. I will argue as well that the "vocabulary" of fundamentalism, and especially that of premillennial dispensationalism through the publication of the Scofield Reference Bible (1909), crept into the pentecostal terminology. Chapter 5 occasions the stability of pentecostal denominations and their adjustment to the emerging fundamentalist network in the early 1920s. Controversy concerning divine healing gained heightened attention in this period, though pentecostals and fundamentalists did share some common thinking on the matter. More importantly, leaders in the AG found it difficult to maintain a pentecostal identity without being overwhelmed by fundamentalist theology. Again, the influence of fundamentalism was most acute in AG eschatology, where the "vocabulary" of fundamentalism shifted to its "content."

Chapter 6 commences the retention stage, whereby the Sunday school assumed an increasingly vital role. This was evident in new periodicals launched specifically for children in the late 1920s and the amelioration of organizational structures at the regional level in the early 1930s (chapter 7) and at the national level in the late 1930s (chapter 8). Meanwhile, the tension between pentecostals and fundamentalists reached its apex in 1928 when the latter officially ostracized the former. Nevertheless, cooperation could still be exhibited at the local level between the two, particular after fundamentalism began to wane in power in the late 1920s. While continuing the retention theme, chapter 7 argues that pentecostals, at least in the AG, had adopted the "rhetoric" of fundamentalism by advocating fundamentalist causes such as evolution, the "scientific" veracity of Scripture and the disdaining of modernist theology. The transition also becomes evident in the CG from the early 1930s, influenced again by "dispensational truths."

Chapter 8 will demonstrate that pentecostal and fundamentalist cooperation first occurred through the Sunday school movement, foreshadowing cooperation in other common interests like revivalism. It will be argued that the influence of fundamentalism had pitched pentecostals against modernists so that cooperation became more likely and even necessary, leading to the formation of the National Association of Evangelicals in 1943. Conversely, there was also a weakening in fundamentalist militancy facilitated by visible loss to the modernists in the denominations, spiritual loss of fundamentalist vitality due to the vapidity of intellectualism evident during the depression, and physical loss of "old-guard" fundamentalists due to death. These events allowed space for cooperation, whereas in the early years of both movements no such fraternal communion could prevail.

Historical Background

Survey of the Religious Landscape, 1860–1900

NEARLY FORTY YEARS AGO, YALE CHURCH HISTORIAN SYDNEY AHLSTROM EXPRESSED THE opinion that "no aspect of American church history is more in need of summary and yet so difficult to summarize as the movements of dissent and reaction that occurred between the Civil War and World War I."[1] It is precisely this period which shaped the religious landscape into which pentecostalism was born. Nazarene church historian Timothy Smith described the last half of the nineteenth century as the "maturation" and "decline" of an evangelical consensus which had existed up to the Civil War.[2] Though Marsden has designated the years 1865-1890 as the "Evangelical Empire,"[3] an important symbolic landmark occurred in 1899 with the passing of D. L. Moody, whose reputation as evangelist and ecumenist was unparalleled in his day. The coalition of evangelicals and modernists whom he invited to Northfield, Massachusetts quickly disintegrated when leadership of his yearly conference passed to his son William.[4]

Dates, arbitrary as they can be, also are valuable in demarcating significant events in the life of a given movement. Among protofundamentalists, 1899 saw the dissolution of the Niagara Prophecy Conference while 1901 launched its successor, the Sea Coast Bible Conference, through which C. I. Scofield would devise the notations that bare his name. In modernism, 1899 witnessed the publication of Washington Gladden's *How Much is Left of the Old Doctrines?*, pealing a death knoll for the old orthodoxy in the mainline denominations, while 1901 witnessed George Gordon's *The New Epoch for Faith*, announcing the optimism of liberal missions. And on New Year's Day of 1901, pentecostalism stirred in Topeka, Kansas, under the tutelage of radical holiness preacher Charles Fox Parham. To understand this sea change within the Evangelical Empire, we turn to a brief survey of American religious and secular history of the nineteenth century.

---

1. Ahlstrom, *A Religious History*, 823.
2. Smith, *Revivalism*, 15.
3. Marsden, *Understanding Fundamentalism*, 12.
4. William preferred modernist speakers like Henry Drummond to the narrow theories of A. T. Pierson and R. A. Torrey, prompting Torrey to start his own conference at his summer home in Montrose, Pennsylvania in 1907. William became belligerent by 1923, defending himself as a fundamentalist, but not in any sense Torrey would have recognized (W. R. Moody, "What is Fundamental?" *RCW* [March 1923] 184–85).

The Great Evangelical Empire, 1860

As John Locke once voiced with a touch of biblical wryness, "In the beginning, all the world was America." From the outset, America had been a vast political, entrepreneurial, and religious experiment. The newness of the land fostered fresh ideas and fresh methods. One of these great experiments was Jefferson's separation of church and state, hitherto unknown in the Western world—probably anywhere in the world. In Europe, one institution had supported the other, providing stability to nations, or so the theory had gone since time immemorial. Dissenters like the Quakers and Pilgrims sought refuge from persecution in colonial America, embarking with hopes for freedom, even if some such as the Puritans later proved a bit intolerant. Raised in a spirit of competition and unequalled opportunity, sects were afforded room to grow.

American religion also exhibited revivalist tendencies since the days of the Great Awakening (1735–1742). Its vaunted spokesman, Jonathan Edwards, highlighted the role of emotion in a Calvinist context in his treatise *On Religious Affections* (1746). For Edwards, conversion without heart-felt conviction cast doubt upon the reclamation of the soul.[5] Emotion played a substantial part in the Second Great Awakening (1800–1835), originating among Presbyterians on the Kentucky frontier. Their model became a hallmark of the "camp meeting" for which the Methodists acquired fame. Emotion also was indicative of the revivals conducted by Charles Finney. More decisively, Finney's exaltation of the role of the will in conversion represented a departure from historic Calvinism. His theology helped tilt traditionally Reformed denominations towards Arminianism.[6] Finney also popularized revivalism, transforming it into something of a profession if not an art. His *Lectures on Revival* (1835) circulated widely and into the next century graced the advertisements of holiness, fundamentalist, and pentecostal magazines alike.

To this was added the rapid expansion of the Methodists and Baptists along the frontiers. These relative newcomers had an advantage in that they did not require high levels of education among their clergy, unlike the older, eastern-based Congregationalists (former Puritans) and Episcopalians (former Anglicans). Their circuit-riders and lay preachers invaded the West by the hundreds. By 1855 seventy percent of church-going America communed with either denomination.[7] One tenet that fertilized Methodism in the mid-eighteenth century was the holiness article of Phoebe Palmer, derived tangentially from John Wesley. Palmer promoted her "scriptural call to holiness" in periodicals, books, and her well-attended Tuesday meetings in New York City. To sum up American religion prior to the Civil War, Robert Anderson succinctly states: "Mined from various veins of the common lode of Christian tradition, forged in the Second Awakening, and hammered out in the intermittent revivals down to 1858, evangelical Protestantism was Arminian in

---

5. Noll, *America's God*, 23–24.
6. Faupel, *Everlasting Gospel*, 67; see also McLoughlin, *Modern Revivalism*, 12–13.
7. Smith, *Revivalism*, 22.

doctrine, revivalistic in method, and perfectionist in purpose; and perfectionism meant the regeneration both of the individual and of society."[8]

Evangelical fervor reached its height in the Prayer Meeting Revival, referred to also as the "Revival of 1857–58," the "Businessman's Revival" and the "Noontime Prayer Revival." Faupel credits Palmer's Canadian campaign in 1857 as the beginnings of the revival, although it was in New York City that it gained prominence.[9] Noontime prayer meetings had been a weekly feature in the metropolis since the fall of 1856, and daily at the Old Dutch Church by October 1857. In that same month, a banking panic paralyzed the economy. Businessmen ordinarily gainfully employed in the financial district suddenly found themselves out of a job and on the street. Many turned from material values to spiritual ones, laying up their treasures in heaven while it rotted on earth.[10] By mid-winter the meetings at the Old Dutch had flowed over into a nearby Methodist church. By April 1858 at least twenty prayer meetings were being held throughout the city while the revival spread up and down the eastern seaboard and into the Midwest.[11] Up to a million converts were reported, mostly in urban areas.

What is significant for our study is that both pentecostal and fundamentalist scholars commend this revival as the inception of their respective movements. In Faupel's natal analogy, pentecostalism was "conceived" in the midst of the 1857–1858 Revival, "gestated" in the holiness movement, and "birthed" in the aftermath of the Welsh Revival of 1904–1905.[12] For David Beale, fundamentalism's roots lie "in America's third Great Awakening—the Prayer Meeting Revivals."[13] Beale then charts the revival's transmission to the British Isles and back again to America through Irish proselyte George Needham, who was instrumental in forming a yearly prayer retreat that morphed into the Niagara Prophecy Conference.[14] Both Marsden and Carpenter indicate that later fundamentalists looked upon the Prayer Meeting Revival as their model and inspiration.[15] Unfortunately, the revival was followed not by the renewal of society but by its rending—a savage war that hastened the collapse of evangelical hegemony.[16]

The Cultural Challenge to the Empire, 1865

Surprisingly, the Civil War resulted in only a temporary interruption to the progress of America. Much of the optimism evident before the war quickly returned to the North.[17]

---

8. Anderson, *Vision*, 29.

9. Faupel, *Everlasting Gospel*, 71.

10. McLoughlin writes that it "scarcely deserved to be called the Third Great Awakening" as it can be attributed to financial pressures (*Modern Revivalism*, 163).

11. Smith, *Revivalism*, 63–63.

12. Faupel, *Everlasting Gospel*, 307.

13. Beale, *Pursuit*, 13.

14. Ibid., 13–19.

15. Marsden, *American Culture*, 11; Carpenter, *Revive Us Again*, 116.

16. Dayton, *Theological Roots*, 75.

17. Handy, *History of the Churches*, 274.

DISFELLOWSHIPED

On the ecclesiastical front, Protestant denominations grew threefold from 1860 to 1900.[18] Black churches with independent organization and leadership sprang up and proliferated in the newly-emancipated South.[19] Though these were cause for celebration, major changes were taking place elsewhere in American society which would permanently alter the religious landscape.

The years of reconstruction (1865–1877) were a time of optimism and expansion. With the slavery debacle decided, America focused her attention westward to complete its inchoate settling. A well-disciplined union army aimed its guns towards the plains Indians as a migratory populace moved in to subdue the land. America had regained its status as a country of opportunity. The transcontinental railroad, connected with a golden spike at Promontory Point, Utah, in May of 1869, spelled the end of hazardous wagon trains and perilous voyages around the Chilean tip. Institutions called themselves "national" even if they were relegated to one coast or the other, for potentially they could reach anyone in the country.[20] The "manifest destiny" that had gripped the East in the 1840s would be fulfilled by the 1890s, when all but five of the fifty states had been affixed to the union.[21]

The post-war years brought prosperity hitherto unknown in America. The demands of the Civil War awakened industrialists of the North to the possibilities of mass-production.[22] This was the age of "robber barons," captains of industry who amassed wealth in staggering proportions. On top of that list was John D. Rockefeller, a devout Baptist and benefactor of the church to some, an unscrupulous thief to others. By 1880 Rockefeller refined 95 percent of the nation's oil and by 1900 had accumulated a fortune of over $200,000,000.[23] But he was hardly alone. Andrew Carnegie in steel, Cornelius Vanderbilt in steamboats and railroads, Philip Armour in meat-packing, J. P. Morgan in finance, George Pullman in railcars, and many others monopolized and channeled the seemingly limitless resources of the country to a growing consumer appetite.

Immigration supplied a ready force who bought the very products they produced. The years between the Civil War and World War I saw the largest influx of new blood America had ever known. Thirteen and a half million immigrants arrived between 1865 and 1900 and in excess of fourteen million in the following twenty years, tripling the total population to 106,000,000.[24] The pivotal year was 1882, where for the first time immigrants who were southern European and Catholic or eastern European and Orthodox or Jewish outpaced those who were northern European and Protestant.[25] This alien contingent did not assimilate into the evangelical ethos as easily as their Protestant confessing neighbors to the North and were increasingly resented by the Anglo-Saxon majority. While Protestant

---

18. Marsden, *Understanding Fundamentalism*, 12.
19. Handy, *History of the Churches*, 271.
20. Schlesinger, *Modern America*, 163.
21. Ibid., 162.
22. Tipple, "Big Businessmen and a new Economy," 14.
23. Collier and Horowitz, *The Rockefellers*, 29, 53.
24. Ahlstrom, *Religious History*, 735; Schlesinger, *Modern America*, 169, 229; Marty, *Pilgrims*, 310.
25. Schlesinger, *Modern America*, 167; Weber, *Shadow*, 84–85.

membership tripled to sixteen million in the three decades following the war, Catholicism quadrupled to twelve million.[26]

Further, accommodations had to be procured for all the newcomers, and those who did not strike out West huddled in the cities. By 1890, four out of five New York residents had either been born outside the United States or born to immigrant parents, and their density exceeded that of Bombay's most congested district and was twice that of Europe's largest slum in Prague.[27] In 1837 Chicago consisted of seventeen shacks on the shores of Lake Michigan. By 1900 it had swollen to the fifth largest city in the world with a population surpassing 1.5 million.[28] While New York doubled and Detroit quadrupled, cities further west like Minneapolis and Omaha increased fiftyfold.[29]

The churches were ill-equipped to handle such influxes of foreigners. They spoke a different language and practiced a different religion. They lived in squalor and kept to their own enclaves in overcrowded conditions. It was an age of corrupt political machines run with immigrant support in a lawless, urban "jungle", like the Chicago of 1906, described by Upton Sinclair.[30] It is little wonder that Mark Twain and Charles Dudley Warner described the opulence of the rich covering over the poverty of the masses as "The Gilded Age."[31] New York possessed one saloon for every two hundred people, and in some localities bars and brothels outnumbered churches by a hundredfold.[32] The cities were ideal venues to implement social reforms like Hull House in Chicago in 1889, and facilitated the rise of the Social Gospel through Washington Gladden in the late nineteenth century and Walter Rauschenbusch in the early twentieth.

Immigrants were not the only ones crowding the cities. America was undergoing a transformation from a rural-agricultural society to an urban-industrial one. In Midwestern states like Illinois and Ohio, the population decreased in over half of their bucolic townships despite dramatic increases in the overall population.[33] In 1850 only six cities contained more than 100,000 people, but by 1900 forty-one such communities existed.[34] It was in fact from these transient laborers that holiness and fundamentalist ranks were extracted, a pattern that would later be repeated among pentecostals. "The old-time religion" catered to those displaced individuals who pined for something of the wholesome hearth that was absent in the fetid big cities.[35]

---

26. Marsden, *Understanding Fundamentalism*, 14.
27. Ammerman, "North American," 12; Schlesinger, *Modern America*, 108.
28. Weber, *Shadow*, 84.
29. Ibid., 84; Balmer, *Mine Eyes*, 247.
30. Sinclair, *The Jungle* (1906).
31. Their joint novel by this title was published in 1873.
32. Schlesinger, *Modern America*, 112, 117.
33. Sweet, *Story of Religion*, 372.
34. Marty, *Pilgrims*, 311.
35. The rural roots of fundamentalism and the holiness movement as it transferred to the cities are cited in Marsden, *Understanding Fundamentalism*, 13; Faupel, *Everlasting Gospel*, 53; and Handy, *History of the Churches*, 264.

Another factor threatened the evangelical empire internally: its newfound affluence. The Methodists for instance had traditionally amassed its communicants from the frontier and the rural south. After the Civil War, Methodism attracted members from the middle and upper classes in the cities. With it came a decrease in personal piety and exuberance of devotion. Padded pews replaced the mourner's bench, robed choirs stifled enthusiastic congregational singing, and indoor lectures curtailed outdoor revivals.[36] These alterations encouraged the Methodist leadership to be increasingly hostile to the holiness movement and its emotional excesses. Methodist historian William Warren Sweet cites wealth as the single greatest mechanism for change within the churches following the Civil War.[37]

The Theological Challenge to the Empire, 1874

Challenge to the health of evangelicalism also emitted from modernism. One early indicator of this emerging movement was the heresy trial of Presbyterian minister David Swing in Chicago in 1874. Swing had been swept into a Methodist revival as a young man. Though he never repudiated orthodoxy, he evinced a sensitivity to the layperson's doubt, inculcating that religion was culturally conditioned, and shied away from the historic creeds. Though exonerated of error, Swing nevertheless resigned from his pulpit and accepted a post at a disenfranchised church the following year, where he preached to thousands each week for the next twenty years.[38] His was a harbinger of trials to come.[39]

Two tenets of the New Theology in particular contested the old faith: evolution and biblical criticism. Darwin published *The Origin of Species* in America in 1860, one year after its British release.[40] Its impact was felt first upon the scientific community and did not produce the theological firestorm that *The Descent of Man* did in 1871. In this latter work Darwin made explicit what was implicit in the earlier treatise, crudely, that humankind was created in the image of monkey rather than in the image of God. Darwin rendered God superfluous to the Creation event and effectively pronounced the Genesis account dubious. It did not endear him to conservative theologians. Charles Hodge responded in 1874 with *What is Darwinism?* by answering, "It is atheism."[41]

Other luminaries were less adverse. Henry Ward Beecher, son of evangelical icon Lyman Beecher, championed Darwinism in *Evolution and Religion* in 1885, and Lyman Abbot applied Darwin to the church in *The Evolution of Christianity* in 1892 and followed that up five years later with *The Theology of an Evolutionist*. Clearly Darwin enjoyed

---

36. Sweet, *Story of Religion*, 345–52; R. Anderson, *Vision*, 30.
37. Sweet, *Story of Religion*, 345–46.
38. Hutchison, *Modern Impulse*, 48-53; Reid, et al., eds., *Concise Dictionary*, 333.
39. Congregational conservatives successfully blocked Nyman Smyth's appointment to Andover Theological Seminary in 1877 and Crawford Toy was removed by Southern Baptists from their seminary in Louisville in 1879. By 1893, however, the conservative party of the Northern Presbyterians' successful prosecution of Charles Briggs resulted in Union Theological Seminary eventually severing its ties with the denomination. See Hutchison, *Modern Impulse*, 77, and Sweet, *Story of Religion*, 343–44.
40. Marty, *Pilgrims*, 299.
41. Beale, *Purity*, 80.

Historical Background

ascendancy in some circles while others remained intransigent.[42] Social Darwinism, the survival of the fittest, was particularly feared by evangelicals. They would later eisegete the fruits of evolutionary theory into German aggression in World War I. The strain would reach its climax in the Scopes Trial in Dayton, Tennessee, in 1925, whereby H. L. Mencken and the demotic press would stigmatize fundamentalism as a "hill-billy" religion.

While evolution undermined the divine origins of humanity, the second issue, biblical criticism, undermined the divine origins of Scripture. "Higher criticism" as it was also known had been an import from Germany. At first disseminated to the English-speaking world through two British writers, Frederick Maurice and Frederick Robertson, prospective American theologians traveled to the Continent to imbibe the procedure directly from the likes of Ernst Troeltsch and Adolph von Harnack, both disciples of Albert Ritschl.[43] They brought back with them the higher critical methods of scholars like Julius Wellhausen along with the pietism of Frederick Schleiermacher.

Young ideologues distributed these principles throughout American seminaries. Seminaries in fact had become changed institutions since the heyday of evangelicalism. Professors were no longer practicing or retired ministers but professional academicians. Andover Seminary, for instance, founded in 1808 as a conservative Congregational alternative to the Unitarian takeover of Harvard, now espoused a liberal theology which the faculty published as *Progressive Orthodoxy* (1886). Other leading modernist lights like Baptist William Newton Clarke at Colgate and Presbyterian William Adams Brown at Union Theological Seminary in New York produced textbooks with inverted titles, *An Outline of Christian Theology* (1898) and *Christian Theology in Outline* (1906).

One pillar which supported their dogma was the idea that God's presence was immanent throughout culture, ensuring the progress of society. It coincided well with American expansionism which pattered after the heels of the Spanish-American War (1898), and nowhere was this more pressed than in the missionary endeavor. Modernists evaluated the increasing influence of American hegemony as an opportunity to "civilize" the heathen through education and medication. In 1895 Boston minister George Gordon trumpeted the "Gospel for Humanity" to the American Board of Commissioners for Foreign Missions, and five years later William Clarke criticized the debonair optimism of winning the world to Christ "in a generation," an obvious slight on the Student Volunteer Missions inspired by D. L. Moody, A. T. Pierson and John Mott.[44] In the words of Clarke, "The rush is over and the steady pull begins."[45]

Evolution and biblical criticism were each grounded in Romanticism, which stressed the process and development of history and its continuity with the past.[46] Gradualness rather the suddenness was the prevailing mood. Scientific gradualism found expression in England in Darwin's friend and mentor Charles Lyell, who introduced epochs of geologi-

---

42. See Boller, "The New Science," 239–57, for a treatment of Darwin's effect upon culture.

43. Hutchison, *Modern Impulse*, 80. Among those who studied in Germany was R. A. Torrey, who turned from liberalism "as though avoiding a cliff."

44. Ibid., 134–35.

45. Quoted in ibid., 149.

46. Marsden, *American Culture*, 225–26.

cal time in the 1830s.[47] Evolutionary development was not revolutionary by Darwin's day except in its application to God's creatures and to the pinnacle of creation, humanity itself.[48] Romanticism also influenced the understanding of Scripture among German intellectuals. They viewed the Bible as a product of culture and therefore subject to criticism like any other mundane document, calling into question the uniqueness of Christian revelation.[49] In comparing the New Testament to other sacred writings, Troeltsch concluded that it presented nothing extraordinary.[50]

The New Theology is said to have arisen among Congregationalists in the Northeast. As Marsden maintains, Romanticism lacked the imprint on America as it had in England and Germany except among transcendentalists and Unitarians in the same northeastern region.[51] Hutchison postulates that modernism originated among these mystically-attuned literati and diffused to Congregationalism through Horace Bushnell.[52] Alternatively, a case can also be made for the influence the New School theology of the 1820s and 1830s which flourished through Finney and his associates Lyman Beecher and Nathaniel Taylor. Finney appealed to the emotions and the will rather than the mind in conversion and had an aversion to confessionalism.[53] It is no accident that Oberlin College fell into the New Theology through Henry Churchill King not long after Finney's departure from this life.[54] Further, the historical link between New School Presbyterians and the New Theology of the Congregationalists to modernism is stronger than through the Unitarians, as evidenced through Lyman Beecher and his son Henry Ward.

For this reason, Faupel is wrong to follow George Fry in asserting that pentecostalism and modernism are "fraternal twins."[55] To be sure, there were similarities between the two movements, but such were only superficial. Both scored the importance of experience and shunned doctrinal formulation. Many of the modernists were reared in evangelical homes and several cherished religious conversion in their youth, like Baptists Shailer Mathews, Harry Fosdick and Douglas Macintosh.[56] Faupel rightly notes that the similarity came

---

47. Lyell's *Principles of Geology* were published from 1830–1833 and championed "uniformitarianism" as opposed to a "catastrophic" view of geology where change happens quickly through powerful events.

48. Marty, *Pilgrims*, 299, cites the 1845 edition of an English work, *Vestiges of the Natural History of Creation*, in which the author, Robert Chambers, taught that life generated spontaneously in "a universal firemist." Chambers believed the process to be controlled by God.

49. Marty, *Pilgrims*, 297–98, 301–2.

50. Dollar, *History of Fundamentalism*, 10.

51. Marsden, *American Culture*, 226.

52. Hutchison, *Modern Impulse*, 9–11.

53. McLoughlin, *Modern Revivalism*, 24–26, 34–35. Finney's attitude toward the Westminster Confession is discussed in Hambrick-Stowe, *Finney*, 26–28. Hambrick-Stowe points out that the attitude toward the Confession in the Western New York Presbytery was generally lax at the time of his examination in the early 1820s.

54. Dorrien, *American Liberalism*, 63–64. King, an Oberlin graduate, later studied under Adolf von Harnack in Berlin and by the turn of the century had assumed Finney's position as theological instructor.

55. Faupel, "Whither Pentecostalism?" 21, citing Fry, "Pentecostalism in Historical Perspective," *The Springfielder* (March 1976) 182, 192. Hollenweger follows Faupel's argument in *Pentecostalism*, 191–92.

56. Dorrien chronicles several of these conversions in *Modern Liberalism*. For Mathews, see 181–85. For Macintosh, see 237–43.

through Arminian theology, but there was a difference between what Roger Olson has called Arminianism of the head and Arminianism of the heart.[57] Furthermore, Faupel under-appreciates the role of pietism in forming fundamentalist spirituality, and also how steeped modernists were in the scientific spirit of the age. For modernists experience was moderated through culture while for pentecostals it was moderated through the Spirit.[58] Moreover, modernists disdained creed because they feared it would straight-jacket their religious notions. Pentecostals disdained creed because they feared it would hinder the work of the Spirit and divide them ecclesiastically. In short, modernists desired freedom to explore the human spirit while pentecostals desired freedom to explore the Holy Spirit. Though there were parallels between the two, they did not stem from the same source.

To pursue the familial analogy, modernism if anything was more like an estranged cousin to the evangelicalism of 1900. Though modernists and fundamentalists co-existed within the same denominations, particularly in the Northern Baptists and Northern Presbyterians, they had drifted apart for some time theologically. Fundamentalism subscribed to the Enlightenment philosophy as expressed by Thomas Reid and Scottish Common Sense Realism as Marsden has traced, while modernism adhered to the Romantic notions as expressed by Finney and the New Theology. While not doubting Finney's impact on revivalists and pentecostals, his theological imprint was felt equally in modernism as well.

Pentecostalism is much more of a fraternal twin to the holiness movement.[59] In the early years, they were virtually indistinguishable to onlookers in temperament and teaching. Pentecostalism posed a greater menace to the holiness movement, hijacking some of its institutions wholesale when it first emerged. Their proximity more than any other factor explains the rancor between them. Fundamentalism, though related by birth through the Prayer Meeting Revival and sharing much of the evangelical DNA with pentecostals, was appalled at pentecostal extremes in biblical interpretation and emotion. Pressing the analogy a step further, fundamentalism was more like an older brother looking upon the antics of a younger sibling. "Grow up!" he would say. And meanwhile he told the neighbors they weren't related.

A Place for Pentecostalism, 1900

In his dissertation, Faupel contends that pentecostalism was born as a pietistic movement in the midst of the Prayer Meeting Revival. He tracks this piety through Jonathan Edwards and Charles Finney in the Reformed-wing and through Methodism and Phoebe Palmer in the Wesleyan. There is much to commend in Faupel's work. As he has ably demonstrated, piety lay at the heart of evangelicalism throughout the nineteenth century. This was coupled with premillennial expectations in the late nineteenth century, particularly fueled by the belief that a spiritual outpouring would precede the Second Advent. Indeed, holiness and fundamentalist brethren manifested many of these elements as well.

---

57. See Olson, *Arminian Theology* (2006).
58. For contrasts between pentecostals and modernists, see Cox, *Fire from Heaven*, 75.
59. See Dieter, *Holiness Revival*, 76.

Alternatively, Robert Anderson viewed the tongues movement as an ecstatic expression of Christianity.[60] As a social historian, he described pentecostalism in Marxist terms, capitalizing on the marginalization of its proletarian station. "Disinherited" from the power structures of society, pentecostals sought solace from their "gruelling, insipid lives" in psychic escape through the euphoria of tongues-speech.[61] In effect, the pentecostal dousing gave voice to the voiceless and purpose to the purposeless. Of course, pentecostals would not think of themselves as "deprived" in the way Anderson envisions. Allan Anderson offers a corrective by stressing that the pentecostal experience touches upon the existential needs of believers at a very human level.[62] Still, Robert Anderson's book remains an invaluable resource in biography and analysis, though pentecostals will disagree with his conclusions.[63]

Edith Blumhofer has flagged the "restorationist roots" of pentecostals in *Restoring the Faith* (1993) and in other publications.[64] The advantage of this position is that it locates pentecostalism in a more spacious context. From this perspective it could be argued that Protestantism in general is a restorationist movement. Certainly the early pentecostals saw themselves in this way. Lewis Wilson complains correctly that Blumhofer at times overstates her case by allocating restorationism to nearly everything pentecostals did.[65] However, as Grant Wacker has advocated, restorationism is what undergirded the movement.[66] In other words, it need not be a prominent theme in order to be present. If nothing else, restorationism provided a theological sinew that connected pentecostals to the past. This motif became important to early pentecostals in defending their apparent "newness," as we shall see.

Steven Ware has applied the restoration theme to the holiness movement, stating that whereas in the pentecostal movement the message was explicit, in holiness it was implicit.[67] Ware draws a helpful distinction between what he calls "spiritual" and "ecclesiastical" restorationism.[68] Though both are present in many Protestant movements, one or the other tends to be emphasized. Pentecostals gravitated towards the spiritual pole. Carpenter noticed the same trait among fundamentalists. However, instead of recovering New Testament Christianity, fundamentalists wished to preserve what had been restored already through the Reformation.[69] They lived out their faith through the epistles whereas

---

60. Anderson, *Vision*, 4. This theme is taken largely from Lewis, *Ecstatic Religion* (1971).

61. Anderson, *Vision*, 96, 240.

62. Anderson, *Introduction*, 229.

63. Wilson has challenged Anderson's position in "They crossed the Red Sea" 159–76. Anderson argued that the pentecostal revival petered out in 1909. For Wilson, theories of psychological deprivation and social displacement fail to explain why the movement has endured while keeping much of its vitality intact.

64. See also Blumhofer, *Assemblies of God*, 1:15. On restoration, see also Blumhofer, "Restoration as Revival," 146–60; and Faupel, *Everlasting Gospel*, 35–56.

65. Wilson, Review of *Restoring the Faith*, 119–22.

66. Wacker, "Playing for Keeps," 205–6. See also Neinkirchen, "Conflicting Visions," 120.

67. Ware, "Restoring the New Testament Church," 241.

68. Ibid., 240.

69. Carpenter, "Contending for the Faith," 101.

pentecostals lived out theirs through the Book of Acts. (We may add here that modernists too recaptured the Bible, which they had reduced to the ethical teachings of Jesus in the Gospels.) The difficulty in viewing pentecostalism strictly through a restorative lens is that it fails to separate it adequately from other movements.

Richard Lovelace correctly observes that pentecostals appeal too frequently to glossolalic precedents to fit their movement into church history. Tying tongues to Mormonism, the Shakers and Montanists should give one pause and ask why the Holy Spirit has such odd theological preferences, says Lovelace.[70] He thinks a better milieu for pentecostalism is within the revivalist tradition. Though he is correct in suggesting that pentecostalism is much closer to evangelicalism than it is to Mormonism, the descent from Reformed revivalism to pentecostalism is not as obvious as one might suppose. Lovelace traces revivalism from Jonathan Edwards to Charles Finney but terminates his argument there, leaving a rather embarrassing gap between Finney and the pentecostals.[71] Likewise, Dale Frederick Bruner claims in his detailed study of pentecostal theology that the line from Finney's revivalism to pentecostalism is a direct one, but he assumes rather than proves his case.[72] A connection likely exists, but it still needs to be made explicit.

Pentecostals enlarged initially through the more extreme ranks of the holiness movement or "radical evangelicals" (as they styled themselves). After the initial stages, they also gathered adherents from the Keswick-wing. Vinson Synan is more adamant than most in underlining the Methodist-holiness roots of pentecostals.[73] Others, mainly AG scholars like William Menzies and Blumhofer, have profiled the Reformed roots of the movement.[74] The Keswick-wing has been an important and at times overlooked addition. Nevertheless, Synan is right to show that sanctification as encapsulated in the Wesleyan-wing forms the main branch of the early pentecostal movement in the United States. That sanctification migrated to receptive Presbyterians and Baptists should not obscure its beginnings. Whether or not pentecostalism would have existed without the prior antecedents in the holiness movement as Steven Land insists, it certainly would have appeared in a different shape if it had.[75] Tongues after all did occur outside the holiness movement, but it is within that movement that the phenomenon of tongues received its theological impetus.

---

70. Lovelace, "Baptism in the Holy Spirit," 101.

71. Ibid., 120.

72. Bruner, *Holy Spirit*, 42.

73. Synan in *Holiness-Pentecostal* focuses on his own tradition in the South, where the holiness roots were more prominent. An excellent study in itself, its main flaw was in focusing too little attention on the Keswick influence on pentecostals. Anderson suggests contra Synan that Parham would never have come to his position on tongues without the intervention of Keswick-fundamentalism (*Vision*, 43, 54).

74. Menzies, *Anointed to Serve,* and "Non-Wesleyan Origins," 81–98; Waldvogel, "The 'Overcoming Life,'" passim, and Blumhofer, *Assemblies of God*, vol. 1.

75. Land, *Pentecostal Spirituality*, 49.

The Holiness Conduit of Pentecostalism

Dayton, Faupel and Blumhofer have each in their own way performed a yeoman's task in uncovering the nineteenth-century precedents of pentecostalism.[76] I do not wish to replicate their efforts here. Pertinent to the thesis however is the transference of Dayton's pentecostal *gestalt* from protofundamentalism to pentecostalism via the holiness movement in the realms of premillennialism, spiritual baptism and divine healing. Due to space, this section will sketch only in bare detail how these teachings filtered through radical evangelicalism. The fourth component, Christ as Savior, was dear to all three through their common evangelical heritage and will therefore not be discussed.

The theology of the baptism in the Spirit was loosely derived by Phoebe Palmer from John Wesley. The Reformed-wing developed its own version of perfectionism from Oberlin College professor Charles Finney and its president Asa Mahan. *The Higher Christian Life* (1858), a momentous volume by Presbyterian layman William E. Boardman, also pollinated the doctrine among like-minded Calvinists. Quakers Robert Pearsall and Hannah Whitall Smith exported it to England in the early 1870s and were instrumental in establishing the Keswick Convention in the Lake District from 1875 onwards. Several protofundamentalists attested to consecratory experiences in their ministries, D. L. Moody in 1871, A. B. Simpson in 1874, and A. T. Pierson in 1875.[77] The experience in each case preceded their adoption of premillennialism.

Jonathan Edwards launched a postmillennial vision of the world upon colonial America, which became standard fare for nineteenth-century evangelicalism. An alternative eschatology was shaped in England through the Plymouth Brethren, a small but influential group. Its leader, J. N. Darby, was an indefatigable traveler and promoter of a system he had developed in the 1830s and 1840s: dispensationalism. In turn, Darby had been influenced by Edward Irving's eschatology, though the two never met.[78] In America, premillennialism made slow but steady headway among conservatives. James Brookes

---

76. Dayton, *Theological Roots*; Faupel, *Everlasting Gospel*; Waldvogel, "Overcoming Life."

77. There is some controversy as to whether Simpson came into the experience during Daniel Whittle's evangelistic campaign in the fall of 1874 or the spring of 1875 (there is also controversy as to when the campaign took place) or as a result of reading Boardman's work prior to the campaign, as McGraw argues. See Thompson, *Life of A. B. Simpson*, 65–67, and McGraw, "The Doctrine of Sanctification," 148–49. I follow McGraw's argument here.

78. Murray makes the case that all the salient features of Irving's theology are present in Darby (*The Puritan Hope*, 200). The influence came from the Albury Conferences (1826–1830) south of London to the Powerscourt Conferences near Dublin (1831–1836). Irving was prominent at Albury, which Lady Powerscourt attended, hosting a similar conference at her estate, which Darby attended and became a leading proponent, though his own thought did not crystallize until about 1840.

became a disciple around 1864,[79] D. L. Moody around 1872,[80] A. J. Gordon around 1874,[81] A. B. Simpson around 1875,[82] and A. T. Pierson around 1879.[83] Brookes was instrumental in organizing the Niagara Prophecy Conferences (1883–1899).[84] One member of his St. Louis congregation, C. I. Scofield, would virtually become synonymous with dispensationalism through his reference Bible (1909).

Healing also secured inroads among protofundamentalists following their consecrations. The doctrine gained currency first in Germany under Jacob Blumhardt and in Switzerland under Dorothea Trudel. An Episcopal physician in Boston, Charles Cullis, considered it in 1864, two years after his encounter with the Spirit.[85] After touring Europe in 1873, meeting with Trudel and George Müller, he incorporated faith healing into his home for consumptives. A. B. Simpson experienced healing in 1882 while on vacation at Cullis's camp at Old Orchard Beach, Maine.[86] In 1883 his daughter was healed of her infirmity, and a year later he opened up the Berachah Home in New York. Not to be outdone, A. J. Gordon's *The Ministry of Healing* (1882) became a template for pentecostals.

Sanctification was already part of the holiness movement, but the National Holiness Association shunned premillennialism and divine healing as inconsistent with its ethos. In 1894 the Methodist church, increasing in wealth and respectability, lost patience with holiness extremes, passing Rule 301 which barred anyone from preaching in a Methodist pulpit without episcopal approval.[87] Additionally, many holiness bands had by this point developed outside Methodism, forming loosely organized associations in their own right.[88]

---

79. Sanders, *Premillennial Faith*, 26–33. Sanders believes that Brookes came into the doctrine through James Inglis in the mid-1860s and not through Darby as Sandeen suggests (*Roots*, 74–75), although Sanders misstates Sandeen's position that they may have met in 1863 and not in 1872. Sanders is correct in that Darby's earlier visits were meant to encourage Brethren fellowships and not spread dispensationalism as his later trips did.

80. Faupel lists 1877 (*Everlasting Gospel*, 99). This is when Moody began to preach regularly on the topic, but I think Blumhofer is right that his conversion to premillennialism happened shortly after his baptism (Waldvogel, "Overcoming Life," 21–22). McLoughlin's guess of the mid-1850s seems hasty (*Modern Revivalism*, 257).

81. Gibson, *A. J. Gordon*, 32–34. Gordon was initially influenced by the Plymouth Brethren but soon resorted to a historicist premillennialist position, one of the few at the Niagara Bible Conference who did so. Sandeen gives evidence that Gordon may have attended Darby's lectures in Boston in 1875 (*Roots*, 78), though the information is inconclusive and he had abandoned dispensationalism by that point at any rate.

82. Sung, "Second Coming," 62–63, notes that Simpson came to doubt postmillennialism shortly after his consecration but did not state why or even how he was influenced, which was abnormal for him.

83. Pierson was influenced in this as in many things by George Müller, who attended the 1833 Powerscourt conference. D. Robert contradicts Delevan Pierson's date of 1878 by showing that Müller preached for Pierson in January 1879 (*Occupy*, 103–4). Dayton's date of 1883 is too late, based on when he began presenting the doctrine ("Christian Perfection," 50). As with Moody, Pierson may have been reluctant to preach the doctrine immediately due to its unpopularity.

84. The conference met at Point Chautauqua, New York for the last two years. Brookes's death in 1895 effectively ended the broad appeal Niagara had to premillennialists of all stripes.

85. Dayton, *Theological Roots*, 123.

86. Thompson, *Simpson*, 72–79.

87. Synan, *Old-Time Power*, 46.

88. Dieter, *Holiness Revival*, 124.

The severance allowed for more radical teachings to enter those who were dissatisfied with Methodism's direction. Two examples will suffice.

Martin Wells Knapp, holiness editor of *The Revivalist* in Cincinnati, proclaimed premillennialism in January 1897.[89] The March edition printed several short excerpts dedicated to the subject, including a selection from Methodist W. E. Blackstone's *Jesus is Coming* and an article by Knapp condemning the fallacy of postmillennialism, citing the escalation of crime and divorce as confirmation that the world was in a deteriorating condition.[90] By 1899, a full page was dedicated to the premillennial theme (usually page six), with the title "Behold He Cometh" (the subtitle to Gordon's *Ecce Venit* [1889]), and another to divine healing (usually page ten).[91] Gordon's writings figured prominently in both columns.[92]

The first radical holiness preacher to separate the baptism of the Spirit from sanctification was Ralph Horner, a Methodist evangelist in Ontario, Canada. In 1891, he argued that Wesley's Aldersgate experience was actually a spiritual baptism and later claimed it for himself as a "qualification to do signs and wonders in the name of the Lord."[93] But the individual who had the greatest impact on pentecostalism was Benjamin H. Irwin. Irwin, a Baptist, ran afoul with the Iowa Holiness Association when he taught a third experience, a "baptism of fire" beyond that of the "Spirit." His "three-blessingism," to which he would later add more experiences, was condemned by IHA president Isaiah Reid. Irwin organized "Fire-Baptized" associations in Iowa, Kansas, and Oklahoma in 1896 and spread the message to the Southeast in 1897.[94] These associations would form the nucleus of the Pentecostal Holiness Church under J. H. King after Irwin fell into "gross immorality" (drunkenness) in the summer of 1900.

Charles Fox Parham's friction with Methodism stemmed from his belief in sanctification and divine healing. Relegated to "supply" status, Parham threw himself into independent ministry in 1895.[95] Inspired by Irwin, whose camp he had attended, Parham came to believe that sanctification and the baptism of the Holy Spirit were separate events, which had not been traditional holiness parlance.[96] Parham also found stimulation in John Alexander Dowie's community in Zion, Illinois, and Frank Sanford's Shiloh complex in Maine, where he heard tongues spoken in 1900.[97] At Parham's training school in Topeka,

---

89. Knapp, "A Great Doctrine Neglected," *TRev*, March 1897, 2; Hills, *A Hero of Faith*, 154.

90. Knapp, "A Post Millennial Fallacy," *TRev*, March 1897, 2; Blackstone, "Jesus is Coming," *TRev*, March 1897, 2.

91. The bulk of 1898 is non-extant. It is likely that the format was changed then.

92. Of eighty articles in 1899 by protofundamentalists, Gordon was reprinted forty times, all but one of them from either *Ecce Venit* (twenty-five times) or *The Ministry of Healing* (fourteen times). See Appendix A.

93. Dayton, *Theological Roots*, 99–100, cf. Horner, *Pentecost*, 138. Quotation from Horner, *Evangelist*, 13–14.

94. Fankhauser, "The Heritage of Faith," 128–32.

95. Goff, *Fields White unto Harvest*, 36.

96. Synan, *Holiness-Pentecostal*, 92.

97. Wacker, *Heaven Below*, 5; Faupel, *Everlasting Gospel*, 164–65.

Kansas, students sought for and received the "Bible evidence" of the baptism with speaking in tongues, starting with Agnes Ozman on January 1, 1901.

Summary and Conclusion

The holiness movement had permeated evangelical attitudes towards spiritual baptism through both its Wesleyan and Keswick wings, though the doctrine was nuanced through Arminian and Calvinist attitudes toward sin. The major difference was that the Wesleyan-wing taught that the baptism of the Holy Spirit eradicated sin from the heart through an instant of sanctification while the Keswick-wing believed that the baptism of the Holy Spirit empowered the believer to "overcome" the stranglehold of sin through holy living and acts of service. The ambiguity of the relationship of spiritual baptism to holiness in the book of Acts allowed for the expansion of a third (and fourth, etc.) baptismal experience in the writings of R. C. Horner, and more importantly in B. H. Irwin.

Meanwhile, the protofundamental emphasis on premillennialism and healing infiltrated radical holiness members in the late nineteenth century. It was among these radical evangelicals that pentecostalism initially found a home. These two doctrines, premillennialism and divine healing, often followed upon the Spirit-baptism experience of protofundamentalists and became nearly a theological package. But protofundamentalists were battling the emerging modernist movement as early as 1874 with David Swing. It was also the beginnings of the prophecy conferences that would form an important venue for developing fundamentalist doctrines along the lines of dispensationalism and the inerrancy of Scripture. These interests would later combine with the Keswick spirituality as it penetrated protofundamentalist ranks by the last decade of the century.

The pentecostal *gestalt* of Christ as savior, healer, baptizer and coming king had been articulated most effectively by protofundamentalists, especially A. B. Simpson. Thus, while pentecostalism began in the context of the holiness movement as will be demonstrated in chapter 3, the protofundamentalist movement established the rubric around which its theology formed. The proximity of pentecostalism to the holiness movement in the religious environment caused great friction between them. Protofundamentalism was further removed and therefore less threatened by pentecostals, though it was not long before it too felt infringed upon by the expanding movement. The protofundamentalist reaction to pentecostalism and the pentecostal response to protofundamentalist critiques will also occupy the next chapter, along with the development of premillennial thought in pentecostalism and the eventual pentecostal shift towards dispensationalism.

PART TWO

Genesis

3

Emerging Pentecostalism (1906–1909)

Introduction

RETURNING TO THE MODEL OF POPULATION ECOLOGY, THE FIRST STAGE CONSISTS OF production, or what I have labeled here *genesis*. In ecological terms it entails the introduction of a new species into an existing environment. In our milieu this translates into a new expression of faith within an existing religious context. The phase is often short and constitutes something of an explosion onto the scene. As chronicled in the previous chapter, many of the foundational themes of pentecostals were transferred to them from protofundamentalism via the holiness movement. From its inception, pentecostalism grew largely but not exclusively within the holiness movement. Keswick protofundamentalists, who formed one branch of the holiness movement, were also susceptible to the fervor of pentecostalism, which in turn inaugurated a muscular response from those leaders whose membership were affected by it. Pentecostals, aware of this reaction, responded by tracing their movement to spiritual precedents throughout church history. They saw themselves as the final manifestation of the reformation of Christendom by recapturing the lost gifts of the early church. Meanwhile, the drift from holiness to fundamentalist modes of thought within pentecostalism began with an acute eschatology informed by the dispensational theology as articulated in the Scofield Reference Bible.

While there is debate as to whether the pentecostal movement began with Agnes Ozman at Charles Fox Parham's Bethel School in Topeka, Kansas in 1901 or with the Azusa Street revival under William J. Seymour in Los Angeles in 1906, this study will begin with Los Angeles, for it is from Azusa Street that the movement spread most rapidly in the United States and Canada. Parham was no doubt an important figure as an innovator of pentecostal theology and instrumental in introducing the doctrine of tongues to Seymour in December 1905. We have traced the development of the baptism of the Holy Spirit from Phoebe Palmer to Parham in the previous chapter and need not reinvestigate that here. Briefly, we will cover how pentecostalism spread from Azusa Street to various religious circles throughout North America.

Seymour, the son of ex-slaves in Mississippi, absorbed Parham's doctrine during a short-term Bible school Parham conducted in Houston, Texas. In keeping with the racial mores of the day, Parham permitted Seymour to sit in the doorway while he lectured from the classroom. He hoped that Seymour would disseminate the Apostolic Faith to the black population of the South, but events intervened. Seymour was called to Los Angeles by a struggling black holiness mission that had only recently broken its ties to a local Baptist church over the issue of sanctification.[1] However, once there, Seymour soon found that the promotion of tongues as the sign of baptism was unwelcome and was subsequently locked out of the church.

Undeterred, Seymour and a handful of the faithful removed to a home on Bonnie Brae Street in February of 1906. He continued to preach on tongues even though he himself was not yet a practitioner. On April 9 the Spirit descended with tongues upon an Edward Lee before his dinner, and then upon others during the evening prayer meeting.[2] Nine days later the Great San Francisco Earthquake sent tremors up and down the West Coast. The "spiritual earthquake" which preceded it at Los Angeles would have a far more lasting and global impact. The attraction which the prayer meeting garnered forced the group to find a larger edifice—the famed mission at 312 Azusa Street, but the revival fires could not simply be contained in their ramshackle building, affectionately known as "the barn." Missionaries were dispatched to the surrounding region and indeed around the world to promulgate the message of this modern-day Pentecost. Having been incubated in the holiness movement, pentecostalism multiplied within its favorable environment.

Early Spread of Pentecostalism

Railroads (and steamships) were to the pentecostal movement what the Roman highways were to the primitive Christians. Cecil M. Robeck has shown that virtually every household in the city of Los Angeles had access to the streetcar system and that six railroad companies connected the city to the rest of the country.[3] Henry Huntington's Pacific Electric Railroad also branched into the outlying areas, making it possible for the revival to reach places like Monrovia and Whittier.[4] By September a band of workers led by Florence Crawford had traveled by train to Oakland to visit a mission run by William Manley, editor of the holiness periodical *Household of God*. During the meetings thirty seekers found their Pentecost.[5] October found Azusa missionaries A. G. and Lillian Garr at their old "band" in Danville, Virginia, where Lillian improved her xenolalic ability to speak in both "Thibetan [sic] and Chinese."[6] Meanwhile, after switching railroad cars in New Orleans, Lucy Farrow arrived in Portsmouth, Virginia. She pleaded for assistance from the Azusa constituency (whether by prayer or in material support is unclear) in ministering to a group of believers there who had neglected to read their Bibles because they claimed Scripture was written to unbelievers only.[7] By November Tom Hezmalhalch had brought Pentecost to a holiness

---

1. Blumhofer, *Assemblies of God*, 1:90.
2. Robeck, *Azusa Street Mission*, 67.
3. Ibid., 54.
4. Ibid., 97, 205.
5. "Fire Falling at Oakland," *AF*(LA) (September 1906) 4.
6. Garr, "Pentecost in Danville, Va." *AF*(LA) (October 1906) 2. "Band" was a common designation in the holiness movement for a gathering of believers.
7. Farrow, "Work in Virginia," *AF*(LA) (October 1906) 3.

mission in Denver run by G. F. Fink, declaring that it was "but the beginning of a work here such as we knew in Los Angeles."⁸ December's issue of *The Apostolic Faith* reported new works in San Diego under F. E. Hill, San Jose under H. M. Turney, Benton Harbor, Michigan under Elsie Robinson, Seattle, Washington under Thomas Junk, and Fort Worth, Texas under Mrs. C. A. Roll, among seven other locales.⁹

Just as importantly, railroads brought many who were receiving news about the revival through *The Apostolic Faith* and various holiness periodicals (both positively like *Way of Faith* and negatively like *The Nazarene Messenger*) to seek their own Pentecost at the Azusa Street Mission. An unnamed Armenian brother came "only" 300 miles in October to examine if the reports he had heard about Pentecost were true. He likened his journey to the Queen of Sheba's investigation of Solomon and, like the fabled Sovereign, left well satisfied.¹⁰ William Durham arrived from Chicago on February 8, 1907 and departed on March 6 filled with the Spirit, stopping off to preach in missions in Colorado Springs, Denver and Des Moines along his way back.¹¹ Having read of Azusa through *Way of Faith*, G. B. Cashwell ventured to California from North Carolina, traveling some three thousand miles over six days. He received his Pentecost shortly after arriving and returned to his home in Dunn, where fifty received tongues under his ministry. He then embarked on a tour of the South as a sort of pentecostal apostle, eventually establishing a mission in Atlanta.¹²

The holiness movement provided the atmosphere into which the pentecostal movement was born and where the effects were first experienced. Most of the preachers who received their Pentecost in these early years like the aforementioned had connections with the holiness movement and many of the lay-people like Florence Crawford and Agnes Ozman were seasoned holiness workers. After seeking earnestly for nine days, the Quaker-holiness educator Levi Lupton received his baptism over a four-hour period at the "10 a.m." night service [sic] on November 30, 1906 at his school in Alliance, Ohio.¹³ During that time he gave multiple messages in tongues and interpretation and was given "other remarkable revelations" which he did not feel at liberty to relate. Like many holiness clergy, J. Jeter of Little Rock, Arkansas struggled to reconcile his sanctification experience with the baptism as evidenced by tongues. Sifting through the "chaff and wheat" of the Azusa Street meetings, he finally gave up his preconceived notions about the baptism and "experienced

---

8. Hezmalhalch, "Pentecost in Denver," *AF*(LA) (November 1906) 1.

9. "Pentecost in San Diego," *AF*(LA) (December 1906) 1; "Pentecost in San Jose," *AF*(LA) (December 1906) 1; "Pentecost in Benton Harbor," *AF*(LA) (December 1906) 1; "Pentecost in Seattle," *AF*(LA) (December 1906) 1; "Pentecost in Fort Worth," *AF*(LA) (December 1906) 1.

10. "Came Three Hundred Miles," *AF*(LA) (October 1906) 3.

11. Durham, "Chicago Evangelist's Pentecost," *AF*(LA) (February 1907) 4.

12. Cashwell, "Came 3,000 Miles for his Pentecost," *AF*(LA) (December 1907) 3; Cashwell, "Hundreds Baptized in the South," *AF*(LA) (February 1906) 3.

13. Lupton, "Holiness Bible School Leader Receives his Pentecost," *AF*(LA) (February 1907) 5.

Jesus" as he never had before.[14] This experience was repeated innumerably throughout the holiness movement.[15]

The awakening transformed not only individuals but also organizations. The Altamont Bible and Missionary Institute, established in 1898 by Presbyterian minister N. J. Holmes near Greenville, South Carolina, adhered to the pentecostal message in 1907.[16] Holmes had already undergone his sanctification experience after listening to D. L. Moody at Northfield in 1891 and later broke with his church. Lida Purkie, a student at the institution, attended a Cashwell meeting in West Union, North Carolina and returned "a confirmed pentecostal."[17] Holmes went to investigate Cashwell's teaching and after a thorough search of the Scriptures became convinced that the experience was real, though he still disagreed with some of Cashwell's points. By April 1907 the staff and student body had rallied to the pentecostal flag. In time Holmes associated himself with the Pentecostal Holiness Church but kept his school independent of denominational control.

Another important venue for the spread of pentecostalism was the camp meeting. Azusa Street had not grown quickly enough in 1906 to impact the camp meeting season that year, which typically ran from June through August, but in 1907 entire camps were being swept into the movement. The Falcon Camp Meeting near Dunn was founded in 1900 by J. A. Culbreth as part of the North Carolina Holiness Association.[18] It became a center for pentecostalism in 1907 following Cashwell's earlier successes in the area. Pentecost came to Durant, Florida by August of 1907, and the nearby camp grounds at Pleasant Grove (originally a Methodist camp established in 1881) became devoted to the new doctrine.[19] Azusa Street itself held its first camp in June of 1907 at a location adjacent to the city limits near the streetcar line to Hermon. Once there the saints were encouraged to pray as loud as they desired amongst the swaying oaks.[20] The conversion of holiness camps to Pentecost was repeated throughout the country.

The northeast was the last sector of the U.S. to develop a viable pentecostal witness. The holiness magazine *Word and Work* of Russell, Massachusetts endorsed the movement with some timidity in its February 1907 issue.[21] The editors, Samuel and Addie Otis, published an anonymous letter from Carrie Judd Montgomery's *Triumphs of Faith* in which the writer remarked that while fanaticism accompanied all revivals he was more concerned

---

14. Jeter, "There is something in this for Jesus," *AF*(LA) (February 1907) 6.

15. E.g., G. Watson, "Testimony," *BM* (15 January 1908) 3; "Get into the Cornfield," *AF*(LA) (October 1906) 1 [from "Brother Hill" (although the name is obscure)—a Nazarene preacher]; J. A. Culbreth, "Baptism and Evidence of Pentecost Foreshadowed," *BM* (15 February 1908) 2. Culbreth compares the Holiness rejection of tongues to the Jewish rejection of Christ.

16. Synan, *Old-Time Power*, 134; V. Synan, "Holmes, Nickels John," 410; Holmes, "Altamont Bible School," *BM* (1 December 1907) 4. The school was renamed the Holmes Bible and Missionary Institute after his death in 1919.

17. Synan, *Holiness-Pentecostal*, 127–28.

18. Synan, *Old-Time Power*, 74–75.

19. "'Everywhere Preaching the Word,'" *AF*(LA) (September 1907) 1; Simmons, "Durant, Florida," *BM* (1 February 1910) 4; "Pleasant Grove Camp Meeting," *PE* (5 June 1926) 12.

20. "Los Angeles Campmeeting of the Apostolic Faith Missions," *AF*(LA) (May 1907) 1.

21. A. Otis, "Apostolic Faith Movement," *W&Wk* (February 1907) 51–53.

with the "conservatism" that would hold the church back from enjoying the pentecostal charisms.[22] By April however *Word and Work* was fully committed to the pentecostal immersion, exhorting readers to by-pass the devil's counterfeits for "GENUINE nuggets of pure gold."[23] Articles appeared in this same issue from pentecostal leaders W. F. Carothers, M. L. Ryan, and J. E. Sawders, as well as a report on "Pentecost in India" and unexpected encouragement from Baptist academician A. S. Worrell.

With ties to *Word and Work*, the last holiness organization to adopt pentecostalism was the First Fruit Harvesters (FFH) of Rumney Depot, New Hampshire at their camp meeting in August 1908. Founded by Joel Wright in 1897 with visions of uniting Christendom under one banner, the group had first heard about tongues in the fall of 1905.[24] Despite misgivings concerning the doctrine of initial evidence, the band experienced tongues with Wright "rolling among the pine needles." By November 1908 Wright's son Elwin reported that some thirty souls had found "Jesus as the latter rain" and that a spirit of unity had replaced "contention and self seeking."[25] Under the leadership of Elwin, the Harvesters became a model of evangelical cooperation in the 1930s, as will be seen later. Though the Northeast was the last region to accept pentecostalism, the last holiness camp I have found in the U.S. to change allegiance to pentecostalism was the Vienna Holiness Association near Bloomfield, Illinois in September 1909.[26]

From the holiness perspective, such meetings were disruptive. John Harris recalled years later the havoc which tongues wreaked upon the Marvin camp twelve miles distant from St. Louis in the summer of 1907. On the evening he arrived a young man cautioned him not to "grieve the Spirit." The pentecostals had already taken over the group's periodical *The Vanguard*.[27] Harris was appalled at the chaos of the meetings. One married man had taken up with a young woman, allegedly at the behest of the Holy Spirit. Luema Angel, a missionary to India, sought tongues "stretched out on the floor, rolling back and forth, seemingly unconscious," her dress up in an "indecent" manner.[28] Over the next three days Miss Angel claimed to speak in twenty languages and left the camp to return to India via her sister's house. Unfortunately, she died just days after arriving at her sister's, attestation to Harris that errant beliefs killed spirit and body alike.[29] The leader of the pentecostal band, a Mr. B., wired California to send for someone to replace him in the revival. The replacement impressed Harris with his knowledge of Scripture but not with his inability to cast demons out of the adulterous lady mentioned above, who had by that time been abandoned and fallen ill.[30] One of the pentecostal participants, S. D. Kinne, condemned

---

22. "Prayer for the Church of God—A Crisis Hour," *W&Wk* (February 1907) 39–40.

23. A. Otis, "Apostolic Work," *W&Wk* (April 1907) 115–16. By 1909 miraculous cures had replaced wellness as the periodical's understanding of healing.

24. Carpenter, *Revive Us Again*, 142; Berends, "Social Variables," 71.

25. E. Wright, "Rumney, N. H.," *W&Wk* (November 1908) 342.

26. Lawrence, "Holiness Camp Meeting went Pentecostal," *TPent* (15 October 1909) 3.

27. Harris, *Tears and Triumphs*, 334 [FPHC].

28. Ibid., 336.

29. Ibid., 337.

30. Ibid., 337–38.

Harris's resistance as akin to the Pharisees attitude toward Jesus, though Harris himself never regretted his opposition.[31] In the end, thirty to forty pentecostal converts vacated the camp and moved into St. Louis, where according to Harris they splintered into four factions, each with a separate leader avowing "he was right and the others wrong."

In many ways their intransigence was understandable. Holiness folk were learning for the first time that they were not baptized in the Spirit when for years they thought they were. Lacking the coveted gift of tongues, they were relegated to "second-class" spiritual status.[32] In the quest for evidences of the baptism, as Grant Wacker asserts, pentecostals beat the holiness crowd at their own game.[33] The witness for holiness folk had been some vague internal euphoria. Pentecostals on the other hand had a demonstrable, audible signal. Wacker posits that the earliest holiness response to pentecostals came in the November 15, 1906 issue of *The Christian Witness and Advocate of Bible Holiness*, but the distinction most likely belongs to C. V. LaFontaine in an article in the *Nazarene Messenger* for July 19, 1906.[34] Based on his sermon "The More Excellent Way" delivered July 8 at the First Church of the Nazarene, LaFontaine objected to the concept of "missionary tongues" being promulgated by Los Angeles adherents. Tongues were an inferior gift at which only "childish" believers in ancient Corinth tried to excel. While the movement should not be condemned wholesale, he advised, a danger remained in that the practice could be self-manufactured or even manipulated by the devil and would most likely lead to fanaticism and an uncharitable spirit, far from the Pauline ideal of love.[35] More articles followed in the *Nazarene Messenger* from editor P. F. Bresee and in other holiness periodicals like *The Gospel Trumpet*, the Church of God (Anderson, Indiana) organ, and *Pentecostal Advocate* of Peniel, Texas, edited by R. W. Huckabee.[36]

Respected peripatetic holiness scholar William Godbey wrote three tracts denouncing "the tongues movement" between 1908 and 1915. The first, *Current Heresies*, defined heresy as that which "separates," dissecting three radical perversions of the holiness movement before addressing the tongues heresy.[37] Godbey toured the West Coast from December 1907 to early March 1908, inquiring as to whether anyone had actually received the "missionary" gift of tongues, which he believed to be a real phenomenon. One woman in Oakland claimed to speak Chinese, but he perceived the declaration to be false.[38] In

---

31. Kinne, "Procession of the Pharisees," *W&Wk* (August 1907) 198–99. This article was reprinted from *The Vanguard*—though Harris is not mentioned by name. Harris claims that the pentecostals had renamed the periodical as *The Banner*. If so, it would have been at a later time.

32. Wacker, *Heaven Below*, 6.

33. Wacker, "Travail of a Broken Family," 41. Spittler raises the issue as to whether any historical link exists between Darwinism and this quest for evidence in "Suggested Areas," 48. An intriguing question it may be, but he admits it would be difficult to test.

34. Wacker, "Travail," 44; LaFontaine, "More Excellent Way," *Nazarene Messenger* (19 July 1906) 10–12 [FPHC].

35. LaFontaine, "More Excellent Way," 12.

36. See Appendix B for a partial list of anti-pentecostal articles in holiness periodicals (1907–1910).

37. Godbey, *Current Heresies*, 8, 12–16 [FPHC]; the three other heresies were "power," "fire," and "water"—the first two the results of the "third blessing" heresy.

38. Ibid., 22–24.

Los Angeles, a man familiar with spiritualists explained to him that much of what passed for tongues was no different from what transpired at a séance. Godbey lamented, "The tongue heresy climaxes all the heresies of all ages in the Holiness Movement."[39] He made the spiritualism charge more explicit in his next critique, *Spiritualism, Devil-worship and the Tongues*.[40] By seeking the gift rather than the giver, "you open wide the door for evil spirits to come in and play the Holy Ghost upon you, thus running you into Spiritualism."[41] Through this avenue spiritualism had subtly invaded the holiness movement, Godbey postulated. His third tract, *Tongue Movement, Satanic*, was published by Alma White's Pillar of Fire in 1918, although he actually scribed it in 1915, leading many to assume falsely that Godbey had first visited Azusa Street in 1909 when in fact it was 1906.[42] Here Godbey recounted his reluctance to preach at the mission, only relenting at Seymour's urging. Asked in the pulpit whether or not he spoke in tongues, he replied in Latin, "*Johannes Baptistes tinxit, Petros tinxit et Christus misit suos Apostolos, ut gentes tingerent*."[43] The impressed worshippers desired that he should oversee their fledgling movement, but Godbey politely declined and walked away.

Alma White truculently opposed pentecostalism, airing her feelings in *Demons and Tongues* after her estranged husband Kent joined the pentecostal movement in England and refused to return with her to America.[44] The book was published in 1910 and reprinted in 1918 and 1936. This last included a severely edited version of Godbey's *Tongue Movement, Satanic* as an appendix, which wrongly supplied the 1909 date. White labeled the movement as "turkey-buzzard vomit" and uncharitably described Seymour, who had visited her mission in Denver on his way to Los Angeles, as "very untidy" and excelling all other "religious fakes and tramps."[45] Her violent reaction can best be explained by the threat which pentecostalism posed to her ministry in lost numbers and revenue and the personal rupture involving her marriage.

Initial Reaction of Fundamentalism

The earliest fundamentalist rejoinder to pentecostalism came from the pen of A. T. Pierson. Pierson, like other protofundamentalists, expected a great outpouring of the Spirit to precede Christ's coming in glory. In a chapter titled "The New Pentecosts" in *The New Acts of the Apostles* (1894) he observed: "Careful comparison of the second chapters of Joel and of the Acts must convince us that the cup of prediction has not yet been full to the brim, and waits for a more copious outpouring. Pentecost was the summer shower after the drought;

---

39. Ibid., 20.

40. Godbey, *Spiritualism, Devil-worship, and the Tongues* (c. 1911) [ATS Arch]. The date for 1911 is based upon the trip of Gorham Tufts to India in 1901, which Godbey reports as having preceded the tract by ten years [cf. Tufts, "Liberated from Dr. Dowie," *Holiness Advocate* (1 August 1901) 2].

41. Ibid., 21–22.

42. See King, "Holiness Preacher," n.p.

43. Godbey, *Tongue Movement, Satanic*, 4–5. The Latin can be translated as "John the Baptist baptized, Peter baptized and Christ sent his apostles that they might baptize the nations" (my translation).

44. Stanley, "Alma White," 81; White, *Demons and Tongues* (1910).

45. Quoted in Blumhofer, *Assemblies of God*, 1:90.

the final outpouring will make springs gust forth and turn the desert into a garden, and a thousand rills, singing their song, shall blend in rivers of grace that roll like a liquid anthem to the sea."[46]

A similar line was taken in 1900 in his retrospective *Forward Movements of the Past Half Century*, where he predicted that the supernatural signs of the past might reappear in the future if "a new Pentecost could restore primitive faith, worship, unity and activity."[47] Samuel Otis, after espousing pentecostalism, appealed to an extensive quote from Pierson to defend the spread of miracles in anticipation of the second advent. "There is every reason to believe," said Pierson, "that the millennial reign of Christ will be introduced by wonders more startling than ever astonished the mind of man."[48] Unwittingly, end-time theorists had given pentecostals an apologia for their existence.

Pierson was not as amiable to the sign of tongues, however. At the Keswick convention in 1905 he took charge of an impromptu prayer meeting that had been overrun with some 300 Welsh enthusiasts. Dana Robert speculates that Pierson may have reacted to apparent "speaking in tongues" among other manifestations at the normally sedate proceedings when he dubbed it a "Satanic disturbance."[49] The Welsh language certainly could have sounded like gibberish to him. In August 1906 he included without comment a report by veteran missionary Minnie F. Abrams on a revival at Pandita Ramabai's home for child-widows in Pune, India, in *Missionary Review of the World* (*MRW*), which he edited. The revival had commenced at the end of June 1905 and was occasion for much repentance and rejoicing among the girls. Abrams was convinced that "the baptism of the Holy Ghost *and fire* is for all who are willing to put themselves wholly at God's disposal."[50] Nowhere in the article did Abrams mention tongues, but clearly she believed that there were two distinct baptisms that awaited all believers—one for service by the Holy Ghost and one for purification by fire.

Pierson answered the pentecostal movement in July 1907 in *MRW*, although he had composed lengthier articles in May for *Life of Faith*, a Keswick-themed weekly based in London.[51] Pierson interrupted a series he had been writing on "The Bible and the Spiritual Life" for *Life of Faith* to author the three anti-pentecostal pieces, perhaps stirred by the devotional lessons for those issues, which covered the original account of Pentecost in Acts.[52] Having tested his judgments on a British readership and heartened by the feedback, he

---

46. Pierson, *New Acts of the Apostles*, 13–14.

47. Pierson, *Forward Movements*, 401. "Forward move" became a demotic catch-phrase among evangelicals, including pentecostals. Any positive development in religion became "a forward movement."

48. Pierson, "What We Need," *W&Wk* (August 1908) 235. The source of this quote is not cited by Otis.

49. Robert, *Occupy*, 261–62; see also A. Anderson, *Spreading Fires*, 28.

50. Abrams, "Baptism of the Holy Spirit at Mukti," *MRW* (August 1906) 619–20, emphasis in original. The revival in India had antecedents in the Welsh revival.

51. Robert writes that the articles appeared in *The Christian* (*Occupy*, 263), but Cartwright is right that they appeared in *Life of Faith* in May and July 1907 in "Everywhere Spoken against," 4.

52. Pierson, "'Speaking with Tongues,'" *LF* (8 May 1907) 403–4; Pierson, "'Speaking with Tongues'—II," *LF* (15 May 1907) 420; Pierson, "'Speaking with Tongues'—3," *LF* (22 May 1907) 441–42. The devotional for May 8 covered Eph 5:17—6:24 and Acts 1:1–26 ["Worship in the Home," *LF* (8 May 1907) 412] and for May 15 Acts 2:1—4:37 ["Worship in the Home," *LF* (15 May 1907) 432].

launched his attack on American pentecostals in two abridged *MRW* articles. In the first part Pierson situated his disputation on 1 Corinthians 14. Tongues, he noted, were the least desirable of the gifts and should be suppressed rather than expressed if an interpreter were not present. Though not denying tongues outright, he thought pentecostals violated the model of order and decency in worship advocated by Paul. Women especially were prone to hysteria, as he had once encountered in a parishioner in his early ministry.[53] Pierson borrowed heavily from Richard Baxter's critique of the Irvingite movement of the early 1830s and from an unnamed correspondent in India, who wrote that hardly any of the more "spiritually-minded missionaries" had fallen victim to the tongues deception.[54] He rued the divisiveness and fanaticism of tongues practitioners, attributing their speech to the mimicry of Satan rather than to an authentic induction from the Father.

Part II of the article appeared two months later, counseling that each case of glossolalia must be judged on its own merit.[55] Conceding that some genuine repentance had taken place, he nevertheless deemed that on the whole the movement suffered from subjective feelings, morbid introspection, and trusted not at all in "His finished work". Throughout both articles Pierson struck a cautionary note against censuring harshly any true work of God and concluded that while such outpourings could descend from God today, what many promoted as tongues was spurious.

Pierson followed these articles with three addendums. In the January 1908 issue he remarked that nearly all the letters had "*fully approv[ed]*" his position but also included some quotations from detractors. One letter cited a prediction that the island of Ceylon (Sri Lanka) would sink into the sea and its capital Colombo be rattled by an earthquake.[56] Another from a pentecostal missionary in Pune regretted that Pierson's article had discouraged some from seeking the baptism; others contained testimonials of miraculous healings from Los Angeles "without comment" so that readers might judge for themselves their efficacy.[57] Pierson was prepared to give glory to God for the true but warned against the deceptions of the devil.

The March issue published the recantation of the anonymous writer who had previously believed in the Colombo earthquake. The expected date had passed, and now he admitted that his faith was shaken as a result.[58] Pierson also inserted news of a fresh awakening in Pune culled from Pandita Ramabai's *Mukti Prayer Bell* along with a case of xenolalia in English—adding a biblical quote from Isaiah 28:11, which pentecostals also often utilized, "For with stammering lips and another tongue will He speak to this people."[59] Despite Ramabai extrapolating at length on tongues, Pierson felt the excerpts fit for print.

53. Pierson, "'Speaking with Tongues,'" *MRW* (July 1907) 488–89.
54. Baxter, *Narrative of Facts* (1833). Baxter was a former member of Irving's church.
55. Pierson, "'Speaking with Tongues'—II," *MRW* (September 1907) 683–84.
56. Pierson, "Speaking with Tongues," *MRW* (January 1908) 60–61.
57. The missionary was a woman who received tongues in Colorado on August 7, 1906, possibly under Andrew Johnson and two "sisters" at Fink's mission. See Hezmalhalch, "Pentecost in Denver," *AF*(LA) (December 1906) 1.
58. "Speaking with Tongues," *MRW* (March 1908) 221.
59. "The Spirit among Ramabai's Girls," *MRW* (March 1908) 166–67.

Ramabai's own vigorous defense of her "hysterical" girls in September 1907 in *The Mukti Prayer Bell* plus the universal respect she garnered among Western evangelicals dissuaded Pierson from further assaults.[60]

The Free Methodist, a Chicago paper, related the earthquake fiasco in December 1907. Missionary Kittie Wood Kumarakulasinghe complained that if America wanted to overflow they should send "sound and sensible people instead of these excrescences of religious life."[61] A group from Ceylon had attended A. G. Garr's pentecostal meetings in Calcutta and imported "the same confusion into this country." Some 25,000 leaflets in both English and Tamil were distributed to the local populace regarding Colombo's imminent demise, resulting in the exit of many natives from the capital. Kittie was certain that no case of xenolalia in the Indian tongue had actually occurred though she did not doubt God's power to do so if He willed. But false prophecies had not endeared the movement to her heart.

Arno Gaebelein reprinted Pierson's *Life of Faith* articles in *Our Hope* simultaneous to the *MRW* appearance in July 1907.[62] Initially *Our Hope* had been circumspect. Early in 1907 G. W. Leavitt reconnoitered Fink's mission in Denver at 19th and Welton and pronounced that much good had been accomplished there. He evaluated Fink as an educated yet humble man who heralded the "second and near coming of Christ"—a laudatory credential to any dispensationalist.[63] Waxing pentecostal, he concluded, "What we need most among our people is heartfelt and Holy Spirit religion, instead of so much 'head religion.'"[64] In July however Gaebelein objected to the idea that supplicants could obtain their "personal Pentecost," for all believers were baptized into the body of Christ at salvation.[65] He also opposed pentecostalism's mixture with "holiness theories"—equally foreign to Scripture, in his opinion—and alleged that the visions from God were actually demonic hallucinations. Gaebelein singled out Levi Lupton's testimonial for the peculiar way in which God "possessed" different parts of Lupton's body before getting hold of his jaw and vocal apparatus.[66] As to Joel 2, Gaebelein contended that pentecostals misinterpreted its context in Acts and that its "fulfillment"—of which Acts was only a foretaste—would occur upon Israel's return to Palestine only after the church had been raptured from the earth.[67] Unlike many protofundamentalists, Gaebelein did not believe in a great outpouring of the Spirit prior to Christ's return, insisting that the church universal was already in a state of apostasy and, therefore, beyond spiritual help.

60. Article cited in Anderson, *Spreading Fires*, 84. Ramabai challenged, "Why should not the Holy Spirit have liberty to work among Indian Christian people, as He has among Christians of other countries?"

61. Kumarakulasinghe, "Tongues Earthquake Scare in Ceylon," *The Free Methodist* (17 December 1907) 811.

62. Pierson, "'Speaking with Tongues,'" *Hope* (July 1907) 35–42.

63. Leavitt, "Gift of Tongues," *W&Wk* (March 1907) 76–77. The article was taken from *Our Hope* [no citation]. Leavitt refers to an editorial in the December issue which was not yet condemnatory.

64. Ibid., 77.

65. Gaebelein, "So-Called Gift of Tongues," *Hope* (July 1907) 13–16.

66. Gaebelein, "So-Called Gift of Tongues," 15; see Lupton, "Holiness Bible School Leader Receives his Pentecost," *AF*(LA) (February 1907) 5.

67. Gaebelein, "Joel ii:28–32," *Hope* (July 1907) 16.

As part of his regular Bible studies in *Our Hope*, Gaebelein targeted tongues speakers when he landed upon Acts in November 1907. He argued that only on the first day of Pentecost were "tongues" intended to be a sign "to the multitude" and that the other examples recorded in Acts such as Cornelius (Acts 10:46) and the Ephesians (Acts 19:6) were forms of "ecstatic speech glorifying God" rather than intelligible rhetoric.[68] To their detriment, contemporary emulators emphasized the least of the gifts and thrust women to the forefront, "acting in many instances as preachers and leaders, and therefore in direct disobedience to the Word of God."[69] Pentecostals reminded him of the prophets of Baal screeching, "Oh God, send the power!" In February 1908 he bound his commentary on Acts 2 into an "attractive pamphlet" which "ought to be circulated freely" but sold for twenty cents a copy instead.[70]

Beginning in February Gaebelein reprinted British fundamentalist Sir Robert Anderson's exposé of pentecostals in a three-part series titled "Spirit Manifestations and 'The Gift of Tongues.'" In the first installment Anderson quoted at length from Baxter's critique of the Irvingites as a historical precedent to the modern movement.[71] The second part attributed pentecostalism's resources to the deception of Satan, who masqueraded as an angel of light.[72] Those who surrendered themselves to the guidance of the Spirit often floundered by straying from the Word, as was the case with H. J. Prince, a leader of the Agapemone movement in the previous century in England.[73] Part Three had Anderson extolling the value of spiritual warfare as a guard against the schemes of Satan. He averred that miracles, though evident in the apostolic ministry during Acts, were not recorded in any of the post-Acts epistles. For instance, Paul escaped from the Philippian jailor in Acts 16 but not from his prison in Rome in Acts 28.[74] Fundamentalists did not deny the supernatural, but many diminished their effectiveness by claiming that though miracles did occur today, they were not "evidential" concerning the truth of Christianity and ought to be avoided if their source was not in God—such as miraculous cures promoted by Christian Science. Anderson did not specify what types of miracles he considered "evidential," but presumably they fell into the fantastical category like tongues. He ended with a brief summation of 1 Corinthians 14: gifts are to be distributed as the Spirit wills and tongues are an inferior gift only to be exercised "under control" to edify the church.

The second chapter of Joel afforded Gaebelein further space to assail pentecostalism in November 1908, this time challenging their interpretation of the "latter rain." He in-

---

68. Gaebelein, "Acts of the Apostles—Chapter II," *Hope* (November 1907) 318–19.

69. Ibid., 320–21.

70. "Pentecost," *Hope* (February 1908) 509.

71. Sir R. Anderson, "Spirit Manifestations and 'the Gift of Tongues,'" *Hope* (February 1908) 535–42. Anderson knew Baxter personally in Baxter's later years (540). "Spirit Manifestations" was also distributed in tract form in New York by Loizeaux Brothers, which by 1909 was in its fourth edition (Wacker, *Heaven Below*, 44). Anderson was a former head of Scotland Yard.

72. Anderson, "Spirit Manifestations and 'the Gift of Tongues,'" *Hope* (March 1908) 600–605.

73. Ibid., 604–605. Gaebelein imported 1,000 copies of Anderson's pamphlet on Prince and sold them for 15 cents.

74. Anderson, "Spirit Manifestations and 'the Gift of Tongues,'" *Hope* (April 1908) 663–73. On Paul, see 667.

sisted that the showers in Joel should be construed literally as the spring and autumn rains of the Palestinian weather cycle and that its lack represented the withholding of God's pleasure and its presence represented the restoration of His favor.[75] The day of Pentecost did not "fulfill" the conditions of Joel 2, he bickered, for Peter's words in Acts 2:16 that "this is that" meant likeness rather than exactness. The Spirit would be poured out on Israel only after she was prophetically restored to Palestine.[76] Nor was there any foundation to project the Spirit's outpouring upon the church into the present age.[77] And yet a decade later, Gaebelein "spiritualized" precipitation when discussing the "refreshing rain" of God's presence as depicted throughout Scripture.[78] Like many fundamentalists, his appropriation of the Word was selective.

William Bell Riley barked against tongues on the evening of August 18, 1907 from his pulpit at First Baptist Church in Minneapolis, just one month after Pierson, whom he quoted, had aired his views in *MRW*.[79] Pentecost first fell in Minneapolis upon Otto Baulin by November 1906, but the first pentecostal mission opened under J. R. Conlee at 320 S. Cedar Street on April 14, 1907 with fifty to sixty seekers, many of them ex-"Dowieites."[80] Riley recognized that the Apostolic Faith movement was an aberration of the holiness movement, but he felt compelled to address the subject because pentecostals embraced premillennialism and because tongues were a biblical phenomenon.[81] Eschatology and the sanction of Scripture built a bridge of kinship between fundamentalists and pentecostals that he could not ignore. Due to time constraints, he had declined invitations to attend Conlee's meetings, which were just over a mile from his office, so he centered his remarks on relevant biblical passages—a purer criterion in his opinion "since observation is often prejudiced."[82] One might argue that so are interpretations, but doubt about the rightness of opinion rarely entered the fundamentalist (or pentecostal) mind.

He divided his topic into three compartments: the promise of tongues, the experience of tongues and the employment of tongues. Like other fundamentalists, Riley believed that tongues were of secondary importance and not the sole mark of Spirit-baptism since all the gifts were to be dispersed as the Spirit determined.[83] Further, the tongues heard at Pentecost were comprehended by the listeners unlike the gibberish of today (not that he had heard it himself). Riley was open to the possibility of glossolalia existing in modern times, for the charisms of the New Testament "were intended for all ages."[84] He

75. Gaebelein, "Studies in Joel—Chapter ii.21–27," *Hope* (November 1908) 335–37.

76. Gaebelein, "Studies in Joel—Chapter ii.28–32," *Hope* (December 1908) 409.

77. Ibid., 407.

78. Gaebelein, "Like the Rain," *Hope* (November 1918) 131–33.

79. Riley, "*Speaking with Tongues*" (Minneapolis: Hall, Black & Co., 1907), 3 [NWC Arch].

80. On Baulin, see "Baptized in Minneapolis," *AF*(LA) (December 1906) 4; Conlee, "In Minneapolis," *AF*(LA) (May 1907) 1. Given the time for mail to be received and letters printed in a monthly, I have used November as when the events likely took place and not the month the letter was printed.

81. Riley, "*Speaking with Tongues*," 3–4.

82. Ibid., 4.

83. Ibid., 6–7.

84. Ibid., 10–12.

was also reluctant to malign any genuine work of God, preferring that his tongue should cleave to the roof of his mouth instead. However, much of what passed for the modern manifestations was unseemly, consisting of contortions, trances, and babble. In the end, he encouraged those who truly possessed the gift to exalt God "as an additional evidence of the enduement of the Spirit," but reminded them that it was better to speak five intelligible words in church than ten thousand unintelligible ones.[85] Like Pierson, Riley refused to dismiss tongues and thereby limit God's power. Both fostered expectations that revival would sweep the world, and, however unlikely it might come through pentecostals, God could still perform wonders.

The Apostolic Faith reported in September 1907 that some of the "people" at Moody Bible Institute in Chicago had received their Pentecost, although "the theologians [were] not accepting it."[86] No allusion was made to the impact it had on the student body in MBI's magazine *The Institute Tie*.[87] Pentecost gripped Moody Memorial Church in 1908, although the exact dating is unclear. Andrew Urshan, a Presbyterian-raised Iranian who emigrated to the U.S. in 1901, was the charismatic leader of a group of Persian Christians who were meeting under Moody's auspices at their Young People's Building on the third floor, which they called the "Upper Room."[88] The pastor of the church and future editor of *The Fundamentals* was A. C. Dixon, a Baptist minister from North Carolina, who had previously shepherded Ruggles Street Baptist in Roxbury, Massachusetts, and had acted as principal of Gordon Missionary Training School in Boston before moving to Chicago.[89] A popular conference speaker and ardent premillennialist, Riley would later eulogize his friend as a "contender of the faith" and a "maker of ministers."[90]

Urshan developed a fondness for holiness fare while attending a Methodist Episcopal Church on the North Side. At a holiness mission—"an old wooden shack-like building"— Urshan received his sanctification and yearned for more of God.[91] Soon afterwards through "providential" circumstances he met a woman from the same assembly who communicated in heavenly languages. Her promotion of the apostolic gifts grated against his Presbyterian-training, which held that the days of miracles were past, yet he could not deny the woman's humility and grace.[92] He attended the pentecostal mission to which she belonged, and though put off by some of the odd manifestations of the Spirit, he was impressed with the demeanor of the people. They seemed to him "just as natural and normal

---

85. Ibid., 16.

86. "[Untitled]," *AF*(LA) (June-September 1907) 1. The article does not specify students, but the context makes it seem likely that it was a student-lead movement.

87. MBI periodicals were successively titled *The Institute Tie* (1891–1893, 1900–1910), *The Christian Worker's Magazine* (1910–1920), *The Moody Bible Institute Monthly* (1920–1938), and *Moody Monthly* (1938–1970), after which it was discontinued.

88. Hall, "Urshan, Andrew David," 866.

89. Beale, *Pursuit*, 222–24.

90. Riley, "A. C. Dixon," 14, 18 [NWC Arch]. Dixon died of a heart attack in Baltimore on 14 June 1925. Riley preached this sermon on August 9 at First Baptist in Minneapolis.

91. Urshan, *Life Story*, 50, 67–71.

92. Ibid., 72–74.

as other church folks"—except they reverenced the Lord quietly to one another while on the street after church instead of "window-shopping."[93]

Still, Urshan was reluctant to devote himself to the novel tenet and asked the Almighty to fill his Persian brethren with the Holy Spirit first. One evening God did just that, with "Abraham" receiving tongues in the Upper Room at Moody. Then followed the Spirit-baptism of an evangelist in the church, and members took notice of the strange happenings. Dixon was alarmed, telling Urshan that he had a grand future ahead of him as an evangelist in the manner of Gypsy Smith if only he would sever company with the "tongue folks."[94] Undaunted, Urshan pushed ahead with his pentecostal vigils in the church. Dixon bludgeoned pentecostalism from his pulpit, accusing it of being full of "spirutulists [sic], and religious fanatics" and proclaiming that tongues were not for moderns.[95] At the conclusion, Dr. Dixon asked that congregants stand in unison against tongues, leaving Urshan, who was sitting near the front, to face the stern countenances of those on the platform when he refused. A voice rang out from the gallery, "Dr. Dixon, this is the rottenest sermon you ever preached!"[96] One of the faculty at MBI, Mr. Hunter, was sent to dissuade Urshan on behalf of the church but to no avail. Urshan and his "Persian boys" were barred from the church, only to plant their own mission on North Clark Street.[97]

Dixon's critique *Speaking with Tongues* could not have appeared before January 1908 as he quoted from a letter from Baptist missionary S. C. Todd with that date.[98] Todd in fact had been associated with N. J. Holmes's ministry and had first-hand knowledge of the movement. Much of Dixon's opus however was culled from Atlanta Congregational pastor J. W. Blosser, whose pamphlet *Fanaticism—Its Cause, Characteristics and Cure* was itself published in mid-1908 at the earliest.[99] Blosser was a trained physician who became concerned with the outbreak of tongues in his area—particularly at the mission hall on Marietta Street which Cashwell had established and from which *The Bridegroom's Messenger* was published. Blosser visited the mission several times and believed that Cashwell induced some hypnotic state in the recipients by having them continuously repeat the words "Glory" or "Praise Him," creating an atmosphere of "suggestibility."[100] Blosser determined that though proponents were sincere, the "delusion, superstitions, and fanaticism" were

---

93. Ibid., 75–76.
94. Ibid., 81, 85.
95. Ibid., 85–86.
96. Ibid., 86.
97. Ibid., 87; Jacobsen, *Thinking*, 238.
98. Todd, "Some Sad Failures of Tongues in Mission Fields," *Baptist Argus* (23 January 1908) 1–2; cf. Stephens, *Fire Spreads*, 221.
99. *Emotional Delusions* was a revised version of *Fanaticism*. Comparing Dixon's quotes from *Fanaticism* with *Emotional Delusions*, there is little reason to suspect that Blosser altered the material much. The only extant copy I have found was at the Congregational Library in Boston, Massachusetts, for which I owe thanks to Jessica Steytler. The date for mid-1908 is based on Blosser mentioning that Godbey had spent 3 months among the pentecostals, which can only refer to *Current Heresies*, which could at the earliest have been published in late March 1908 but more likely April or later. This would put Dixon's pamphlet to late 1908, although the sermon may have been earlier.
100. Blosser, *Emotional Delusions*, 5–6.

made possible by "the disposition of ignorant people to accept natural mental phenomena as supernatural and divine manifestations."[101] It is doubtful that Blosser had much sympathy with fundamentalism and was therefore more inclined to attribute pentecostalism's power to psychological excesses than satanic forces.

Dixon commenced his tract with a short exposition of Acts. Unlike Gaebelein, he appraised Joel's prophecy as partially fulfilled on the day of Pentecost, but it was not an experience to be repeated, as he had explained to Urshan. Dixon tried his utmost to dispel the notion that tongues implied an unknown language. Neither the Ephesians nor Cornelius's household spoke in "other" tongues, and the "new tongues" mentioned in Mark 16:17 "does not necessarily mean 'other tongues.'"[102] The tongues which Paul referred to in 1 Corinthians were distinguished from the tongues of Acts—the former being personal and the latter being corporate. Dixon's unique understanding based on Luke 24:27 was that the word *translate* (or interpret) should be rendered "to explain the meaning of" and had no relation to foreign speech. The church in Corinth therefore should have implemented tongues only if someone were present who could explicate the reason for their joy, otherwise "inexpressible ecstasy" should be kept to oneself.[103] For Dixon tongues were a sign of unbelief in the practitioner, for "God's word is sufficient basis for faith. To demand more in the way of miraculous signs is to dishonour His word."[104] The phenomenon of tongues could have three sources: physical (e.g., from lack of sleep), psychological (i.e., hypnotism), or spiritual (i.e., demonic imitation).[105] Dixon concluded that while rhapsodic adoration can be appreciated, it was not to be sought. The demand for a "sign" was the surest mark of immaturity.

One of the first "martyrs" of the fundamentalist reprisal was William Trotter, superintendent of the Union Rescue Mission in Los Angeles. Trotter underwent pentecostal effervescence in the summer of 1907 and informed his board about it. If he had expected sympathy, he was disappointed and summarily dismissed.[106] The founder of the mission, Lyman Stewart, subsidized Trotter after he joined Florence Crawford's Apostolic Faith mission in Portland, Oregon. Mel Robeck has shown just how dependent Trotter was on Stewart and how close their relationship was.[107] Stewart supplied Trotter with testaments of John from 1909 onwards, sharing his financial wealth in a way that Robeck describes as "sustained and substantial."[108] Trotter would even name one of his sons after his patron.[109] Stewart, co-founder of Union Oil and co-funder with his brother Merrill of *The Fundamentals*, proved to be impartial in the distribution of his gifts to both pentecostals and fundamentalists. In 1908 he also inaugurated the Bible Institute of Los Angeles (Biola),

---

101. Ibid., 9.
102. Dixon, *Speaking with Tongues*, 1–2. Dixon's tract was reprinted in *KB* in January 1922 (pp. 14–19).
103. Ibid., 4–5.
104. Ibid., 7–8.
105. Ibid., 17–20.
106. "[Untitled]," *AF*(LA) (June–September 1907) 1.
107. Robeck, "Florence Crawford," 219–35.
108. Ibid., 233.
109. Ibid., 405 n. 85.

a leading fundamentalist institution that had R. A. Torrey as its dean and editor of the school's periodical, *The King's Business*, which pentecostals would frequently reference.

Pentecostal Defense of the Movement: Historical

Pentecostals were desperate to connect their quickening with church history. The maiden issue of *The Apostolic Faith* trumpeted historical precedents for the Spirit's work, citing such diverse examples as the Huguenots, the Quakers, the Irvingites, a Swedish revival in 1841 and the Ulster revival of 1859.[110] In the second issue, a writer, most likely Seymour, oriented the reader to Azusa's locus amongst the annals:

> All along the ages men have been preaching a partial Gospel. A part of the Gospel remained when the world went into the dark ages. God has from time to time raised up men to bring back the truth to the church. He raised up Luther to bring back to the world the doctrine of justification by faith. He raised up another reformer in John Wesley to establish Bible holiness in the church. Then he raised up Dr. Cullis who brought back to the world the wonderful doctrine of divine healing. Now he is bringing back the Pentecostal Baptism to the church.[111]

The charge that pentecostals were ahistorical is untrue. It seemed as though God had transported them back to the first century, yet they could not ignore their orthodox heritage if they were to avoid confusion with cultism by their evangelical peers. It had long been assumed in holiness circles that the apostolic gifts had been lost since the days of Constantine when the church exchanged her spiritual power for temporal power. Pentecostals viewed themselves as both culmination of the Reformation and as restoration of the New Testament church.

Already in this edition Azusa was responding to the criticisms of holiness leaders. "Father has certainly opened up His house on Azusa street [sic] for the return of the prodigals," it said, employing familial imagery.[112] A veritable party had been thrown, but "the elder brother is angry and will not come in to the feast." Pentecostal "wastrels" were dancing drunk in the Spirit while their sanctified siblings huddled outside glumly condemning tea, coffee, pork, and neck-ties. The illustration was apt for the moment. Holiness folk mistook pentecostal ravings for extravagance and devil-possession, an accusation which would not readily evaporate. The mark of fanaticism, pentecostals countered, was harshness toward others while the Azusa revival was punctuated with love, meekness and purity.[113] Fundamentalists would use pentecostal excesses for fodder in future.

V. P. Simmons, a regular contributor to *The Bridegroom's Messenger*, scoured history for specimens of glossolalia. He found it the chronicles of the *Library of Universal Knowledge* and Philip Schaff's *History of the Christian Church*. The post-apostolic father Irenaeus of

---

110. "Promise Still Good," *AF*(LA) (September 1906) 3.

111. "Pentecostal Baptism Restored," *AF*(LA) (October 1906) 1. The remainder of the article concerns Charles Parham's ministry and his anticipated arrival at Azusa Street, referring him "an apostle of the doctrine of Pentecost."

112. "Elder Brother," *AF*(LA) (October 1906) 2.

113. "Marks of Fanaticism," *AF*(LA) (October 1906) 2.

Lyons stated in *Adversus Haereses* that "we have many brethren in the churches having prophetical gifts, and by the Spirit speaking in all kinds of languages."[114] Simmons then moved to the Huguenots, the Camisards (a prophetic Huguenot group), and Irving, while mentioning the early Quakers and Methodists only in passing. Simmons also championed a little known group in America known as the "Second Adventists." One B. G. Mathewson erupted in tongues in 1864 while Edwin Burnham provided the translation. A smaller group called the "Gift Adventists" had similar experiences in 1872. Simmons finished his overview with a manifestation of tongues in Charles Finney early in his career, knowledge of which Simmons insinuated was suppressed by friends.

Simmons furnished a more personal defense of the movement in an article written for a Florida paper, *The Observer*, for August 17, 1909, and reprinted in *BM*.[115] After rehearsing his account of the "Gift Adventists," he informed his readers that the pentecostal people were "sweet-spirited," ran for no political offices (though they voted occasionally), sued no one, and served others before themselves. Far from being uncharitable, "[you] cannot be with this people [*sic*] long without feeling the warmth of their Christian love."[116] Simmons would make a more biblical apology in December, arguing that Paul only restricted the public use of tongues when no interpreter was present.[117] He considered the opposition of even "seemingly conscientious" ministers to be astonishing. The enmity was so bitter that it bordered on the satanic, while pentecostals possessed a "heavenly countenance" which they manifested in "loving service bestowed upon others." Opponents saw nothing but extremism and dissipation; adherents only holy ardor for God and humankind.

Samuel Otis selected an 1887 work from Plymouth Brethren author G. H. Pember to bolster the pentecostal viewpoint. In *The Great Prophecies* Pember utilized the "latter rain" analogy to argue that a parallel stirring could be expected in the last days.[118] For Pember as for pentecostals, the gifts of the Spirit had been evident amongst ecclesiastics up to the fourth century. The intermittent period up to the Reformation he expected to be "dry," and so it was. Since then, the lapse between renewals had become ever shorter. From Luther to Wesley, Pember marked two hundred years, but only seventy or eighty from Wesley to the Prayer Meeting Revival (1857–1858). Could it be that a great harvest was at hand? Pember hinted as much, and pentecostals were convinced that they were the cutting edge of the scythe.

---

114. Simmons, "History of Tongues," *BM* (1 December 1907) 2. The article was later put into a tract ["Some Good Tracts," *BM* (1 May 1909) 2]. Simmons returned to this theme two months later in "Historians Dodging Tongues," *BM* (1 June 1909) 2. C. E. Preston, an Episcopal turned pentecostal minister, may have had familiarity with this group, although the information is too vague to give a positive answer. He was in "Narragansett Bay" and knew of tongues speech around 1874—see Preston, "Some Manifestations of the Spirit Thirty-five Years Ago," *LRE* (February 1909) 22–23.

115. "Bro. V. P. Simmons, of Frostproof, Florida," *BM* (15 September 1909) 2.

116. Ibid., 2.

117. Simmons, "'Forbid not to Speak with Tongues,'" *BM* (1 December 1909) 3. Simmons made a similar but shorter assessment earlier in "Forbid Not," calling pentecostals "the best people I ever known" [*W&Wk* (August 1908) 233].

118. Pember, "Latter Rain," *W&Wk* (December 1909) 286–87.

Pentecostal Defense of the Movement: Experiential

Pentecostalism was buttressed by Baptists outside the movement as well. A. S. Worrell, an elderly scholar known for his translation of the New Testament, parried assailants in November 1907 in *Triumphs of Faith* and again in August 1908 in *Word and Work*. In the first article, he challenged the logic of the sweeping indictment that "all" pentecostals were possessed by the devil.[119] Its fallacy lay in allowing for no exceptions, and if the critic had not investigated each case, then it was both morally and logically inconsistent. Would demon-ravaged believers become more aware of their sin and exalt the blood of Jesus as pentecostals did? In the second article, like Simmons, Worrell praised pentecostals as "wonderfully joyful people" who extolled the name of Christ far beyond other believers.[120] He then compared the attitude of opponents to the Jews' rejection of Christ, warning that "if it was a fearful sin to ascribe the works of Jesus, done in the power of the Holy Spirit, to Satan, must it not be a horrible sin to ascribe to Satan the works of the Spirit in those who are filled with His holy Presence?"[121] Given the shortness of the hour and the burden of evangelism, critics were answerable for preventing God's children from receiving His blessings. Worrell's support was widely appreciated by those who lacked the stately respect he merited.

George Horr, editor of an independent Baptist paper in Boston, agreed about the wholesome character of pentecostals: "They are humble, earnest and devout Christians, and have shown no exceptional tendency to aberration, religious or otherwise."[122] Inquiries had been made into the manifestation of tongues in India through the letters of a Mrs. A. H. Downie and also in Los Angeles and Alliance, Ohio. The editor had "no good reason" to doubt the veracity of tongues because of the sincere testimony he had read from pentecostals and other observers. Though trances could be discounted, xenolalia provided convincing proof of the genuineness of the gift. Perhaps Horr had read the case of Lewis Rudner, reported in *Word and Work*, then headquartered in Western Massachusetts, in February 1909. Rudner, a Jewish Austrian immigrant in Seattle, had stumbled into a holiness mission the previous winter and heard Thomas Junk repeating Isaiah 53, Junk's wife singing a Jewish New Year's song, a girl of twelve repeating Psalms 6 and 12, a "colored" woman repeating part of Jeremiah 33, and a Scandinavian woman pointing at him, declaring that he was lost and needed God, and all of it in Hebrew.[123] One can imagine the impression it made upon Rudner, who quickly submitted to the Messiah.

---

119. Warner, "Worrell, Adolphus Spalding," 903; Worrell, "Open Letter to the Opposers of this Pentecostal Movement," *TF* (November 1907) 246–49.

120. Worrell, "The Crisis Now On," *W&Wk* (August 1908) 236. This article was reprinted from *Gospel Witness* [no citation] and reprinted in *Good Tidings* [no citation] and *ELCOGE* (15 October 1910) 4–5.

121. Ibid., 237.

122. "Speaking with Tongues," *W&Wk* (October 1909) 221. Reprint from *The Watchman*—Otis describes the editor as "an impartial observer." Reprinted by *Word and Witness* in October 1913 under same title (p. 4). The nearest article I could find in *The Watchman* affirming revivalist movements, including tongues, was "The New Revival" (*The Watchman* [9 September 1909] 7).

123. "Is this of the Devil?" *W&Wk* (February 1909) 27–28.

Experience was the trump card of the pentecostal apology. Mrs. A. F. Rawlson protested that she was under no hypnotic spell when tongues emitted from her lips, almost willing herself to not to succumb to the event as she made a "complete surrender" to God.[124] Only through consecration could the Holy Spirit gain mastery over mind and mouth and only through obedience did she have the boldness to deliver the medley of syllables. An editorial in *Trust*, a Rochester, New York periodical, speculated that fear of the pseudo-spiritual, which often accompanied revivals, kept many from seeking God's bounty. Like other apologists, Sister Duncan did not think it necessary to answer every critique lobbed at them, for "God has graciously granted us a 'real' experience, [and] we should set forth the benefits of this rather than expatiate upon the dangers of counterfeits."[125] Above all, pentecostals believed that the blood of Christ would form an aegis against the bombardments of the enemy. A. A. Boddy was particular about this protection in *Confidence*, a British syndicate popular on American shores. By pleading the blood while tarrying, "he [sic] will not be frightened of mixture or counterfeit."[126] In good Anglican fashion, he even prescribed a prayer to be recited for protection against the machinations of the devil while seeking the baptism.

Pentecostals were well aware of their own excesses and constantly tried to mitigate against them—at least by argument if not in practice. An unnamed source in *Word and Work* acknowledged the blending of the false with the true: "I know that inconsistencies and failures and counterfeits and different grades of experience follow along with this movement, and so have they with every real work of God that was ever started on earth. But that does not any more argue that this is of the devil than the terrible failures and falls of Adam and Aaron and Moses and David and Judas and Peter prove that the work of God with which they were in touch was of the devil."[127] The writer then listed nine fruits evident in the lives of pentecostals: their faith in God, their union in spirit, their missionary endeavors, their love for the Word, their consecration, their magnification of the blood, their happiness, their passion for souls, and their good deeds. Frank Bartleman judged the denunciations from those who had not sought God whole-heartedly to be hypocritical. The spiritual sensitivities of opponents could not be trusted, and, furthermore, "they would rob us of what we have and give nothing in return."[128] Elizabeth Sexton feared for those who disparaged a Holy Ghost-instigated progress. There had always been counterfeits in any awakening, including false conversions and sanctifications, but the misuse of the gifts did not negate authentic renewal.[129] Despite their idiosyncrasies, pentecostals were card-carrying evangelicals to the last.

The drama of Spirit-baptism stamped its indelible imprint on the individual, but experience alone was insufficient to sustain the whole. The burgeoning movement needed stability from leaders who were theologically well grounded if it were to survive beyond

---

124. Rawson, "Hypnotism," *W&Wk* (August 1908) 244–45.
125. "Counterfeits," *W&Wk* (October 1908) 301 [reprint from *Trust*].
126. Boddy, "Pleading the Blood," *Conf* (August 1908) 4.
127. "The Pentecostal Movement," *W&Wk* (November 1909) 254–55. Reprint from *A Call to Faith*.
128. "Letter from F. Bartleman," *BM* (1 March 1908) 2; written from Pasadena on February 7.
129. Sexton, "'O, Man, Greatly Beloved, Fear Not,'" *BM* (15 July 1908) 1.

the initial euphoria. One of these was D. Wesley Myland, a CMA-educated pastor and teacher. At the Stone Church Convention in Chicago, May 26–27, 1909, Myland was the first to place pentecostalism within a biblical framework beyond the usual location of Acts as part of God's overarching plan for the universe—the "latter rain covenant." Myland based his lectures on Deuteronomy 11:10–21 concerning Israel's entrance into Canaan.[130] Three layers comprised his interpretative schemata: the literal, the spiritual and the prophetic (dispensational). Physically the covenant was fulfilled when Israel entered Canaan; spiritually it was fulfilled through the early church at the original Pentecost; prophetically it was being fulfilled through its current devotees. In his fifth session, Myland demonstrated that just as precipitation had increased in Palestine from 1860 to the present, so the Spirit's refreshing had also been increasing upon the church and "will never be taken away from her, but it will be upon her to unite and empower her, to cause her to aid in God's last work for this dispensation."[131] His use of "dispensation" was generic—what he defined as the unfolding of "God's plan for the ages." Evangelical Publishing House, a wing of Stone Church, produced *The Latter Rain Covenant* late in 1910.[132]

Pentecostalism and the Christian and Missionary Alliance

Myland severed his ties to the Methodist Episcopal Church shortly after his sanctification experience. He joined the CMA in 1890 and acted as its first superintendent over Ohio.[133] In November 1906 he became the first CMA pastor to acquire tongues and remained a shepherd to several CMA congregations afterwards.[134] His transfer from Methodism to CMA to pentecostalism demonstrates the fluidity through which the holiness teaching flowed. Care should be exercised when tagging groups "holiness," "evangelical," or "fundamentalist." While such distinctions did exist, they were not impermeable fixtures. Such was the case with the CMA, which at its heart was a hybrid of holiness and fundamentalist interests.

Pentecost infiltrated CMA churches through Warren Cramer in Cleveland, Ohio, Glenn Cook in Indianapolis and J. E. Sawders in Homestead, Pennsylvania in January 1907.[135] The deepest impact transpired at the CMA Convention in Nyack, New York, from May 28–31, where AG notable David McDowell among others was immersed in the Spirit. Prior to the convention, foregleams of glory descended upon the Baccalaureate service held in the Training Institute chapel on May 26. CMA historian Paul King theorizes that it was Cramer who stood up and "suddenly burst out in an unknown tongue" while students implored heaven for a fresh baptism.[136] King has ably documented the spread of tongues

---

130. Myland, "Latter Rain Covenant," *LRE* (June 1909) 15–22; see *FSRB*, Dt. 30.3.
131. Myland, "Fifth Latter Rain Lecture," *LRE* (September 1909) 13.
132. "Latter Rain Pentecost," *BM* (1 December 1910) 2.
133. Robinson, "Myland, David Wesley," 632–33; Blumhofer, *Assemblies of God*, 1:122.
134. King, *Genuine Gold*, 61.
135. Ibid., 69–75. It should be noted that these meetings were not universally endorsed by the CMA leadership. See also Bundy, "G. T. Haywood," 239–40, on Cook and the CMA response in Indianapolis.
136. King, *Genuine Gold*, 79.

among the CMA and the numerous connections which existed between them and pentecostals, particularly with the AG, citing 211 leaders in the CMA who had pentecostal experiences and 79 CMA churches that were charismatic in nature, most of these by 1908.[137]

The movement also spread to various CMA camp meetings from June 1907. In August, revival sparks flared at the primary CMA grounds at Old Orchard Beach, Maine, where at Frank Bartleman's urging several were ushered into the experience—but only in the woods, for as he recalled, "we were not allowed to tarry on the camp grounds."[138] Sam Otis attended the last three days of the gathering, spying participants from the First Fruit Harvesters and a "Sister Garragus" (Alice Garrigus—who would later introduce pentecostalism to Newfoundland).[139] Those desirous of a deeper infilling removed to an Advent Christian church, where some lay "prostrate under the power," and continued meetings in a rented barn for several days afterwards. Otis characterized the camp as a "spiritual feast," though he does not mention Bartleman in his account.[140]

CMA founder A. B. Simpson maintained an amiable relationship with many pentecostal leaders even while he graced fundamentalist pulpits like that of Moody Church. In 1883, four years after her wondrous healing from a fall, a young Carrie Judd met Simpson and served as recording secretary at the first CMA organizational meeting in 1887.[141] Simpson later conducted her marriage to George Montgomery in 1890, and the couple held leadership positions in the CMA even after receiving their Pentecost in 1908.[142] Carrie regularly spoke in CMA churches and also gave her testimony at Old Orchard in 1909 and at Simpson's church, the Gospel Tabernacle, in New York in 1909 and 1910.[143]

Simpson most likely met British pentecostal leader A. A. Boddy in 1889 on one of the inveterate traveler's journeys to North America.[144] In 1909 Simpson hosted Boddy for lunch at Nyack. Boddy described him as "a healthy, wholesome combination of a capable business man and a gentleman farmer . . . He is just a true, healthy Christian."[145] At the end of the visit, Simpson invited Boddy to speak at Gospel Tabernacle and repeated the request three years later on Boddy's second pentecostal tour, which Boddy regrettably declined as he was already aboard ship.[146] Simpson also enjoyed the hospitality of both Boddy

---

137. Ibid., Appendices I and II (n.p.).

138. Bartleman, *Azusa Street*, 109. Bartleman records an extensive ministry among CMA churches from 1907 to 1908, see pp. 99–137, where he preached in at least thirteen different locales, some numerous times. Just prior to the CMA meeting, he had been at a holiness camp at Wilmore, Kentucky, home of Asbury College, where S. B. Shaw was present.

139. Otis, "Campmeeting at Old Orchard, Me.," *W&Wk* (September 1907) 242–43.

140. Ibid., 243.

141. Storms, "Montgomery," 274–76.

142. King, *Genuine Gold*, 175; Storms, "Montgomery," 278.

143. Storms, "Montgomery," 284.

144. In 1914 Simpson introduced Boddy to an audience at Gospel Tabernacle as "a friend twenty-five years' standing" (Boddy, "Westward Ho!" *Conf* [October 1914] 183–86). Wakefield describes his three journeys in *Alexander Boddy*, 46–50. According to Wakefield, Boddy did not record these journeys in detail and does not mention Simpson. However, the last of these journeys in 1889 coincides with Simpson's remarks.

145. Boddy, "Across the Atlantic," *Conf* (September 1909) 199.

146. Boddy, "Transatlantic Experiences," *Conf* (April 1913) 70. The journey took place in 1912, though it was serialized through several issues up to April 1913. Boddy attended the Old Orchard camp meeting in

and Baptist minister Graham Scroggie, with whom Boddy was also on friendly terms, at Sunderland, England towards the end of 1909.[147] On Boddy's final trip to America in 1914 he finally had opportunity to expound on divine healing at Simpson's tabernacle on Friday July 17—though he confessed he would have preferred to have heard Simpson on the subject.[148] The genial Anglican and the magnanimous Presbyterian were alike in age, intellect, and temperament.

Simpson was favorably disposed toward the gift of tongues, though he consistently opposed it as the only "sign" of baptism. On this he and Boddy agreed. The evidence for the baptism extended beyond physical manifestations to the fruits of the Spirit, though Boddy expressed his hope that someday he should hear of Simpson entering into the pentecostal experience.[149] In *The Gospel of Healing* (1885) Simpson intimated that the gift of tongues had been continuously present in the church along with counterfeits and had even been realized in the current generation.[150] He first responded to the emerging pentecostal movement on September 22, 1906, striking a cautionary note between the twin rocks of frenzy and frigidity—a theme that would be constant throughout his ministry. He wrote in an editorial, "God will not be displeased with us if we are conservative and careful in investigating all such alleged facts and guarding against fanaticism, human exaggeration, or spiritual counterfeits ... But on the other hand, let us also guard against the extreme of refusing to recognize any added blessing which the Holy Spirit is bringing to His people in these last days."[151]

King opines that Simpson became aware of the movement through California friends Joseph Smale, the Montgomerys, and J. Hudson Ballard.[152] Simpson followed up the editorial with an article, "All the Blessings of the Spirit," in which he affirmed that while tongues were for today, one should not seek after "the strange and wonderful gifts" but let Him choose which gifts to impart.[153] At a 1907 conference in Chicago, he supplied much the same answer to future AG evangelist Mae Eleanor Frey, a position he would maintain unto his death in 1919.[154] Simpson has been described as a pentecostal forerunner by Charles Nienkirchen, which accounts for his earlier response to pentecostalism than other protofundamentalists like Pierson.[155] The difficulty is that he does not fit neatly into one category or another. Ever sensitive to the promptings of the Holy Spirit, he was a pro-

---

1909 where he met future AG leader D. H. McDowell, but there is no record of him speaking at Simpson's Gospel Tabernacle in New York at this time. Boddy spent two months away from his parish.

147. Scroggie wrote an antipentecostal tract called *The Baptism of the Spirit: What Is It?* (n.d.).

148. Boddy, "Westward Ho!" *Conf* (October 1914) 183. Boddy arrived in New York on the morning of July 17, met with Simpson, then went to a camp meeting in New Jersey.

149. Boddy, "Across the Atlantic," *Conf* (September 1909) 199–200.

150. Simpson, *Gospel of Healing* in Graf, ed., *Healing*, 313.

151. *Christian and Missionary Alliance Weekly* (22 September 1906) 177; quoted in King, *Genuine Gold*, 57–58.

152. King, *Genuine Gold*, 57.

153. *Christian and Missionary Alliance Weekly* (29 September 1906) 198; King, *Genuine Gold*, 58.

154. Frey, "An Evangelist's Story," *PE* (22 May 1926) 8.

155. Nienkirchen, *A. B. Simpson*, 8.

tofundamentalist with a charismatic-holiness asterisk. In terms of sanctification, Bernie van de Walle has demonstrated that Simpson most closely mirrored the Keswick theology of Bishop Handley Moule, who emphasized the indwelling presence of Christ in the believer.[156]

Early Pentecostal Eschatology

Early pentecostal eschatology was initially inherited from its holiness roots, which tended to divide dispensational history into three phases: the Old Testament, Christ's earthly ministry in the Gospels, and the New Testament age of the Church or of the Spirit, which continued to the present. These periods were roughly synonymous with Jonathan Fletcher's dispensations of Father, Son, and Holy Ghost—although not always expressed in those terms.[157] For the most part, this eschatology can be described as "expectant." Pentecostals looked forward to the soon return of Christ, which in turn fuelled their missionary zeal to claim as many souls for the kingdom as they could—time was running short. Faupel and R. Anderson assert that premillennialism formed the integrating core of pentecostal theology, while Dayton believes it was only one of four strands.[158] Faupel also remarks that early pentecostal eschatology was dependent on dispensationalism, but Dayton states otherwise, insisting that their view of history differed significantly from that of dispensationalists, to which I concur.[159]

Radical holiness groups adopted a premillennial outlook prior to the pentecostal movement, as already seen. The Pentecostal Holiness Church incorporated premillennialism into their disciplines as early as 1902.[160] Martin Knapp of Cincinnati gravitated toward premillennialism in January 1897. Seymour imbibed premillennialism as a young man and briefly attended Knapp's school in the early 1900s because of it.[161] He regarded the Azusa Street revival as an indication that Jesus' Second Advent was near, and, judging by how quickly Pentecost was spreading, would materialize "very soon." "We are only in the A.B.C. of this wonderful power of God that is to sweep over the world," he surmised in 1906.[162] William Kostlevy's study on the Burning Bush Movement in Los Angeles (in which A. G. Garr was a pastor) notes a number of theological similarities between it and Seymour, though Kostlevy does not specifically address eschatology and overstates the influence of the Burning Bush on Seymour.[163]

---

156. Van de Walle, *Heart of the Gospel*, 103–10.

157. Dayton, *Theological Roots*, 150.

158. Ibid., 144–47; Faupel, *Everlasting Gospel*, 21–23; R. Anderson, *Vision*, 80, 90.

159. Faupel, *Everlasting Gospel*, 29; Dayton, *Theological Roots*, 145–46. Dayton adds a further danger, which is to take one's sources strictly from the AG which did have more fundamentalistic elements early in its formation. For now we look only at the period prior to 1910.

160. Synan, *Old-Time Power*, 71, cf. *Discipline* (1902) 11.

161. Nelson, "For such a Time as This," 163–64. Seymour was also attracted by Knapp's egalitarianism according to Nelson, which led him to the "Evening Light Saints" and sanctification.

162. [Seymour], "Hallelujah for the Prospect," *AF*(LA) (October 1906) 4.

163. Kostlevy, "Nor Silver, nor Gold," 244–45.

DISFELLOWSHIPED

At the risk of oversimplification, pentecostalism at its genesis was dispensational in its eschatology but not in its view of biblical history. In other words, it was dispensational about the future age but not about the ages past. September 1906 glimpsed this distinct theology when an anonymous writer (probably Seymour) declared that the redeemed who partake in the "first resurrection" (i.e., the rapture) will reign with Jesus over "unglorified humanity" during the millennium.[164] In the January 1907 issue, Seymour focused on the parable of the ten virgins, hinting that only those who sought more oil (the baptism of the Spirit) would meet the bridegroom in the air while the ordinary regenerate would have to wait.[165] For June-September 1907 the paper compared Jesus' second coming to the ark. As Noah was lifted above the flood, so Christ would rescue believers from the great tribulation.[166] The following edition was more explicitly dispensational in predicting two appearances of Christ, "The first appearance is called the Rapture, when He comes as a thief in the night and catches away His bride; the second is called the Revelation, when He shall come with ten thousand of His saints and destroy the wicked with the brightness of His coming, and when His feet shall touch the same mount from which He ascended."[167] Then the triumphant will reign with Christ on earth as "His queen the Lamb's wife" and rule "this old world in the millemnium" [sic] and afterwards adjudicate with Him on the Great White Throne. Elements of dispensationalism are evident in these passages without reference to Darby's seven "ages." In other words, pentecostals were speaking the language of dispensationalism without adopting its necessary content.

The Bridegroom's Messenger knew of the rapture, dedicating a poem to that theme in February 1908. The author, C. R. Kent of Halifax, Nova Scotia, expressed the hope of many pentecostals that they would "behold" Christ returning on the clouds "far brighter than pure gold."[168] On November 19 or 29, 1908, shortly after receiving her infusion of the Spirit, a Mrs. E. L. Murrah entertained a vision of Christ's return.[169] It seemed to her that the Holy Ghost was dispatching invitations to the marriage supper to those willing to press into the baptism, which sadly many "good Christians" were resisting. Elizabeth Sexton spoke of the "catching away" of the saints while the world went about its wickedness as in "the days of Noah."[170] Knowing of His soon coming was for her adequate motivation to "help us watch our ways."[171] This preparation for the marriage supper was indeed the concept behind the periodical's title. She adjured, "we have no time for backsliding, we must get ready ... [W]e are marching to quickstep music now. Hallelujah!"[172]

---

164. "The Millenium [sic]," *AF*(LA) (September 1906) 3.
165. Seymour, "Bridegroom Cometh," *AF*(LA) (January 1907) 2.
166. "Type of the Coming of Jesus," *AF*(LA) (June-September 1907) 4.
167. "Notes on the Coming of Jesus," *AF*(LA) (September 1907) 4.
168. Kent, "The Rapture," *BM* (1 February 1908) 1.
169. Murrah, "My Testimony," *BM* (1 January 1908) 3. The date is obscure.
170. Sexton, "Editorials," *BM* (15 September 1908) 1.
171. Sexton, "The Field is the World," *BM* (1 November 1909) 1.
172. Sexton, "'And There Shall be no more Curse," *BM* (5 June 1908) 1.

In July 1908 Sexton postulated that as soon as the "latter rains" ripened the harvest fruit the great tribulation would quickly ensue.[173] Sexton had once been a worker in the CMA and followed the *Alliance Weekly*'s perspective on Palestine in November 1908. The Turks who still ruled the region figured prominently in the prophetic restoration of Israel, according to dispensational dogma. All the pieces signifying the Lord's return had been arranged except a few details like the Jewish repopulation of Palestine, which was occurring in earnest.[174] It wasn't until 1909 when the Scofield Reference Bible had been published that the more dire aspects of dispensationalism crept into the paper. In March of that year Sexton highlighted the "Laodicean church," widely paraded by dispensationalists as a symbol of apostate Christianity prior to the rapture—a church that was monetarily flush but spiritually impoverished.[175] In August in an article significantly titled "The End Near," she quoted a report from *The Apostolic Light* concerning the increase of earthquake activity throughout the world, and by January 1910 her editorial had become positively alarmist. Brandishing secular press reports, she divulged that social unrest and war threatened to upset civilization as calamity awaited an "ungodly world and sleeping church."[176]

Throughout early pentecostalism, there is a pronounced expectation of the soon return of Christ. Two gospellers in Minneapolis simultaneously slipped into a trance, receiving the same vision of the "New Jerusalem," and were notified by the Spirit that scant time remained to labor for the harvest.[177] Mary Galmond, overwhelmed by her insight into future earthquakes disassembling Chicago and tossing Pasadena into the ocean, was comforted that Christ would rescue her ere she died.[178] C. J. Quinn entertained a longer perspective than most when he foresaw in 1908 that there would be "seven years of plenty" followed by "seven years of famine" (referring to the seven-year tribulation), which extended to pentecostals five more years of missiological activity.[179] Quinn adduced a definite dispensational plot in this prophecy—promising that the church would be whisked away in the rapture and swoop down with Christ again to establish His millennial kingdom. Thus, while dispensationalism was not absent, neither was it central to pentecostal eschatology—nor did it evoke in its earliest stages the type of pessimism articulated by dispensational pundits. The popularity of Scofield assured that they would not remain immune for long.

Summary and Conclusion

Pentecostalism emerged in the milieu of an existing holiness movement that had been radicalized at the end of the nineteenth century through the protofundamentalist teachings of premillennialism, healing and a Keswickian view of baptism in the Holy Ghost. It spread rapidly in its genesis stage through the various holiness missions and campgrounds

---

173. Sexton, "'O, Man, Greatly Beloved, Fear Not,'" *BM* (15 July 1908) 1.
174. Sexton, "What does it Mean?" *BM* (15 November 1908) 1.
175. Sexton, "The Laodicean Age," *BM* (15 March 1909) 1.
176. Sexton, "The End Near," *BM* (15 August 1909) 2; Sexton, "Signs of the Times," *BM* (1 January 1910) 1.
177. "[Untitled]," *AF*(LA) (October 1907—January 1908) 2.
178. Galmond, "Testimony and Prophecy," *AF*(LA) (October 1906) 2.
179. Quinn, "The Blessed Hope," *TPent* (September 1908) 5.

scattered around the country. Holiness organizations like the Church of God (Cleveland, TN) and the holiness school of N. J. Holmes in Greenville, South Carolina, were swept into its wake. Reaction was severe, beginning in the summer of 1906. Holiness leaders were threatened by the potential loss of prestige and power through the ebbing of their constituency. Camps were split, organizations rent asunder, and relationships (not to mention Alma White's marriage) severed.

The fundamentalist reaction was slower, not gaining significant momentum until the summer of 1907. Though Minnie Abrams had reported on tongues in August 1906 to A. T. Pierson, Pierson did not respond until July 1907 in America. Having opened the doors for criticism by this senior spokesman, other fundamentalists like A. C. Gaebelein, W. B. Riley and A. C. Dixon voiced their opposition. Their critiques were based not on first-hand experience but on second-hand reports. Assuming a scientific method to combat modernism, their rationalistic approach was repelled by emotional excesses in the new movement. Nevertheless, pentecostalism posed a potential threat to their leadership. Thus Riley and Dixon addressed their concerns from the pulpit and distributed tracts to parishioners, who in turn distributed them to friends.

Pentecostals did not directly respond to these criticisms until the following decade. Instead, they developed a twofold defense of their practice. Firstly, aware that they were advocating something new to evangelicalism, they linked their movement to historical precedents, consulting the annals of church histories for spiritual manifestations similar to their own. They invoked the Reformers and the Wesleys to establish a line of restorationism congruent with an orthodox reading of history. God was restoring His gifts to the church so that revival might usher in the denouement. Though they did not acknowledge it, they were indebted to protofundamentalists like Pierson and Torrey, who predicted a final harvest of souls before the millennium would commence.

Secondly, pentecostals appealed to their experience as an incontestable proof of the genuineness of tongues. For many, the experience was simply overwhelming. The body was filled with an electric presence, the mouth was loosed in uncontrollable syllables, the soul was lit up in ecstasy. What others interpreted as hysteria or even demon possession, they considered to be the Spirit of God. They objected that the devil would not exalt the blood of Christ so highly as they did in their meetings. Furthermore, the messages they received through the Spirit warned of Christ's imminent return, a theme dear to the protofundamentalist scheme which even Riley could recognize.

It was this commitment to premillennialism which most closely bound the two movements. It would also be the instrument through which fundamentalism made its initial impact upon pentecostalism, as will be shown in the next chapter. Early pentecostals were expectant that the Second Advent was only a few years away as their missionaries scattered across the globe. Stories of successful evangelism through xenolalia were relatively rare, setting up many missionaries for great disappointment. That failure somewhat dampened their eagerness and opened them up to the gloomier brand of dispensationalism, presented logically and consistently through the Scofield Reference Bible. Meanwhile, the rapid growth and ill-defined structure of pentecostalism would be cause for dispute and division in the following decade, to which we now turn.

PART THREE

Adaptation

4

Forming Denominations (1910–1919)

Introduction

THE WUTHNOW-LAWSON ECOLOGICAL MODEL STRESSES THE COMPETITION THAT EX-ISTS between similar species or, in our case, similar religious movements, evident in the struggles witnessed in the previous chapter. As pentecostals forged an identity apart from the holiness movement, they also found it necessary to differentiate themselves internally from one another. Alister McGrath has distinguished the formation of "doctrine" as arbitrated by the community of believers from that of "dogma," which is derived from the teachings of the authorities over believers.[1] Aside from its theological implications, doctrine also operates with social and political dimensions. Socially, it serves to separate those who belong to a particular religious community from those who do not. In such a case, McGrath observes, "The general phenomenon of 'doctrine'—although not specific doctrines—is linked with the perceived need for social definition, especially when other factors do not adequately define a group."[2] This is born out in the *adaptation* stage wherein pentecostals adjusted to one another within newly conquered holiness territory. Fiercely independent and loosely interconnected, the movement split asunder along theological fissures that lay just beneath the surface.

William Durham, the Finished Work, and Dr. Dixon

If anyone can be blamed for this rift, it is William Durham, the Chicago pastor baptized at Azusa Street in February 1907. Durham's doctrine of the Finished Work, expounded upon at the Stone Church Convention in Chicago in May 1910, projected pentecostalism on a course of division and consolidation along both ecclesiastical and geographical lines.[3] His innovation collapsed the generally accepted tri-tiered formula (justification precedes sanctification which precedes Spirit-baptism as distinct experiences) into two tiers (sanctification commences with justification, followed later by Spirit-baptism). This novelty appealed largely though not exclusively to those descended from the CMA and Baptist

---

1. McGrath, *Genesis*, 8–11. McGrath follows the work of Niklas Luhmann here.

2. Ibid., 37. McGrath lists 3 other functions of doctrine aside from the "social": doctrine is generated by and interprets Christian narrative, it interprets Christian experience, and it makes truth claims.

3. Faupel, *Everlasting Gospel*, 237. Anderson has dated Durham's attack on the "second work" theory to the launching of his periodical in 1908 (*Vision*, 166).

denominations, both with Reformed roots, as well as the disciples of John Alexander Dowie—a former Congregational minister from Scotland.

Durham's theology and the subsequent rupture it caused have long been points of contention between holiness- and Keswick-pentecostals, both then and now. One attempt to heal this breach by Allen Clayton threads a continuous strand of "Jesus piety" through the early pentecostal movement to the oneness issue a decade later.[4] In Clayton's analysis, pentecostals so exalted the name of Jesus that exclusive attention to it resulted in a trinitarian conflation. Alternatively, Faupel has called attention to a "paradigm shift" in Durham induced through his pneumatobaptism, an experience that compelled him to reorient his theological underpinnings.[5] Elsewhere, Jacobsen discards Dale Simmons's attempt to link Durham's theology with that of Keswick-inspired docent E. W. Kenyon.[6] Blumhofer invokes Durham's Baptist upbringing as the primary catalyst for his rejection of sanctification. She has demonstrated that one year prior to his licensing by the World's Faith Missionary Association of Shenandoah, Iowa, the group printed an article titled "It is Finished" in their periodical *Firebrand*.[7] This same organization harbored ties with the CMA, including two of Durham's colleagues, H. L. Blake and George Morgan.[8] Finally, R. Anderson opines that the Finished Work represented a compromise with the emerging fundamentalist ideology.[9]

One argument contra Anderson is the vehemence with which Durham opposed fundamentalism. He was well aware of the intellectual trappings that were entailed within fundamentalism. As Jacobsen comments, "he saw modernism and fundamentalism as, in essence, conspiring together to eliminate the supernatural from the present-day experience of Christian faith, and of those two he probably viewed fundamentalism as the greater threat."[10] On the modernist front, Durham was one of the first in pentecostalism to attack higher criticism, which he viewed as faith-destroying.[11] In his view, many students at the nation's seminaries either became infidels or "higher critics, which amounts to about the same thing."[12] His two-part article on "The Great Crisis" launched a full scale assault on formalism in the churches and the aridity of their theology, particularly among Methodists.[13] He relegated the lukewarm denominations to tribulational fires, out

---

4. Clayton, "Significance of Durham," 27–42.

5. Faupel, *Everlasting Gospel*, 267.

6. Jacobsen, *Thinking*, 380–81 n. 42. Faupel however was more amenable to Simmons' thesis (*Everlasting Gospel*, 264 n. 148, cite Simmons, "'I Love You but I Just Can't Marry You'" paper presented to the Twenty-fifth Annual Meeting of the Society for Pentecostal Studies, Toronto, March 9, 1996).

7. Blumhofer, "Durham," 126–27. Personal tragedy also affected Durham, losing his wife in August 1909 and his daughter in February 1910 (pp. 135–36).

8. King, *Genuine Gold*, 71. Blake accompanied Durham to Azusa and likely knew him from when Durham lived in Tracy, Minnesota. Morgan often ministered in Tracy (cf. Blumhofer, "Durham," 127).

9. See Anderson, *Vision*, 171–73. Anderson sees the conflict as between Calvinists and Wesleyans within pentecostalism. Church background however cannot be considered a decisive factor as many Baptists and Quakers were staunch "second work" advocates and numerous Methodists joined the AG.

10. Jacobsen, *Thinking*, 356.

11. Durham, "Word to Ministers, from a Minister," *PT*, March 1909, 10.

12. Ibid., 11.

13. Durham, "Great Crisis Number Two," *PT* (July 1910) 1–4. "The Great Crisis" also appeared in *W&Wk*

of which only a few would be saved.[14] Pentecostals rarely sustained their comminations against modernism at this stage, occasionally mentioning the issue in brief paragraphs but not in dedicated articles. Modernism was as yet a distant menace.

Durham was equally suspicious of the dry rationalism of the fundamentalists. In July 1910 he leveled at Dixon's diatribe against tongues in an article titled "Doctor Dixon Answered." He acknowledged that pentecostals themselves were partly at fault for the stiff opposition from fellow evangelicals, for pentecostalism attracted "every flighty, or visionary, fanatical, or mentally or otherwise unbalanced person."[15] But this did not excuse opponents from misrepresentation and from failing to investigate them fairly. He had already lodged a similar complaint in March 1909 when he noted that none of the fundamentalist leaders who lived in Chicago deigned to attend their meetings.[16] Durham first heard Dixon fulminate against tongues in 1907, when Dixon attributed the phenomenon to ecstasy.[17] Durham opened his article with his profound respect for the honorable cleric as a steadfast defender of God's Word. However, Dixon had instigated a fresh campaign against pentecostals and published a "recent" booklet censuring them, which Durham dared not leave unchallenged.[18] It is impossible to say how recently the booklet had been published, for conceivably such booklets could circulate for years before they were answered. Probably it was a reissue of *Speaking with Tongues*.

Durham confronted three specific items in Dixon. First, he contended that Pentecost was not a single occurrence as Dixon claimed since it was repeated in the case of Cornelius in Acts 10 and was commanded by Jesus in Mark 16.[19] Second, he was astounded that Dixon considered tongues to be mere "ecstatic joy" and not a supernatural event, and that "interpretation" meant nothing more than an explanation of that ecstasy. In a typical pentecostal maneuver, he recalled his own simulation of tongues, which were produced neither by "my happiness, nor emotions."[20] Third, he doubted that the Lord intended tongues to be "a sign of unbelief" as Dixon suggested, unless Dixon believed that Paul lacked faith because he engaged in glossolalia.[21] Durham regretted that he had not space enough to refute Dixon fully and summoned him to a public duel in which he himself would rent the hall if Dixon would only lay his case open before the pentecostals.[22] Durham's invitation went unheeded.

(March 1910) 80–82 in an abridged form.

14. Durham, "Great Crisis Number Two," 4; Jacobsen, *Thinking*, 354. Durham divided the world into three classes: the unbelieving world, the unbelieving church, and the saints.

15. Durham, "Great Crisis Number Two," 3.

16. Durham, "Word to Ministers, from a Minister," 11

17. Durham, "Doctor Dixon Answered," *PT* (1 July 1910) 13. Durham does not provide a specific date, only saying it was "three years before."

18. Ibid., 12. Dixon had preached twice against tongues "in the last few months," according to Durham.

19. Ibid., 12–13.

20. Ibid., 13.

21. Ibid., 14.

22. Ibid. Durham left over half of Dixon's material untouched, most of which concerned S. C. Todd and Blosser's pamphlet on "emotionalism."

Faupel and R. Anderson have each adequately demonstrated the effect of the Finished Work on the pentecostal movement in their respective surveys. At the time of Durham's premature death in 1912, over half of the pentecostals in North America had been persuaded to his position, mostly outside of the Southeast, where 80 percent retained their loyalty to Wesleyanism.[23] Durham's associate Frank Ewart observed that pentecostalism gained wider acceptance among the "nominal churches" as a result.[24] If Anderson is correct that the controversy was an accommodation to fundamentalism, it was only so at a subconscious level. It is also an open question as to what degree Durham's Baptist background influenced his theology. Many Methodists would join the AG and many Baptists the CG; therefore denominationalism alone cannot explain its popularity. The Finished Work would not have transpired had not Durham been forced to reassess his sanctification experience through the lens of his Azusa Street experience—a "paradigm shift" as Faupel asserts.

Formulation of Creeds

Pentecostals have long blamed "creedalism" as a source, if not *the* source, of Christian disunity, placing the proverbial horse before the apple cart. This anti-creedal stance, something of a "creed" in itself says Land, was prevalent among radical evangelicals in the late nineteenth century.[25] Godbey voiced his dissatisfaction, claiming creeds had "done more to sunder and alienate the body of Christ than any other influence."[26] In *The Return of Jesus*, Godbey and collaborator Seth Rees proclaimed that the holiness folk had no creed but the Bible, adding: "they only take the Bible; but they take it all, and take it just as God gives it."[27] Such naïve truisms spilled over into the pages of *The Revivalist*, to which Godbey and Rees were frequent contributors. Holiness preacher Louis Hawkins wrote that creeds were the product of uninspired men, as "liable to err . . . as any other good men [sic]."[28] The attitude was summed up well by Methodist evangelist Sam Jones: "If I had a creed, I would sell it to a museum."[29] A pentecostal crowd would have nodded its approval.

Such sentiments were detectable in *The Apostolic Faith*. The first issue assured readers that "we are not fighting men or churches, but seeking to displace dead forms and creeds and wild fanaticisms with living, practical Christianity."[30] In November 1906 Seymour

---

23. Faupel, *Everlasting Gospel*, 256. Durham never made a planned trip to the South. Faupel speculates that even the South might have joined him had he done so.

24. Quoted in Faupel, *Everlasting Gospel*, 260. Faupel adds, "It must be noted however, [sic] that those who retained the Second Work view were also enmeshed in an emerging fundamentalist mentality."

25. Land, *Pentecostal Spirituality*, 106.

26. Godbey, *Autobiography*, 445.

27. Godbey and Rees, *Return of Jesus*, 41.

28. Hawkins, "Creed vs. the Bible—I," *TRev* (20 September 1900) 7. In context, Hawkins was protesting against an article by Daniel Steele opposing premillennialism.

29. Cited in Ahlstrom, *Religious History*, 746.

30. "Apostolic Faith Movement," *AF*(LA) (September 1906) 2; also cited in Blumhofer, "Restoration as Revival," 148.

offered gratitude that the "freedom in the Spirit" loosed men from the "boundary lines of human creeds."[31] However, in January a recognition for the role of confessionalism had crept into the paper, likely spurred by an unnamed controversy:

> The Lord will hold you just as responsible for believing a lie as He did Adam. False doctrine kills the soul. If we get out of the Word of God and believe a lie, we lose the Blood and lose the life out of our souls. Let no one, not even if he comes as an angel of light, nor your own church or pastor, it may be, get you to doubt the Word of God and believe a lie.[32]

Early the next year the paper listed seven "principles of the doctrine of Christ," namely the "five-fold" gospel plus repentance and final judgment.[33] The last issue warned that "the only way to keep foul and false hellish spirits out of the church of christ [sic] is to have sound doctrine."[34]

Members of the CG studiously avoided creeds. In its pre-pentecostal days, in response to an inquiry as to which denomination they belonged, they replied that they did not subscribe to any formulation and were "strictly undenominational."[35] They further enshrined the Bible as their only doctrine and love and obedience as their "fundamental principals" [sic]. The general assembly of 1906 expressed its desire that the minutes would never be abused "as articles of faith upon which to establish a sect or denomination."[36] The Finished Work doctrine precipitated change. In 1911 the church's council adopted a twenty-five point document, based on "the whole Bible rightly divided," but circumspectly referred to it as a "teaching" and not a creed.[37] Each tenet was submitted without elaboration but with copious scriptural support.

This pattern was mimicked in the AG, amalgamated from loosely affiliated bands in the Midwest in 1914. The proposal to organize sounded through E. N. Bell and Howard Goss on December 20, 1913 in *Word and Witness*, which they published from Malvern, Arkansas.[38] More than three hundred persons swarmed to the resort of Hot Springs, Arkansas from April 2–12, 1914, some 128 of them ministers.[39] M. M. Pinson titled his keynote address "The Finished Work of Calvary."[40] Given their general suspicion of ecclesiasticism, the leaders had to convince attendees that they were not concocting a new denomination. Just as intolerant of dogmatics, they would not suffer a theological statement by which they might define themselves.

---

31. Seymour, "River of Living Water," *AF*(LA) (November 1906) 2.
32. "[Untitled]," *AF*(LA) (January 1907) 4.
33. "[Untitled]," *AF*(LA) (October 1907–January 1908) 4.
34. "[Untitled]," *AF*(LA) (May 1908) 2.
35. "The True Worshipers," *The Way* (June 1904) 3.
36. Preface to *Minutes of the First Annual Assembly*, cited in Conn, *Like a Mighty Army*, 65.
37. Listed in Conn, *Like a Mighty Army*, 118–19.
38. Nichols, "Pentecostalism," 220; "General Convention of Pentecostal Saints and Churches of God in Christ," *W&Wt* (20 December 1913), 1; "April Convention," *W&Wt*, 20 December 1913, 2.
39. Menzies, *Anointed to Serve*, 97. The cheaper "winter" railway tickets were only available up to April 20, which explains the dates for the meeting ("General Convention of Pentecostal Saints," 1).
40. Faupel, *Everlasting Gospel*, 243.

The first resolution that was approved by the convention laid a biblical foundation for organization, acknowledging Christ as their Head and "the holy inspired Scriptures" as "the all-sufficient rule for faith and practice."[41] They insisted that they did not "believe in identifying ourselves into a sect or denomination which constitutes an organization which legislates or forms laws and articles of faith and has jurisdiction over its members and creates unscriptural lines of fellowship and disfellowship."[42] A second resolution affirmed that they would not "legislate laws of government" nor "usurp authority" over its assemblies, reiterating their commitment to hold to "scriptural methods" of unity. Finally, they agreed to appellate their churches by the "general scriptural name" of "Assembly of God" both for convenience and legal documentation.

This lack of doctrinal affinity provided ample opportunity for invention. Indeed, the pentecostal dynamic encouraged reception of imaginative "revelations" from the Spirit, and if not balanced by Scripture could result in fanaticisms, as one author fretted.[43] The "new issue" which rent the AG concerned whether believers ought to be water baptized "in the name of the Father, Son and Holy Ghost" or "in the name of Jesus" only. This latter recipe first surfaced at the April 1913 Arroyo Seco camp meeting in California, although it did not become controversial until the third General Council of the AG, which convened in St. Louis in October 1915.[44] For a time the new issue even swayed chairman E. N. Bell into its fold. As R. Anderson shows, a CMA faction within the council, spearheaded by J. Roswell Flower, saved the fledgling denomination from total meltdown.[45] In the end 156 out of 585 ministers deserted the AG to shape various "oneness" unions of their own.[46]

The near disaster necessitated the move toward doctrinal precision at the next council. They labeled it the "Statement of Fundamental Truths"—only one year after the twelfth and final pamphlet of *The Fundamentals* had been distributed to Christian workers throughout the world. More immediate to the context, the *Weekly Evangel* issue that announced the 1916 conclave also copied a brief report from *The Presbyterian* under the heading "Back to the Fundamentals."[47] Enmeshed in controversy between modernists and fundamentalists, eighty-eight Presbyterian clergy and laymen signed a declaration on April 15, 1915, which bade the denomination to reaffirm its 1910 resolution that constituted the "fundamentals of our common faith" and make it binding upon ministers assuming new pulpits. The resolution successfully passed in 1916, confirming their commitment to the authority of the Bible, the deity of the Lord Jesus, His vicarious atonement and His bodily

---

41. Menzies, *Anointed to Serve*, 99–100.

42. Quoted in Menzies, *Anointed to Serve*, 100.

43. "[Untitled]," *AF*(LA) (January 1907) 3, "The way people get into fanaticism is to put aside the Word and go to following the Spirit. If you do this, you will get full of spirits—you will get into Spiritualism. But if we keep close to the Word of God, there is no danger of going into fanaticism."

44. Menzies, *Anointed to Serve*, 106–21; Faupel, *Everlasting Gospel*, 279–304. Reed has exposed the influence of proto-/fundamentalist writers like Gordon, Simpson, Scofield and Gaebelein on the "Jesus only" piety of oneness pentecostalism. According to Reed, these commentators focused on "Jesus" as opposed to "Jesus Christ" as a designation for the Son (*"In Jesus' Name,"* 39–65).

45. Anderson, *Vision*, 183–84.

46. Synan, *Holiness-Pentecostal*, 157.

47. "Back to the Fundamentals," *WE* (23 September 1916) 7.

resurrection from the dead.[48] Curiously, the *Weekly Evangel* report omitted the virgin birth, which formed the fifth element of the Presbyterian resolution, commonly known as the "Five Points of Fundamentalism." Commented *WE*:

> The churches are awakening to the danger confronting them through the attacks of deluded ministers on the Fundamentals of the Faith. It is high time that all christendom [*sic*] arises and throws off the yoke of toleration to any doctrines which destroy the fundamentals relating to the deity, Sonship of Jesus and in Jesus, salvation, etc. Sound the alarm![49]

In this era of rising militancy both political and spiritual, the AG supported those conservative elements in other denominations from which they drew inspiration. Whereas their reaction to modernism had been visceral, their own internal battles nudged them toward their rationalistic peers. By adopting "fundamental truths" the AG unwittingly participated in a wider religious controversy.

Overall, the statement reflected the doctrines and polity of the CMA. Its "four cardinal truths" copied the fourfold gospel of A. B. Simpson. "Sanctification" however was left deliberately vague to include both "Finished Work" and "Second Work" adherents.[50] Not surprisingly, the doctrine of the Trinity figured prominently in the statement. In the following year, the PHC added a trinitarian formula to its teachings as a response to events in the AG.[51] Furthermore, as Gerald Sheppard has revealed, the AG statement also neglected the fundamentalist concern for the virgin birth of Christ, which was adopted in 1961, the year after AG superintendent Thomas Zimmerman was elected president of the NAE.[52] At the same time, the 1916 statement improved upon the 1914 preamble with words like "infallible" and "revelation" in order to provide a rational basis for doctrine, an appeal reminiscent of fundamentalism's quibble with modernism. Indeed, the "new issue" forced the AG to think along these fundamentalist lines.

This shift became more explicit by the end of the decade. In May 1919 the first World Conference on Christian Fundamentals was held in Philadelphia. It was a direct outgrowth of the sixth and last international prophecy conference which had taken place in November 1918, also in Philadelphia, and from it would emerge the World's Christian Fundamentals Association (WCFA), with W. B. Riley at its head.[53] Its doctrinal statement, crafted by Wheaton College president Charles Blanchard, received encomium from the AG. While they faulted Blanchard for failing to mention "repentance" and "baptism" (both

---

48. The resolution passed again in 1923, albeit by a slight majority, and was never brought up again. W. J. Bryan's failed attempt to become moderator of the Presbyterian Church in 1923 spelled the end of fundamentalist influence over the denomination. The list in *WE* did not include the Virgin Birth, although it was part of the resolution. See Beale, *Pursuit*, 149; Sandeen, *Roots*, xiv–xv.

49. "Back to the Fundamentals," 7.

50. Faupel, *Everlasting Gospel*, 258.

51. Synan, *Old-Time Power*, 41.

52. Sheppard, "Word and Spirit," 20.

53. Ammerman, "North American," 23; Marsden, *American Culture*, 31; Weber, *Shadow*, 161. The purpose of the meeting, attended by some 6,000 delegates, was to broaden the prophecy conferences' concerns over premillennialism and biblical criticism to wider issues confronting the church such as evolution in the public schools and the "modernist" drift of the churches.

by water and the Spirit), still they thought it "so good that we gladly print the same for our readers."[54] The AG report endorsed the association for making "a strong protest against the atheistic 'Modernism' that is sapping the life of the churches of today." Pentecostals were not invited to this evangelical party, but they surely felt they had a stake in it.

Fundamentalist Critiques

Philip Mauro, a patent lawyer who converted to evangelical faith at Simpson's Gospel Tabernacle in 1903, scathingly upbraided the tongues movement in *Our Hope* in a three-part series, commencing in March 1911. Mauro situated his gravamen on First Corinthians, where he considered tongues to be the least of the charisms.[55] Far from being a cessationist, he utterly rejected the notion that the miraculous "signs" had disappeared with the apostles. So long as the current dispensation lasted, he was confident that spiritual gifts would accompany the church. However, like Dixon, he asseverated that tongues were a "sign-gift" to unbelievers and were not intended to edify the body of Christ. Mauro assumed for the purposes of argument that select Christians possessed the genuine ability today. But in examining the spiritual conditions at Corinth, where tongues proliferated, he rated the believers to be less than exemplary models. In comparison to the churches at Ephesus and Colossae, whose Pauline epistles did not address tongues, the Corinthians were immature and carnal.[56] This did not bode well for modern proponents.

In the second article, he pursued this puerile theme further, observing that "childhood, whether natural or spiritual, is not a reproach, unless it be a case of arrested development."[57] Mauro classed tongues as an unsuitable exercise for mature Christians along with all "such emotional experiences as are sought so ardently by our 'latter-rain' brethren."[58] As at Corinth, pentecostal obsession to split into rival factions attested to their carnality. They lacked the requisite "spiritual intelligence" to discern the things of God, which Paul could not share because of their Corinthian preoccupation with things seen (wonders) and heard (tongues). Another indication of pentecostal immaturity was their eagerness to condemn other believers, being themselves spiritually "puffed up."[59] Paul's prohibitions against women in ministry seemed to him singularly appropriate for pentecostalism, where women seized a "prominent, dominant and often lawless part," especially the married ones.[60] He concluded that tongues were appropriate only for "childish" saints

---

54. "Doctrinal Statement," *CE* (28 June 1919) 8.

55. Mauro, "Concerning Spiritual Gifts—Especially Tongues," *Hope* (March 1911) 615.

56. Ibid., 617–18.

57. Mauro, "Concerning Spiritual Gifts—Especially Tongues," *Hope* (April 1911) 670.

58. Mauro conscientiously avoided "tongues movement" so as not to denigrate genuine believers and thus preferred "latter-rain" for his designation, regardless of whether or not Joel's prophecy was applicable to the church.

59. Mauro, "Concerning Spiritual Gifts—Especially Tongues" *Hope* (April 1911) 672. Mauro spends little energy chastising pentecostals for cases of "gross immorality," amounting to a brief paragraph on page 673.

60. Ibid., 676. Mauro points out unjustly that only "men" spoke in tongues at Corinth without considering the inclusive use of gender in the Greek text.

but refused to stigmatize all pentecostals as illegitimate children of God or automatically deceived by Satan's counterfeits (though some undoubtedly were).

In the final article, Mauro contested phrases like "Pentecost," "signs following" and "latter-rain" as erroneous.[61] First, Scripture made no mention of a "personal" Pentecost. Second, Mark 16:17 depicted tongues as only one sign that escorted faith. Third, though not mentioning Myland by name, he believed "the latter rain covenant" to be a misnomer. There was to him as with Gaebelein no inference that a latter rain revival would fall at the end of this age.[62] Mauro recognized that most pentecostals were redeemed but thought them odd for coveting "immature" gifts. His parting advice was to treat pentecostals like infants, forbidding them to seek after their signs but at the same time patiently commending them to discover the "more excellent way."

James Gray, president of MBI and editor of *The Christian Worker's Magazine*, conceded that not all pentecostals were "thoughtless, excitable fanatics": "Some are sober students of the Word of God even though they may be mistaken in some points."[63] Lest he appear too cordial, he added that even sober Christians may "fall under the control of demons" and yield to "spiritual influences that are not of God."[64] A correspondent of the magazine championed "the latter rain" interpretation of Joel as a predictor of future revival without referencing the pentecostal movement, complaining that "prophetic students, [sic] see only the gloom and not the glory of the last days," a reference to pessimistic dispensationalism.[65] Five months later another letter writer requested that the editorial board supply a definition for the "latter rain." The reply correlated the former rain to Pentecost in the "springtime" of the Christian era and the latter rain to "another similar effusion of the Holy Spirit" which was to precede the "harvest," precisely what pentecostals had argued for.[66]

Like many Keswickians, Gray advocated having a "second blessing," which he identified as a crisis whereby the Christian yields him or herself fully to the Lord in consecration for service.[67] Some designated this as the baptism of the Spirit, he continued, though technically it was initiated at conversion and could theoretically be experienced then—though for many it alighted later in life. As to tongues, the editor was confident that the Spirit could distribute them today just as in "the Apostolic days".[68] Thus, Gray, and to a certain degree Mauro, bore grudging acknowledgement that tongues might be a genuine gift for today but exhibited grave doubts that they were much honored by its modern practitioners.

---

61. Mauro, "Concerning Spiritual Gifts—Especially Tongues," *Hope* (May 1911) 752–58.

62. Ibid., 757.

63. "Practical and Perplexing Questions," *CWM* (February 1913) 392. This column was sometimes answered by a committee and sometimes by an individual. Individual replies were sometimes identified in the text, as in this case with Gray, but most often they were not.

64. Ibid., 392.

65. "Practical and Perplexing Questions," *CWM* (December 1913) 252.

66. "Practical and Perplexing Questions," *CWM* (April 1914) 536. This "latter rain" question and answer were repeated in the July issue (p. 736).

67. "Practical and Perplexing Questions," *CWM* (July 1914) 735.

68. "Practical and Perplexing Questions," *CWM* (February 1915) 370.

R. A. Torrey tackled tongues in his regular "Questions and Answers" column in *The King's Business* in July 1913. Responding to the inquiry "Is the present 'Tongues Movement' of God?," he answered emphatically, "It is not."[69] To him, it was as "clear as day" that pentecostals contradicted "the plain teaching of God's Word." Specifically, tongues were not the only sign given in Scripture. They were one of the least profitable, while the Bible recommended believers to crave the greater—like prophecy. Furthermore, pentecostals disregarded the injunction in Corinthians by permitting the multitude to speak in tongues simultaneously without any interpreter present. In these comments he did not differ much from other fundamentalists.

If that were not satisfactory, Torrey accused the movement of gross immorality, most particularly in the lapse of its leaders—one (Parham) whose sin he could not specify in print (sodomy) and another from Ohio (Lupton) whose sin he could (adultery). In recent meetings conducted in Los Angeles by a woman (Maria Woodworth-Etter), hypnotic methods felled men and women, who lay indecently supine for hours.[70] He was unwilling to denounce every pentecostal, but he spent a good third of the article impugning their character.[71] He implied that the movement possessed the hallmarks of demonic activity just as had their predecessors in the Irvingites and the Mormons. He allowed the possibility of tongues could be given in our day ("if God sees fit to do it, He can do it and will do it"), but so many errors occurred both at Corinth and in the current expression that one should be exceedingly careful. In sum, "it is a movement that every one who believes and obeys the Word of God should leave severely alone except to expose . . . the gross errors and evils connected with it."[72] In taking his own advice, Torrey shied away from it as he would a disease.

Henry Frost of the China Inland Mission discredited the scriptural basis for pentecostalism in *The King's Business* in 1915.[73] Frost focused the bulk of his discussion on 1 Corinthians regarding the employment of tongues. The Spirit's manifestation should never excuse the loss of self-control, especially in women, who were prone to emotionalism.[74] He denied that Pentecost as a "known tongue" (xenolalia) could be repeated again, for it was distinctly a "dispensational and Jewish" phenomenon. After Acts 2, the gift was not generally practiced in the church as it was only recorded in Corinthians and was not extolled

---

69. Torrey, "Questions and Answers," *KB* (July 1913) 360–62. This article was published as a tract of the same title: "Is the Present 'Tongues Movement' of God?" The handwritten date on the tract at FPHC has "1915?," but 1913 seems more likely given the article's appearance in *KB*. The tract had been published hastily as it retained the numerical mistakes of the article. Torrey supplied seven reasons for rejecting the movement but counted the number "5" twice, leaving him with six.

70. According to Frank Ewart, Torrey had asserted that pentecostalism had been founded by a "Sodomite," but Torrey avoids the term here and in the tract. Unless he had spoken it, Ewart either inferred the term or heard it from an intermediary source. [See Ewart, "Last Great Crisis," *Meat in Due Season* (July 1916) n.p.]

71. Torrey, "Questions and Answers," (July 1913) 361–62.

72. Ibid., 362. A model of scientific fundamentalism, Torrey regarded the doctrines of scripture as "unmistakable" and "plain."

73. Frost, "Gift of Tongues," *KB* (August 1915) 695–96.

74. Ibid., 696.

as the "supreme gift." Unlike Torrey before him, Frost refrained from heaping opprobrium on its leadership.

Harry Ironside ventured into the melee with *Apostolic Faith Missions and the So-called Second Pentecost*. Earlier Ironside had denigrated his Salvation Army roots in *Holiness, the Fake and the True* (1912). In this newest opus, Ironside composed a crude historical sketch of the pentecostal movement, which arose among "colored people" at Azusa Street.[75] Ironside noted that many who had started in the movement had withdrawn from it for multiple reasons, but many others had compensated for the erosion. Divisions were plentiful, including "Finished Work" folk, who were repulsed by the Apostolic Faith Mission in Portland, and a recent "Jesus only" contingent. As he alludes to the World-wide Camp Meeting which gathered at Arroyo Seco in April 1913 and to Durham as still residing in Los Angeles, it is likely that he wrote this around the same time as Torrey but was unaware of Durham's death the previous year.[76] Ironside reprinted the doctrinal statement of Florence Crawford's Apostolic Faith mission, remarking in a footnote on the absence of any reference to Jesus as Lord or God as Father.[77] This lack formed the kernel of his grievance against pentecostalism.

Ironside personally surveyed several missions across the country, but felt it necessary to elaborate on two as indicative of the whole. In San Francisco, "a large fleshly woman" warned her audience that "two enemies of the truth ha[d] just come in" soon after Ironside and his accomplice perched themselves on a bench. After the session, Ironside confronted the woman for not being as "sinless" as she pretended. She in turn reproved the pair as emissaries from the devil. Five men loitered afterwards to hear what Ironside and his associate had to say. On the whole, he was unimpressed with the worship and heard no proclamation that Jesus was Lord. At the Burnside Street Mission in Portland, what they witnessed beggared description.[78] One man spouted tongues for half a minute while a woman translated for five, leaving Ironside to wonder at the "amazing condensation" of tongues. More seriously, in a gross misstatement of pentecostal beliefs, Ironside charged the movement with the ancient heresy of Gnosticism, for they promulgated a human Christ who could not minister except under the power of the Spirit.[79] Ironside replicated his allegation that Pentecostals did not hail Jesus as Lord, basing his conclusions on a single issue of *The Apostolic Faith* (Portland) and from his observations of their meetings.[80] Though Ironside's mind may have been jaundiced, he had at least investigated empirically what he eschewed.

D. R. Parker lumped pentecostals together with the holiness movement in the *Florida Baptist Witness* in May 1915, indicating that the two movements had not grown suffi-

---

75. Ironside, *Apostolic Faith Missions* (c. 1913) [ATS Arch].

76. Ibid., 6–7, 13. Blumhofer suggests a date of 1914 or 1915 (*Restoring*, 112 n. 98). I prefer an earlier date (1913) as Ironside does not mention the AG as a "Finished Work" entity.

77. Ibid., 6.

78. Ibid., 9.

79. Ibid., 13.

80. Ibid., 14–15.

ciently apart to warrant distinction by the author.[81] He probed seven fallacies of holiness proponents: sinless perfection, divine healing, tongues, the second blessing, the "rolling fallacy," women exhorters, and "fighting the churches." He declared that tongues vanished in the apostolic era, one of the first fundamentalists to clearly state so. As to females commandeering the pulpit, "Were there any women among those first preachers? Can you find one in the Bible who ever preached?"[82] And as to the "holy rollers," well, "why roll in the dust as a mark of humility?" He had never read such shameful displays recorded in the book of Acts. Parker treated each anomaly as though it formed a separate branch within the holiness movement and not overlapping parts of it or even distinct from it like pentecostals, demonstrating only the faintest familiarity with either movement.

The "new issue" caught the attention of a Wisconsin Sunday school worker in 1916, raising the matter with Charles Trumbull, editor of the popular weekly, *Sunday School Times*. The unnamed inquisitor feared that the heresy had become widespread in the Middle West and wanted clarification as to why the trinitarian formula was not used in Acts 2:38. Trumbull reasoned that "the name of Jesus carries with it all the power of the triune God" and saw no justification for believers to be re-baptized in a second ceremony.[83] Gaebelein swiped at pentecostals in a 1917 editorial, reproaching them for thinking they needed the Spirit to enter into them when He indwelled them already as believers.[84] A year later he chastised them for valuing "revelations" by the Spirit above the revelation of the Word.[85] In the 1920s Gaebelein's philipics would air more frequently and vehemently.

Many fundamentalists at this stage were reluctant to damn pentecostalism outright, preferring instead to reprimand its excessive emotionalism and indict it for hypnotism, demonic influences, unsavory and unstable characters, and misguided and ungrounded faith. The notion that fundamentalists uniformly believed that the spiritual gifts had ceased with the apostles is errant if applied to pre-WWI writers, though this would change after the publication of *Counterfeit Miracles* (1918) by B. B. Warfield. Many abandoned caution after WWI, fuelled both by the increasing militaristic mentality which inculcated the movement in its battle with modernists and by the increasing threat that Holy Ghosters posed to their flocks. Other than Ironside, who displayed no trepidation at walking into a pentecostal gathering, fundamentalists were too remote from the movement to have direct contact with it and thus depended upon hearsay from members and quick perusals of available literature. Besides, they subscribed to the modern impulse that cognition was the most reliable path to truth, therefore appeals to Scripture and not experience weighed heavily in their assessments.

---

81. Parker, "Fallacy of the Modern Holiness Propaganda," *Florida Baptist Witness* (13 May 1915) 2–3.
82. Ibid., 3.
83. "Baptized into what Name?" *SST* (20 May 1916) 322.
84. Gaebelein, "Be Filled with the Spirit," *Hope* (July 1917) 7–9.
85. Gaebelein, "Word and the Spirit," *Hope* (November 1918) 260–62.

Pentecostal Responses

Isaac Haldeman, a firebrand dispensational pastor in New York, denounced the pentecostal movement from his pulpit in 1915. Haldeman's complaints can be pieced together from Robert Brown's lengthy rejoinder on December 19 at Glad Tidings Hall (AG).[86] Of the seventeen charges, some were petty, such as Haldeman's insistence that the term "pentecostal" was unscriptural, or his assertion that pentecostals lay on their backs impertinently toward the sky when "slain in the Spirit" rather than penitently on their faces before heaven.[87] Others were simply incredibly, such as when Haldeman posited that only eleven disciples were baptized by the Spirit at the founding of the church and that no women were involved. Unlatching the text, Brown reminded his congregation that in fact 120 were collected in the Upper Room, including Jesus' mother Mary, and that "ALL" were filled and spake in tongues (Acts 1:12–15; 2:4).[88]

Other points were more contentious. Like Gaebelein, Haldeman linked Joel 2:28 with the restoration of Israel, thus dismissing the possibility of a second outpouring of the Spirit prior to the millennium.[89] His polemic was typical of dispensationalism: tongues were given prior to the written record of the NT and were withdrawn after their completion. "This is partly true and partly false," Brown retorted.[90] The Spirit did descend at Pentecost prior to the penning of any epistle, but Paul condoned tongues to the Corinthians—itself part of the written record—and there was no expectation that tongues would diminish.[91] To the point that tongues were the least of the gifts because it was listed last in 1 Corinthians 12:28, Brown countered (as most pentecostals did) that according to Haldeman's logic "charity" must then also be regarded as a lesser gift, for in chapter 13 it followed after faith and hope, contradicting Paul's statement that charity was the greatest of these. Brown conceded that without interpretation, tongues were inferior to prophecy, but Haldeman egregiously omitted this stipulation when quoting from 1 Corinthians 14:5.

Haldeman also assailed the dominance women had over pentecostalism, which Brown refuted by showing that Paul sanctioned women to prophesy in church, that Philip sired four prophetesses (Acts 21:8-9), and that Mary Magdalene was the first to announce the gospel after Christ's resurrection. Brown did grant that women ought not to teach "with authority" in the church, despite the fact that his wife Marie founded Glad Tidings.[92] He cited Joel 2:28 against Haldeman, where God promised that His Spirit would be poured

---

86. Brown, "Reply to Dr. I. M. Haldeman," *MC* (March 1916) 5–10.

87. Ibid., 5, 7. Brown asserted that the "humble, expectant suppliant, waiting for the power to come down." is more likely to fall backwards "with his [sic] face toward heaven, rather than to fall forward with his face toward hell."

88. Ibid., 5.

89. Ibid., 5–6.

90. Ibid., 6.

91. Scofield's note on 1 Cor 14 stressed that the chapter regulated "the ministry of gift in the primitive, apostolic assembly of saints." On tongues, he wrote that they "and the sign gifts are to cease." (*FSRB*, p. 1224). The implication is that "sign gifts" will cease at the end of the apostolic age.

92. Ibid.," 7–8. Brown's wife, Marie Burgess, began Glad Tidings in 1907 before they had even met. They married in 1909 with W. H. Piper presiding.

out upon "ALL flesh," including His daughters. In Brown's hands, Haldeman appears as a chauvinist who wrongly handled the word of truth.

Using Mark 16:17-18 as his text, Brown dismissed Haldeman's notion that miracles were not to be expected in this age except through the power of Satan.[93] Nor was there evidence that "those who prophesied" in Jesus' name and subsequently suffered His rejection (Matt 7:22–23) had done so under the power of the Spirit. In the end, Brown mourned Haldeman's opposition, which was born of either ignorance or a willful perversion of truth. If ignorance, then it was incumbent upon Haldeman to repent; if willful, then he was culpable of blaspheming the Holy Spirit, a most serious charge.[94] By taking Haldeman head on, point by point, Brown demonstrated as much skill in handling Scripture as the prestigious Baptist minister. Brown felt in no way inferior to his fundamentalist brethren.

CG General Overseer A. J. Tomlinson, restrained from apologetic maneuvers until August 1915, taking umbrage with D. R. Parker. Justifying his tactical volte-face, he dared "this friend" who drew first blood to "show one article where any of our people have arraigned the Baptists with the same disrespect and hatred and ridicule that is shown in his article."[95] His opening salvo blasted Parker's last proposition. Far from being rampant heretics, CG embodied the whole Bible while denominations like the Methodists and Presbyterians—whose names were not suggested in Scripture as "Church of God" was—were guilty of perverting truth by ignoring tongues and healing. And if, as Parker claimed, pentecostalism siphoned the most sordid elements from their churches, then why should they be so solicitous? Tomlinson insisted that it was the most godly Baptists who had departed, which accounted for Parker's anxiety.[96] Just as one dispensation waxed and another waned, so the denominations were being eclipsed by a vital progress in religion, Tomlinson advanced two weeks later.[97]

He intended to grapple with each of Parker's disputations in reverse order but instead devoted his next four articles to the status of women, spilling much more ink on this point than Parker had in his terse article. He noted that female oracles were only required to cover their heads when "prophesying," which included "preaching" within his definition.[98] If the laudable Baptist had his way, even Mary would have been forbidden from testifying to the risen Lord. As to women keeping silent, Tomlinson consented that they should have no authority over men, which he limited to the "business meeting"; in other matters they had great liberty to speak.[99] "As the age is fast drawing to a close . . . many good women are held in check, and energies and abilities are lying dormant because of traditional in-

---

93. Ibid., 9.

94. Ibid., 9-10.

95. Tomlinson, "Zealous for the Truth," *COGE*, 7 August 1915, 1. Tomlinson mistakenly calls the paper the *Florida Baptist Advocate* in this first article. "Advocate" was a common appellation for Methodist journals, like the *Florida Methodist Advocate* in Tampa.

96. Tomlinson, "Which is it the Church of God or Something Else? [*sic*]," *COGE* (14 August 1915) 1.

97. Tomlinson, "Be Wise and Careful," *COGE* (21 August 1915) 1.

98. Tomlinson, "Women Preaching Continued," *COGE* (4 September 1915) 1, 4.

99. Tomlinson, "Women Preaching Continued," *COGE* (11 September 1915) 1, 4; "Paul's Statement Consider'd: If Woman should Preach in Church, what does it mean?" *COGE* (18 September 1915) 1, 4.

terpretations of these Scriptures," Tomlinson lamented.[100] Like many nascent movements, pentecostalism created space for women to labor, but Tomlinson scratched a line at the upper echelons of leadership.

Not satisfied to let matters lie, Tomlinson responded in March 1917 to an article titled "Gift of Tongues 'Unknown'" from a "Mississippi paper" by one "W.M.B." First, Tomlinson denied that the "tongues of fire" that appeared on the day of Pentecost were an OT symbol for purification since fire connoted the presence of God.[101] Second, while W.M.B. claimed that "tongues" meant simply "speaking the mighty works of God," accusing "holy rollers" of manufacturing mere babble, Tomlinson responded that Paul communicated in "unknown tongues," the usual translation in 1 Corinthians 14. He swept aside W.M.B.'s insistence that tongues ceased after Pentecost with extracts from Acts, Eusebius, and John Chrysostom. Tomlinson did not fault his opponent for warning fellow Baptists of the "tongues movement," "for thousands of Baptists are getting saved in our meetings and making fine members of the Church of God."[102] If their churches were vacuous, the blame lay at their own feet.

A Mr. Wheatlake of Urbana, Illinois provided enough material for Tomlinson to scribe four articles in June 1917.[103] Apparently it had not been Wheatlake's first disparagement of tongues.[104] Wheatlake purported that in the pentecostal services he monitored many shouted in tongues at once while Paul's injunction curbed the number to two or three.[105] Tomlinson argued that Scripture made a distinction between the "sign" and the "gift" of tongues. The "sign" marked the initial moment of baptism while the "gift" referred to an ongoing faculty under the believer's control.[106] In his ultimate article, he countered Wheatlake's prosaic assertion that tongues were the least of the gifts by divulging that Jesus placed "tongues" near the top in Mark 16 while Paul listed "charity" last in 1 Corinthians 13.[107] Surely by Wheatlake's standards love should be reviled. While Tomlinson often incorporated folksy illustrations in his logic, he vindicated himself by being at least as adept with biblical passages as his opponents.

Tomlinson's colleague and successor Flavius J. Lee reacted to Dr. Torrey's pamphlet on tongues in February 1916 with thirteen refutations.[108] Lee agreed with Torrey that the devil could parody tongues but also maintained that those who acquired the genuine abil-

---

100. Tomlinson, "Paul's Statement Consider'd," 1.

101. Tomlinson, "Opposition Weakening," *COGE* (3 March 1917) 1.

102. Ibid., 2. No doubt the number was embellished somewhat, though hundreds would have sufficed.

103. Tomlinson, "Confidence Unshaken," *COGE* (2 June 1917) 1. This was S. K. Wheatlake, a Free Methodist minister.

104. Tomlinson, "On the Bible Line," *COGE* (16 June 1917) 1. Wheatlake's article appeared in "a Chicago paper" (probably *The Free Methodist*) under the title "Is the Modern Tongues Movement Scriptural?," though no date is given.

105. Ibid., 1.

106. Tomlinson, "The Gift of Tongues," *COGE* (23 June 1917) 1. Tomlinson quotes from the Syriac version, 1 Cor 14:14.

107. Tomlinson, "Covet the Best Gifts," *COGE* (30 June 1917) 1.

108. Lee, "'Is the Present Tongue Movement of God?'" *COGE* (26 February 1916) 1–2. Lee noted that the pamphlet had been "extensively circulated."

ity led exemplary lives. Like other pentecostals, he separated the "sign" of tongues at baptism from Paul's "gift" index in Corinthians.[109] As to tongues having lesser value, Lee noted that Torrey deleted (as had Haldeman) the critical words "EXCEPT he interpret" from the text. Coupled with her sister "interpretation," "she [tongues] is the greatest of all gifts."[110] As to women keeping silence, Lee asserted like Tomlinson that Paul's command applied only to the "business session," otherwise they enjoyed every liberty that men had. Lee admitted that there were "skunks" in the movement and that some may have behaved in "disorderly" fashion, but equally Paul's actions would probably have shocked many people's sensibilities today.[111] As to the gifts having been removed from the church, he counseled Torrey to "lift your eyes see the thousands receiving [sic]."[112] Lee's wife for one had preached in tongues "to the Spanish people" in Tampa, admonishing them to quit tobacco. For his clinching argument, he reasoned that since tongues were a sign to unbelievers who still populated the earth, then the gift must be in continuance.[113] Like Tomlinson, Lee wielded passages in greater depth than opponents, lending biblical weight to his beliefs which should not have been cavalierly dismissed.

Andrew Urshan incriminated "the majority of denominational churches" for promoting the cessationist position at a convention in Ottawa on the evening of January 29, 1917, which appeared in three successive installments in *WE* starting February 24.[114] (Hattie Barth lay similar blame against "many" and Durham against "learned divines," but neither specified who had cast these charges.)[115] However, as was God's prerogative, it was through humble servants (like pentecostals) and "not the best educated" that He operated.[116] Urshan ascertained a biblical rationale for the continuation of miracles in that God had not altered His ways (Heb 13:8) and that Jesus promised His followers that they would perform greater works than He (John 14:11). The source of these miracles was His compassion, which Urshan illustrated from a number of passages.[117] The conduit of miracles was faith in Christ, which God expected to be exercised through the church today.[118] And as miracles were testimony to Christ's divinity on earth, so the church would testify to His

---

109. Ibid., 1.

110. Ibid., 1, capitals in the original. Reference to 1 Cor 14:5. Like Tomlinson, Lee also cited that the order in which gifts appear is irrelevant as "charity" also appeared last after "faith" and "hope."

111. Ibid., 1.

112. Ibid., 1. Torrey believed that tongues had been withdrawn temporarily because of their "abuse" at Corinth but could be restored by God at any time (Torrey, "Is the Present 'Tongues Movement of God?'" 9).

113. Ibid., 2.

114. Urshan, *Life Story*, 74.

115. Barth, "Things of the Kingdom," *BM* (15 March 1909) 4; Durham, "A Word to Ministers, from a Minister," *PT* (March 1909) 10.

116. Urshan, "Are the Days of Miracles Passed?" *WE* (24 February 1917) 2.

117. Ibid., 2-4. Among the illustrations were the Good Samaritan (which Urshan highly allegorizes), the Prodigal Son (reclaiming backsliders), the casting out of demons from the Gadarene, raising the dead and healing the sick.

118. Urshan, "Are the Days of Miracles Passed?" *WE* (3 March 1917) 4–5.

divinity through miracles today.[119] If they had ceased in the intervening years, the fault lay with the impoverished faith of the church and not God's faithlessness.

In July 1917 former CMA missionary W. W. Simpson rebutted criticisms leveled at pentecostalism in *Scofield's Question Box* (1917).[120] He also defamed the Scofield Reference Bible, which had been revised that year. His first task dealt with Scofield's "sweeping" assertion that the NT discouraged believers from seeking the baptism of the Holy Spirit. In Luke 11:13, had not Jesus assured the disciples that the Father would "give the *Holy Spirit* to them that ask Him?"[121] In particular, Simpson challenged Scofield's belief that the "normal" pattern of Spirit-reception for the Gentile church was instituted with Cornelius.[122] It was in fact Cornelius's experience that was abnormal, having received the baptism at his conversion, mainly to convince Jews that the Lord had extended salvation to the uncircumcised.[123] Simpson lobbied for the 120 who tarried at Jerusalem (Acts 2:38–39) as the normal pattern, rallying Samaritans (Acts 8), Paul (Acts 9) and the Ephesians (Acts 19) to his support. Each had received their Pentecost after some temporal delay. Dismantling the dispensational distinction between the "Jewish" and "Gentile" periods of the early church inaugurated with Cornelius, Simpson noted how Paul laid hands on the Ephesian converts ("the normal pattern") and how they spoke in tongues after receiving the Spirit. "Oh, Paul! why did you spoil that beautiful and learned theory?" Simpson mocked.[124]

Dispensational theology taught that the Jewish nation should have proclaimed Christ as their king within seven years of His resurrection. According to their reading of Daniel 7, the Messiah's crucifixion took place on the 69th week dating from Artaxeres' proclamation to restore the temple (c. 445 BC), provided that one week was the prophetic equivalent of seven years. The failure of the Jews to acknowledge the Christ by the end of the 70th week (or seven years after the resurrection) led to the suspension of biblical prophecy concerning the Jews and the establishment of the Gentile church (the "church age") with Cornelius up until the time of the rapture—a period known as the "Great Parenthesis"—after which the prophecies would be reinstated and the 70th week fulfilled in the "Great Tribulation."

---

119. Ibid., 5; Urshan, "Are the Days of Miracles Passed?" *WE* (10 March 1917) 4–5.

120. Simpson, "Baptism in the Spirit—A Defense," *WE* (14 July 1917) 2–6. Simpson also noted the attacks of Haldeman, Gaebelein, A. B. Simpson and two members of the China Inland Mission, D. E. Hoste and Henry Frost, though he chose to dispute only with Scofield. *Scofield's Question Box* was compiled by Ella Pohle from Scofield's Correspondence Course and a column in *Record of Christian Work*. *Question Box* addressed "the Holy Spirit" on pp. 47–53 (including "baptism in" and "filled with") and "tongues" on pp. 153–54. The four points Simpson handles were under "tongues." "The Holy Spirit" gives Scofield's view of Spirit-baptism along Keswick lines.

121. Simpson, "Baptism in the Spirit—A Defense," 2, italics in original. Simpson criticized Scofield's notes on this verse for not admitting that it referred to baptism. Scofield wrote that "none of the disciples ... asked for the Spirit in the faith of this promise" (*OSRB*, 1090). Scofield's point is that the Spirit was given to those who did not seek for the baptism (see also *Question Box*, 48).

122. Scofield commented for Acts 10:44, "Heretofore the Gospel has been offered to Jews only ... But now the normal order for this age is reached: the Holy Spirit is given without delay, mediation, or other condition than simple faith in Jesus Christ" (*OSRB*, 1164).

123. Simpson, "Baptism in the Spirit—A Defense," 3.

124. Ibid., 4.

Simpson's second point challenged Scofield's rendering of both Acts 2:8 and 1 Corinthians 14:2, where Scofield had claimed that "tongues" signified a "known" language.[125] In a novel interpolation, Simpson hypothesized that the outpouring of the Spirit on the day of Pentecost happened in two stages. At the initial moment the 120 spoke in unknown tongues, but when their ebullience attracted non-believers, the Spirit gave them utterances in known tongues.[126] Simpson further accused Scofield of contradicting Paul's command to "forbid not tongues," and "may God pity him for he is dangerously near speaking against the Holy Spirit."[127] Thirdly, Scofield supposed that when properly employed tongues convicted unbelievers of sin, which pentecostal "gibberish" certainly failed to do.[128] Simpson countered that the primary purpose of tongues was private communication with God. Fourthly, whereas Scofield wrongly conjectured that Paul rebuked the Corinthians for speaking in foreign languages at their gatherings, Simpson surmised that the rebuke resulted from the absence of someone to translate the otherwise undecipherable speech.[129] Simpson dispatched a letter to Scofield on April 16, 1917, challenging him on these points. In reply, Scofield merely acknowledged that he had perused it.[130]

In an editorial aside to Simpson's article, Bell remarked that while these revered preachers had maligned them, "it is no reason for our discounting all their good works."[131] In particular, "the Scofield Reference Bible, which contains no attacks on the Pentecostal or any other movement, is still highly esteemed among us . . . We continue in our recommendation of the Scofield Bible as the best work of its kind that has ever been published."[132] Bell betrayed his reliance upon fundamentalists in admitting that "many of their writings show signs of divine inspiration."[133] A year later he endorsed both the Weymouth and Scofield Bibles—"but not everything in them," emphasizing his differences with Scofield regarding the baptism of the Spirit. He advised subscribers to "take the many good things in his Bible, and pass these mistakes up to his ignorance of full Pentecostal light."[134] Indeed, the works of fundamentalists were trumpeted in pentecostal periodicals.

A survey of advertisements for Christian literature in the *CE* and *WE* for 1915 discloses that of the eleven titles presented that year, four were pentecostal, one was proto-

---

125. Scofield suggests "a tongue" instead of "an *unknown* tongue" in the marginal note for 1 Cor 14:2. Simpson agreed with Scofield that Acts 2:8 should be translated "language." He says the meaning in Acts 2:11 is uncertain, but I see no reason for him to reject Scofield's use of "languages" rather than "tongues."

126. Simpson, "Baptism in the Spirit—A Defense," 4–5. Simpson's interpretation seems unnecessary, as the "tongues" if "known" at Pentecost would still have been "unknown" to the original speakers and only "known" later as others heard them. He was looking for a way to refute Scofield's rendering of "tongues" as "language" in the note.

127. Ibid., 5.

128. *Scofield's Question Box*, 154.

129. Scofield believed that tongues only referred to "known" languages (*Scofield's Question Box*, 154, his fourth objection), an interpretation which pentecostals consistently rejected, especially in 1 Cor 14.

130. Simpson, "Baptism in the Spirit—A Defense," 1. Scofield's letter was dated April 26.

131. Ibid., 6.

132. Bell added that "hundreds" of pentecostal preachers and workers used Scofield.

133. Simpson, "Baptism in the Spirit—A Defense," 6.

134. Bell, "Note on Modern Bibles," *CE* (1 June 1918) 5.

fundamentalist, two were fundamentalist, four were evangelical, and none were holiness.[135] For 1920, fundamentalists figured even higher, comprising thirty-seven out of ninety-seven titles, while protofundamentalists filled thirty-three spots, pentecostals fourteen, evangelicals thirty-three, and holiness none.[136] The prominence of Finney's *Lectures on Revival* among the works in 1915 contrasted with the more theological works of the fundamentalists advertised in 1920. Already a shift from enthusiastic revivalism to a more sedate fundamentalism was taking shape.

In another editorial in 1919, Bell responded to a chiding from the Cumberland Presbyterians.[137] But Bell reminded his brethren that their own denomination catapulted into existence out of a revival (Cane Ridge) where physical sensations such as "violent shaking" and "awkward jerks" were manifest.[138] As for the clamor of pentecostals, had they not heard that "a mighty rushing wind" accompanied the chosen Jerusalemites in their frenzied speech?[139] "Quietness" was a hallmark of spirituality neither in the NT nor for today. The Welsh miners, for instance, were universally acclaimed for their spirituality and spontaneity, meriting the accolades of G. Campbell Morgan.

After appraising Torrey's pamphlet in 1919, Stanley Frodsham volunteered some correctives.[140] At many junctures he felt Torrey to be mistaken and ill-informed. Like other pentecostals, he separated the "sign" from the "gift" of tongues. Assuming that Torrey's criticisms pertained to the "World Wide Camp Meeting" in Los Angeles, Frodsham, who unlike Torrey was an eyewitness, assured him that his allegations were spurious. Frodsham's wife for one had been cured along with many others, and the results were permanent in her.[141] He considered it unfair for Torrey to judge the movement by the unseemly behavior of a few; after all, one of Torrey's own assistants confessed to a drug addiction and to "sins of immorality," yet that did not taint Torrey's integrity. After rehearsing his baptism in the Spirit in 1908, Frodsham touted early pentecostal familiarity with fundamentalist doctrine,

> To a man we stood for the infallibility and verbal inspiration of the Bible. We all believed in the virgin birth, the resurrection and miracles of our Lord that are being deuled [sic] on every hand by modern churches. We all made much of the atoning

---

135. See Appendix C. For convenience, I have counted protofundamentalists as having died before 1920 and fundamentalists as having died after 1920, the year "fundamentalism" was coined. See note in Appendix C.

136. See Appendix D.

137. Bell, "Gentlemanliness and the Holy Ghost," *CE* (28 June 1919) 4.

138. Cumberland was an outgrowth of the Cane Ridge revival, though it did not organize until 1810 in Tennessee.

139. Bell, "Gentlemanliness and the Holy Ghost," 4.

140. Frodsham, "Why We Know the present Pentecostal Movement is of God: An Answer to the Tract, 'Is the present "Tongues" Movement of God?'" *CE* (9 August 1919) 4–5.

141. Ibid., 4. Alice Frodsham tumbled down a flight of stairs fifteen months before the meeting and was in "great pain." Since receiving prayer, she had been pain free. Once more, the handling of those seeking healing was not "violent" as Torrey had insisted.

blood of Christ that cleanseth from all sin. We were all looking for the near and premillennial coming of the Lord Jesus Christ.[142]

As to ethics, "I was delighted to find that the Pentecostal people were an unworldly people, a people that never attended shows, movies or other places of amusement." Like other conservatives, they did not revel in the modernist penchant for the "ice cream social" or "oyster supper," nor did they abuse alcohol or tobacco "in any form." In all aspects pentecostals imitated fundamentalists save in spiritual aptitude. Frodsham was eager to display just how much they shared in common.

Pentecostals sustained a mettlesome defense of their uniqueness. CG pastor Sam Perry reminded detractors that pentecostals were "very strict as to their standard of morals."[143] The ground for comparing them to Mormons and spiritualists was slippery in his view, for infamy would then have to be attached to the apostles as well since they too spoke in tongues. Meanwhile, the Holy Spirit had bypassed the holiness movement for others more receptive than they, he stated in another contribution.[144] To C. C. Martin and J. A. Davis, far from being the puppets of malicious spirits, pentecostals could pride themselves in embracing the entirety of divine inspiration, which advocated tongues.[145] If their opponents were accurate, then "the Apostles were of the devil," a view to which no Christian should acquiesce. Many nominal believers saw no harm in dance halls, but dance in church and they say you are demon possessed. To the authors, it was the devil's logic to hate holiness and love sin.[146] The moral credentials of pentecostals were impeccably evangelical throughout.

Pentecostals continued their appeal to church history for validation. Like *AF*, *COGE*'s premier edition viewed the CG as the fulfillment of gospel truths encapsulated in the Reformation.[147] Luther and Wesley may not have ensconced "Pentecostal fullness," but their ideals laid the groundwork for it. Tomlinson propped up George Fox, early Methodists, Cane Ridge and Charles Finney as their precursors.[148] *LRE* also featured Cane Ridge in March 1911, painting a vivid portrait of its effervescence.[149] One Mrs. E. E. Duncan of London invoked Chrysostom in her struggle against the cessationists.[150] It seemed to her that the devil borrowed even pious minds to combat the pentecostal message. Max Wood Moorhead recounted the tumult surrounding the Irvingites. In his opinion, Irving's discipline Richard Baxter had been entrusted with burdensome responsibility at a young age and prophesied "wildly," even fixing a date for the Lord's return. Therefore, "we are not

---

142. Ibid., 5.
143. Perry, "Why Reject Speaking in Tongues," *COGE* (6 October 1917) 3.
144. Perry, "'What is the Matter with the Holiness People," *COGE* (20 October 1917) 3.
145. Martin and Davis, "Did the Devil write the Bible?" *COGE* (18 August 1917) 3.
146. Ibid., 3.
147. "Latter Rain Revival," *ELCOGE* (1 March 1910) 3.
148. Tomlinson, "Manifestations of the Spirit," *ELCOGE* (1 November 1910) 3–5.
149. "Outpouring of the Spirit in 1800," *LRE* (March 1911) 12–13.
150. Duncan, "Lessons from the Past," *LRE* (September 1916) 18–19.

greatly surprised that he repudiated the work of the Holy Ghost."[151] Nor was he astonished that the Holy Ghost had deserted the movement, which deteriorated into a "dead formalism" after Irving's demise.

Elizabeth Sexton targeted her sights on John Wesley in several op-eds. In her estimation, pentecostalism would have visited Methodism had it not lost its early fervor.[152] She reprised this observation two years later when she copied an account from Phoebe Palmer's *The Promise of the Father* concerning tongues speech among Wesley's disciples.[153] Warnings were proffered against those who resisted the Holy Spirit or criticized His work. Moorhead described a truculent German reverend who became ill, repented of his opposition to tongues and subsequently recovered his health, and a young Indian woman who died of cholera after spurning pentecostal fellowship.[154] J. Roswell Flower applauded Gamaliel's prudent orientation towards Christianity in Acts and David's refusal to wound God's anointed, King Saul, encouraging pentecostal enemies to be more circumspect.[155] The AG organ *CE* reprinted an article from *Trust* in which the Dean of Canterbury extolled charismatic vitality during the reign of Nero in a fictionalized form.[156] In a series of thirteen articles detailing the rise and spread of pentecostalism, B. F. Lawrence dedicated three pieces to church history, including the spiritual practices of Francis Xavier, the Camisards, the Quakers and an obscure sect in Rhode Island.[157] William Schell provided incidents from the post-apostolic Fathers proving the Spirit's enduring presence among them in three articles in early in 1916.[158]

Cooperation and Discord with the Christian and Missionary Alliance

Not all fundamentalists were antagonistic to the movement. Charles Blanchard, an honorary vice-president in the CMA and president of Wheaton College in Illinois, exhorted the congregation at Stone Church in Chicago both to "prepare ye the way of the Lord" and "prepare ye the way of the people" on October 6, 1912.[159] *LRE* also dedicated five pages to his sermon "The Two Preparations" in the March 1913 volume. Spirit-baptized CMA leaders Ira David and William MacArthur frequently graced the Stone Church pulpit. And

---

151. Moorhead, "Rise and Fall of Irvingism," *LRE* (March 1917) 10.

152. Sexton, "Early Methodism," *BM* (15 September 1910) 1.

153. Sexton, "Did Wesley and Some of the Early Methodists Receive the Pentecostal Baptism?" *BM* (1 June 1912) 1.

154. Moorhead, "Friendly Letter to Christian Critics of the Latter Rain," *BM* (15 August 1912) 4.

155. Flower, "Important Warning," *TPent* (1 April 1910) 6.

156. "Glossolalia in the Early Church," *CE* (22 August 1914) 3.

157. Lawrence, "Tongues in History," *WE* (15 January 1916) 4–5; "Work of the Spirit in Rhode Island," *WE* (22 January 1916) 4–6; "Incidents of the Spirit's Work from 1890 to 1900," *WE* (29 January and 3 February 1916) 4–5. This series was followed by another 13-part series by Lawrence on the current movement throughout the world.

158. Schell, "Manifestations of the Holy Spirit in Post-Apostolic Times," *WE* (15 January 1916) 6–9; Schell, "Manifestations of the Holy Spirit in Post-Apostolic Times," *WE* (12 February 1916) 5,7; Schell, "Manifestations of the Holy Spirit in Post-Apostolic Times," *WE* (19 February 1916) 6–7.

159. Blanchard, "Two Preparations," *LRE* (March 1913) 2–6; King, *Genuine Gold*, 151.

pentecostal patriarch Jonathan Paul of Germany was afforded opportunity to preach at the CMA Gospel Tabernacle in New York in 1912.[160]

The Stone Church invited A. B. Simpson to its podium in 1911. He prayed for seventeen-year-old Alfred Bostrom, who instantly mended from a life-threatening illness and survived another seventy years as a minister in both the AG and CMA.[161] After 1912, however, a bitter dispute between Simpson and CMA missionary W. W. Simpson (no relation) over the doctrine of initial evidence soured the CMA founder on "dogmatic" pentecostals. He and the CMA maintained that "the chief evidence of the baptism in the Spirit was a holy life," rejecting both Wesleyan eradicationism and Keswick suppressionism.[162] Doctrinally it put him at odds with the "finished work" teaching supported by so many ex-CMA workers.

More problematic however were the numerous CMA churches seceding to the AG or opting for independence. In May 1912 the CMA amended its constitution with a "reversion clause" which stated that the property of any church that no longer supported its position would revert to the CMA.[163] Consequently, several CMA luminaries absconded, leaving historians with an impression that the CMA had hardened its stance against pentecostalism. Charles Nienkirchen asserts that Simpson had privately sought glossolalia from 1907 onwards and, after five years of failure, abandoned the project, about which, according to future AG assistant superintendent David McDowell, Simpson later expressed regret.[164] King persuades that Simpson's "regret" did not refer to him altering his opinion about tongues, which he did not, but to the decision to append the "reversion clause" in the CMA constitution.[165] Simpson did not waver from his middling approach to pentecostalism in rejecting the "sign" of tongues but not the "gift." Thus, many pentecostals felt that Simpson rejected tongues altogether when in fact he only regretted the CMA approach to charismatic churches. Misunderstanding fermented on both sides, though many pentecostals remained loyal to the CMA.

Impact of Dispensationalism on Pentecostalism

Meanwhile, dispensationalism augmented its steady incursion into pentecostal thought. For example, from 1910 *The Bridegroom's Messenger* became ever more alarmist. Under the editorial "Signs of the Times"—a typical posting of dispensationalists—Elizabeth Sexton expressed the tension between apocalyptic termination and inchoate longing: "The all-absorbing theme of Pentecost and its significance regarding the early appearing of our Lord . . . keeps us in a hopeful and expectant attitude . . . But there is also to be a terrible

---

160. King, *Genuine Gold*, 152.

161. Ibid., 147.

162. Ibid., 148.

163. Ibid., 155. King, citing Faupel (*Everlasting Gospel*, 256), says that no "mass exodus" occurred at this time, as a number of leaders had already left.

164. Nienkirchen, *A. B. Simpson*, 105–7.

165. King, *Genuine Gold*, 158–60.

day for the ungodly world and the sleeping church."[166] Among the dolorous tokens Sexton culled from various news reports were global unrest, the aggrandizement of destructive armaments around the world, and agitation in Europe for revolution and war. Another theme, "apostasy," appeared for the first time in 1911, stolen from *LRE*. Reacting to a proposed merger between Episcopalians and Methodists, the anonymous source bristled that it "only speaks loudly of the apostasy of the Methodist church."[167] Infidelity permeated both Protestantism and Catholicism, quoting at length from A. C. Gaebelein, who equated Rome with the whore of Babylon and "the hub of an apostacized Christendom."

The first portent of the end for Arch Collins was the "falling away" of the church. "Spiritualism, Eddyism, Russellism, Romanism, ad infinitum" fulfilled the requirement handsomely, not to mention the reduction of spiritual power in the denominations.[168] Furthermore, fires, comets, earthquakes and a Costa Rican snowstorm buttressed physical omens, while the risk of war despite the recent push for international peace constituted a political omen.[169] According to evangelist L. C. Hall of Chicago at the close of 1913, war loomed in Europe. Armies and arms were escalating and pupils in the military academies were mastering the art of war, which "is only legalized killing."[170] Even the invention of the "war air ship" in Germany was predicted in Habakkuk 1:8. Hall mourned that the failure of evangelicals "to declare the *whole word of God*" (i.e., spiritual truth) had bequeathed to a godless world the miseries of the antichrist.[171]

LRE reflected dispensational concerns soon after the launch of the Scofield Reference Bible on January 1, 1909. In February 1909 C. E. Preston, a former Episcopal rector who had heard tongues in the Rhode Island revival of 1874, presumed that history had reached "the ten toes" in Nebuchadnezzar's dream (Dan 2:42) just before the rock of the blessed kingdom would seal "this dispensation."[172] Moreover, "Whitbyanism" (postmillennialism) was seldom promoted anymore because "the 'signs of the times' all indicate that we are living in the last days." William Piper was more explicit. Citing Matthew 24, he chronicled a litany of disasters that had pummeled the earth—"famines, pestilences, and earthquakes"—from India in 1877 to Persia in 1908.[173] Hostilities had ravaged the nations from the American Civil War to the Boer conflict, while the near "dissolution" of Turkey paved the way for Armageddon. In the midst of his homily, someone broke forth in tongues which another interpreted, "The Lord is coming soon . . . Oh that thou wilt watch and pray as He hath told thee."[174] Piper, suitably encouraged, discoursed on the antichrist

---

166. Sexton, "Signs of the Times," *BM* (1 January 1910) 1.
167. "Growing Apostasy," *BM* (1 June 1911) 4.
168. Collins, "Signs of the Times," *W&Wt* (20 September 1913) 2.
169. Collins, "Signs of our Times," *W&Wt* (20 October 1913) 1.
170. Hall, "Great Crisis Near at Hand," *W&Wt* (20 November 1913) 1.

171. Hall's "whole word of God" was essentially the fourfold gospel with one change, substituting "power" for "redemption" but leaving in "baptism of the Spirit." Habakkuk 1.8 reads in part, "their horsemen shall come from far; they shall fly as the eagle that hasteth to eat" (KJV).

172. Preston, "Some Manifestations of the Spirit Thirty-five Years Ago," *LRE* (February 1909) 23.
173. Piper, "Lord is at Hand," *LRE* (April 1909) 13–14.
174. Ibid., 16–17. Piper also quotes W. Blackstone on p. 19.

and the Great Tribulation, which would ultimately conclude with the triumph of Christ, quoting from William Blackstone along the way. Future editions of *LRE* obsessed over the probability of war right up to the outbreak of the Great War in 1914.[175]

Another prominent signal was the enlargement of Islam and "heathen" religions, themes emphasized by dispensationalists. Islam had swept the Sudan and threatened to overwhelm western societies with its mosques. A feared alliance between Jews and Muslims could spell disaster for "apostate Christendom."[176] One author lamented that the exposure given to eastern religions at the Congress of Religions at the World's Fair in Chicago in 1893 would delude many into sun-worship, Buddhism, Islam and Hinduism while disguising their "degradation of women."[177] "There never was a time when the forces of evil were so subtily [sic] at work as they are today in the false religious systems," said another.[178] Human and chthonic forces were conspiring to forge a dreaded "one world government" and "one world religion" through which the antichrist would oppress the world: "All these things show us how fast the darkness is increasing, and that the hour of Satan's rule is fast coming to a climax, from which it will come to a sudden end."[179]

R. V. Miller's "signs of the times" in *Word and Work* in 1907 mirrored dispensational prognostication: apostasy, lawlessness, the Jewish migration to Palestine, the peace movement and the popularity of spiritualism.[180] Another writer saw the fulfillment of Nahum 2:3–4 in automobiles that raged like chariots in the streets with headlights that burned like torches.[181] Albert Weaver selected Christian Science, the Layman's Missionary Movement, and the Hague tribunal as harbingers of impending collapse.[182] After the Scofield Reference Bible was published, excerpts extracted from prophetic periodicals like *Signs of the Times*, *Our Hope* and *Morningstar* projected a speedy decline in morals and faith.[183] For J. C. Wheeler, worsening conditions like financial trusts that controlled so much wealth in the U.S. were ripening the country for anarchy.[184] Scanning the globe of 1913, he saw Europe ready for conflict, although his news briefs were somewhat dated as he had plagiarized his information from an article in *BM* from more than three years before.[185]

---

175. E.g., "Wars and Rumors of Wars," *LRE* (December 1911) 12–13; "Wars and Rumors of Wars," *LRE* (November 1912) 12; "Wars, Pestilence and Famine," *LRE* (December 1912) 12–13.

176. "The Rapid Spread of Islam," *LRE* (November 1909) 24—copied from *Herald of Truth*. Other articles on Islam—"Islam and Judah are Uniting, Will their Union Produce Antichrist?" *LRE* (October 1909) 14–15 [also from *Herald of Truth*]; "A Great Crisis," *LRE* (October 1913) 2–7.

177. "Deadly Peril," *LRE* (February 1912) 20–22.

178. "Encroaches of Heathenism," *LRE* (March 1911) 14–15.

179. "Massing of Forces: A Sign of the Times," *LRE* (August 1912) 22–24 [from *Herald of Truth*].

180. Miller, "Christ's Coming Nigh at Hand," *W&Wk* (March 1907) 70–72.

181. "Signs of His Coming," *W&Wk* (May 1907) 132 (from *Apostolic Faith*).

182. Weaver, "Latter Day Delusions and Counterfeits," *W&Wk* (February 1909) 22–24.

183. "Growing Infidelity," *W&Wk* (October 1909) 235 [*Signs of the Times*]; "Increase of Iniquities," *W&Wk* (February 1910) 46 [*Hope*]; "Antichrist," *W&Wk* (March 1913) 77 (*Morningstar*).

184. Wheeler, "Worse and Worse," *W&Wk* (July 1913) 200.

185. Compare Wheeler, 201–2, to Sexton, "Signs of the Times," *BM* (1 January 1910) 1, noted above. The end of Wheeler's article is taken verbatim from the middle of Sexton's, nine paragraphs in all.

W. H. Cossum dedicated eight lectures to the Jews and prophecy at the Stone Church in 1910. He considered the study of prophecy as the key to balancing the dry intellectualism of the churches with the exuberance of pentecostals.[186] Though the Jews had been scattered among the nations, he predicted that they would return as a *whole* and not as a remnant, for Palestine was capable of supporting the world's twelve million Jews and more.[187] After charting the rise of the Zionist Movement, Cossum persuaded his audience that revival would seize the assembling Jews just as it had the pentecostals.[188] His treatment of the history of Jerusalem was largely conceived along dispensational lines, such as the antichrist duping the Jews after 1,260 days of halcyon co-existence.[189] Also, Pentecost demarcated the suspension of God's dealing with Israel until the end times—forming a "parenthesis" in prophetic history, just as dispensationalists maintained.[190] Cossum proved to be knowledgeable about prophetic history of both Palestine and the Bible, giving long discourses on Zionism and its relation to Scripture.

As Cossum's discourse finished, Myland's lectures on the book of Revelation began. And like Cossum's, the series was published in book form by the Stone Church. Myland confessed to joining the "harmonic school" of Revelation in 1892 after praying with F. L. Chapell, principal of A. J. Gordon's missionary training institute in Boston before Dixon. This hermeneutic combined elements of the preterist, historicist, and futurist theories into one, for "a great deal of Scripture, [sic] is double-barrelled and some even three-barrelled. That is, it has a literal, a spiritual and a dispensational bearing."[191] Of the three, Myland preferred the spiritual, at least at the beginning of his lectures. For instance, in his exposition of the letters to the seven churches (Rev 2–3), he scrupulously avoided historicizing the letters into periods as was typical of both historicists and futurists.[192] Myland divided biblical history into four dispensations, the patriarchal, the Levitical (priestly), the prophetical and the Gospel, which he likened to the four living creatures in Revelation 4:6–8.[193] Like dispensationalists, he equated the Great Tribulation with Daniel's seventieth week.[194]

---

186. Cossum, "Mountain Peaks of Prophecy and Sacred History," *LRE* (March 1910) 5.

187. Cossum, "Mountain Peaks of Prophecy and Sacred History: The Indestructible Jews," *LRE* (April 1910) 4. 731 BC represents the first deportation of the Jews under the Assyrians.

188. Cossum, "Mountain Peaks of Prophecy and Sacred History: The Zionist Movement," *LRE* (May 1910) 8.

189. Cossum, "Mountain Peaks of Prophecy and Sacred History: Jerusalem the City of History and Destiny," *LRE* (July 1910) 8–13.

190. Cossum, "Mountain Peaks of Prophecy and Sacred History: The Jew and Pentecost," *LRE* (August 1910) 2.

191. Myland, "Book of Revelation of Jesus Christ," *LRE* (December 1910) 4. The preterist views prophecy as having taken place during the lifetime of the hearers, the historicist looks at prophecy as being fulfilled throughout history up to the present, and the futurist treats the majority of prophecy, especially Revelation, as yet future. Myland placed G. H. Pember in this last camp.

192. Myland, "Book of the Revelation of Jesus Christ: The Messages to the Churches," *LRE* (February 1911) 2–6; Myland, "Book of the Revelation of Jesus Christ: The Messages," *LRE* (March 1911) 2–6; Myland, "Book of the Revelation of Jesus Christ: The Messages," *LRE* (April 1911) 3–8.

193. Myland, "Book of Revelation of Jesus Christ: The Four Living Creatures, Four and Twenty Elders, the Bride—Resurrection Order," *LRE* (May 1911) 15.

194. Myland, "Book of the Revelation of Jesus Christ: An Exegesis of Sixth and Seventh Chapters," *LRE*

Unlike dispensationalists, he forecast four raptures, one before and three during the tribulation, estimating that three hundred million would be saved *in toto*.[195] Like the angels in heaven, a third of humanity would be lost to Satan but two-thirds redeemed through the Blood. Myland exhibited independence in his interpretation, not holding slavishly to one tradition or another.

Prophecy, World War I, and the Denominations

The Great War solidified dispensationalism's hold upon pentecostal eschatology, for not only had dispensationalism provided a theological framework for understanding the outpouring as at first, but now the war confirmed its predictions that the world was headed for catastrophe and not improvement. Armageddon seemed closer than ever. *CE* announced the conflict with a gargantuan headline, "Take WARning," beneath which George Carlyle expatiated on the Great Tribulation.[196] Increasingly, the identity of the antichrist became a matter of speculation. The editors of *CE* guarded against choosing a specific person but were certain he would appear once the Holy Spirit withdrew His presence from the world.[197] In 1917, J. T. Boddy contrasted the kingdom of the antichrist, which ruled the present world, with the future kingdom of Christ.[198] For Weaver the spirit of the antichrist was ubiquitous, though he rejected the notion that the antichrist would be the pope, who traditionally upheld the deity of Christ.[199] Even so, his sentiment that civilization teetered on the "fringes of Tribulation Days" was electric throughout the movement.

Like their fundamentalist mentors, pentecostals examined WWI through the lens of prophecy. Premillennialists had long yearned for the Jewish repopulation of ancient Israel as a catalyst of Christ's next advent. The appointment of a free parliament by the Sultan of Turkey in 1908 set Sexton to ruminating on its implications for Jewish settlement.[200] Four years later she celebrated the establishment of forty new kibbutzim in Palestine with the expectation that a state of Israel would soon emerge.[201] *WE* admitted that one of its principle interests in the war concerned the Jews, "It is only a matter of time until this prophecy is fulfilled, and in this present war we see conditions ripening fast which indicate that the time is at hand."[202] For the writer of "The Jew, the Gentile, and the Church of God" (a title which matched the first chapter of Scofield's *Rightly Dividing the Word of Truth*, which appeared as an appendix to his reference Bible), God was dealing with all three simultaneously through the war while in the past He had handled only one or two at a

(June 1911) 4.

195. Ibid., 8; Myland, "Book of the Revelation of Jesus Christ: Opening the Seventh Seal," *LRE* (July 1911) 9; Myland, "Book of the Revelation of Jesus Christ: The Consummation of all Things," *LRE* (March 1912) 14.

196. Carlyle, "Great Tribulation," *CE* (5 September 1914) 1. Carlyle's identity is uncertain.

197. "Editorial," *CE* (31 October 1914) 2; "Who is the Anti-christ?" *CE* (21 November 1914) 4.

198. Boddy, "The Antichrist," *WE* (20 January 1917) 4–5.

199. Weaver, "Antichrist and his System," *CE* (3 October 1914) 3.

200. Sexton, "What does it Mean?" *BM* (15 November 1908) 1; W. J. Ohan, "Day of Miracles in Turkey," *BM* (1 December 1908) 1. The Sultan's legislation was signed July 25.

201. Sexton, "Jews and the Holy Land," *BM* (1 December 1912) 1.

202. "Preparations for the Return to Palestine," *WE* (7 August 1915) 3.

time.[203] Prophetic pundits everywhere were stirred when British foreign secretary Lord Balfour committed his country to establishing a Jewish home in Palestine.[204] The capture of Jerusalem by General Allenby in November 1917 added further validity to dispensationalism. Said Arch Collins, "More than thirty years ago students of prophecy said that 1917 would be a year of 'terminal crises' and we have lived to see it so,"[205] counting 1335 lunar "years" (days) as instructed by Daniel 12:12 from the founding of Islam in AD 622.

COGE has a woeful collection of pre-WWI material—most of 1912 and 1913 are missing from the record. What remains betrays little of the apocalyptic gloom that crept into other periodicals. With the war, eschatological speculation improved. In January 1915, Sam Perry asked what many had been wondering, "Is this Armageddon?" No, he replied, supplying three reasons: the battles were in all the wrong locations, the war did not involve "all nations," and as yet no single supreme power dominated the world.[206] Perry commented, "The present war no doubt will go far to shaping the nations for the reception of anti-christ, and perhaps open the way for the Jews to get possession of Palestine." As Britain pushed towards Palestine in the fall of 1917, Perry became more impassioned, "From many indications it seems that the time is very near when Israel is to be a nation again."[207] He assumed that most Christians believed that God had cast off Israel forever when the nation rejected the Messiah in the first century, and he set out to correct this misunderstanding, laying great stress on the Zionist movement. However, a year passed before *COGE* bothered to print the news that Allenby had ousted the Turks from Jerusalem.[208] Perry did not remark on its implications until near the conclusion of the war.[209] When it came to the prophetic perspective, the CG lagged behind the AG in both content and time.

Tomlinson reluctantly approached the Revelation of John, largely avoiding it until February 1918. He divided scholarly opinion about it into three classes: the figurative, who applied it "according to their own knowledge," the literal, who applied it to the future and would never see it, and a mixture of the two.[210] Scholarly confusion was the cause for him remaining silent on the subject. "I never wanted to guess at its meaning or put an interpretation upon it that would prove false," he explained. Surveying the world situation, he thought that many professing Christians were unaware of what prophetic students strategically knew, that we were indeed living in "perilous" times.[211] He could hear the gallop of

203. "Jews, the Gentiles and the Church of God," *WE* (26 January 1918) 6. The most likely candidate for this article is AG chairman J. W. Welch.

204. "Palestine for the Jews," *WE* (1 December 1917) 4; compare to A. E. Thompson, "Ought the Jews to have Palestine?" *SST* (1 December 1917) 691–92.

205. Collins, "The Capture of Jerusalem," *WE* (23 March 1918) 13. The dating of Islam in the prophecy indicates that this was a historicist premillennial prediction. On the same page, *WE* advertised commentaries on Revelation by Myland and Gaebelein.

206. Perry, "Is this Armageddon?" *COGE* (16 January 1915) 3.

207. Perry, "Jews have a Future," *COGE* (1 September 1917) 3.

208. "Palestine Liberated from Turkey for the Jews," *COGE* (12 October 1918) 4.

209. Perry, "Palestine, Jews, Time of the End," *COGE* (2 November 1918) 4.

210. Tomlinson, "Mark of the Beast," *COGE* (9 February 1918) 1.

211. Tomlinson, "Last Days," *COGE* (23 February 1918) 1.

the four horsemen; the white horse of peace had already fled while the red war horse and black horse of price-controls were now rampaging.[212] Had he written during the influenza epidemic later that year, doubtless the pale horse of pestilence would have followed upon their heels. "The last days have come, the prophecies are fulfilling rapidly now and the time is at hand," he declared.[213] The expansion of CG was further evidence for him that persecution and deliverance were soon to follow, as forecast in prophecy.[214]

However, Tomlinson eschewed dispensationalist speculation which had gripped the AG. He professed weariness with Bible teachers who "make charts and paint them in glaring colors and long and short curved lines to represent certain periods or certain dispensations."[215] Daniel's auguries were mysteries, and those who "unwisely" built theories about "secrets" were dabbling in the hidden things of God. Such predictors were so much at odds with one another that "we are afraid of all of them, so we have decided to watch."[216] He had little time for those who proclaimed with certitude that they had discovered the "Mark of the Beast" while he confessed his own ignorance.[217] He did infrequently employ the phrase "rightly dividing the word of truth," though for him it consistently meant the fivefold gospel.[218] Otherwise, he shied away from the dispensationalist scheme, but future CG leaders proved more pliable.

Blumhofer hints that most pentecostal periodicals were dispensational by the time WWI commenced. While many who had sympathies with the CMA (Sexton, Otis, Myland, the AG) gravitated toward dispensational themes, there was still too much eschatological ingenuity to warrant such a judgment. The term "dispensation" was widely bantered about in premillennial circles whether it minded Darby or not. Most of what was said centered on apocalyptic literature and not on the historical dispensations as Scofield envisioned them. This would change as pentecostals ingratiated themselves with the emerging fundamentalist movement in the next decade.

Summary and Conclusion

As pentecostalism expanded it had to make room for diverse theological opinion which its converts imported from their previous upbringing and experiences. The apparent cohesion espoused by early believers fragmented under geographical and organizational pressures. The CG in the South, much more steeped in Wesleyan theology and polity, maintained a more unified episcopal approach to church government and thus was able to stave off the sea-change taking place in other quarters. The Midwest, the Northeast and the West, say from Arkansas northwards and westwards, loosely identified themselves with

---

212. Ibid., 1. The AG took a similar stance early in the war in "Prophetic War Horses Sent Out," *CE* (29 August 1914) 1.

213. Ibid., 1.

214. Tomlinson, "Enlargement and Deliverance," *COGE* (23 March 1918) 1.

215. Tomlinson, "Translation Power," *COGE* (2 March 1918) 1.

216. Ibid., 1.

217. Tomlinson, "Mark of the Beast," 1.

218. E.g., Tomlinson, "Dividing the Scriptures," *COGE* (14 July 1917) 1.

the emerging pentecostal network. These formed the nucleus of the AG in 1914, which split two years later under the "new issue" controversy. The noble ideal of a creedless faith floundered in the wake of the need for identification. The formation of denominations addressed this need.

The adjustments in their own living space also jostled against the space of fellow religionists. Church splitting only multiplied pentecostal efforts rather than weakened it. Competing for the hearts and minds of an American populace, fundamentalists denounced the pentecostals from pulpit and in print. Anti-pentecostal literature circulated in these conservative churches, superseding tracts on the Holy Ghost that might attract parishioners to the new sects. With the lack of a state-controlled church system, open competition forced both pentecostal adherents and detractors into an aggressive campaign with forceful words to convince and cajole others into their camp. In the genesis stage, pentecostals were obliged to defend their beliefs generally, but now in the 1910s the apologetics became more sophisticated against specific charges from specific foes.

Fundamentalists felt intellectually and socially superior to pentecostals, but this explains only in part their vehement reaction to the movement. To have agreed with pentecostals would have been an admission of wrong. It would have meant a loss of prestige and power. They had nothing to gain by joining pentecostals, and so their most active defense against this threat was actually an offense. Some like Gray could recognize that pentecostals were sincere but misguided believers, but others like Mauro and Gaebelein were not so kind. They saw the new movement as the activity of Satan designed to dupe believers into apostate forms of Christianity.

Whatever their reaction, pentecostals were genuinely hurt at the repulse. Pentecostals almost universally admired these leaders and often referred to their books. Neither pentecostals nor holiness folk had books of equal theological acumen to compare with proto-/fundamentalists. Figures like Pierson, Torrey, and Gray were national spokesmen for their common evangelical beliefs. Despite pleas to the contrary, they longed for fundamentalist recognition as comrades in arms against the tide of modernism. They were as committed to missions and evangelism as any fundamentalist preacher and would have preferred cooperation to antagonism. But such was not yet to be.

The growing strength of fundamentalism as indicated by *The Fundamentals* made inroads into pentecostalism. More importantly, the Scofield Reference Bible enjoyed unprecedented access into pentecostal homes. Pentecostals were picking up the "vocabulary" of fundamentalism though not necessarily the "content," which would come later. Moreover, AG pentecostals were much more susceptible to the fundamentalist message, being both theologically and geographically closer to fundamentalist centers of power in the Northeast, Midwest, and West. They also had a close affinity with the CMA and were more comfortable with the Keswick brand of Christianity than the holiness version in CG. Tomlinson however proved far more attracted to fundamentalist themes than his successors, as will be evident in the next two chapters. He was more combative in temperament and more aware of fundamentalist concerns, perhaps because of his roots in Indiana as a holiness Quaker and because of his earlier interest in the CMA.

5

Emerging Fundamentalism (1920–1924)

Introduction

Pentecostals completed their major period of internal strife by the end of WWI and discovered themselves to be in a stronger position than they could otherwise have expected. They consolidated their gains and shifted focus from organizational to institutional development. Bible colleges acquired a more definitive role within their denominations. In the doctrinal battles besieging the mainline churches, they aligned themselves with the fundamentalist cause, though they did not take an active part in this dispute. Dispensationalism in particular gripped the AG. Immersed in prophetic literature, it was inevitable that they should soak up a fundamentalist mentality. This chapter highlights this growing alignment with fundamentalism.

The Rise of Fundamentalism

In the aftermath of WWI, the newly christened movement of "fundamentalism" took shape. In the summer of 1918, several leaders of the prophecy movement, who had recently hosted a conference in Philadelphia, gathered at the summer-conference home of R. A. Torrey in Montrose, Pennsylvania, including W. B. Riley, John Campbell, W. H. Griffith Thomas, R. M. Russell, H. W. Jones, William Evans, and Charles Alexander.[1] According to Riley, the meeting was instigated at Dixon's behest, although other sources indicate that Dixon was living in London at the time and could not have been present at the meeting.[2] Those who did gather planned a World Christian Fundamentals Conference for May 1919 in Philadelphia, which attracted some six thousand participants uniting their voices against modernism. This conference also birthed the World's Christian Fundamentals Association (WCFA), electing Riley as its president. Thus, fundamentalism gained its first viable organization.

Riley was also instrumental in fomenting opposition to modernism in his own denomination, the Northern Baptist Convention. In late May 1920, three days prior to

---

1. Sandeen, *Roots*, 243 n. 12. Beale, *Pursuit*, 107 n. 6, mistakenly accuses Sandeen of leaving off Riley and A. C. Dixon, but Sandeen only doubts Dixon's presence as recorded by Cole. Sandeen is correct in that Dixon was in England at the time. See H. Dixon, *A Romance of Preaching*, 241. Riley gave evidence supporting Beale's point in *Conflict of Christianity*, 129–30, but wrote this twenty years after the fact.

2. See Riley, "Christian Fundamentals Movement," n.p. [NWC Arch].

their annual convention in Buffalo, New York, a group of "fundamentalist Baptists" rallied together in a pre-convention uproar. Dixon assisted Riley in his efforts along with J. C. Massee, who proved less enthusiastic for the faction in the long run. Curtis Lee Laws, the sympathetic editor of the Baptist paper, *The Watchman-Examiner*, commended their idealism, coining the term "fundamentalism" in process.[3] The modernists were lead by Harry Emerson Fosdick, Cornelius Woelfkin, and Shailer Mathews, backed by the deep pockets of J. D. Rockefeller.

The Expansion of Pentecostalism

Meanwhile, an expanding pentecostalism could not help but benefit from the post-war economic boom, evident in the procurement of new buildings. In the cities, the mass production of the automobile facilitated the move of professionals to the outskirts, taking their congregations with them. Pentecostals snapped up the abandoned buildings. Robert Brown's Glad Tidings in New York bought a Baptist sanctuary in 1923, while the faithful of Rochester purchased a Methodist one.[4] In rural areas where no urban elite existed, pentecostals constructed their own edifices, often small, boxy structures fit for the circumstances. An assembly in Pottersville, California, for instance, poured the foundations for their forty-four-by-eighty-foot sanctuary in September 1923.[5] Such advancement was repeated across the country.

While growth continued in the CG, gut-wrenching changes wracked the denomination in 1923 when it was alleged that A. J. Tomlinson had mishandled funds. Flimsy as the evidence may have been, Tomlinson nonetheless found himself voted out of the church he had done so much to establish.[6] The ordeal resulted in several courtroom clashes in the ensuing years; indeed the issue of a name was only resolved in 1952 when the courts ordered Tomlinson's breakaway group to use "Church of God of Prophecy" in its correspondence so as not to confuse the postal workers.[7] In all, a third of the pastors maintained loyalty to Tomlinson, leaving Flavius J. Lee in charge of the main body. By 1924 Lee felt sufficiently secure to declare that the rupture was behind them.[8]

The AG took more definite organizational shape by augmenting the number of its district councils. The Southern California District formed in August 1920, Louisiana in January 1921, Maryland in July, and North Central, which covered the Upper Midwest, in December 1922.[9] Later in the decade, shut out of local ministerial associations by

---

3. Laws, "Convention Side Lights," *Watchman-Examiner* (1 July 1920) 834.

4. "Expecting Great Things," *PE* (3 February 1923) 1; "Rochester, N.Y.," *PE* (31 March 1923) 14.

5. Gregg, "Pottersville, Calif.," *PE* (6 October 1923) 11.

6. Stone, *Church of God of Prophecy*, 39–43. The lack of clear record keeping and the fact that Tomlinson kept a tight control of finances opened him up to charges of misappropriation regardless of what actually happened.

7. Conn, *Like a Mighty Army*, 176–79, 188.

8. Lee, "Final Victory is Sure," *COGE* (28 April 1924) 1.

9. "Notice of Formation of Southern California District Council," *PE* (7 August 1920) 11; "New District Council," *PE* (22 January 1921) 14; "New District Council," *PE* (9 July 1921) 14; "North Central District Council," *PE* (23 December 1922) 14.

both fundamentalists and modernists, AG clergy arranged their own fellowships, first in California and then along the east coast.[10] CG had always been more tightly knit through its bishopric structure, lending itself to a more insular fellowship, although cooperation with other ministers was welcomed when available.

Pentecostals mirrored their fundamentalist peers in their institutions. Bible colleges long formed a mainstay of fundamentalist education, developing into regional networks unaffiliated with denominations. Early attempts at pentecostal education were often conducted through short-term Bible schools like those of D.C.O. Opperman, through already established holiness schools which adopted pentecostalism like the one operated by N. J. Holmes, or through programs initiated by larger churches like the one at Bethel Assembly in Newark. By the 1920s the need for more substantial education had become apparent. Jesus had not returned as soon as many had predicted, and the rising second generation of pentecostal leaders needed instruction in the tradition. Furthermore, the post-war boom made these institutes sustainable.

Central Bible Institute opened in September 1922 at AG headquarters in Springfield, Missouri, taking over from the defunct Auburn school in Nebraska.[11] Frank Boyd, who joined the faculty the following year, taught courses on dispensationalism, prophecy and the Pauline epistles.[12] In the CG, the yen for a Bible school had preoccupied Tomlinson since 1916, but a place could not be built until 1919.[13] Jacobson critiques Blumhofer for assuming that pentecostal schools were based on fundamentalist ones.[14] But on the whole, Bible institutes were originally a fundamentalist phenomenon, and again A. B. Simpson was influential. D. W. Kerr, who helped form both CBI and Southern California B.I., was one of many products of Nyack in the AG. R. Spittler believes that fundamentalist volumes were used as textbooks in pentecostal schools by "at least as early as the 1940s," but a review of the CBI catalogue from 1922 reveals that dispensationalism was taught by D. W. Kerr from its inception.[15] A robust pentecostal literature did not yet exist. The most trusted source for conservative, evangelical theology came from fundamentalist pens, as our literary review indicates in chapter 4.

The Rise of the Healing Evangelists

Divine healing was a core component of the pentecostal message—a "cardinal doctrine" in the AG and near the top among CG priorities. F. A. Yoakum, a Los Angeles physician, found early success on the healing front, establishing Pisgah house in 1907. Another healing home belonged to Carrie Judd Montgomery. She had been miraculously healed in

10. "Fellowship Meeting of S. Cal. And Arizona," *PE* (5 February 1927) 9; "San Jauquin Fellowship Meeting," *PE* (14 May 1927) 12; "Minister's Meetings," *PE* (5 May 1928) 9.

11. Kerr, "Heart Talks on the Bible School," *PE* (19 August 1922) 4.

12. "C.B.I. Correspondence Course," *PE* (18 December 1926) 7.

13. Tomlinson, "What shall We Do?" *COGE* (16 September 1916) 1.

14. Jacobsen, "Knowing the Doctrines," 105–6 n. 7, cite Blumhofer, *Restoring*, 150.

15. Spittler, "Are Pentecostals and Charismatics Fundamentalists?" 108; *First Annual Catalog: Central Bible Institute, 1922–1923* (CBC Arch). Kerr taught "Ages and Dispensations" and "Eschatology" among his 5 courses while Peirce taught "Old and New Testament Prophecy" and "Typology" among his 4 courses.

1879 in Buffalo and opened a healing home soon afterwards, relocating later to Oakland. Maria Woodworth-Etter became an early star on the pentecostal circuit, authoring two books that sold widely. She eventually settled in Indianapolis, erecting a tabernacle there in 1918.[16] Unlike others, she operated no healing home, modeling a traveling ministry for those who would imitate her. Many fundamentalists accepted divine healing in principle but were repulsed by pentecostal practice and theory.

Aimee Semple McPherson and Healing Literature

The touchstone of controversy was Aimee Semple McPherson. McPherson conducted revivals in fundamentalist-leaning churches in Washington, DC, Philadelphia, and San Jose. Charles Shreve, pastor of McKendree Memorial Church (Methodist) in the nation's capital, hosted McPherson in March 1920.[17] At the end of the year, L. W. Munhall, a senior among Methodist fundamentalists, spoke glowingly of McPherson's crusade at Mt. Airy in Philadelphia and licensed her for ministry.[18] In March 1922 at First Baptist in San Jose, Pastor William Keeney Towner ordained McPherson following his baptism in the Spirit.[19] His initial invitation to McPherson was a desperate act to revive a dying and financially insolvent church after a year of frustration.[20] In August, McPherson conducted a longer crusade in Towner's church that attracted thousands. Shreve became an evangelist with the AG and brought Santa Cruz Baptist preacher J. N. Hoover into the pentecostal experience at Towner's church in 1925.[21] Hoover in turn became an important conduit for fundamentalist ideas in pentecostal churches, which we will explore in a later chapter. Through McPherson's efforts, Pentecost made inroads among fundamentalists at a nationally recognized level. Frodsham attributed her success shortly after the McKendree meetings to her uncompromising presentation of tongues, her compassion for people and her sure faith in divine healing.[22]

Relations between McPherson and mainstream pentecostals were uneasy. She had been uncomfortable with some aspects of pentecostalism since 1919 when the local press

---

16. Woodworth-Etter, "Woodworth-Etter Tabernacle Going up in Indianapolis," *WE* (9 March 1918) 9.

17. Shreve, "Great Outpouring in Washington," *BC* (May 1920) 13; "How Pentecost Came to McKendree," *LRE* (July 1922) 13–15.

18. J. Wilson, "Great Days in Philadelphia," *BC* (December 1920) 20; McPherson, "Methodism and Pentecost," *W&Wk* (January 1921) 14; Sutton, *McPherson*, 42. Gaebelein would later express his disappointment in Munhall (see "McPhersonism Repudiated," *Hope* [January 1925] 402).

19. Sutton, "Wildfire," 172–73; "San Jose Vicinity," *W&Wk* (March 1923) 10–11.

20. Towner, "'An after that Experience'," *GGr* (September 1926) 18–19. Blumhofer calls the meeting a ploy to attract large crowds (*Restoring*, p. 167). While it was hoped to do that, it should also be remembered that it was squeezed into McPherson's schedule at the last minute to fill space between campaigns in San Diego and St. Louis. A second campaign in August that year was more intentional. Previously, Towner had pastored the largest Baptist church in Oakland.

21. Hoover, "Baptism and Ministry of the Holy Spirit," *LRE* (July 1930) 5–7, 21. An AG church that formed in Santa Cruz in October 1923 reported "much opposition" in the area, although it cannot be ascertained if Hoover was among the opponents (Tussey, "Santa Cruz, Calif.," *PE* [19 January 1924] 13).

22. Frodsham, "From the Pentecostal Viewpoint," *PE* (24 July 1920) 8.

commented on her "wild" meetings in Baltimore.[23] "Backwater" pentecostals could not provide her with the respect she craved. In June 1921, when asked about her affiliation with the Methodists, E. N. Bell defended her in print, assured by her in a personal letter that she wished to remain "undenominational."[24] However, in January 1922 McPherson surrendered her AG credentials and dropped the title "Pentecostal" from the banner of her periodical *The Bridal Call*. Later that summer in Wichita, Kansas, she emphatically declared herself to be a Baptist, using her ordination by Towner to further distance herself from the AG. To a local reporter she disclaimed any connection with pentecostalism, declaring, "I am not one of the cult . . . I have done everything in my power to curb the apparent wildness of the Pentecostal believers."[25] At her original ordination service in San Jose in March, she had told the audience that she seldom spoke in tongues but preached the Cross.[26] Nonetheless, she did relay a message in tongues from the platform during the revival, which inspired many to seek the Lord for power.[27] Even so, the AG office lamented that her "power" had receded as a result of her disavowal of them and prayed that she might some day be restored to the "full Pentecostal faith."[28]

In 1921, Lyman Stewart published McPherson's sermons on healing, employing the same press that now churned out *The Fundamentals*.[29] W. J. Bryan confessed that he altered his opinion on healing after hearing her preach on the subject.[30] After Stewart's death in 1923, Biola partisans felt free to abandon Stewart's strict policy which forbade any criticism of pentecostals.[31] "Fighting" Bob Shuler, pastor of Trinity Methodist in Los Angeles, questioned McPherson's doctrine in sermon and in print early in 1924.[32] R. A. Torrey, now the former dean at Biola, offered his own evaluation in *Divine Healing* (1924). He objected not so much to the doctrine as to the practice of certain "adventurers and adventuresses."[33] After all, Jesus the exemplar did not draw attention to himself through mass rallies as modern advocates did, nor did anyone He touch fail to be healed. Torrey imagined that he too could have succeeded as a healing evangelist had pentecostal methods been biblically sanctioned. In private meetings after concluding evangelistic services, he stated that many

23. Epstein, *Sister Aimee*, 161.

24. Bell, "Questions and Answers," *PE* (25 June 1921) 10 (No. 1041).

25. "Is Mrs. McPherson Pentecostal?" *PE* (10 June 1922) 9.

26. Sutton, *McPherson*, 42. The local Baptist council had split 21–21 on recommending her for ordination, but Towner proceeded without their approval. See also "Is Mrs. McPherson Pentecostal?" 9.

27. Towner, "'An after that Experience,'" 22.

28. "Is Mrs. McPherson Pentecostal?" 9. McPherson responded that pentecostalism was marked not by hysteria but by "deep, holy, sober, godly, reverent, prayerful exaltation of the gentle Christ of Galilee" (quoted in Blumhofer, *McPherson*, 185–86).

29. Sutton, "Wildfire," 171.

30. Ibid., 180.

31. The break from Stewart's policy in part led to the resignation of T. C. Horton from Biola, see Draney, *When Streams Divide*, 102. Biola's leadership passed a resolution condemning pentecostalism and McPherson by name on September 30, 1924.

32. Shuler, "Is McPhersonism Apostolic, Biblical or Dispensational?" *Hope* (March 1924) 559–68; Shuler, *McPhersonism* (Los Angeles: author, 1924).

33. Torrey, *Divine Healing*, 6–7.

had been healed under his ministry. An excerpt from *Divine Healing* of such instances appeared in *PE*, which gladly sold it for forty cents.[34] Like many fundamentalists, Torrey believed that God could heal people of physical ailments, so long as the method adhered to Scriptural prescription, such as the calling of elders (Jas 5:14).

Though not directly assailed by Torrey, F. F. Bosworth published a compilation of sermons as *Christ the Healer* (1924) in response to numerous demands from followers, spurned doubtlessly by Torrey's volume. It likely came out shortly after a May campaign in Toronto that attracted the largest indoor audience in Canadian history to that point. In defense, Bosworth emphasized that healing crusades were often an avenue for conversion, as his own ministry demonstrated.[35] Most importantly, he lay "healing in the atonement" as the foundation for his ministry as well as the "name it and claim it" theology that later healing evangelists would imitate. He also incorporated material from CMA pastor Kenneth Mackenzie's 1923 volume, *Our Physical Heritage in Christ*.[36] F. J. Lee added his own thoughts on the topic with a twenty-eight-page pamphlet in 1925, though its contents differed little from other pentecostal efforts.[37]

Other fundamentalists who weighed in on the issue included A. C. Gaebelein, unsurprisingly against it in *The Healing Question* (1925), and John Roach Straton, who favored it in *Divine Healing in Scripture and Life* (1927), from which *PE* printed two portions.[38] A Spirit-filled Baptist, B. C. Miller, challenged his fellow fundamentalists to embrace the whole truth of the Word and accept healing, proclaiming that the pentecostal dispensation had arrived.[39] Others like conservative S. D. Gordon addressed healing among his "Quiet Talk" series in 1924, and *PE* featured Anglican healing minister J. T. Butlin's *A Handbook on Divine Healing* in a 1924 article.[40] In short, healing intensified the rivalry between pentecostals and fundamentalists that both in principle accepted as biblical.

A. C. Gaebelein's Battle with McPherson and Pentecostalism

McPherson first stepped into Gaebelein's sights in 1920 when a United Brethren parishioner from Baltimore queried him concerning her evangelistic campaign at his church. Gaebelein, himself a former United Brethren minister in Baltimore, replied that tongues were "a form of religious hysteria."[41] Gaebelein's gravamen inferred that women occupied the principal position in pentecostal meetings and more actively sought the

---

34. "A Fundamentalist's Testimony to Divine Healing," *PE* (26 July 1924) 8.

35. Bosworth, *Christ the Healer*, 73.

36. Mackenzie, *Our Physical Heritage in Christ* (1923). Bosworth (*Christ the Healer*, 29–31) quotes R. E. Stanton, Charles Brent and James Hickson directly from Mackenzie (ibid., 89–90).

37. Lee, *Divine Healing* (1925).

38. Gaebelein, *Healing Question* (1925); Straton, *Divine Healing in Scripture and Life* (1927). *PE* articles from Straton's book: "God's Conditional Covenant to Heal His People" (*PE*, 8 September 1928, 2–3) and "God's Conditional Covenant to Heal His People" (*PE*, 15 September 1928, 2–3).

39. Miller, "The Fundamentalist and Divine Healing," *GGr* (July 1926) 5.

40. Gordon, *Quiet Talks about the Healing Christ* (1924); "An Episcopal Minister's Testimony," *PE* (24 May 1924) 8.

41. Quoted in Frodsham, "From the Pentecostal Viewpoint," *PE* (21 August 1920) 6.

baptism than men. In response, Frodsham pointed out that women had been conspicuous in Paul's ministry and that men participated as much if not more than women in the current movement.[42] Furthermore, while pentecostals admitted to being "sanctified" as Paul commended and Gaebelein condemned, no one in the movement taught that sin could be "eradicated" as certain holiness folk did. Frodsham also chastised Sir Robert Anderson for mishandling Mark 16. In return, Gaebelein threatened to reprint Anderson's tract in *Our Hope*, making good in May 1921.[43]

Gaebelein's reply faulted Frodsham for misconstruing Paul's "divinely inspired statement" concerning the "women leaders of their cult," rallying 1 Timothy 2:11-14 and Ephesians 5:21-32 to his succor.[44] He also grumbled about Frodsham's application of Psalm 68 to the modern church when in dispensational hermeneutics the passage could only refer to the "Congregation Israel." In the previous issue Gaebelein acknowledged the myriads of pentecostals who lodged grievances at his criticism of McPherson. Citing one letter from Wellesley, Massachusetts, Gaebelein reiterated his contention that Joel 2 was a prophecy yet to be fulfilled in literal Israel.[45] For him pentecostalism wavered on "an unscriptural basis." Asked if he believed in the baptism with the Holy Spirit, he affirmed that he did, for "there was ONE Baptism, which was given on the day of Pentecost."[46] The Holy Spirit had dwelt within the church ever since, he insisted, and no fresh outpouring should be expected until after the Lord's return. For him, the power of God lay in "Divine Truth" as mediated through the Spirit.[47] In other words, power was manifested through the Word and not through apoplectic demonstrations.

Our Hope opened up a veritable barrage on pentecostalism. Plymouth Brethren preacher George Soltau dismissed the pentecostal use of Acts as biblical precedence for their movement.[48] Each example of tongues in Acts was unique to the occasion rather than a template for modern Christians. Moreover, he feared that tarrying meetings misled sincere believers into thinking they could attain more fullness of the Spirit than others. Pentecost was a Jewish celebration which happened to mark the church's birth, not an essential event intended for duplication.[49] In January 1921 Gaebelein launched an exposition on demon possession, including the deception of Satan through "destructive criticism," "hypnotism," and "Spiritism."[50] Pondering whether Christians could be thus subjected, he quoted at length from a case in Britain where a preacher who spoke in tongues had demons cast out of him by a fellow worker, who determined him to be thus afflicted.[51] "May

---

42. Frodsham, "From the Pentecostal Viewpoint," *PE* (21 August 1920) 6.
43. R. Anderson, "Spirit Manifestations and 'The Gift of Tongues,'" *Hope* (May 1921) 658-79.
44. Gaebelein, "'Pentecostal' Mis-interpretation," *Hope* (December 1920) 321-23.
45. Gaebelein, "Is it that?" *Hope* (November 1920) 258-60. McPherson's book *This is That* was published in 1919.
46. Ibid., 261.
47. Gaebelein, "Eyes are Opened," *Hope* (November 1920) 263-64.
48. Soltau, "'Tongues Movement,'" *Hope* (December 1920) 357-60.
49. Ibid., 361-62.
50. Gaebelein, "Demon Possession," *Hope* (January 1921) 403-5.
51. Ibid., 407-10.

this serve as warning," Gaebelein concluded for those who wished to seek something God had not ordained. Fundamentalists were quite willing to appeal to experience when it suited their purposes, though they did so less frequently than pentecostals.

Later in life, Gaebelein recalled an incident at a favorite mission in Winnipeg, where he spoke disparagingly on the "Pentecostal-Gift of Tongue" delusion.[52] He noticed the presence of a number from the "deluded sect" in the crowd and felt "an awful antagonism" oppressing him. Whispering to a brother beside him, he asked for prayer that a special anointing might embolden him for the task before him.[53] "When I got up to speak," he testified, "it seemed as if an unseen hand tried to keep back my words, and while I struggled for expression I cried to the Lord, and all at once there came another power upon me; it was the Holy Spirit."[54] By the end of his hour-long harangue, approbation had replaced the recalcitrance of the "deluded," enlightened no doubt by his inspired speech. Gaebelein was unremitting in his opposition to tongues, taking nearly fifty jabs against it in editorials and commentary between 1920 and 1925 in *Our Hope*, exclusive of contributions from associates like Haldeman.[55] It is rather ironic that biographer David Rausch dubbed Gaebelein an "irenic fundamentalist"—for no one of type was more truly pugnacious than he.[56]

Another Plymouth Brethren combatant, F. C. Jennings, sliced through McPherson's sermon "Lost and Restored," where the evangelist had put forward the demotic notion that modern pentecostalism represented the restoration of the Spirit's gifts to the church. Jennings, in concord with Brethren theology, asserted that "all true Christians [were] baptised into the one Body."[57] He contested that tongues were not the only hallmark of the baptism, for charisms were distributed throughout the holy community at the Spirit's pleasure. Further, he found no scriptural grounds for McPherson's division between the "GIFT" ("known") and "gift" (sign) of tongues.[58] Jennings attributed the strength of pentecostalism to "feeble" Christians who were weak in the Word; "it can but speak of how easily and quickly will all apostate Christendom be swept off its feet."[59] He discerned in McPherson the palpable swelling and deceitful pride of Satan.

---

52. Gaebelein, *Half a Century*, 177. Gaebelein regularly preached at the Elim Chapel in Winnipeg, though he does not give a date for this incident. Fundamentalism was represented there from 1917 onwards. As Gaebelein was preoccupied with WWI, and in fact there was a lull in attacks in against pentecostalism in *Our Hope* from Philip Mauro in 1911 until Gaebelein's attack on McPherson in 1920, the early 1920s is the mostly time period.

53. Likely this was Elim Chapel founder Sydney Smith, a prominent businessman and president of the WCFA in 1925. See Hindmarsh, "Winnipeg Fundamentalist Network," 303–19.

54. Gaebelein, *Half a Century*, 177.

55. See Appendix E.

56. Rausch, *Arno C. Gaebelein, 1861–1945: Irenic Fundamentalist and Scholar* (1983). D. Weber makes a similar comment about Rausch in "Portrait of a Premillennialist," 5–6. In one incident, a woman approached Gaebelein and asked if he could be a little more like John, the apostle of love. Gaebelein replied, yes, but he also wanted to be like John Boanerges—"a son of thunder" (*Half a Century*, 160–61).

57. Jennings, "Pentecostal Movement and the Standard of Truth," *Hope* (January 1921) 413.

58. Ibid., 415.

59. Ibid., 417.

Like Gaebelein, Soltau and Haldeman, Jennings saw in the movement the evidences of apostasy, while other less dogmatic dispensationalists like Riley and Torrey had seen in it the possibilities of revival.[60] The difference hinged on their respective views of the church and Israel. Those who maintained a clear separation between those prophecies relating to the church and those applied to Israel were more apt to condemn pentecostalism as diabolical. True spiritual revival belonged to national Israel during the Great Tribulation. Those who regarded the renewal of the church in passages like Joel favored the view that the church would be revived before the Great Tribulation and thus help usher in the Lord's return. For them, pentecostals were mistaken saints, perhaps even deceived by Satan, but not demon possessed apostates.

Frodsham was not humored. He too like Jennings desired to go "to the laws and to the testimony."[61] The great apostasy, he countered, was signified by men "having a form of godliness but denying the power thereof." By contrast, pentecostals had uncovered lost truths, just as Josiah had uncovered the neglected Book of the Law. Frodsham described this process amongst his co-religionists: "Our souls chafed under the unreality of a religion that was utterly lifeless and powerless," but "how grateful we are to our God that . . . there has been a revival of the primitive faith."[62] He chastened Gaebelein for lumping pentecostals together with cults who did not confess Christ and for parading the vague British example of demon possession, which withheld names and therefore could not be verified. He also refuted Gaebelein's earlier averment that Joel 2 referred not to the church but to some future event.[63] It was after all the Spirit that prompted Peter to connect the two events in his sermon and not some invention of pentecostals.

As to Jennings's slander upon McPherson, Frodsham too veered away from some details in her book, which she had not submitted to the council for correction. Still, her ministry needed no vindication as God had validated it through "the salvation of thousands and in the healing of hundreds."[64] As to fundamentalists, their hard hearts might resist the Lord even as Michal despised the dancing of her husband David, but "we need to pray for these people." Frodsham concluded, "There is some good stuff in some of these critics, and they could be useful men for God if the scales could be removed from their eyes."[65] Indeed, Gaebelein was an authority on prophecy for many pentecostals. His commentaries on Revelation and Ezekiel were commended by *PE*, as was his book *The Conflict of the Ages*.[66] However, *COGE* gave little if any press to Gaebelein, and during most of the

---

60. Soltau and Jennings were both Plymouth Brethren, as was Haldeman's publisher F. F. Fitch. Fitch was also influential in bringing Gaebelein to dispensationalism at the Niagara conferences.

61. Frodsham, "From a Pentecostal Viewpoint," *PE* (19 February 1921) 3.

62. Ibid., 3.

63. Ibid., 3. Frodsham does not specify the article, but Gaebelein made this point in "Is it that?" (see above).

64. Ibid., 7.

65. Ibid.

66. "Important Books on Revelation," *CE* (10 August 1918) 7; "Prophet Ezekiel," *PE* (1 November 1919) 9; "Recommended Books," *PE* (24 February 1934) 11.

1920s through 1938 Frodsham shunned *Our Hope* as well, indicating how relevant the two wars were for prophecy and how tendentious Gaebelein was towards pentecostals.

Canadian pastor A. G. Ward rebutted Gaebelein in 1923. He could apprehend only one explanation for Gaebelein's virulence, quoting from William Paley: "contempt prior to examination."[67] Like Frodsham, Ward showed that Joel 2 was partially fulfilled at Pentecost.[68] The desideratum of the church was spiritual power, for the "promise of the Father" extended to all believers regardless of the era. Ward picked his way through several texts extrapolating this promise. To ancient critics of Pentecost, the event would have seemed disorderly, for the 120 spoke in bedlam, contradicting Paul's prohibition to the Corinthians as Gaebelein charged—unless one distinguished the "sign" of tongues from the "gift" as pentecostals consistently did.[69] Though Dr. Gaebelein was articulate on some matters of biblical interpretation, Ward wished the doctor had been more attentive to passages about Spirit-baptism and refrained from "nonsensical statements."[70]

Other Healing Evangelists and the Churches

Rarely did modernists become pentecostals. One notable exception was Charles Price. But even Price had been tempted by the Azusa Street revival, though he was discouraged by a fellow minister from going there to pursue Spirit-baptism.[71] In the event, Price fell into modernism, eventually shepherding a Congregational church in Lodi, California. In August 1922 he reconnoitered First Baptist in San Jose in order to discredit McPherson's ministry. He was surprised when Dr. Towner, a ministerial acquaintance, greeted him with a zesty "Praise the Lord."[72] The only space available in the packed auditorium was up front among "the cripples," who were expecting their miracles. Sister Aimee's sermon and the enthusiastic response to her altar call impressed him. Laying aside all pretension, he knelt, appropriating the baptism for himself. As a result, his ministry was rejuvenated, with the weekly prayer meeting at his church increasing from fifteen to three hundred in six months.[73] Soon he was promoting the pentecostal message of baptism and healing around the country. His false conceptions about the virgin birth and resurrection of Christ had been corrected, although fundamentalist doctrines were never central to his platform.

Price gained notoriety for his healing campaigns, especially in Canada. His appearance in Vancouver in May 1923 attracted thousands, including pastors from mainline denominations.[74] The local ministerial association formed a committee to investigate 350 reported cases of healing and concluded in a January 1924 report that only five could be

67. Ward, "Pentecostal Testimony according to the Scriptures," *PE* (26 May 1923) 2.
68. Ibid., 2–3.
69. Ward, "Pentecostal Testimony according to the Scriptures," *PE* (2 June 1923) 2.
70. Ward, "Pentecostal Testimony according to the Scriptures," *PE* (9 June 1923) 6.
71. Sumrall, *Pioneers of Faith*, 125–26.
72. Price, "Personal Testimony," *W&Wk* (October 1922) 4.
73. Ibid., 4–5.
74. "Gospel of Redemption and Healing, Vancouver," *PE* (14 July 1923) 9; "Victoria and Vancouver Stirred by Revival," *LRE* (August 1923) 10. Price misidentified as a "Baptist" in *LRE*. *PE* reported some 4,000 attendees at the beginning of the revival, and *LRE* some 8,000 by the end.

counted as authentic, and further insinuated that these could have been as facilely cured through medicine.[75] A Methodist minister in Vancouver charged the committee with bias, noting that some five thousand had been prayed for and that the ministerial association had already pronounced judgment against Price before the committee was even appointed.[76] For his part, Gaebelein "exposed" the supposed healing of one Reginald Edwards, now deceased, and of a cancer victim who claimed to be healed despite evidence to the contrary.[77] "The harm which is being done cannot be over estimated," he stated, warning "sane and spiritual believers" to avoid all such "healing cults."[78] Though some protested against Gaebelein's "unfair" treatment of pentecostals, the feisty editor stood firm—accusing Price of incorporating hypnotic methods to seduce his audience.[79] In the ensuing months, he vigilantly conjured up those whose health had failed and whose faith was shattered as a result. One Presbyterian minister indicted Price for praying only for those he believed had sufficient faith to be healed.[80]

T. J. McCrossan, a Presbyterian who regularly assisted Price, also earned Gaebelein's opprobrium. Gaebelein endorsed McCrossan's admission that a "strange power" had enveloped him as he interceded for the infirm, but Gaebelein would not attribute the power to the Holy Spirit.[81] McCrossan had taught Greek at Riley's Northwestern College in Minneapolis during its primitive days before tutoring students at the University of Manitoba in Winnipeg and later relocating to the Vancouver-Seattle area. He received his pentecostal immersion under Price in 1922, contributing regularly to his periodical *Golden Grain*. McCrossan's daughter Charlotte would later marry the son of South African pentecostal leader A. H. Cooper.[82] McCrossan joined the CMA in 1923, postulating that tongues were a gift rather than a sign of baptism as Simpson had.[83] In 1930 he penned a volume championing healing in the atonement.[84]

F. F. Bosworth, one-time music director for Dowie in Zion City, parted ways with the AG over the doctrine of initial evidence in 1918, affiliating with the CMA.[85] He established a church in Dallas, which facilitated a 1912 revival engineered by Maria Woodworth-Etter. Like those of McPherson and Price, Bosworth's campaigns were marked by their interdenominational character. A 1917 tent meeting in Dallas featured his brother Bert guiding a Methodist-filled choir, who warbled from a Billy Sunday hymnbook. Meanwhile, prayer conclaves met at the Cole Avenue Methodist Church, and Presbyterian minister William

---

75. W. Sipprell, "Divine Healing a Present Day Reality," *LRE* (January 1925) 8.
76. Ibid., 8.
77. Gaebelein, "Another Healer," *Hope* (August 1923) 81–83; "Untruths," *Hope* (August 1923) 83–84.
78. Gaebelein, "Untruths," *Hope* (August 1923) 84.
79. Gaebelein, "Perplexed Christians," *Hope* (October 1923) 208–11.
80. Gaebelein, "Light on 'Dr. Price,'" *Hope* (November 1923) 271–73.
81. Gaebelein, "What Power," *Hope* (February 1924) 465–66.
82. "Glorious News from South Africa," *PE* (25 December 1937) 12.
83. McCrossan, *Speaking with other Tongues*, 184–204.
84. McCrossan, *Bodily Healing and the Atonement* (1930).
85. Bosworth, *Do all Speak with Tongues?* (1918).

Holderby delivered some of the homilies, receiving his own Pentecost in the process.[86] In 1928, ex-Moody Church pastor Paul Rader, who headed the CMA from 1920 to 1924, invited Bosworth to hold a successful campaign in his independent Chicago Gospel Tabernacle.[87]

I. M. Haldeman disputed Bosworth's atonement theory of healing in *Our Hope*. Haldeman tended toward hyper-dispensationalism which insisted on a sharp distinction between prophecies intended for Jews and those for Gentiles. From his perspective, Isaiah 53:4—"he bore our griefs"—applied to Jesus' earthly ministry while verse 5—"he was bruised for our iniquities"—applied to His crucifixion.[88] In a rather dubious argument, he decided that the healings "were not given to us, the Gentiles, at all. They were given to the Jews, and to them exclusively."[89] Like other fundamentalists, he declared himself to be pro-physical healing through prayer. But as a thoroughgoing dispensationalist, he spared NT saints from the curses of the OT.[90] Haldeman clinched his argument with Paul's thorn in the flesh, which he assumed to be an eye condition. If God had not relieved such an exemplary Christian from distress, why should modern sickness constitute a curse from God?

Bosworth initiated a campaign in Toronto's Massey Hall in 1921. The meetings were hosted by Oswald Smith, who had recently switched allegiances from the Presbyterians to the CMA.[91] Smith suffered from occasional eye trouble himself, which were exasperated by intense headaches. Blurry vision once hindered him from noticing Bosworth's presence when Bosworth slipped into his church. As a test of faith, Smith stopped wearing his glasses. His eyesight gradually improved while the headaches dissipated. Smith defended Bosworth by confirming the healing of three other participants in the meetings.[92] Though approving of Bosworth's ministry, he was still critical of pentecostalism. In a 1936 trip to Sweden, he praised Lewi Pethrus's church for being "sober" pentecostals, unlike their North American counterparts, whom he considered to be unruly by comparison.[93] It is possible that Smith was unaware that Bosworth was a tongues practitioner.

Paul Rader had long been suspected of being a tongues speaker by fellow fundamentalists, partly because of his magnetic personality and partly for his emphasis on the Holy Spirit, such as a 1917 message titled "Let the Spirit have His Way."[94] That same year

---

86. "Bro. F. F. Bosworth," *WE* (25 August 1917) 16.

87. "Chicago's Visitation of Miracles of Healing," *LRE* (February 1928) 14.

88. Haldeman, "Did Our Lord by His Death on the Cross Atone for Bodily Sickness and Disease: No! Never!" *Hope* (February 1923) 486–88.

89. Ibid., 487. Haldeman selectively ignores the Syro-Phoenician woman (Matt 7:26) and the centurion's servant (Matt 8:6).

90. Ibid., 491–94.

91. Smith, *Great Physician*, 124.

92. Ibid., 112–21.

93. Reported in Stemme, *Pentecostal Christian*, 32–33. Stemme quotes from *The People's Monthly* for December 1936 concerning Smith's trip that summer.

94. Rader, "Let the Holy Spirit Have His Way," *CWM* (September 1917) 16–18. He spoke at an MBI conference on the need for the baptism of the Spirit for power by surrender. However, he stated here that "some of the most carnal Christians . . . in the Bible spoke with tongues" and the Spirit will "never knock a man down to give him the fullness."

Riley pestered Rader to find out if the rumors were true. Rader steadfastly denied that he had ever exercised tongues, though he acknowledged it as a genuine gift of the Spirit. He deemed many pentecostals to be godly servants; however, the movement itself had deposited "a slimy trail" behind it.[95] The topic of tongues resurrected in 1926 when he supplied McPherson's pulpit in Los Angeles. One could almost hear D. M. Panton's sigh of relief when Oswald Smith, who worked closely with Rader, denounced the charges as utterly fallacious.[96]

Nonetheless, pentecostals devoured Rader's sermons in print.[97] Morse Markley, an ex-Methodist pastor, appreciated Rader's ten-day Asbury Park, New Jersey campaign in 1925, where a "clear note was given . . . on the lines of salvation and the Word of God and its authority."[98] In 1928 Rader addressed the "Central States Gospel Rally" at Trinity Tabernacle (AG) in St. Louis, which assembled its "largest crowd ever."[99] He also had a long-standing relationship with McPherson and frequented Angelus Temple along with other fundamentalist dignitaries like L. W. Munhall, William Biederwolf, W. J. Bryan, and Oswald Smith,[100] demonstrating again how solidly McPherson stood at the crossroads between pentecostals and fundamentalists.

Another renowned healer was Ray Richey. WE spotlighted his 1917–1918 efforts to evangelize servicemen in Houston through the "United Prayer and Worker's League."[101] Music, led by Bosworth, was a major component of the services where thousands of "doughboys" were reached.[102] Richey left the AG for the CMA in 1922 but returned in 1936.[103] His healing campaigns were well attended by those of other denominations—Presbyterians, Methodists, Baptists and Congregationalists. A seven-week crusade in Houston in 1922 harvested four thousand souls for the kingdom.[104] William Holderby rejoiced at the miraculous repair of his lame leg in Chicago and showered superlatives upon Richey's engagement in Milwaukee that same year.[105] Six to seven thousand convened each night at Richey's Fort Worth campaign in 1923 with Methodist evangelist Frank Morris

---

95. "Paul Rader and the Gift of Tongues," *SC* (December 1917) 222.

96. Panton, "Supernatural Deception," *Dawn* (15 June 1926) 100; Panton, "A Correction," *Dawn* (14 August 1926) 211.

97. E.g., *Hell, and How to Escape* and *Signs of the Times* ["Inexpensive Books," *PE* (10 July 1920) 11; "Some of Paul Rader's Works," *PE* (24 July 1926) 15]. Several articles by Rader were duplicated as well, like "Observation from a World Tour" (*PE*, 4 September 1926, 7) and "When the Modern Tide Struck our Home" (*PE*, 28 January 1928, 8).

98. Markley, "St. Louis, Mo.," *PE* (28 November 1925) 12.

99. L. Lohmann, "Great Crowds in St. Louis," *PE* (30 June 1928) 9.

100. Blumhofer, *McPherson*, 264. Biederwolf denounced the doctrine of healing in the atonement in his provocatively titled *Whipping-Post Theology* (1934).

101. "United Prayer and Worker's League," *WE* (8 September 1917) 5.

102. "Telegram from Houston," *WE* (2 February 1918) 3.

103. King, *Genuine Gold*, Appendix II. King misspells "Richey" as "Ritchey" in this chart. Richey's marriage to a divorced woman in 1921 was the cause for his departure (Blumhofer, *Restoring*, 168).

104. L. DeWeese, "Brother Richey's Revival Meetings," *PE* (5 August 1922) 9.

105. Holderby, "Great Campaign in Chicago," *PE* (30 September 1922) 9; Holderby, "Revival at Milwaukee," *PE* (11 November 1922) 17.

joining him on stage and many denominational pastors baptized in the Spirit.[106] In Tulsa, a procession of recovered invalids marched down Main Street, pursued by a truck loaded with their discarded crutches.[107] Ten thousand reported conversion, nine thousand professed healing and at least one CMA church was born. Cooperation permeated Richey's ministry as he healed the sick from town to town.

Less celebrated healers in the AG plied their trade in ecumenical settings across the country. Pastor W. A. Jordan of Central Baptist in New Orleans attested to some 1,400 healings at his church under AG evangelist Warren Collins, bolstered by a cadre of prayer warriors in 1920.[108] Methodist and Baptist churches in New Mexico welcomed Willard Pope, Irving Meier, and the "Four Fold Gospel" in the summer of 1922.[109] The United Brethren at Terre Haute, Indiana accommodated afternoon tongues seekers under A. W. Kortkamp and provided a quartet for the evening service.[110] In Binghamton, New York, members from eleven different traditions attended A. H. Argue's healing campaign.[111] In 1925, a committee chaired by a Presbyterian cleric invited May Turner to orchestrate a revival in Tulsa, where ex-Methodist Jonathan Perkins was pastor. Elmer Muir, a Baptist preacher overflowing with the Spirit, elucidated gospel insight in the morning services. A Salvation Army band played at one of the services, and at least one Baptist and one Presbyterian pastor succumbed to the power of the Spirit.[112]

Evangelist S. K. Biffle secured the approval of local Methodists and Presbyterians in Washington, Missouri, where some were slain in the Spirit and others healed.[113] Frank Lindbald witnessed pentecostal manifestations at a Baptist church in 1924 that had been "hungry" for years.[114] Ray Fostekew oversaw both a pentecostal church and a Congregational church near Medina, Ohio, with several members of the latter receiving baptism.[115] The Salvation Army and a Methodist church openly backed Watson Argue at the opera house in Kalispell, Montana.[116] J. J. Ashcroft's meetings in St. Paul saw "the usual prejudice swept aside" as many denominational people heard him evangelize.[117] In Hattiesburg, Mississippi, members of Gypsy Smith's "Flying Squadron" assisted the A. H. Argue revival at Red Circle Auditorium, and some of them sought baptism.[118]

---

106. Mrs. J. C. Wilder, "Fort Worth Revival Meeting," *PE* (3 February 1923) 14; "Forth Worth, Texas" *PE* (23 June 1923) 10.

107. "Triumphs in Tulsa," *PE* (4 August 1923), 8; King, *Genuine Gold*, 199.

108. "A Pentecostal Brother has a Ministry of Healing in Baptist Church," *PE* (10 July 1920) 4.

109. Pope and Meier, "Good Meetings in Northern New Mexico," *PE* (25 November 1922) 19.

110. Kortkamp, "Great Revival at Terre Haute, Ind.," *PE* (14 October 1922) 25.

111. J. Kellner, "Argue Campaign in Binghamton," *PE* (4 August 1923) 11.

112. Perkins, "Tulsa, Okla,," *PE* (20 June 1925) 13.

113. Biffle, "Washington, Mo.," *PE* (30 May 1925) 13.

114. Lindbald, "Pentecostal Revival in a Baptist Church," *PE* (12 January 1924) 11.

115. Fostekew, "Medina, Ohio," *PE* (19 January 1924) 14.

116. E. E. Hoiland, "Kalispell, Montana," *PE* (19 January 1924) 14.

117. "St. Paul, Minn.," *PE* (9 May 1925) 12.

118. J. Savell, "Hattiesburg, Miss.," *PE* (15 March 1924) 9. The Gypsy Smith team led some of the devotional services during the revival, and several non-pentecostal pastors assisted in the meetings.

Though healing evangelists were officially condemned by fundamentalist leaders, local churches often aided them. Fundamentalist parishioners buttressed mass rallies, which navigated hundreds of them to encounters with the Spirit. The need to revitalize the local churches could at times outweigh the resistance to the pentecostal message, particularly in churches that were dying or in individuals who felt themselves spiritually vapid. Shepherds, no matter how diligently they guarded their flocks, could not prevent their sheep from grazing in other fields.

Marsden correctly observes that pentecostals were only tangentially part of the fundamentalist movement.[119] Further, he adds that the influence ran largely in one direction. This was partly true in that fundamentalist literature reached the hands of thousands of pentecostals. The effect was top-down. But at another level pentecostals impacted mainline congregations through the healing evangelists; here the influence was bottom-up. It was hardly the case that every fundamentalist was scurrying to a pentecostal healing service, but there were enough to arouse solicitude. Their churches were leaking members and occasional splits occurred where healing was emphasized, such as at United Presbyterian in Albany, Oregon in 1929.[120] Fundamentalists struggled with balancing the spark of renewal within their churches while dousing pentecostal fires from without, potentially alienating those they were trying to revive. Reacting against the effervescence of pentecostalism, and, on a larger stage, battling modernism with intellectual weaponry, fundamentalism in cases became emotionally constrained. It is little wonder that they strove against the healing "fakirs," as Gaebelein labeled them.

Pentecostals and Fundamentalism: Alignments and Disputes

Mae Eleanor Frey was a Spirit-filled Baptist pastor when she attended the Northern Baptist Convention in Buffalo in 1920. "Fundamentalist Baptists," led by Riley and Dixon, gathered in a pre-convention protest against the Interchurch World Movement and the modernist obscurantism in NBC colleges and seminaries. "It is easy to see that a split in the denomination is pending," she divulged to her *PE* readers.[121] The "conservatives" prevailed over the "liberals" at many points by halting publication of the left-leaning *Baptist*, clearing the schools of tepid theology and opening the door for women to preach. (Not all fundamentalists were afraid of female ministers.) They could not however prevent the Promotion Board from controlling many of the denomination's institutions by disbanding it.

Frey (née Edick) "got saved" as a young cub-reporter covering a revival sometime in the mid-1880s.[122] She and her husband became Baptist ministers, joining the NBC from its inception in 1905. Her baptism in the Spirit came at the annual Easter convention at Bethel Pentecostal Assembly in Newark, New Jersey in 1919.[123] She remained as pastor of Echo Park Baptist in Paterson, New Jersey for at least a year before transferring her license

---

119. Marsden, *American Culture*, 94.
120. Gaebelein, *Half a Century*, 227–28.
121. Frey, "Crisis in the Baptist Church," *PE* (10 July 1920) 5.
122. Frey, "An Evangelist's Story," *PE* (15 May 1926) 8.
123. Frey, "An Evangelist's Story," *PE* (5 June 1926) 8.

Emerging Fundamentalism (1920–1924)

to the AG as an evangelist and cooperated frequently with Baptist churches thereafter. Her 1922 revival in Edmonton drew many Baptists to C. H. Cadwalder's church.[124] She conducted revivals at First Baptist in San Jose in July 1924, where Dr. Towner styled her the best evangelist in the country next to McPherson, Tower Grove Baptist in St. Louis in March 1925, and the old First Baptist in Canton, Illinois in April 1926.[125] In the fall of 1926 she spoke to businessmen at a Baptist church in Denver.[126] Her ministry continued among Baptists in the 1930s with revivals in Lyons, New York and Greenwood, New Jersey.[127] As a reconstituted fundamentalist, she found doors opened for charismatic gifts where most pentecostals would have been ejected.

Pentecostals were aware of the emerging fundamentalist movement. *COGE* endorsed the Southern Baptists' plea for pentecostal power in 1920 as recorded in a Nashville paper.[128] A. J. Tomlinson boasted of the "Fundamentalist Baptists" in 1922 when the Northern cohorts descended upon Indianapolis, noting with glee the split that had developed between their conservative and liberal branches.[129] He recognized his kinship with their biblicist and premillennial demeanor, for they practiced most of what the Good Book said with the exception of tongues. Further, many Baptist churches had stepped "lock, stock, and barrel" into the CG. Beyond this, however, fundamentalism received little direct attention from CG. With Tomlinson's departure in 1923, replies to fundamentalist malevolence halted until Frank Norris's bombardment in 1936.

Norris was the executive of the largest congregation in the U.S. at around 15,000: First Baptist in Fort Worth, Texas. On September 2, 1923 the "Texas Tornado" spurred his listeners to seek "power on high," lamenting its lack in the modern church. "I don't care what a man's connections are," he thundered, "if the Spirit of the Almighty gets hold of him, he is going to be changed and doing everything different. Do you believe that? If you do, what holy zeal should fire us!"[130] The *PE* applauded, quoting from the sermon where Norris said, "I believe, with all my soul, in the Baptism of the Holy Ghost."[131] Norris admitted in this blurb that some had gone to extremes because the doctrine had become faddish but called upon believers to commune for ten days of prayer. What *PE* did not note were their differences in understanding. For Norris, baptism had the Keswick-ring of enduement of power for witness and not the ability to speak in tongues. Pentecostals tended to latch on to these similarities in language.[132] Both movements curried power through the Spirit, but they did so with alternative results in mind.

124. Caldwalder, "Seasons of Refreshing at Edmonton, Canada," *PE* (14 October 1922) 26.

125. Towner, "'Pentecost' in a Baptist Church," *PE* (16 August 1924) 9; "St. Louis, Mo.," *PE* (11 April 1925) 12; Frey, "Hungry Audiences," *PE* (8 May 1926) 12.

126. S. Patterson, "Good Meeting in Denver," *PE* (7 August 1926) 12.

127. Frey, "Rain on Thirsty Land," *PE* (7 February 1931) 11; Frey, "God Visits Beauty Spot," *PE* (27 June 1931) 19; Frey, "Lyons, N.Y.," *PE* (3 April 1937) 10.

128. "Baptists Praying for Power," *COGE* (29 May 1920) 1.

129. Tomlinson, "God Bless the Fundamental Baptists," *FS* (July 1922) 24.

130. Norris, "Power from on High our Supreme Need," *Search* (28 September 1923) 1.

131. "A Fundamentalist Speaks Out," *PE* (10 November 1923) 5.

132. An extreme case of this was "Did Martin Luther Speak in Tongues?" (*PE*, 30 October 1920, 3) in which Ernest Ruff found in a church history volume that "Dr. Martin Luther was a prophet, evangelist, speaker in tongues, and interpreter, in one person, endowed with all the gifts of the Spirit," perhaps not realizing

DISFELLOWSHIPED

Once again, Gaebelein was not so amicable towards Norris. In his sermon, Norris had appraised McPherson, "an ordained Baptist preacher," as a model worthy of emulation for seminary students beyond their courses in homiletics and church history.[133] Gaebelein adjudged his task of reprimanding Norris as unpleasant, but the fight for truth compelled him onwards. Would the apostle Paul have raved about the "fine figure" cut by a woman as Norris had? Gaebelein likened Norris to the indecisive Gamaliel, who refused to take a stand for or against Christianity.[134] He called upon the WCFA to condemn women in leadership, the "Pentecostal delusion" and "healing cults" in one swoop. Gaebelein as always drew a strict line between orthodox fundamentalists and pretenders, and Norris had bungled the test.

The situation was quite different in the AG. Asked whether it was permissible to fellowship with those who gainsaid tongues, E. N. Bell responded positively so long as the detractors held to the "fundamentals of Christ as Lord and His atoning blood."[135] Such fellowship was not tantamount to approving of their doctrine. Pentecostals were to remain "longsuffering" in the face of opposition, he added. Though craving recognition from fundamentalists, the relationship was uneasy. In 1922, *PE* voiced support to the Bible Union of China, a fundamentalist organization formed in 1920 to thwart the increasing influence of modernism in mission societies.[136] Missionaries who presented Darwin rather than Christ and parceled out doubt through higher criticism would "reap a bountiful harvest for their error," it read, citing several fundamentalist articles that highlighted the antagonism of secularized Chinese professors against Christianity.[137] The article urged pentecostals to petition heaven that their missionaries would "confound the wisdom of this world" with "power and signs and wonder." While fundamentalists wrestled with the principles of the mind, pentecostals wrestled against "principalities in the air."

Their alignment was particularly uncomfortable with the chief dispensational source, the Scofield Reference Bible. Frank Boyd at CBI recommended Scofield to all his pupils so long as they were aware of tenets pentecostals found objectionable: the cessation of tongues, the postponement of the "kingdom of heaven," eternal security and the designation of the "sermon on the mount" as "pure law" (i.e., belonging to the Jewish dispensation).[138] Still, many in the AG assessed it as indispensable. In a letter to secure his ordination papers in 1916, W. E. Moody inquired to J. W. Welch about Bible prices, declaring, "No other Bible but Scofield will do."[139] W. I. Evans once averred that he would only accept a large sum

---

that "speaking in tongues" simply meant the ability to speak a foreign language. The phrase is also found in Shakespeare in *The Two Gentlemen of Verona* where the Second Bandit asks Valentine, "Have you the tongues?' (IV.i.32), but has nothing to do with the apostolic gifts.

133. Gaebelein, "Gamaliel Route," *Hope* (November 1923) 267.

134. Ibid., 268–69.

135. Bell, "Questions and Answers," *CE* (20 September 1919) 5 (No. 739).

136. Baptist Harry Emerson Fosdick would use a trip to the Orient to preach a sermon at his Presbyterian church in New York titled "Shall the Fundamentalists Win?" which sparked much of the controversy that embroiled the Northern Baptists for the next several conventions.

137. "Great Battle on between Forces of Evil and Good in China," *PE* (10 June 1922) 12.

138. "Great Move Forward," *PE* (1 May 1926) 3.

139. Moody to Welch, letter dated 5 December 1916 (FPHC).

of cash for his Scofield if no other could be found. Welch would have taken $50 but only if he could buy another, a price which Bell then upped to $100.[140] Misgivings were stern enough for the executive presbytery to ban the advertising of Scofield in *PE* in 1924, but the decision was rescinded two years later.[141] By 1935 Stanley Frodsham had worn out four successive copies of Scofield, heralding it as the "best Bible yet published."[142] Miss L. M. Mackinlay, in an article reprinted from *Friends' Witness*, challenged Scofield's assertion that believers were baptized in the Spirit at regeneration.[143] She endeavored to prove that the experience was at times immediate and at others subsequent. Despite any disagreements, Scofield had no peer, and pentecostals could settle with no substitute.

Former Southern Baptist minister Arch Collins felt obliged to refute Riley's anti-pentecostal tract "Speaking in Tongues"—thirteen years belated. He acknowledged that Riley stood "four-square for the fundamentals of Christianity" and appreciated his frankness on the occasions he had heard him speak.[144] He also notched eight points at which he concurred with Riley, such as not shortening Mark's ending and not limiting tongues to the apostles. "Never before from any of our critics have I read so many favorable admissions concerning speaking in tongues," he conceded.[145] Nonetheless, Riley could not escape censure for inconsistent utilization of Scripture and for associating tongues with spurious religions like "Sandfordism," "Dowieism," "Millennial Dawnism," and "Christian Science." "This he will have to answer for before the judgment seat of Christ," he admonished, not recognizing the debt pentecostals owed to Sanford and Dowie, nor the fact that pentecostals often cited other prophetic movements as their own precedents, including Mormonism. Collins protested that the "burden of our ministry" was Christ crucified and not tongues as Riley assumed, though he agreed that fanaticism ought to be deplored. As to Riley's quarrel that Isaiah 28:11 did not refer to tongues, why then had Paul quoted it in 1 Corinthians 14:21? At the end, Collins reiterated that "the Pentecostal people [stood] for the fundamentals of Christianity as does Dr. Riley" but asked readers not to be prejudiced by his sermon.[146]

Pentecostals likened the hostility they faced to that which Jesus faced from religious authorities. One editorial asked, "Where is the opposition coming from today?

---

140. "Great Move Forward," 3; "Scofield Reference Bible," *PE* (6 July 1935) 15.

141. "Great Move Forward," 3. The committee consisted of General Superintendent W. T. Gaston, Assistant Superintendent David McDowell, General Secretary J. R. Evans, Missions Secretary William Faux, editor Stanley Frodsham, Bible school principal Frank Boyd, plus Ernest Williams, S. A. Jamieson, and J. N. Gortner. W. I. Evans was also present at the 1926 meeting. In 1924, J. W. Welch was serving as General Superintendent (or "Chairman" as was the original title) and J. Roswell Flower as Missions Treasurer, a responsibility that went to Faux in 1925.

142. "Scofield Reference Bible," *PE* (6 July 1935) 15. See also Frodsham, "Editor's Bible," *PE* (11 December 1937) 5.

143. Mackinlay, "Experience of Pentecost—Is it for Today," *PE* (6 August 1921) 3, 9. This article was followed up two years later by Mackinlay with "Experience of Pentecost: Is it for Today?" *PE* (16 June 1923) 7–9.

144. Collins, "Review of Dr. W. B. Riley's Tract 'Speaking with Tongues,'" *PE* (17 April 1920) 8.

145. Ibid., 8.

146. Ibid., 9.

From the world? No. It is from the spiritual leaders so-called."[147] In November 1921 Frodsham noted to his consternation the myriad of tracts and articles being published against pentecostals "in which we are assured that tongues, visions and miracles are not for today."[148] He blamed it on an "aversion to the supernatural" and a "gangrenous formalism" that had "eaten the very vitals of modern Christianity." As on earlier occasions, he reminded pentecostals to remain above the fray and imitate the lesson of Jesus towards his tormentors by forgiving them.

Pentecostals pleaded for fairness in their dealings with their critics. George Ridout, a Methodist, battered pentecostalism in *The Pentecostal Herald*, a holiness periodical which had turned fundamentalist in tone.[149] For too long, Ridout said, he had held his tongue against the tongues artifice and the havoc it wreaked upon weak Christians. His charges were answered by J. M. Pike, long a holiness booster of pentecostalism, and reprinted in *PE*.[150] Pike gauged Ridout's deprecation to be both ignorant and uncharitable. The *PE* was also appreciative of John Scruby, publisher and editor of *The Standard Bearer* in Dayton, Ohio.[151] Scruby sponsored McPherson's campaign in his city and defended her in print. God had providentially raised up defenders on their behalf outside the movement, a later *PE* article proposed, and therefore they need not defend themselves.[152]

Though pentecostals said they were too busily engaged in evangelization to bother about what others thought of them, the attacks did not pass without comment.[153] Some perceived a parallel in the treatment the Messiah had endured at the hands of the Pharisees. As the rulers rejected Christ, so fundamentalists had rejected pentecostals.[154] Thus history repeats itself. Similar observations were made anonymously in 1923 and by Eddie Young in 1924.[155] They gained encouragement from Charles Finney to live "above the world and walk with God."[156] Just as Festus accused Paul of madness, so the unspiritual reckoned the spiritual to be deranged. One author asked readers to ponder if they were "temple" (i.e., nominal) or "upper room" (i.e., spiritual) Christians.[157] The disciples were surely in the vine of Christ after the resurrection but still lacked God's essential power on their lives, the

---

147. "Overcoming Man-Child," *PE* (30 October 1920) 4.

148. Frodsham, "Opposition to Pentecost," *PE* (26 November 1921) 4.

149. Ridout, "Satan's Devices Deceiving the very Elect," *PH* (1 September 1920) 4–5. Editor H. C. Morrison founded Asbury Seminary in 1923 as a fundamentalist institution to stem the tide of modernism in the Methodist church. The Nazarene church was undergoing a similar process of "fundamentalization" as the AG in this time period. See Ingersol, "Strange Bedfellows," 123–41.

150. "Was it Wise or Charitable?" *PE* (27 November 1920) 7. Pike's article titled "The Tares and the Wheat."

151. "Lovers of Fair Play," *PE* (8 January 1921) 4. Scruby had also published Bosworth's *Do all Speak with Tongues?* in 1918.

152. "Keep on Believing," *PE* (19 March 1921) 4.

153. "Too Busy at Evangelizing, no Time for Controversy," *PE* (20 January 1923) 1.

154. "Have many of the Rulers Believed on Him?" *PE* (2 September 1922) 8.

155. "Answer to Critics of Latter Rain," *PE* (11 August 1923) 5; Young, "Cast Out," *PE* (29 March 1924) 5.

156. "Misunderstood," *PE* (22 December 1923) 6.

157. "Are You a Temple or Upper Room Christian?" *PE* (11 August 1923) 7. This anonymous article was also distributed as a tract.

implication being that many Christians (i.e., fundamentalists) reposed their faith in the Savior but shied away from the profits of the Spirit.

The margin between pentecostals and fundamentalists was slight. "We see all they see, but they don't see what we see," Daniel Kerr wrote, determining (contra Bell) that they could not fraternize with those who disdained pentecostal truth.[158] Canadian editor R. E. McAlister similarly registered his affinity "with all evangelical churches" in proclaiming the total depravity of the human race and the necessity of blood atonement, even if they disagreed on Spirit-baptism.[159] Holy unction saturated pentecostals with such fervency that evangelist Billy Sunday admired them for their exuberant prayers and caused Toronto fundamentalist pastor Peter Philpot to wonder why his most spiritual members had joined them.[160] Blumhofer is correct that pentecostals juxtaposed the "full gospel" with the "partial" faith of fundamentalists. The extra ingredient of the Holy Ghost added a fieriness to pentecostal verve.

At an AG executive council meeting in 1924, David McDowell opined that pentecostals were "fundamentalists plus," meaning they possessed both the wisdom of the Word and the power of the Spirit. Frodsham agreed, stipulating that they had no sympathy for the "unproved theory" of evolution or the denial of the supernatural so prevalent among modernists, whom he compared to the Sadducees.[161] He stated, "We stand one hundred per cent with all who believe in the verbal inspiration and absolute inerrancy of the Scriptures of truth." Responding to modernists' claims that hell did not physically exist, Max Wood Moorhead compiled a list of Christ's notions about divine retribution extracted from W. C. Proctor's contribution on hell to *The Fundamentals*.[162] He may very well have been one of the missionaries to whom the series was distributed. A correspondence course would later be offered through CBI entitled "Fundamentals of the Faith 'Plus,'" designed by D. W. Kerr and billed as a doctrinal study of the "Great Teachings of the Bible,"[163] Pentecostals were reliant upon fundamentalist textbooks like MBI professor William Evans's *Great Doctrines of the Bible* (1912) but felt they had something more to offer besides dry erudition.[164]

As their movement took shape in the early 1920s, fundamentalists buttressed their arguments with the theory that miracles had ceased, as Flower observed above. Though

---

158. Kerr, "Basis for our Distinctive Testimony," *PE* (2 September 1922) 4.

159. McAlister, "The Pentecostal Movement," *PE* (13 May 1922) 5.

160. Ibid., 5. Philpot sat on the first council of the WCFA along with Riley, Torrey, James Gray, Haldeman, Scofield, Straton, Rader, Munhall, Charles Alexander, Lewis Sperry Chafer, and W. H. Griffith-Thomas, basically a "who's who" of fundamentalism.

161. "'Fundamentalists Plus,'" *PE* (12 July 1924) 4.

162. Moorhead, "What Christ Teaches about Future Retribution," *PE* (11 November 1922) 6-7; see also W. C. Proctor, "What Christ Teaches concerning Future Retribution," in Torrey, ed., *The Fundamentals*, 2:53–63.

163. "C.B.I. Correspondence Course," *PE* (18 December 1926) 7; "Why be Ignorant of what your Bible Teaches?" *PE* (29 June 1935) 15.

164. E. S. Williams had a copy in his personal library along with books by A. T. Pierson (*Keys to the Word*), James Gray (*Synthetic Bible Studies*), G. Campbell Morgan (*The Gospel according to Mark*), and A. C. Gaebelein (*God's Masterpiece*) (CBC Arch). He was hardly dependent on fundamentalists. Other works included *Systematic Theology* by A. H. Strong, *Clarke's Commentary*, *Wesley's Notes on the New Testament* (7 vols.), and *First Epistle to Timothy* by H. C. G. Moule.

dispensationalism had been the lens through which pentecostals conceptualized the Latter Rain, dispensationalists like Gaebelein cut off the days of miracles at the apostolic age.[165] The outstanding theologian articulating this position was B. B. Warfield. His *Counterfeit Miracles* (1918) targeted various healing factions such as Christian Scientists, the Lourdes phenomenon, the Irvingites and contemporary faith healers, including A. J. Gordon, whom he otherwise respected.[166] Warfield's argument was largely historical rather than theological, challenging the idea held by pentecostals (and holiness adherents before them) that miracles had diminished after Constantine ascended to the throne. In fact, said Warfield, recordings of miracles proliferated in the fourth century and only increased over the centuries, informed by an influx of pagan converts who shallowly adopted their new faith.[167] Fortified by Warfield's exposé, fundamentalists latched on to the cessationist position with alacrity.

However, the theory was not universally accepted in fundamentalist circles, particularly in the realm of divine healing. In 1921 *The King's Business* printed an excerpt from A. T. Pierson in which he argued that healing "continued to be wrought through the apostolic age" and had never wholly ceased throughout church history: "The Scripture certainly suggests and favors the healing of the body in answer to prayer; and as no hint is there found that such signs would cease, the burden of proof is with the opponent, not the advocate of such healing. From the word of God alone no one would gather that such supernatural signs any more than promises to prayer were confined to the apostles or apostolic age."[168]

Likewise, Riley would remark that same year, "We can find no warrant whatever for the contention that miracles were only temporary and intended to prove the deity of Christ, nor do we discover anywhere a hint of that other teaching that miracles 'were limited to apostolic days' and possibly to answers to apostles' prayers," though he did not refrain from assaulting the Bosworth brothers and McPherson for their methodology.[169] Self-promotion, exaggerated claims, and shady "money-getting" were the primary complaints he lodged against them. Though a bit later, Harry Ironside would make a similar observation, asserting that every New Testament believer must recognize the power of God to heal both body and soul today. He only questioned, as Torrey had, whether Jesus would have directed mass healing campaigns, as some modern healers did.[170]

---

165. Gaebelein, *Healing Question*, 49–50.

166. Warfield, *Counterfeit Miracles* (1918). Ruthven, *On the Cessation of the Charismata*, 54–55, contends that Warfield was also counteracting modernism, based on an article by R. Mullin and a reference to H. Bushnell's *Nature and the Supernatural* (1858). However, Warfield's only reference to a contemporary modernist, Charles Briggs, indicates otherwise. Here Warfield questions Briggs's subsuming of the supernatural into the natural, reducing Jesus into some sort of occult healing figure (*Counterfeit Miracles*, 163–64). Warfield's intent was to counteract the modernist habit of removing supernaturalism from the biblical account.

167. Warfield, *Counterfeit Miracles*, 9–24, 61–69, 73–84.

168. Pierson, "What about Divine Healing? Have Supernatural Signs Ceased?" *KB* (March 1921) 231.

169. Riley, "Divine Healing and the Dangers Incidental to the Doctrine," *CFSC* (April-June 1922) 10–11.

170. Ironside, *Divine Priorities*, 96.

Confirming a Pentecostal Identity

Even as the AG veered towards fundamentalism, they struggled to keep their pentecostal identity. But Frodsham took comfort in the example of John the Baptist. Though the Pharisees had rejected John's authority, the prophet was not disturbed in the least. Had he exchanged his camel's hair shirt for priestly garments, he would have lost his power as a forerunner of Christ. As John was called to be a harbinger of Christ's first coming, so pentecostals should witness to His second. "Don't compromise, forfeit, sell nor [sic] barter your high calling," Frodsham admonished.[171]

Addressing the CBI student body in 1925, J. R. Flower arranged the pentecostal movement into three stages. Drawing on imagery from Pharoah's dream in Genesis, the first phase commenced at Azusa Street in 1906 with "seven years of plenty," followed by the new issue controversy in 1913, resulting in "seven years of trouble."[172] The third and current epoch squeezed pentecostals between the Sadducees (modernists) who denied the supernatural and Pharisees (fundamentalists) who believed in it but relegated it to the past. Imitating the stance of St. Paul, Flower called himself a "Fundamentalist of the Fundamentalists"—and that of the strictest sect. He worried however that some "great men" had watered down their distinctive so as not to offend critics. Like Jewish proselytes to Christianity, will pentecostals avoid the "cross" and hush their "hallelujahs" or escort those who fall under the power into some back room? "Satan is luring us into a position of compromise . . . Shall we fall into the snare?"[173] The danger of losing the supernatural to placate fundamentalists was worrisome to him. Flower's anxiety signaled the pentecostal adjustment to the growing strength of fundamentalism. How closely could they align themselves with it without obliterating their identity?

Donald Gee, a British pentecostal, only a short time before had grappled with that very issue in *PE*. A friend had encouraged him to abandon tongues so that he could enjoy fellowship with other evangelicals. Despite his "hearty agreement on every Fundamental Doctrine of Christian Faith," Gee found himself an outcast because of "those dreadful tongues."[174] Several eminent pentecostals in Britain had rescinded their testimony, so why shouldn't he? Not surprisingly, Gee's personal acquaintance with tongues furnished his apology. He was unwilling to dishonor God by discounting an experience which had been so precious to him, nor would he compartmentalize his faith by speaking in tongues in private as his friend suggested. "To publicly deny what I privately believe is an outrage on moral character which none would tolerate who love the truth."[175]

PE took the offensive with a "Special Pentecostal Number" in September 1922 and again in August 1923.[176] Articles promoting their "distinct testimony" included "How can

---

171. Frodsham, "Shall We Compromise our Pentecostal Testimony?" *PE* (15 September 1923) 4.

172. Flower, "Present Position of Pentecost," *PE* (13 June 1925) 7.

173. Ibid., 13.

174. Gee, "Shall We Give Up Tongues? A Reply," *PE* (7 March 1925) 6.

175. Ibid., 6.

176. "Special Pentecostal Number," *PE* (30 September 1922) 4—referring to the September 2 issue; "Circulate the Pentecostal Message," *PE* (11 August 1923) 8.

We know that We have received the Baptism?" by Bert Williams, "Pentecost Restored" by United Brethren pastor A. J. Covington, "Have any of the Rulers believed on Him?" and "Have you received the Holy Ghost since Ye believed?" both likely by Frodsham, "The Bible Evidence of the Baptism with the Holy Ghost" by Daniel Kerr, and "An Answer to Critics of the Latter Rain," again probably by Frodsham.[177] "Become a candidate for a personal Pentecost and open your being for all God has for you," Frodsham implored, referencing Andrew Murray's spiritual baptism, followed by a piece on how to tarry for the Spirit.[178] The inclusion of Covington was designed to entice fundamentalists, while the inclusion of boxer Eddie Young's testimony capitalized on the sports craze of the post-war era.[179] Another issue in August 1921 highlighted a pentecostal revival among British fundamentalists connected with the Prophetic Society, a major source for dispensational thought in London, featuring a laudatory article by the Presbyterian secretary of the society, Ernest Goode.[180]

Subscribers were encouraged to purchase these issues in bulk and distribute them to interested and not so interested persons. Thirty thousand copies beyond the regular membership of the September 1922 edition were dispersed to neighbors, relatives and congregants of other denominations.[181] In a 1924 entreaty, Frodsham asked readers to forward ten dollars and ten addresses so that ten families may enjoy "Pentecostal Fundamentalism" in their homes for a year.[182] None in their movement doubted the inerrancy of the Bible, denied the virgin birth of Christ or nourished sympathy for evolution propounded by "learned ignoramuses," he pointed out, but they also believed in the "Fundamental of Service"—the baptism of the Holy Ghost.

Pentecostalism and Dispensationalism

The AG turned increasingly to apocalyptic themes in the 1920s. Stanley Frodsham's column "From the Pentecostal Viewpoint" in particular reflected dispensational peculiarities. One portent of the end was an apostate church. Modernism had ravaged the Student Volunteer Movement, which in Frodsham's estimation was "advancing backwards" by promoting the benefits of civilization over the message of the gospel.[183] Likewise, Baptist icon Russell

---

177. Williams, "How can We Know We have Received the Baptism?" *PE* (2 September 1922) 2–3; Covington, "Pentecost Restored," *PE* (2 September 1922) 8; [Frodsham], "Have any of the Rulers Believed on Him?" *PE* (2 September 1922) 8; [Frodsham], "Have you received the Holy Ghost since Ye believed?" *PE* (11 August 1923) 1; Kerr, "Bible Evidence of the Baptism with the Holy Ghost," *PE* (11 August 1923) 2–3; [Frodsham], "Answer to Critics of the Latter Rain," *PE* (11 August 1923) 5.

178. [Frodsham], "Return to Pentecost," *PE* (2 September 1922) 5; [Frodsham], "Tarry until Endued," *PE* (2 September 1922) 5.

179. Young, "From Prize Ring to Pulpit," *PE* (11 August 1923) 4–5.

180. Goode, "Pentecostal Revival in London," *PE* (20 August 1921) 11.

181. "Circulate the Pentecostal Message," *PE* (11 August 1923) 8.

182. Frodsham, "Dear Evangel Reader," *PE* (5 April 1924) 15. Publishing special editions incurred "plenty-cost," he added.

183. Frodsham, "From the Pentecostal Viewpoint," *PE* (10 January 1920) 4.

Conwell was now attuned to the voice of his deceased wife in séances instead of God.[184] "Religion was never so popular and never so powerless" as in these last days, Frodsham insisted.[185] The world was degenerating in the same way that King Nebuchadnezzar's vision of the statue declined in quality from a head of gold to feet of clay, he observed in another article,[186] employing similar imagery to that used by Panton in a 1915 article in *PE*.[187] In the midst of the disarmament movement following the Great War, Frodsham noticed from a London prophetic journal edited by Panton that arms were proliferating instead of diminishing.[188] Panton's 1922 predictions for yet another war, possibly by 1927, were reprinted in *PE*.[189] In fact, between 1920 and 1925 sixteen articles written by Panton appeared in *PE*, at least nine of which were eschatological in nature.[190]

The Interchurch World Movement, a cooperative affair to evangelize the world, was also put under a microscope. Fundamentalists and pentecostals scrutinized it as a precursor to a one world religion that would introduce the antichrist. Riley denigrated the movement in June 1920 as further evidence of apostasy.[191] J. T. Boddy, temporary editor at *PE*, chastised the Interchurch founders for fellowshipping with "Universalists, Unitarians and other unorthodox bodies."[192] The expenditure for their program was a colossal waste of resources in Frodsham's view. The ten-year, $3.5 million rental for their New York offices alone would have deployed a 5,000-strong force of pentecostal missionaries on the field with considerable comfort.[193] Elizabeth Sisson suggested that Interchurch was Satan's duplicate of the pentecostal revival. For her, everything spiritual was yoked to its fake, such as "Christ the Lamb" versus "Anti-Christ the Beast." The true pentecostal revival had inundated the world, but a counterfeit revival was being swallowed by "unwitting, but precious blood-washed saints," whose "closeness to the Word of God [had] been sacrificed to breadth of opinion."[194]

The League of Nations fared no better since it foreshadowed a one-world government. In dispensationalism, a regenerated Roman Empire, represented by the ten toes in Nebuchadnezzar's dream (Dan 2:42), would prepare the world for the coming of the antichrist. No matter how many nations united with the League, predicted Bell, at some

---

184. Ibid., 4. Frank Bartleman had been an active member in the 1890s of Conwell's church, Temple Baptist in Philadelphia, before studying at Moody Bible Institute.

185. Ibid., 4.

186. Frodsham, "From the Pentecostal Viewpoint," *PE* (13 November 1920) 3.

187. Panton, "Democracy and the End," *WE* (17 April 1915) 1. The Scriptural passage Dan 3:31–45 was wrongly cited in the title (Dan 2:31–45). The same mistake was repeated in *Word & Witness* (*W&Wt*, May 1915, 5). The timing suggests that *W&Wt* copied it from *PE*. *KB* used this image in poetic form in "League of Nations: A Prophetic Forecast (Daniel 2:28–45)," *KB* (September 1919) 878.

188. Frodsham, "From the Pentecostal Viewpoint," *PE* (21 June 1924) 4.

189. Panton, "Another War in 1927?" *PE* (1 April 1922) 7; see also Panton, "Coming War," *PE* (25 November 1922) 10.

190. See Appendix F.

191. Riley, "Interchurch World Movement," *SC* (April-June 1920) 320–25.

192. Boddy, "Substituting Doing for Being," *PE* (21 February 1920) 5.

193. Frodsham, "Interchurch World Movement," *PE* (1 May 1920) 10.

194. Sisson, "Two Revivals," *PE* (29 May 1920) 6.

point ten would dominate and "complete the prophecy concerning the final drama before Jesus will come."[195] Daniel 7 and Revelation 17 spoke of the certainty of such a League as now existed and out of this would come the "godless beast, who will fall in with the popular religion of the day."[196] All differences in religion would dissolve while external worship replaced "real salvation" so that even the very elect would nearly be deceived. To J. T. Boddy, visions for world peace were nothing but "optimistic delusions."[197] The weakness of the League to institute disarmament became apparent in the late 1920s and thus garnered further derision.

Fundamentalist and pentecostal pundits echoed the prophet Jeremiah: "Peace, peace, when there is no peace!" William Burton McCafferty blamed the "Higher Critics" for preaching the gospel of pacifism. Ironically, according to McCafferty, they desecrated the literal interpretation of Scripture while it was "being literally fulfilled in the very midst of their efforts to disannul it."[198] British fundamentalist Percy Hicks's appearance in *PE* touched upon the League. Brazil had blocked Germany's admittance into that irenic institution in 1925 and thus unintentionally preserved the prophetic number of ten on the Council.[199] One writer for *PE* was unimpressed by the signature of fifteen nations to the Briand-Kellogg Peace Pact in 1928, for "in the midst of man's arbitration, damnation is slumbering behind."[200] The ultimate failure of the League to impose permanent disarmament was a sign of its futility. Peace, they believed, would only clothe this world when Christ reigned over it.

Following the Great War, prophetic charts and conferences proliferated. Kerr designed a chart with his son-in-law Willard Peirce and took it with him when visiting churches.[201] During a three-week evangelistic campaign in the nation's capital in April 1924, Peirce and Kerr presented noon lectures on the book of Revelation and evening talks on the dispensations of the ages one hour before the regular service. H. L. Collier, pastor of the thriving Full Gospel Assembly, described his congregation as eager to delve into the Word of God and found Kerr's lectures most beneficial for the "living way" in which he disseminated the truth.[202] In their "Chart of the Ages," first conceived in 1920 with illustrator Lee Dilts, Kerr and Peirce divided history into similar dispensations to those of Scofield with miniscule variation.[203] Unlike fundamentalists, they promoted both a pre- and a post-tribulation

---

195. Bell, "League of Nations: Preparing the Way of the Beast," *CE* (8 March 1919) 2.

196. Ibid., 2.

197. Boddy, "Optimistic Delusion," *PE* (29 May 1920) 4.

198. McCafferty, "'There Shall be Wars,'" *PE* (2 May 1925) 5.

199. Hicks, "League of Nations and Germany," *PE* (22 May 1926) 9.

200. "Death Throes of a Wicked Generation," *PE* (22 September 1928) 8.

201. Peirce married Kerr's daughter Christine. He had been the first secretary of the Southern California District while Kerr served as chair in 1920 and joined the first faculty of CBI, which Kerr headed.

202. Collier, "Washington, DC," *PE* (28 June 1924) 13.

203. Kerr and Peirce, "Chart of the Ages or Great Events and Crises in Bible History" (FPHC). They divided time into nine "ages" instead of seven "dispensations," but each age was divided into four stages as Scofield taught (light, declension, apostasy and judgment). The two additional ages were "pre-history" and "creation" (not strictly dispensations since there is no apostasy or judgment involved). Otherwise, the names of the "ages" matched Scofield's dispensations.

rapture. Those in the first wave would belong to the church saved during the present Age of Grace and those in the second wave saved during the tribulation.[204] Pentecostals still showed independence from fundamentalist schemes at this stage; nevertheless, the influence was heavy upon the AG and would only increase over time.

The AG became obsessed with the Mark of the Beast. Citing Panton, *PE* spotted Bolsheviks sporting "Anti-Christ" bands around their sleeves, while a secret society of French atheists known as "*Les Frères de la Côte*" had tattooed "A.D."—abbreviating *Anti Dieu* (Against God)—on their arms.[205] Some pentecostals were so paranoid that they refused cooperation with other Christians for fear of taking the Mark upon themselves, a position clearly erroneous and against Scripture in Bell's viewpoint.[206] By the same token, the AG was guiltless in having "incorporated" in accordance with the laws of the land just because it required a seal from the government. An article copied from *The Apostolic Evangel* discouraged any involvement in labor unions unless one was prepared to suffer through the Great Tribulation.[207] Bell assuaged one farmer's angst that he would be taking the Mark for joining the local agricultural association, although he advised the agrarian to quit it if the association advocated anything contrary to the Word.[208] He did opine that the Mark would be physical, such as a tattoo inked onto the skin, or another sign that could be permanently displayed.[209] Beyond that he dared not venture.

With the attention to things apocalyptic came speculation as to who the antichrist might be. Bell confessed that he did not know if it would be a "Turk, Jew, or the pope," though he did believe it would be some political leader.[210] Mussolini became a prime candidate after seizing power in Rome. In *LRE*, Panton feared the twin dictators of Trotsky in Moscow and Mussolini would terrorize the world. Mussolini had resurrected the Prætorian Guard, "which made and unmade emperors, and so ruled the world," setting the stage for the final drama.[211] Frodsham later quoted from Panton's article to warn readers of the peril this revived Caesar posed, who "drove his own car and everything else in Italy."[212] In a lengthy 1926 article, Arthur Frodsham asked, "Is Mussolini the Antichrist?," although his conclusion was a tentative "perhaps."[213] Dispensationalists of all stripes were wondering and watching in anxious guessing.[214]

While ever mindful that the end was near, CG did not take as speculative an approach to the apocalypse as the AG. Wars, earthquakes, and pestilence were signs of impending

---

204. A pre-tribulation rapture was based on Rev 4:1 and 12:5; a post-tribulation rapture on Rev 7:14.
205. "Mark of the Beast," *PE* (10 December 1921) 4.
206. Bell, "Questions and Answers," *PE* (12 June 1920) 5 (No. 846).
207. A.E.R., "Mark of the Beast," *PE* (25 December 1920) 3 (identity of author unknown).
208. Bell, "Questions and Answers," *PE* (28 April 1923) 8 (No. 2058).
209. Bell, "Questions and Answers," *PE* (4 February 1922) 6 (No. 1144).
210. Bell, "Questions and Answers," *PE* (14 April 1923) 6 (No. 2048).
211. Panton, "Moscow and Rome," *LRE* (September 1923) 10.
212. Frodsham, "Fear Not: A Word for the New Year," *PE* (5 January 1924) 2–3.
213. A. Frodsham, "Is Mussolini the Antichrist?" *PE* (30 January 1926) 4–5.
214. "Man the World is Watching," *PE* (28 June 1924) 9.

doom, but Mussolini did not enter CG vocabulary until 1928—and not again until 1934.[215] There were many antichrists whose spirit opposed the gospel, but they refused to name names.[216] Through much of the 1920s CG ministers were less likely to quote the daily papers when discussing eschatological matters. F. J. Lee's explication of drought compared the prophecies of Joel to conditions in China, but that was as far as he extended.[217] Lee's dispensational thought was much more evident in *Book of Prophecy* (1923), which he presented in a Q&A format on the "entire book of Revelation." For instance, he accepted that we were currently living in the "Great Parenthesis" between Calvary and the "Great Tribulation," but he studiously avoided identifying any individual as the antichrist and denied that the United States represented the false prophet.[218] Frank Lemons solely appealed to Revelation for his understanding of the Millennium, not the Russian menace or Roman resurgence.[219] Compared to AG pundits, CG was more theoretical than practical, demonstrating its relative distance from fundamentalist thinking at the time. Fundamentalism had not yet encroached upon the South by this juncture. Though many southerners were religiously conservative, the controversies of the North had simply not filtered down to the confederate states. CG was more heavily rural than the AG, and after the removal of Tomlinson, became evermore isolated.

Summary and Conclusion

The early 1920s witnessed the consolidation of gains in pentecostal denominations. Rising incomes allowed them to erect new edifices in rural towns or purchase abandoned ones in the cities. They also turned to the needs of educating the next generation of ministers by investing in Bible schools. These schools were patterned after familiar fundamentalist institutions like MBI, Biola and Nyack. The textbooks most congenial to their needs were fundamentalist in nature, and Scofield enjoyed a prominent place in the education of AG clergy. The transition had begun from the adaptation to the retention stage, which would be characterized by the elevation of Sunday schools.

But first, pentecostals found themselves adapting to the emerging voice of fundamentalism. Criticism stormed around Aimee Semple McPherson and other healing evangelists of the age, viz., Charles Price, F. F. Bosworth, and Ray Richey. Most fundamentalists were at least theoretically committed to divine healing, but they objected to massive campaigns that paraded invalids and to the doctrine of healing in the atonement, which in their eyes reduced faith to a simplistic formula. They also questioned the validity of many of the claims. Pentecostals for their part were indebted to protofundamentalist writers like A. J. Gordon and A. B. Simpson for their resources.

---

215. R. Seyda, "Approaching of Devils—Doctrines," *COGE* (16 March 1928) 2; "Dictatorship," *COGE* (3 March 1934) 5 (the other dictators were Stalin, Hitler and Roosevelt).

216. "Beware of Antichrists," *COGE* (28 May 1927) 3.

217. Lee, "Day of the Lord is at Hand—Indicated by Pests, Drouth [sic] and Fires," *COGE* (19 September 1925) 1.

218. Lee, *Book of Prophecy*, 14–19, 114–15.

219. Lemons, "The Millennium," *COGE* (4 August 1923) 1.

One unspoken contention was the numbers of fundamentalists who were attending pentecostal healing services. As much as they tried to deride pentecostals from the pulpit, fundamentalists could not prevent parishioners from escaping at night to the evening services in pentecostal churches. Indeed, many pentecostal churches experienced higher attendance Sunday evenings than they did on Sunday mornings. As a result, a number of fundamentalists joined pentecostal ranks. It was enough to cause concern. Fundamentalist leaders complained that their members were more susceptible to the pentecostal message than modernists were, as we will see later.

To counteract fundamentalist attacks, pentecostals repeatedly flaunted their evangelical credentials. McPherson in particular distanced herself from pentecostal extravagance in order to gain acceptance and a wider hearing among fundamentalists, entertaining luminaries like Rader, Munhall, and Bryan. Denominational pentecostals like the AG were reluctant to make such concessions. Having carved out their own existence in the religious environment, giving ground to fundamentalists by denying their unique expression would have involved a loss of power that they had worked so hard to create. It placed them in a sort of identity crisis. While still longing for acceptance from the wider religious community and the fundamentalists they so admired, they could not do so without losing their identity as pentecostals. Instead, they became "fundamentalists plus," thus improving upon their evangelical heritage by adding a "full gospel" experience to salvation. If fundamentalists espoused an inerrant Word, pentecostals practiced it.

By advancing the fundamentalist mantra, the AG moved from the "vocabulary" to the "content" of fundamentalism. This was most evident in the near universal adoption of dispensationalism in the AG. Stanley Frodsham was most responsible for bringing this to pentecostal attention, though he was hardly alone. Dispensational charts found homes in pentecostal churches and attracted large crowds of those interested in the future age. Along with this adoption of dispensationalism came the adoption of fundamentalist concerns, often copied from fundamentalist magazines. The end times would be preceded by the apostasy of the church. One issue that came to define fundamentalism was the fight over evolution. It also marked an alignment with fundamentalist issues beyond dispensationalism that would shape a fundamentalist mentality in pentecostals. In the next chapter, the pervasive influence of dispensationalism will help transition pentecostals from the "content" to the "rhetoric" of fundamentalism, where evolution will take center stage.

PART FOUR

Retention

6

Battling One Another (1925–1929)

Introduction

THE ROARING OF THE 1920S AND THE INABILITY OF THE COUNTRY TO ENFORCE PROHIbition put many religious conservatives on their heels. Evangelicals of all stripes were swimming against a cultural current that threatened to drown out their protests against the chugging of intoxicating liquor and the scandalous dancing of the "Chattanooga Choo-choo"—sensible activities to the modern world. In 1925, fundamentalism fell into disgrace in the wake of the Scopes trial in Dayton, Tennessee, depicted in the popular press as an intellectual backwater. Pentecostals were cast in the same pall by their enemies. On the doctrinal front, with the official condemnation of the pentecostals by the World's Christian Fundamentals Association in 1928, the donnybrook between the two movements reached its apex. Nonetheless, there were indications that cooperation could be brokered between them on a national scale.

Evidence for the beginnings of the retention stage can be seen in the AG in the formation of young people's societies and an increasing number of publications designed to retain their loyalty before they could drift off to college and away from the faith. In the early years many pentecostal converts had young families, such as William and Mary Piper, whose six children were all under ten when they joined the movement. As the movement aged, so did the average age of its members. By the 1920s sufficient numbers of young people had grown up into their teen years to warrant the organizing of youth societies. In the AG it began in 1925 and flourished in the years following, as will be demonstrated at the end of this chapter.

Pentecostals and Evolution

"As Vinson Synan has observed," to quote Ronald Numbers, "the most outspoken defamers of Darwin during the Scopes trial 'were not the "Holy Rollers on Shinbone Ridge," as H. L. Mencken implied, but the Presbyterians, Baptists and Methodists in the Courthouse.'"[1] The anti-evolution campaign was not primarily a pentecostal concern. Fundamentalists such as William Jennings Bryan and William Bell Riley led the crusade. And yet neither were pentecostals oblivious to what was being taught in the schools. Early leaders for the

1. Numbers, *Darwin*, 119.

most part had not participated in the upper echelons of education where evolution had been taught up to the early twentieth century. Few Americans graduated from high school in the nineteenth century, and fewer attended college. But by the 1920s pentecostal children were attending schools where such things were being taught.

As I have argued elsewhere, the primary impetus that got pentecostals involved with the fight was their children's education.[2] This same concern motivated the likes of Bryan and fundamentalist lawyer Philip Mauro, whose *Evolution at the Bar* (1922) was available to *PE* readers.[3] Mauro warned, "It is high time for parents to be awakened out of sleep as the dangers to which their children are exposed in our modern schools."[4] To Mauro, the halls of education were filled with more peril than the streets of mean cities. Similarly, Bryan expressed the apprehension of many believers when he quoted a hypothetical parent in a 1925 *PE* article, "I sent my boy or my girl [to college] a Christian and they came back an atheist."[5] Bryan's sermon on evolution at Moody Church in Chicago was reprinted in the *LRE* in 1923.[6] *LRE* editor Anna Reiff explained well the pentecostal position in introducing Bryan's address, "We know that our readers do not need this for themselves, but those who are sending their children to school need to be informed of what they are being taught, for we learn that even in the grades the pupils are taught by their instructors that the Bible is not true."[7] She offered her magazine for twenty-five cents for a three-month subscription as a spiritual anchor to save souls against the shoals of infidelity. In 1924, Reiff echoed Bryan's sentiments for parental control over the curriculum, blaming the increase in crime on the lack of moral and religious education in schools. "Filling the school-room with child experts in biology, zoology and geology does not train the children to honesty, trustworthiness and integrity," she opined.[8]

Pentecostals eulogized Bryan as a hero following his death one week after the Scopes trial. "The nation bows its head in mourning on account of the deceased of one of the greatest men it ever produced," J. S. Llewellyn commented in *COGE*.[9] The writer had listened to Bryan deliver his address "Is the Bible True?" at Ryman Auditorium in Nashville in January 1924, where Bryan estimated all the books on evolution to be worthy of the "humor section" of the library.[10] Llewellyn urged believers to fulfill Bryan's legacy and "make an offensive attack against those who would make our nation a nation of infidels."[11] The editors at *PE* hailed Bryan as a "sturdy champion of the faith" in August 1925 and reprinted his *LRE* speech in truncated form under the title "A Defense of the Faith once

---

2. King, "Evolving Paradigms," 93–114.
3. "Evolution at the Bar," *PE* (28 October 1922) 5.
4. Mauro, *Evolution at the Bar*, 72.
5. Bryan, "Defense of the Faith once Delivered to the Saints," *PE* (8 August 1925) 3.
6. Bryan, "Moses vs. Darwin," *LRE* (February 1923) 2–6; *LRE* (March 1923) 2–7.
7. "Solemn Warning," *LRE* (February 1923) 14.
8. "Need of Religious Instruction," *LRE* (February 1924) 11.
9. Llewellyn, "Nation Mourns," *COGE* (1 August 1925) 1.
10. Bryan, *Is the Bible True?* (1924), 17. Llewellyn mistakenly calls it Rymer Auditorium.
11. Llewellyn, "Nation Mourns," 1.

Delivered to the Saints," a phrase borrowed from Jude 3.[12] The August 15 issue of *PE* printed Bryan's denunciation of apostasy in the churches and advertised five of his works on the back cover.[13] In October *PE* offered his posthumously published "last message," which had originally been slated to be delivered during the Scopes trial.[14]

Aimee Semple McPherson took the battle cry seriously, again demonstrating her alignment with fundamentalist causes. In 1926 she promoted an anti-evolutionary law in California. Bryan had spoken twice at Angelus Temple on the matter and considered McPherson a comrade in arms.[15] Her drive failed after her mysterious disappearance later that year, reportedly drowning during a swim off a Santa Monica pier. The circumstances surrounding the event, allegations of an affair and her seemingly incredible claim that she had been kidnapped by Mexican drug dealers, resulted in a civil lawsuit that forced her to withdraw from political involvement. She did not combat evolution again until 1931 when she debated atheist Charles Smith. McPherson's activism was not typical of pentecostalism. Though Sutton depicts McPherson as representative of the pentecostal alliance with fundamentalism, her political views differed from that of pentecostal leaders like E. S. Williams, as Sutton himself admits, and therefore she should not be taken as the measuring stick of pentecostal attitudes.[16] More accurately, as with prohibition and other social issues, pentecostals sided with fundamentalists but did not actively participate in the legislative processes except to cast ballots when necessary.[17]

The first sustained decrial of evolution in *PE* emanated from Dr. A. P. Gouthey, a Presbyterian evangelist from Seattle who frequently preached in AG churches.[18] Gouthey delved into the inability of proponents to agree on a definition of evolution and their failure to explain both the origins of the universe and the origins of life.[19] "All hail Nothing!" he mocked, "Thou didst lay the foundations of the universe upon nothing, using nothing as thy building material, and out of thy nothingness . . . thou hast created the multiplied millions of stars."[20] Gouthey accepted an old earth but noted the lack of intermediary life forms in the geological record. Citing three surveys regarding the paucity of Bible knowledge among the day's youth, he sounded the fundamentalist trumpet-blast over declining

---

12. Bryan, "Defense of the Faith once Delivered to the Saints," *PE* (1 August 1925) 2; "Defense of the Faith once Delivered to the Saints," *PE* (8 August 1925) 3; Carpenter has labeled this phrase the mantra of fundamentalism (*Revive Us Again*, 64).

13. Bryan, "Great Apostasy," *PE* (15 August 1925) 2–3, 5. The four books were *Seven Questions in Dispute*, *Famous Figures of the Old Testament*, *The Bible and its Enemies*, and *In His Image* ("Books by William Jennings Bryan," *PE* [15 August 1925] 16).

14. "Last Message of William Jennings Bryan," *PE* (10 October 1925) 15; Bryan, *Last Message of William Jennings Bryan* (1925). Bryan's planned oration was deftly pre-empted by Darrow calling him to the stand on Monday July 20. The address was published through a sympathetic editor in Chattanooga.

15. Sutton, *McPherson*, 122.

16. Ibid., 215.

17. Anderson, *Vision*, 204; Wacker, *Heaven Below*, 223.

18. "Another Wonderful Year at C.B.I.," *PE* (9 June 1928) 6; Robinson, "Big Fish Story," *PE* (30 June 1928) 3. Gouthey also gave the CBI Baccalaureate address for 1928, titled "The How of Best Living."

19. Gouthey, "Is Evolution an Established Fact?" *PE* (21 July 1928) 1, 6–7.

20. Gouthey, "Is Evolution an Established Fact?" *PE* (28 July 1928) 4.

morals with an impassioned plea for his listeners to purge their churches of modernist ministers (hardly a pentecostal problem) and petition schools and politicians to curb the teaching of evolution.[21] Many were impressed with Gouthey's six-week campaign at the Full Gospel Tabernacle in Springfield, but AG General Secretary J. R. Evans was not among them. He couldn't fathom why so many flocked to hear Gouthy "as there was absolutely nothing to his message except fighting evolution" and had in his opinion "almost ruined" the church he attended (Central Assembly) by drawing away the crowds.[22] Gouthey served as study leader for W. J. Bryan's Bible class in Miami and actively promoted AG minister Charles Robinson's book *Praying to Change Things* to his audiences.[23]

Despite Cleveland being just twenty-three miles from Dayton, COGE took little notice of the trial. The earliest mention of evolution came in 1919 when an anonymous author declared that it did not matter to him whether man evolved from mud or monkey; either way it was a miracle.[24] The article was introduced with a caveat in which Tomlinson explained that some pentecostals encountered "higher criticism" as a matter of course and not because they sought it out. Evolution was not alluded to again until the Scopes trial. In June, an untitled piece likened the process of squaring Scripture with evolution by ignoring Genesis to the discarding of the foundation of one's house in order to construct an aeroplane—an idea floating in mid-air as it were.[25] An excerpt on the same page suggested that those who accepted the principles of evolution displayed sense equivalent to a monkey. In April 1926, F. J. Lee retold the story of creation, contrasting the two competing theories concerning man's origins: "the genuine Christian belief" of special creation and "evolution by dead force."[26] He found the debasing story of evolution to be far inferior to the noble story of creation in Genesis. Franklin Bowles assembled a lengthy but crude exposé of Darwinism in July.[27] Aside from a brief mention in March 1928 of belief in evolution as a sign of the end of this age, COGE abandoned the topic until 1934 with an article printed from *MBIM* with the permission of James Gray, further evidence of CG's shift to fundamentalism in the 1930s.[28]

Frank Masserano has shown that *PE* advertised fundamentalist titles from Gray, Gordon, Pierson, et al., 255 times from 1924 to 1928.[29] However, such a picture is incom-

21. Gouthey, "Is Evolution an Established Fact?" *PE* (4 August 1928) 6–7.

22. Evans letter to E. S. Williams (18 June 1928) (FPHC).

23. Gouthey, "The How of Best Living," *PE* (9 June 1928) 1, 7; "Appreciative Presbyterian," *PE* (7 July 1928) 17.

24. "Opposition of Science Falsely so-called," *COGE* (28 June 1919) 1–2, quoted in Numbers, "Creation, Evolution, and Holy Ghost Religion," 134–35.

25. "[Untitled]," *COGE* (13 June 1925) 2.

26. Lee, "Story of Creation," *COGE* (3 April 1926) 1–2.

27. Bowles, "God, Science, Evolution, and the Bible," *COGE* (24 July 1926) 1; Bowles, "God, Science, Evolution, and the Bible," *COGE* (31 July 1926) 1.

28. "Some Signs of the Last Days: We are Living in the Saturday Evening Age of Time," *COGE* (3 March 1928) 1–2; "Last Days of Charles Darwin," *COGE* (20 January 1934) 3, 12.

29. Masserano, "Study of Worship Forms," 52–53 (CBC Arch). Masserano makes a distinction between fundamentalist and Keswick authors, listing Bryan, Gray, Gordon, Pierson, Blackstone, Mauro, Scofield, and Charles Eerdman in the former and Simpson and Torrey in the latter. I find it puzzling that Torrey should

plete without comparing how many pentecostal and holiness writers were also featured in the same period. Taking 1925 as a representative year, I have found eighty-five different fundamentalist titles from twenty-seven authors offered a total of 130 times. Additionally, thirty-two protofundamentalist works were advertised fifty times from fifteen pens, with Andrew Murray topping the list at six.[30] Tallying these figures together, they represent 117 works from forty-two authors 180 times. Excluding children's books, eleven pentecostal writers with seventeen titles were featured eighty-six times. Three holiness titles appeared just six times in the same year. Compared to my earlier statistics on 1915 and 1920 in chapter 4, fundamentalist authors as a total were more heavily represented than in the past. Holiness writers also increased their mark, but their presence was still negligible compared to fundamentalist contributions.

Fundamentalist Interaction and the WCFA

In 1928 the WCFA passed the following resolution at their annual convention in Chicago:

> Whereas, the present wave of Modern Pentecostalism, often referred to as the "tongues movement," and the present wave of fanatical and unscriptural healing which is sweeping over the country today, has become a menace in many churches and a real injury to the sure testimony of Fundamentalist Christians . . .
> BE IT RESOLVED, That this convention go on record as unreservedly opposed to Modern Pentecostalism, including the speaking in unknown tongues, and the fanatical healing known as general healing in the atonement, and the perpetuation of the miraculous sign-healing of Jesus and His disciples, wherein they claim the only reason the church cannot perform these miracles is because of unbelief.[31]

As Russell Spittler has pointed out, unlike the other resolutions at the convention, this one failed to pass unanimously.[32] President Riley, for instance, did not think such an anathema was necessary since "the fanatical advocates of tongues" supported the inspiration of Scripture and the deity of Jesus Christ. Furthermore, Riley felt that their resolve fell outside the parameters of their nine-point confession to thwart modernism. Given his earlier support for healing, he may also have been uncomfortable with the latter part of the statement. Nevertheless, their attitudes had hardened.

Another factor contributing to their denunciation of pentecostalism was the reproach of modernists, who lumped the two movements together. "Modernism has left no stone unturned in its endeavor to discredit Fundamentalism," complained Riley in the official WCFA organ in 1926.[33] "It is not at all unusual to have them identify the [WCFA] with Pentecostalism." He added, "The great majority of Fundamentalists would not at all agree with Pentecostal leaders" and would rather, like Paul, speak five intelligible words than in

---

be "Keswick" and Pierson "fundamentalist." A better distinction would be between proto-fundamentalist/Keswick and fundamentalist.

30. See Appendix G.
31. Quoted in Spittler, "Are Pentecostals and Charismatics Fundamentalists?" 115–16 n. 11.
32. Spittler, "Are Pentecostals and Charismatics Fundamentalists?" 115–16 n. 11.
33. Riley, "Fundamentalism Knows No Relation to Pentecostalism," *CFSC* (January-March 1926) 31.

tongues. Riley appended these short comments with a slightly altered version of his 1907 sermon "Speaking with Tongues," significantly omitting the final paragraph in which he had encouraged those pentecostals who truly manifested the gift to render glory unto God.[34] Even so, that same year he affirmed his position that all the gifts including tongues "were intended for all ages [and are] not the subject of doubt with some of us."[35] The 1928 repudiation of pentecostalism by the WCFA was no doubt occasioned by these modernist slights on their movement. And though Riley had become less tolerant of tongues, the rebuke had not been instigated by him.

To pentecostals, ever craving respect from fundamentalist peers, the philip stung. Frodsham vented his displeasure with the WCFA in an op-ed aptly named "Disfellowshiped!"[36] In it he reiterated pentecostals' commitment to the fundamentals of the faith, listing a string of doctrines that composed a fundamentalist creed: Christ's virgin birth, deity, humanity, Lordship, vicarious death, bodily resurrection, ascension, and imminent return. He then articulated the pentecostal distinctives of tongues and healing as signs which shall follow believers. In other words, he appealed to the inerrant Word, proving that pentecostals accepted its whole counsel in practice as well as in theory. Pentecostals interpreted Scripture even more literally than fundamentalists, embodying the NT in a way that fundamentalists could not. Thus, David McDowell could state confidently that the AG constituted "the only truly fundamentalist fellowship [of size] over the earth today."[37] Frodsham also recognized that some fundamentalists like Torrey concurred with them that healing was provided for in the atonement. "Although we Pentecostal people have to be without the camp, we cannot afford to be bitter against those who do not see as we do," he concluded, encouraging his readers to pray for and love their brethren.[38]

AG evangelist Jacob Miller characterized fundamentalist opposition as a reaction to pentecostal success. It had so disturbed the churches that they were "trying with their skill and training to explain it all away."[39] Here again we find the fundamentalist resort to cessationism. By the late 1920s it had become their most effective retort against a movement that was sapping its strength. Miller referred to the tongues experience as a counter measure. He considered the Bible to be as reliable as the Sears and Roebuck catalogue; it both promised tongues and delivered. To an Oklahoma preacher who considered Paul's tongues a gift to preach in several languages, Miller demonstrated that Paul claimed to speak in "unknown tongues." But any fundamentalist would have agreed with Miller's conclusion: "It is no use to fight any longer when you can not use the Bible for a weapon."[40]

The AG had drawn inspiration from the WCFA in the past. *LRE* printed two addresses from its second conference when members had met at "Moody Tabernacle" in

---

34. Ibid., 31–35.
35. Quoted in Melon, *We've Been Robbed*, 40–44, cf. Riley, *Bible of the Expositor and the Evangelist* (1926).
36. Frodsham, "Disfellowshiped," *PE* (18 August 1928) 7.
37. McDowell, "A Parting Word," *PE* (8 September 1928) 7.
38. Frodsham, "Disfellowshiped," 7.
39. Miller, "Standing for the Pentecostal Testimony," *PE* (8 September 1928) 4.
40. Ibid., 4.

Chicago in 1920.⁴¹ The observer, probably Reiff, expressed assurance that the gathering would have a lasting impact in offsetting "the apostasy and infidelity that is sweeping the nominal church of today."⁴² In 1924 the WCFA field secretary for Illinois, a Presbyterian named Louis Stumpf, preached the first week of services for AG pastor Carl O'Guinn and the newly erected "Full Gospel Tabernacle" in Granite City with souls "saved and filled with the Holy Ghost."⁴³ That same year *PE* dedicated nearly a full page to a statement from the sixth WCFA convention in Minneapolis concerning their desire for revival.⁴⁴ A similar WCFA resolution pleading for intercession on the Fourth of July was endorsed two years later.⁴⁵ In its battle against modernism for the soul of America, such fundamentalist entreaties carried patriotic overtones, and pentecostals lined up to support them.

AG pastor A. G. Osterberg in Southern California participated in the 1930 WCFA conference in Los Angeles. The meeting stood firmly for the Bible but "was marred by a speaker taking a tremendous stand against the speaking in tongues in this day," fixating on the biblical phrase "tongues shall cease."⁴⁶ Osterberg also commented that the WCFA had taken a more pessimistic stance concerning the encroachment of modernism in the churches than in years past.⁴⁷ On the same pages that Osterberg's activities were recorded, Stanley Frodsham—who was hosting Osterberg at his home in Springfield—echoed his support for a "great three years' program" of the fundamentalists to unite evangelicals worldwide to promote missions, Bible conferences, evangelistic campaigns and state organizations, but he hastened to add that whereas human plans may fail, "one word given in the power of the Holy Ghost is worth more than ten thousand spoken in the feverishness of our own verbosity."⁴⁸ Despite their differences, pentecostals were one in spirit with fundamentalists when it came to world evangelization and national revival, but the feeling was rarely mutual.

John Roach Straton and Uldine Utley

One exception was John Roach Straton, who sponsored pentecostal child evangelist Uldine Utley in a New York campaign. Straton first heard Utley at a Bible conference in Green Cove Springs, Florida in February 1926. The platform included Canadian fundamentalist T. T. Shields, whose delayed train providentially allowed Utley to greet the initial evening

---

41. L. Broughton, "Bringing Back the King," *LRE* (July 1920) 18–21; G. Johnson, "Christ the Door of the New Christianity," *LRE* (August 1920) 6–10. The *LRE* also reprinted material from MBI conferences such as Founder's Week (e.g., H. Long, "Where the Hidden Things are Found," *LRE* [April 1921] 18–19).

42. [Reiff], "A Timely Conference," *LRE* (July 1920) 13.

43. O'Guin, "Dedication of New Tabernacle at Granite City," *PE* (20 September 1924) 13. The church had started in 1920 with a handful of believers in a saloon building but now had one of the nicest buildings in the city, according to the local paper.

44. "Coming Revival," *PE* (12 July 1924) 7.

45. "July 4th as a Day of Intercession," *PE* (12 June 1926) 13. This article was repeated the next week.

46. Frodsham, "Editor's Notebook," *PE* (27 September 1930) 4.

47. Frodsham, "Editor's Notebook," *PE* (4 October 1930) 4.

48. Frodsham, "Editor's Notebook," *PE* (27 September 1930) 4–5.

session alongside Straton.[49] Straton was so enthralled that he immediately invited her to preach at a Baptist conference in West Palm Beach. Due to illness, Straton was unable to speak to the faithful at First Baptist, so Utley delighted the audience in his stead. "Surely we are seeing the fulfilment of the ancient prophecy 'that our sons and our daughters would prophesy' and . . . 'A little child shall lead them,'" he wrote in a letter introducing her to the congregation.[50] Already a seasoned preacher since her first sermon in Oakland in 1921 following her conversion under McPherson, Utley commanded large crowds wherever she went.

Upon Straton's request, Utley arrived in New York for a summer campaign, opening with a sermon on June 13, 1926 at Calvary Baptist. Her charm and innocence attracted the attention for which Straton was hoping, resulting in widespread publicity in the local papers.[51] The campaign concluded at Madison Square Garden on October 31 with fourteen thousand attendees.[52] To the hundred-strong Baptist Ministerial Association gathered at Madison Avenue Baptist, she discoursed for an hour, garnering their unanimous approval.[53] Utley took New York by storm and won the hearts of all who heard her.

When she wasn't conducting services in civic auditoriums, she often could be found in the pulpits of mainline churches, particularly Methodist and Baptist. In the winter of 1926–1927 she addressed Greene Avenue Baptist in Brooklyn, Olivet Covenant Presbyterian and Simpson Methodist, both in Philadelphia, and Trinity-Hedding Methodist in Jersey City, New Jersey.[54] In May 1927 she was at Carnegie Hall, just across the street from Calvary Baptist, laboring in the city until August 21. She also spoke at the Winona Lake Bible Conference on August 14, where fundamentalist stalwarts like Sunday and Bryan had summer cottages.[55] 1927 marked her height and decline, largely because she was passing puberty and the innocent "child evangelist" was losing effect.[56] Unable to handle the stresses of adulthood, perhaps little prepared for life off the stage, she had a nervous breakdown and was committed to an asylum, institutionalized for the remainder of her life. In Blumhofer's words, "in the end [she] became a tragic victim of her own success."[57]

Blumhofer considers Utley to be "not a Pentecostal," but Utley's influence on Straton's son Warren seems to have been instrumental in his encounter with the Holy Spirit, at least according to his brother in a 1990 interview.[58] Besides, though her messages were not

---

49. Blumhofer, "A Little Child," 309; Lavigne, comp., *Utley*, 12–13, 59 (FPHC).

50. Lavigne, *Utley*, 15.

51. Articles on Utley were reported in the *New York Times, The World, New York American*, and *New York Herald Tribune* on the following day (see Lavigne, *Utley*, 26–28).

52. W. Pigueron, "Closing Campaign," *Petals* (October 1927) 8.

53. Lavigne, *Utley*, 77–78, quoting from *Petals* (November 1926) 6, 11.

54. "In the Churches," *Petals* (February 1927) 8–9.

55. Utley, "Wanted—A Workshop," *Petals* (October 1927) 1, 4.

56. Blumhofer, "A Little Child," 315.

57. Ibid., 317. Utley died in 1995 in San Bernadino, California.

58. Ibid., 312; George Douglas Straton, interview by Wayne Warner, 1990 (FPHC). George Straton was not certain if the baptism of his brother happened directly under Utley but attributed her influence as the major contributing factor towards it. Sadly Warren died in a car accident in 1966.

generally pentecostal in nature as a reading through her periodical *Petals from the Rose of Sharon* will indicate, she nevertheless was identified as pentecostal in the literature of the time and came through a pentecostal conversion. She preached on the Baptism of the Spirit in Straton's pulpit in September 1926, resulting in conversions and "reconsecrations"— though no tongues were reported.[59] Straton believed her to be pentecostal and also entertained one other female pentecostal evangelist, whom his son George tentatively identified as Amy Stockton.[60] The Straton family also enjoyed McPherson's message at Glad Tidings in New York in 1928.

Ever combative, Straton defended Utley's ministry to his own ranks. According to an Associated Press report in the *Springfield Leader*, his son Warren lay prone on the floor during a Monday night young people's meeting at Calvary Baptist in June or July 1927, though it is unlikely that Utley was present.[61] Warren sang in an unknown tongue "in a most beautiful way" while his face appeared "illuminated by joy," according to the elder Straton. After the event, Warren, already ordained in the Baptist ministry by his father, showed marked interest in Bible study, with an improvement to both his spiritual and physical condition. Pressure mounted at Calvary Baptist the following evening when five deacons resigned over the pastor's introduction of "Pentecostalism" to the church. Despite the defection, Straton remained steadfast in his support of Utley. Early in 1928 he preached twice for the newly installed pastor L. R. Keys at the AG "Full Gospel Tabernacle" in Fresno, California, where his services were followed by 13-year-old evangelist Helen Campbell.[62]

Straton's advocacy of pentecostal theology was also evinced in his *Divine Healing in Scripture and Life* (1927), stenographically copied while he preached. He had first witnessed miraculous healing through the deacons of his Baltimore pastorate twenty years before but felt obliged to write on this "sorely neglected truth" after Utley's "remarkable revival."[63] He believed that "healing in the atonement" in no way detracted from the Cross of Christ or the faith of the believer, appealing extensively to A. J. Gordon.[64] "Neither sin nor disease was natural or native to man," he observed, but the atonement "was designed to nullify and overcome *all* the works of the devil."[65] *PE* reprinted his seventh sermon as a two-part series under the title "God's Conditional Covenant to Heal His People."[66] Straton conducted healing services in the fall of 1927, which the American Association for the Advancement of Atheism attempted to stop by charging him with "practicing medicine without a license." *LRE* encouraged his efforts at healing while applauding his opposition to modernism, "Dr. Straton is the author of several books on Evolution, but the manifestation of the power of God in his meetings will build up faith in the living Word and destroy

---

59. Lavigne, *Utley*, 69

60. Douglas Straton interview, 1990.

61. "Pastor Tells of Visitation," *PE* (9 July 1927) 9.

62. Mrs. W. F. Fiese, "Progressive Work," *PE* (17 March 1928) 13.

63. Straton, *Divine Healing*, 7–8.

64. Ibid., 109–11.

65. Ibid., 111–12, emphasis in original.

66. Straton, "God's Conditional Covenant to Heal His People," *PE* (8 September 1928) 2–3; *PE* (15 September 1928) 2–3. See *Divine Healing*, 96ff.

unbelief far more than arguments or debates ever could."[67] Straton felt likewise towards Utley, having called her the greatest weapon against modernism "in all its forms."[68]

Pentecostals and the Bible

Pentecostals never doubted the inspiration of Scripture, but the AG discussed it in earnest only in the later half of the 1920s. Frank Peckham's graduation speech at CBI in 1926 betrayed his desire that the upcoming generation of pentecostal leaders be inculcated in fundamentalist theology. His major points were those which any fundamentalist might have employed against the higher critics, and he depended upon Straton for much of his information in verifying the authenticity of the Bible.[69] The Bible was true because it claimed to be so and had been preserved through history despite all attempts to annihilate it. Its unity and fulfilled prophecy gave it internal consistency, and the changed character of those who imbibed from it confirmed its revolutionary power. His logic in calculating the probability that Christ could fulfill 333 OT prophecies was fundamentalist in tenor.[70] He affirmed the AG fundamental truth that it was an "infallible" book throughout while avoiding the fundamentalist litmus-word "inerrant." Also, the "scientific" proof of Holy Writ that fundamentalists used was still a few years away.

Earlier attempts at the defense of Scripture were usually no more than declarations of its authority or inspiration by the Spirit. One appeal to its power came in a 1917 *PE* article titled "The Bible—Its own Advocate." However, it was not from a pentecostal pen but from an excerpt by J. W. W. Moeran, an Irish clergyman, relating a conversation he had had with Charles Spurgeon in the previous century.[71] The anecdotal purport was telling: pentecostals could understand stories; didactic arguments did not "preach." On December 31, 1921, Jethro Walthall, provoked by a "man of skeptical trend of mind," demonstrated the Bible's veracity at a conference in Wesson, Arkansas. His case fell into four categories: the unity of Scripture, the account of creation versus evolution, the prophetic accuracy of the OT, and the indestructibility of the Bible in the face of opposition.[72] The content from this former Baptist was similar to Peckham's—minus the detailed analysis. In the postwar environment there are hints of an emerging fundamentalist-consciousness within pentecostalism.

Pentecostals relied upon fundamentalists in defending the Word. Burt McCafferty, evangelist and teacher, supplied eight reasons for believing the Good Book, although he compiled his list from other sources.[73] An article on the inspiration of Scripture in October 1924 was reprinted from evangelical magazine *The Christian* (London), and the

67. [Reiff], "'With Persecution,'" *LRE* (December 1927) 13.

68. Quoted in Blumhofer, "A Little Child," 314.

69. Peckham, "Bible is the Word of God," *PE* (3 July 1926) 5–6. Peckham does not name which of Straton's works he drew from.

70. Ibid., 6. The probability was one in 84 billion.

71. Moeran, "The Bible—Its own Advocacy," *WE* (13 January 1917) 5.

72. Waltham, "What Proof have we that the Bible is the Word of God," *PE* (15 April 1922) 6.

73. McCafferty, "Eight Reasons We Believe the Bible is the Word of God," *PE* (17 May 1924) 6.

one in February 1925 from *Missionary Review of the World*, edited by A. T. Pierson's son Delevan.[74] Ivan Panin, a Russian émigré who used "numerics" to prove the Bible true, received attention in *PE* in 1924 and 1928 under "Inspiration of Scripture Scientifically Demonstrated," which had first appeared as a letter in the *New York Sun* in 1899.[75] Charles Robinson later devoted an entire appendix to Panin in *God and His Bible* (1939).[76] *PE* printed a full article from James Gray in 1929, demonstrating the reliability of the biblical text.[77] Many of Gray's books were offered through the *PE*, including *How to Master the English Bible* (1904), *Synthetic Bible Studies* (1906) and the single volume *Christian Worker's Commentary* (1915).[78] Another Moody Press writer who made his way into *PE*'s pages was J. H. McConkey, purveying tips on how to study the Word.[79]

As the decade progressed, pentecostals lent more aid to protecting the Bible from higher criticism, cued by the fundamentalists. Pentecostalism was inherently open to direct revelation, though wise leaders cautioned that "prophetic" words be confirmed through Scripture itself. In 1915 D. W. Kerr advocated what he called "Spontaneous Theology," that is, perceiving the Word through immediate revelation—though he did not deny the value of systematic study.[80] Fundamentalists would have thrown hermeneutical conniptions at such a suggestion. By the 1920s the tone had changed. Donald Gee was more sensitive than most to "destructive" criticism. "We are only just beginning to reap the harvest in every sphere—religious, moral, and political," he feared.[81] He defended the Bible on grounds of Jesus' testimony, the "wonder" it instilled (including a bit on "numerics"), the unity it possessed, its endurance over the centuries, and its power to change lives.[82] Early pentecostals would not have denigrated these claims, but such attestations seemed unnecessary then. They assumed they were biblicists and had no enemies within the camp to challenge it.

Likewise, evangelist Bert Webb asked in 1929 whether indeed the Word of God was inspired or not. As with Gee, Webb blamed the slack spiritual condition of the country on higher criticism and its undermining of faith in the denominations.[83] Webb too appealed to the unity of the thirty-eight writers and to the Bible's popularity. He also upheld the authenticity of Jonah and the big fish. Webb charged "modernistic, infidelic 'preachers'" with robbing Christianity of salvation through Christ. In light of the evidence, he implored readers to "affirm our unalterable allegiance to the precepts of His Word and stand firm

---

74. "How We Know the Bible is Inspired," *PE* (11 October 1924) 4; "What a Bible Can Do," *PE* (28 February 1925) 4.

75. Panin, "Inspiration of Scripture Scientifically Demonstrated," *PE* (8 March 1924) 9, 14; *PE* (26 May 1928) 6–7.

76. Robinson, *God and His Bible*, 131–60.

77. Gray, "Tracing the Bible through the Centuries," *PE* (2 March 1929) 6–7.

78. "Suggestions for Christmas Gifts," *PE* (1 December 1923) 24; "Helpful Books," *PE* (19 July 1924) 13; "Books & Bibles," *PE* (10 January 1920) 9.

79. McConkey, "How to Study the Word," *PE* (20 July 1929) 3, 8–9.

80. Kerr, "Spontaneous Theology," *WE* (17 April 1915) 3.

81. Gee, "Proving the Bible True," *PE* (11 September 1926) 6.

82. Compare Gee on the number seven to Panin in Robinson, *God and His Bible*, 155.

83. Webb, "The Bible: Is it the Inspired Word of God, or the Work of Man?" *PE* (24 August 1929) 7.

as the Rock of Gibraltar for the entire Bible."[84] This reaction to modernism would become more prominent in the next decade, pushing pentecostals and fundamentalists strategically towards one another against a common foe.

In 1928 Charles Robinson asked for the first time in *PE*, "Modernism—What is it?" He found consolation in a recent book, *The Bible under Fire* by John Campbell, professor at Carson and Newman College in Jefferson City, Tennessee, and for sale through Gospel Publishing House. Robinson requested that pentecostals purchase Campbell's book to distribute to friends and donate to public libraries "for the discomfiture of the enemies of the Bible."[85] William Moody (no relation to D. L. Moody) was saddened when a candidate for the Methodist ministry was rejected for adhering to the Bible. The church where he had been spiritually nourished had betrayed the faith. "What is thy name?" he lamented. "Shall I write it *Modernist*? Nay, rather *Traitor* seems to be more fitting."[86] Hope however could be discovered in the first column of the same page in *PE*, where a Methodist church in Bellville, Illinois reportedly accepted pentecostalism following a campaign under Charles Price.[87] The pastor was baptized in the Spirit along with a local Baptist preacher as a result. The panacea of education and legislation could not solve the world's problems, declared acting editor Harold Moss a week later,[88] and soon the world would feel the pinch of the depression clamping down upon it.

Pentecostals, Bible Conferences, and Dispensational Charts

Bible conferences were a trademark of the fundamentalist movement. Winona Lake was one of the more famed. The training school which developed from the summer courses there was administered at one time by G. Campbell Morgan. Its centrality in Indiana made it an ideal crossroads for itinerant Bible teachers on the conference circuit. Another, Montrose Bible Conference in Pennsylvania, was initiated by R. A. Torrey in 1907 as a reaction to the increasingly liberal bent of Northfield under D. L. Moody's son. Riley established Medicine Lake, Minnesota, for his summer retreats, Gaebelein held his on Long Island, and Moody Bible Institute sponsored one at Cedar Lake, Indiana. Other venues included Red Feather Lakes in Colorado, Lake Geneva in Wisconsin, Eagles Mere in Pennsylvania, and the Boardwalk Conference in Atlantic City, New Jersey, among dozens of others great and small.

Holiness folk on the other hand had conducted camp meetings, and pentecostals followed in their walk by either taking over existing holiness camps or establishing their own. The earliest church-sponsored Bible conference in the AG came in 1919 at Bethel Temple in Los Angeles.[89] By the mid-1920s Bible conferences increased in popularity, reflecting

---

84. Ibid., 7.

85. Robinson, "Modernism—What Is It?" *PE* (10 November 1928) 9. J. Campbell, *The Bible under Fire* (1928). Campbell attacks higher criticism, modernists and evolutionists. As Robinson justly stated, "It is a splendid and very readable book."

86. Moody, "A Searching Question," *PE* (5 January 1929) 5.

87. "Two Preachers Baptized," *PE* (5 January 1929) 5. Forty-eight were baptized in water.

88. Moss, "World's Need," *PE* (12 January 1929) 1.

89. Gortner, "Ex-Dancing Master Receives his Pentecost," *CE* (22 February 1919) 7.

the growing influence of fundamentalist norms upon the AG. The Southern Missouri District held its first "Bible convention" in 1924, mostly for the encouragement of ministers.[90] When Tennessee came under Southern Missouri auspices in 1925, it immediately planned a Bible convention in Sharrion for December.[91] Many conventions both local and regional had a prophetic flare to them, such as those held by evangelist Frederick Childe in seven California locations from February to June 1928.[92] His two-week long "chart lecture" at Monrovia in December 1929 stirred the interest of people from "other churches."[93] J. N. Hoover, the Baptist from Santa Cruz baptized under Shreve in 1925, traveled widely through AG churches. His April 1929 afternoon lectures on prophecy at Collier's church in Washington, DC, attracted delegates from "50 miles distant," including a number of denominational pastors.[94]

Finis J. Dake excelled at his interpretation of Revelation. Dake graduated from CBI in 1925 and found his niche in teaching. By 1928 he was principal of the Texico Bible Institute in Dallas, which later united with Southwestern, where he adopted the mantle of Dean of Men. In 1932 he relocated to Zion, Illinois and established Shiloh Bible Institute in Dowie's old home, which morphed into Great Lakes Biblical Institute before merging with CBI. Dake spent much of his time toting his dispensational chart "The Plan of the Ages" to churches and conventions. Amy Yeomans described it as a "very fine chart" at the Lake Geneva camp in Alexandria, Minnesota.[95] Appearing with Price for the 1935 Illinois camp meeting, he was appreciated for his ability to handle "puzzling questions" in Scripture.[96] Dake's elaborate, hand-drawn chart could be ordered in two sizes (2'x 6' or 4'x 16 ½') and referred to alongside his books *Dispensational Truth* and *Revelation Expounded* (1931).[97] He also hawked "dispensational notes" for church classes of twelve or more at a discounted rate. Parts of his drawings look suspiciously similar to *The Book of Revelation* (1919) by Clarence Larkin, a Philadelphia draftsman and ardent fundamentalist.[98]

Such charts and evangelists proliferated in the 1930s as a resurgent pentecostal faith offered hope to a depressed population. Not to be outdone by Dake, "Brother Bragg" carried a chart measuring 4'x 22', "which was of great help in explaining the dispensations."[99] Roxie Alford lectured on Daniel and Revelation from "a large chart" for a week at Anacortes, Washington, where Baptists and Free Methodists were filled with the Spirit under her and

---

90. "Notes from So. Missouri District," *PE* (19 December 1925) 12.

91. "Tennessee Bible Convention," *PE* (5 December 1925) 22. The AG struggled to maintain a presence in Tennessee, which is why the presbytery decided to subsume it under the much stronger Southern Missouri District to the protest of Arkansas leader Jethro Walthall.

92. "California Prophetic Bible Conferences," *PE* (18 February 1928) 14.

93. C. Sigafoose, "Bible Conference," *PE* (14 December 1929) 12.

94. Collier, "Bible Conference," *PE* (25 May 1929) 12.

95. Yeomans, "Echoes from Lake Geneva Camp," *PE* (9 August 1930) 13.

96. G. Phillips, "Lincoln, Ill.," *PE* (10 August 1935) 12.

97. See Dake, *Revelation Expounded*, 255.

98. E.g., Dake's illustration of the Babylonian statue from Daniel 2 used in his dispensational chart is identical to that drawn by Larkin, *Book of Revelation*, 51. Cf. Marsden, *American Culture*, 51–54.

99. B. Greene, "Maud, Okla.," *PE* (20 June 1936) 12.

her husband's ministry.[100] Ora De Von was especially active in bringing the dispensational message to churches. "We were able to see so much as he taught from his 24 foot chart, also using several small ones," Pastor E. F. Hewitt of Denver exulted.[101] Lectures concerning the future were useful evangelistic tools and guided conservative believers through pentecostal doorways.

Under the dispensational rubric, two books received special attention: Daniel and Revelation. A. S. Copley had established an independent pentecostal mission in Kansas City. The first Bible conference at his Christian Assembly was held from October 16 to November 16, 1924. His assistant in ministry, Mary Bodie, spoke on Daniel while Copley delved into Revelation.[102] After retirement in 1946, J. N. Gortner published only two commentaries on the Bible, Daniel and Revelation, based on lecture notes from classes he had taught at Glad Tidings Bible Institute in San Francisco since the '30s.[103] Likewise, Myer Pearlman also wrote devotional commentaries on Revelation (1941) and Daniel (1943).[104] For him, Revelation was "The Drama of Dramas," as he titled an address to a crowd at Eureka Springs in 1930.[105] Even so, Pearlman, ever attentive to spiritual application, was not slave-bound to the dispensational scheme and did not hold to literalistic interpretations of Scripture. His Jewish upbringing would not stand for it.

Though we anticipate here, in the late '30s these Bible conferences transformed into "Deeper Life" conventions—strikingly reminiscent of the "Victorious Life" conferences inaugurated by Charles Gaulledette Trumbull, editor of *SST* and a disciple of Scofield. "Deeper Life" services were conducted at the Eastern District Camp in Green Lane, Pennsylvania in 1935, with conventions appearing in Syracuse, New York in September 1935, in Granite City, Illinois in August 1936, which brought "spiritual awakening," and in Cincinnati in September 1938 under evangelist Hattie Hammond, which attracted many from outside the denomination and were "owned and blessed of God."[106] "Deeper Life Books" featured meditative works by William Biederwolf, Oswald Chambers, Andrew Murray, Hannah Whitall Smith, Brother Lawrence, Donald Gee, and Alice Flower.[107] MBI professor Max Reich's *The Deeper Life* (1936) and W. B. Riley's *The Victorious Life* (1937) were both sold through GPH. Pentecostals drank from the writings of these deeper life thinkers and mimicked their meetings in a uniquely pentecostal way. As the depression turned people inward in the 1930s, "deeper" spiritual themes resonated with the despondent and hungry.

---

100. W. Lewis, "Ancortes, Wash.," *PE* (15 August 1936) 10.
101. E. Hewitt, "Denver, Colo.," *PE* (7 May 1938) 12.
102. Franklin, *Copley*, 81–82.
103. Gortner, *Studies in Daniel* (1948); Gortner, *Studies in Revelation* (1948).
104. Pearlman, *Windows into the Future* (1941), Pearlman, *Daniel Speaks Today* (1943).
105. Pearlman, "Drama of Dramas," *PE* (4 October 1930) 1, 6–7.
106. W. Palmer, "Eastern District Camp," *PE* (19 October 1935) 21; "Deeper Life Convention," *PE* (24 August 1935) 13; E. Chamberlain, "Granite City, Ill.," *PE* (22 August 1936) 12; O. Nash, "'Deeper Life' Convention," *PE* (13 August 1938) 13; H. "Cincinnati Convention," *PE* (5 November 1938) 18–19.
107. "Deeper Life Books," *PE* (15 January 1938) 16.

Fundamentalist Attacks

D. M. Panton, dubbed the "prince of prophecy" in England, launched his own periodical in 1925. It wasn't long before *The Dawn* targeted pentecostalism *á la* Gaebelein. Quoting from *Watch and Pray* in California, one article warned Christians to test the "spirits" lest they find they had been "honouring and even worshipping a demon who has masqueraded as the blessed Holy Spirit."[108] Panton intimated that Satan's first deceit in the Garden of Eden was to imitate tongues through the serpent.[109] The modern gift for him was a mockery of the "covetable charisma" of the apostles. He printed George Kennan's description of trances of certain mystics in Siberia who suffered from "Anadyrski sickness," named after a regional village. These women allegedly produced foreign languages, usually identified as "Gakout," demanding they be given peculiar objects from places they had never visited in order to pacify them.[110] The connection to pentecostalism was tenuous at best, but that mattered not to Panton. It was a clear case of demons manipulating the oral faculty.

Panton derided tongues as a branch of "hydra-headed spiritism" along with Montanism and the Irvingites.[111] Spiritualists too had their glossolalic practitioners, but in his opinion no true miracle had taken place since the close of the apostolic age.[112] He blasted evangelicals who merely cautioned against the excesses of tongues as tepid, "half afraid and wholly uninformed."[113] Tongues were the latest manifestation of a satanic conspiracy to dupe believers in the end times. In his mind, spiritualism and pentecostalism had mixed to such a degree that they were inseparable.[114]

And yet his charge on the cessation of miracles was inconsistent. Where he said on one page "no signal miracle has ever been wrought since the death of the last Apostle" he wrote seven pages later that he and his supporters were "no enemies of the miraculous" and that he was "aware of no proof that the gifts of the Holy Ghost were ever withdrawn on the part of God."[115] However, these miracles were to be restored "at a future, unknown date," presumably upon Jews during the Great Tribulation. The key to the distinction is Panton's use of "signal," which designated the miraculous as a sign of apostolic authority. Thus fundamentalists who used the cessationist argument could still hold to the presence of modern miracles (salvation, providence and even divine healing [in Warfield's case through medicine]) without betraying their revivalist convictions.

Gaebelein was on the warpath as much as ever. He complained of McPherson's ostentatious float at the annual Rose Bowl Parade for New Years in 1925.[116] Her lavish costume—adorned like a "cabaret queen" as the *New York Herald-Tribune* put it—was evidence of her

---

108. "Tongues," *Dawn* (15 February 1926) 483.

109. Editorial note to Kennan, "Demonic Gift of Tongues," *Dawn* (15 September 1926) 275.

110. Kennan, "Demonic Gift of Tongues," 275–78.

111. Panton, "Spirit Tests," *Dawn* (15 January 1927) 435–36.

112. Panton, "Glossolalia," *Dawn* (15 October 1928) 290–91; Panton, "The Miraculous," *Dawn* (15 October 1928) 291.

113. Panton, "Miraculous Gifts," *Dawn* (15 October 1928) 292.

114. Panton, "Modern Irruption of Demon Powers," *Dawn* (15 October 1928) 293–98.

115. Panton, "The Miraculous," 291; Panton, "The Modern Irruption," 298.

116. Gaebelein, "Mrs. McPherson's Expensive Float," *Hope* (April 1925) 626–27.

un-Christ-like character.[117] Leaving no doubt as to his feelings, he detested the "Nauseating Picture" she gave him.[118] One of her followers, Cecile Kraum, attempted suicide, confessing that she no longer believed in McPherson's "rah-rah religion."[119] Gaebelein perceived that insanity reigned supreme in the movement, filling the asylums of the Pacific Coast with its babbling wreckage. He felt it his duty to expose its misguided fanaticism and save Christianity from its diabolic snare.

Lewis Sperry Chafer, pastor of Scofield Memorial in Dallas, rued the crosscurrent between fundamentalists seeking power and pentecostals supplying it in their churches. Like a car discharging its tank by running too fast, so these ministers had been bamboozled by Satan into a spiritual dynamic beyond the bounds of the sacred text.[120] Chafer quoted in full from Norris's 1923 statement as it appeared in *PE* as an example of such wayward thinking.[121] Through dispensational acumen, Chafer dissuaded would-be exegetes from confusing the anointing fire at Pentecost (Acts 2) with the purifying fire proclaimed by John the Baptist (Matt 3). One need not linger for ten days for the Spirit since He already descended at Pentecost and now baptized believers at the new birth.[122] The bulk of his grievance was dedicated to this last point. In this Chafer adhered closely to the arguments of Scofield, whom Chafer had assisted as minister in Northfield, Massachusetts and as educator with Scofield's correspondence courses in New York.

While fundamentalists were genuinely repelled by pentecostal practices, they struggled to ascribe an active role to the Holy Spirit in the lives of Christians that was not mere negation of pentecostal beliefs. R. A. Torrey issued *The Holy Spirit* in 1927, just two years before his death. He had by this point abandoned his post at Biola to pursue full-time evangelistic work. In an earlier treatise, *The Person and Work of the Holy Spirit* (1910), he had rejected tongues as the necessary sign of baptism on the grounds that many charisms were distributed by the Spirit and because it was the least important of the gifts.[123] To his credit, Torrey's position changed little if at all over the years since *The Baptism with the Holy Spirit* had come out in 1895. He still maintained in *The Holy Spirit* that baptism was induced after conversion and that one could obtain it through seven precise steps, which included repentance, obedience, and asking for it by faith.[124] The only notable difference is that he expanded his illustrations over the years. The absence of remarks against pentecostalism in *The Holy Spirit* cannot be attributed to any aversion to controversy. More likely he had said what he wanted in 1913 and did not want to distract the reader with undue focus on glossolalia.

Robert McQuilkin, founder of Columbia Bible School in South Carolina, challenged pentecostalism's assumptions in a two-part article in *SST* in 1929. McQuilkin demonstrat-

---

117. Gaebelein, "The Notorious Woman Leader Leaves for Europe," *Hope* (November 1928) 300.
118. Gaebelein, "A Nauseating Picture," *Hope* (September 1929) 137.
119. Gaebelein, "The Rah-Rah Religion of Mrs. McPherson," *Hope* (October 1927) 232–33.
120. Chafer, "Careless Misstatements of Truth," *Hope* (March 1924) 540–41.
121. "A Fundamentalist Speaks Out," *PE* (10 November 1923) 5. Chafer quotes entire text on 541.
122. Chafer, "Careless," 542–44.
123. Torrey, *Person and Work of the Holy Spirit*, 184–85.
124. Torrey, *The Holy Spirit*, 154–92.

ed a reasonable familiarity with pentecostal tenets and struck an irenic tone in explicating them.[125] He had spoken in at least one pentecostal church and knew several of its leaders. He admitted that at first glance the pentecostal precepts appeared cogent. The chief difficulty lay in their emphasis on Acts, thus basing their doctrine on a single book. Liberals, he pointed out, were guilty of the same misuse of Scripture by locking into the Gospels.[126] In keeping with a fundamentalist motif, McQuilkin suggested that one's understanding of Spirit-baptism should center on the epistles. Here there was only one mention of baptism where Paul averred that believers were baptized into one body (1 Cor 12:13). As for the four baptisms recorded in Acts (the Jews at Pentecost, the Samaritans, Cornelius the Gentile and John's schismatic disciples at Ephesus), each incident was a unique case to demonstrate that God was representatively enfolding different ethnic and religious groups into the expanding church.[127]

In the second article McQuilkin compared the list of charismata in 1 Corinthians 12 to that found in Romans 12, noting that they were nearly identical.[128] The gist was that the Holy Spirit empowered what seemed to be mundane talents like tithing and showing mercy alongside the spectacular gifts of tongues and prophecy. He was reluctant to dismiss the vitality of his pentecostal acquaintances, such as a young unnamed British minister whose skill at soul-winning he coveted.[129] But neither could one ignore the validity of those through whom God performed miracles but did not exercise tongues. McQuilkin drew just such a comparison between two missionaries in India, one a pentecostal and the other not.[130] Both displayed exuberant joy and harvested many souls. We should expect a great outpouring of the Spirit, for Joel 2 remained unfulfilled and the age of miracles had not passed, he argued. The key for McQuilkin, a prominent advocate of Keswick, was to abide in Christ, the source of power.

Pentecostal Responses

Frodsham detected a certain "softness" in fundamentalism, siding with a "well-known evangelist" who said that conservatives were too timid to "split" from ecclesial hierarchy over the deity of Christ and His atoning blood.[131] He expressed his gratitude when T. T. Shields absconded with eighty-two churches after being voted out of the Ontario-Quebec Baptist convention in 1927, hoping that "a similar healthy separation will come about in the Baptists and Presbyterians in this country."[132] Such would happen with the Bible Baptist Union, a more radical group than the Fundamentalist Fellowship of the Northern Baptist Convention, but not until 1932, forming the General Association of Regular

---

125. McQuilkin, "What is Pentecost's Message Today?" *SST* (12 January 1929) 19, 22.
126. Ibid., 19.
127. Ibid., 22.
128. McQuilkin, "What Is Pentecost's Message Today?" *SST* (26 January 1929) 52–53.
129. Ibid., 52.
130. Ibid., 53.
131. Frodsham, "No Separation," *PE* (4 June 1927) 5.
132. Frodsham, "Outlook and Uplook," *PE* (14 January 1928) 3.

Baptists.[133] (Riley did not participate in the revolt, though many of his former pupils from Northwestern did.) Likewise, Princetonian J. Gresham Machen severed his roots in 1936 to help establish the Orthodox Presbyterian Church. These developments were too slow for Frodsham, who was still complaining of fundamentalism's gelatin nature in 1930.[134]

Confronting fundamentalist assaults, Frodsham disclaimed the notion that pentecostals were prone to "fits and ravings" as *Our Hope* had charged. As to the assertion in *The Dawn* that pentecostals did not "test the spirits," Frodsham referred to Donald Gee's article "Trying the Spirits" in *PE*, which in his view Panton had misrepresented.[135] He pronounced an unsigned disparagement from *SST*, reprinted in *Our Hope*, worthy of the wastebasket.[136] The article recounted one woman's dubious experience with tongues and her eventual renunciation of the pentecostal movement after conflicting with her husband, whom she had rejected as her "spiritual head." (The woman, as it turns out, was a member of Louis Bauman's United Brethren church in Long Beach, California.) He noted that a recent book, *The Leaven of the Sadducees* (by Ernest Gordon), skewered "atheistic Modernism" while decrying "the miraculous in Scripture."[137] Equally he felt that pentecostals must be warned of the "leaven of the Pharisees." Frodsham did not expect modern Pharisees to be any more appreciative of miracles than their ancient namesakes.

Pentecostals were just as adamant to protect their territory as fundamentalists were to attack it. It was likely Frodsham who penned "As the Spirit Gave them Utterance" for November 1926. "Why do people oppose us?" he asked. "Man [sic] fights it because the devil hates it. All the more reason why we should contend for it," he answered.[138] In typical pentecostal fashion, he warned that those who attributed the work of the Holy Spirit to the devil were guilty of blasphemy, an application fundamentalists should have recognized from Scofield.[139] It may well have been Frodsham two months later who condemned the Pharisees for condemning others, just as Simon the Pharisee had pronounced judgment on Jesus.[140] The editor was well versed in fundamentalist literature and could not easily let a slight go unanswered, despite his protestations to the contrary.

In their casting of stones at pentecostals, their enemies had overlooked the gold lying underneath, according to Percy Corry, a British pentecostal missionary to Afghanistan. Mental capacity alone would not advance the kingdom of God, he insisted. "Can you afford to sit longer on the fence and look askance at this blessed gift of tongues?"[141] Corry

133. Trollinger, *God's Empire*, 60.

134. Frodsham, "'Too Soft to Split,'" *PE* (28 June 1930) 7.

135. Gee, "Trying the Spirits," *PE* (17 April 1926) 2–3; Gee, "Trying the Sprits," *PE* (24 April 1926) 2–3.

136. "My Experience of Speaking in Tongues," *Hope* (May 1927) 684–86. The *SST* article ran for February 19, 1927.

137. Frodsham, "From the Pentecostal Viewpoint," *PE* (9 July 1927) 4. *The Leaven of the Sadducees* was written by A. J. Gordon's son Ernest in 1926.

138. [Frodsham], "As the Spirit gave them Utterance," *PE* (6 November 1926) 1, 6.

139. Scofield describes the "unpardonable sin" (Matt 12:31) as "ascribing to Satan the works of the Spirit" (*OSRB*, 1013).

140. "In which Class are You?" *PE* (1 January 1927) 5.

141. Corry, "First Corinthians Fourteen," *PE* (30 October 1926) 9.

concentrated his intellect on 1 Corinthians 14, a letter scribed for "ALL the churches."[142] He recognized that worship should be executed "decently and in order," but this applied to both pentecostals and their detractors. For example, he once reprimanded a brother for speaking in tongues during a communion service because no interpretation had been given.[143] If one allowed for gifted teachers and preachers, then one must allow for all the spiritual gifts in Corinthians—including Paul's direction to "forbid not tongues."[144] In his view, fundamentalists were culpable for partially reading Scripture, the very thing for which they accused pentecostals.

Ernest S. Williams parried a "Fundamentalist Magazine" published in Denver. The author of the piece inadvertently supported the pentecostal position that the gift of tongues in Acts was "an evidential sign."[145] Williams parted from the author's contention that tongues ceased before the completion of the NT. Quoting from Anglican commentator F. W. Farrar, he countered that the Corinthians spoke in "unknown" tongues during the epistles' compilation. "The statements . . . only show how orthodox men will, through prejudice, distort truth and slander a God-fearing people."[146] Christianity was powerless without the demonstration of the Spirit and the personal revelation of Christ to believers. Williams feared that the modern church was endangered without the witness of the Spirit. The remedy was "not another gospel, but a fresh outpouring of the Holy Spirit."[147]

William Booth-Clibborn took this argument a step further. To evangelicals who hypothesized that soul-winning had become a more difficult activity as of late, he agreed that for them it was.[148] Though some in the denominations had not "surrendered to the modern drift of worldliness" (i.e., fundamentalists), they discouraged others from seeking the Holy Ghost. In doing so, they had shunned the one operative that could have aided them in evangelism. Booth-Clibborn explained the dilemma in terms of the Latter Rain, "God knew the world would become harder about this time; that is why He sent the Pentecostal Outpouring."[149] Fundamentalists accentuated the "gloomy side" of the Last Days which predicted the apostasy of the church. Pentecostals on the other hand expected a "restoration" to accompany the denouement.[150] He pitied the poor fundamentalists, for *sans l'esprit* it was surely getting harder for them.

Booth-Clibborn's optimism that "we are living on the threshold of the greatest revival time the world has ever seen" stood in sharp contrast to the negativity of some fundamentalists at the end of the 1920s. Their energy spent on lost causes like the reclaiming of their denominations and the failure of the evolutionary campaign had left them forlorn. Reading through *Our Hope*, one may be forgiven for thinking it should have been titled

---

142. Ibid., 8.
143. Corry, "First Corinthians Fourteen," *PE* (6 November 1926) 8.
144. Corry, "First Corinthians Fourteen," *PE* (13 November 1926) 6–8.
145. Williams, "Pentecostal Movement under Fire," *PE* (23 July 1927) 2.
146. Ibid., 2.
147. Ibid., 3.
148. Booth-Clibborn, "Is it becoming Harder to Win Souls?" *LRE* (November 1928) 16–17.
149. Ibid., 17.
150. Ibid., 18–19.

DISFELLOWSHIPED

Our Hopelessness. In 1929 Riley quit as president of the WCFA, which for all intents and purposes had become moribund. An irreparable rift developed between Riley and Norris when the latter changed the name of his paper from *The Searchlight* to *The Fundamentalist* in 1927, upstaging Riley's more cumbersome title, *The Fundamentals in School and Church*. Fundamentalists were deeply divided and unable to cooperate with each other. Perhaps Booth-Clibborn's observation was not so far off. The pentecostal spirit appeared more hopeful in trying times.

Pentecostals forged ahead despite the opposition. Our revivals need Holy Ghost power, said Charles Robinson, while some critics only complained that the "the day of miracle is past" and thus missed their opportunity.[151] Harold Moss conceded that some criticism against them was just; nevertheless pentecostals embraced what was essential in Scripture, the presence and power of the Spirit.[152] Likewise, Gee could admit to extremes among some, but many of the "stock tales" floating about were either unfounded or exaggerated.[153] He accused dispensationalists of arbitrarily dividing the current church age into smaller epochs that truncated the Spirit's work. Nonetheless he detected a certain lessening of the more acrid attacks against them.[154] M. M. McGraw excoriated preaching against "bobbed hair" and "flesh-colored stockings" in lieu of repentance and conversion. "Because a few Fundamentalist brethren have declared the Pentecostal movement not of God, let us not worry. Let us preach Christ who can save from sin."[155] Most pentecostals condemned conformity to the world as heartily as any rabid fundamentalist, but McGraw was aware of the distraction it might create.

Norwegian pentecostal leader T. B. Barratt encountered the cessationist argument in a pamphlet by A. E. Bishop while browsing through the Moody Bookstore in Chicago in 1928. The 24-page booklet by the cofounder of the Gospel Missionary Union in Kansas City had been scribed in 1920 with C. I. Scofield's approval.[156] "How Mr. Scofield could lend his name to anything of so low an order ... is more than I can understand," Barratt grumbled.[157] Pentecostals were rightfully "fundamentalist" because they stood for "the WHOLE Bible," which stipulated that "God has NEVER recalled His promises and His Gifts." Bishop had asserted that the sign-gifts had been removed from the church at the close of Acts. The lack of a scriptural reference did not concern him, for neither did the Bible explicitly state that "Christ is divine."[158] Barratt quickly exploited this omission, "There is not a single proof ... that the GIFTS are recalled,"[159] and countered that they were in fact irrevocable (Rom

---

151. Robinson, "A Great Forward Step," *PE* (6 August 1927) 1.

152. Moss, "Our Distinctive Ministry," *PE* (19 January 1929) 4.

153. Gee, "Why is Pentecostalism Opposed?" *PE* (18 May 1929) 2–3.

154. Ibid., 3.

155. McGraw, "Fundamentalism," *PE* (27 October 1928) 3.

156. Bishop, *Tongues, Signs and Visions* (1920). The mission was established together with Torrey and George Fisher in 1892. See Balmer, *Encyclopedia of Evangelicalism*, 295.

157. Barratt, "Tongues, Signs, and Visions, God's Order Today," *PE* (8 December 1928) 6.

158. Bishop, *Tongues, Signs and Visions*, 13. Bishop's citation on this point is to "one of Dr. Scofield's comments."

159. Barratt, "Tongues, Signs, and Visions," 7.

11:29). Moreover, the purpose of apostolic miracles to confirm the Word was as pertinent today as then.[160] Nor was it true that "some of the most renowned Bible teachers" were unanimous in their opinion with Bishop. Barratt cited a 1923 Episcopalian statement favoring divine healing as one example.[161] Barratt judged Bishop's depiction of pentecostalism as uncharitable and his theology as unsustainable.

In February 1927 Gustave Schmidt advised against contributing to the Russian Missionary Society, which harassed its pentecostal workers. "I have gone through the mill," he reported, "and know positive facts."[162] After three years with them, he and Douglas Scott had withdrawn from this Baptist entity in 1924.[163] He contended that working with them was an impossibility without compromising one's pentecostal ardor. Two helpers showed up at the AG doorstep a few months later, having resigned from the society.[164] C. W. Swanson was a businessman vitally interested in missions, and Paul Peterson was a missionary now desiring amity with the AG. Peterson canvassed AG churches, telling of the harsh conditions Christians suffered under the Soviet regime.[165] He and Schmidt incorporated the Russian and Eastern European Mission in Chicago in June and maintained an at times stormy relationship with the AG until severing connections in 1940.[166]

Another missionary who had succumbed to pentecostalism was reported through Mark Matthews, a Seattle fundamentalist and former moderator of the General Assembly of the Presbyterian Church. In a letter written to Pastor Matthews, Adelaide Woodward glowed about her pentecostal experience, "Then, I cannot say how it came about, but I was lifted up and flooded with joy, and wanted to sing and praise Him ... I heard myself say some strange words and asked if I had been speaking in tongues."[167] Not only had she, but those around her avowed that she also had sung beautifully in tongues. Ms. Woodward attested that several others in the mission station had also been transformed by similar experiences. Christ was real to her, the Bible was real, "And this Baptism of the Holy Spirit is more real than anything that has ever come to me."[168] Matthews did not remark on the letter, but pentecostals gauged it as God's validation of their movement.

Paul Bettex's missionary heroics graced *SST* for February 4, 1928. Paul was the issue of Swiss theologian Jean Fredrick Bettex, contributor to *The Fundamentals* and other apologetic works of orthodoxy.[169] Frodsham recited his story in *Wholly for God: A Call to*

---

160. Ibid., 6. Bishop spent time as a missionary in South America.

161. The healing movement swept into the Episcopal church under Dr. James Hickson. A commission was launched to investigate the wholesomeness of the movement and is quoted in Bosworth, *Christ the Healer*, 30–31. Another pro-healing Episcopalian was J. T. Butlin, whose *A Handbook on Divine Healing* (1924) was sold and quoted in the *PE*.

162. Schmidt, "A Word of Warning," *PE* (26 February 1927) 12.

163. "Withdraws from Russian Missionary Society," *PE* (3 January 1925) 11. Schmidt joined it in 1921.

164. "Visitors at Headquarters," *PE* (9 April 1927) 5.

165. Peterson, "Russia," *PE* (26 November 1927) 8, 17.

166. Peterson, "Preaching the Whole Gospel," *PE* (15 September 1928) 11; Salzer, "Danzig Gdanska Institute of the Bible," 9; McGee, "Working Together," 12.

167. "Fellowship of His Suffering," *PE* (29 October 1927) 1.

168. Ibid., 1.

169. Bettex, "The Bible and Modern Criticism" in Torrey, *The Fundamentals*, 76–93; Bettex, "The Bible and Modern Criticism" in Dixon, ed., *Back to the Bible*, 103–23.

DISFELLOWSHIPED

Complete Consecration in 1934. The Bettex family descended from Huguenot stock, and Paul converted to the Salvation Army under Catherine Booth's persuasive preaching while studying at the Sorbonne.[170] According to Frodsham, Bettex spoke in tongues while consecrating his life to God at Princeton in 1890.[171] He also mastered thirteen other languages through vigorous study and once trekked 8,000 miles from Argentina to El Paso, Texas. Eventually, he married a Spirit-filled believer in Hong Kong in 1910, but she died two years later, and he himself was shot dead with three bullets in Canton in 1916, a victim of xenophobia.[172] Bettex's life was a testament of devotion and absolute surrender to the Lord for fundamentalists and pentecostals alike.

Reviewing the intervening two decades, David McDowell espied eight scriptural confirmations for the movement: a revelation of the Cross, a renewed vision of Christ, a vibrant missionary thrust, miracles of healing, an emphasis on premillennialism, the persecution of the devil, and a love for Christ and the Word.[173] Instead of languishing as many had foretold, pentecostalism had multiplied, forming "one of the greatest factors in the support of belief in the fundamentals of the Scriptures." He maintained as he had in 1924 that pentecostals were "Fundamentalists Plus."[174] Intellectual knowledge was commendable, but the devil hated the "plus," for it resulted in a life anointed by God. Railing against the "observing of precepts and dogmas," pentecostals had something more than an arid version of Christianity as espoused in fundamentalism. Indeed, in McDowell's view, they were on the move. The attitude stood in contrast with fundamentalists who seemed on the retreat.

Sunday School and Youth Work

One area of intersection with increasing importance to both movements was the Sunday school. In 1929 the AG solicited names for a free booklet, "The Second Coming of Christ," to mail to every fundamentalist superintendent who was not using GPH materials. The advertisement stipulated that the Sunday school head must be dissatisfied with the literature she or he was currently using, or, if she or he was not using any, be interested in a sample of pentecostal work.[175] Like many denominations, the AG complied with the International Sunday School Lessons but had been augmenting the curriculum with its own quarterlies "from the Pentecostal viewpoint" since 1918, prepared at first by Frodsham, Bell, and Alice Flower.[176] In 1927 they started a supplemental guide called *Pentecostal Teachers' Quarterly*.

---

170. "A Remarkable Pentecostal Missionary," *PE* (25 February 1928) 4. Catherine was the eldest daughter of General William Booth and husband of Arthur Booth-Clibborn, who became a pentecostal along with son William in 1907. Another son, Eric, died as a pentecostal missionary to the Congo in 1924.

171. Frodsham, *Wholly for God*, 7.

172. Anderson, *Spreading Fires*, 117, 278. Bettex blamed his wife's death in part on a lack of financial support from the U.S.

173. McDowell, "The Lord's Doings—Marvelous in our Eyes," *PE* (9 July 1927) 2.

174. Ibid., 2.

175. "Free Booklet," *PE* (30 November 1929) 22.

176. "Our Sunday School Literature," *CE* (9 August 1919) 7.

This text was written by Milton Fish, a Baptist minister—at least up until he inconveniently spoke in tongues.

Our Pentecostal Boys and Girls, a four-page paper geared towards children, was first produced in July 1921.[177] Many of the tales authored by Frodsham were spun into children's books, such as *Happy Hours with Little Folks* (1924), which was "most heartily recommended" by *SST*,[178] *Little Folk's Story-Hour* (1925), *The Boomerang Boy* (1925), *The Boomerang Boy Again* (1926), *Around the World with the Boomerang Boy* (1926) and *Slumber Time Stories* (with Clara Clark, 1926). Amy Yeomans penned *The Golden Bird and other Stories* in 1924. Also, Vacation Bible Schools, a staple summer fare in fundamentalist churches since the turn of the century, were inaugurated in AG churches by 1927. George Jeffrey's Central Gospel Tabernacle in Long Beach, California was among the first to conduct such a program "along Pentecostal lines."[179] Its enrolment reached 94 by July 15 and saw one student and one assistant baptized in water.[180]

More importantly, a concerted effort was made to indoctrinate the youth before they entered the "lion's den" of secular campuses and to attract their impressionable peers in the high schools. A fresh column, "Young People's Meeting," enhanced *PE* from January 1925 after substantial demand from readers.[181] Youth societies emerged in AG churches from 1925, such as the "Pentecostal Young People's Meeting" at Columbus, Georgia.[182] An inaugural "Young People's Convention" gathered in Oakland, California in May 1925 under the encouragement of Pastor Steelberg, followed by another in October in nearby Stockton.[183] Under Steelberg's impetus, the group fashioned themselves into the "Pentecostal Ambassadors for Christ" and applied to AG headquarters for their own periodical. Dozens of clubs sprang up across the country by March 1926, proving to be a great asset to the local churches.[184] Taking their cue from a fundamentalist group, "The Bible Crusaders," Harry Collier's church organized the militant-sounding "Young Crusaders."[185] April 1926 saw the inception of *Christ's Ambassadors* for the "young people." *Gospel Gleaners*, aimed at a slightly younger crowd, launched in April 1928.

Pentecostal Eschatology

Pentecostal eschatology continued apace with dispensationalism in the later half of the 1920s, particularly in the AG. The first book of prophetic import from GPH was Frank Boyd's *The Budding Fig Tree* (1926). A heraldic, trumpet-blowing angel announced on the

---

177. "Sunday School Literature," *PE* (14 April 1923) 15.
178. "An Appreciative Review," *PE* (10 January 1925) 14.
179. Jeffrey, "A Prospering Pastorate," *PE* (25 June 1927) 12.
180. Jeffrey, "Prosperous Long Beach," *PE* (6 August 1927) 17.
181. "Young People's Meeting," *PE* (3 January 1925) 8–9. The Bible lesson was on creation (Gen 1), and the moral lesson was about stewardship based largely on George Müller's life.
182. J. Graham, "Columbus, Ga." *PE* (2 May 1925) 12.
183. M. Tacker, "'Pentecostal Ambassadors of Christ," *PE* (23 January 1926) 12–13.
184. "Our Pentecostal Young People," *PE* (13 March 1926) 7.
185. "Young Crusaders Revival in Washington," *PE* (13 November 1926) 13–14.

back cover of *PE* that the writer had situated the world's finale in its political context from both "Gentile and Jewish viewpoints."[186] Much of the work discussed the possibilities of a Jewish state in Palestine in light of World War I. Chapter 15 on the Jewish restoration particularly reflected a dispensational scheme for climactic events.[187] Another theme was the prevailing lawlessness in America, supported by statistics from James Beck, Solicitor General of the U.S., and a host of secular news agencies. Boyd heaped much of the blame for the country's woeful moral condition upon modernism and evolution.[188] Aside from the Bible, he also engaged Nathaniel West (a prominent Methodist premillennialist), D. M. Panton and A. T. Pierson as authorities.

Stanley Frodsham composed *Things which must shortly come to Pass* in 1928, an alarmist volume which Moody radio station WMBI endorsed in 1930.[189] Each chapter contained the word "Coming," indicating from a premillennial perspective what the future would entail (e.g., "The Coming Apostasy"). Frodsham seamlessly blended biblical prediction with current affairs. Rarely did he dip into fundamentalist sources, but their imprint can be detected on every page. He discerned in Mussolini the forerunner to the antichrist and was hopeful the Jews would establish a contemporary Israel.[190] In keeping with dispensational theology, the apocalypse would commence gorily in tribulation but finish gloriously in triumph.

Alice Luce's *The Little Flock in the Last Days* (1927) qualified as another essential work for grasping the prophetic, but hers, like Pearlman's later work, focused on spiritual values rather than on the speculative. Luce was an Anglican of Huguenot descent who served in India with the London-based Church Missionary Society before embracing pentecostalism in 1910.[191] While she accepted a general dispensational framework as the background of her thesis, it did not figure prominently in her interpretation. She mentioned only in passing the seven ages as Scofield enumerated them and assumed his chronology for the book of Revelation (Rapture—Tribulation—Parousia).[192] For her it was imperative that one prepare for the second coming rather than guess whether the antichrist should hail from Greece or Syria.[193] Neither Luce nor Pearlman were raised in a conservative American religious climate, thus they were not subject to the forces which shaped Bell and Boyd. Frodsham on the other hand was born into the British Nonconformist tradition and readily subscribed to dispensational doctrine.

All prophetic eyes were fixed on Mussolini and the likelihood of a revived Roman Empire. At General Council, former Baptist minister J. N. Hoover provocatively inquired, "Mussolini: Is the World Preparing for Antichrist?"[194] He concurred with "our most emi-

186. "The Budding Fig Tree," *PE* (2 January 1926) 24.
187. Boyd, *The Budding Fig Tree* (1926); Boyd, "The Jews—Their Future," 111–17.
188. Boyd, *The Budding Fig Tree*, 74–75.
189. "Endorsed by Moody's," *PE* (7 June 1930) 14.
190. Frodsham, *Things Which must shortly come to Pass*, 49–51, 84–90.
191. Wilson and Wilson, "Alice E. Luce," 159–61.
192. Luce, *The Little Flock*, 41, 50.
193. Ibid., v–vi.
194. Hoover, "Mussolini: Is the World Preparing for Antichrist?" *PE* (26 November 1927) 1, 6–7.

nent prophetic scholars" in forecasting the swallowing up of ecclesiastical powers under the Italian government. Mussolini may not be the "Empower of the new Empire," but his role would be pivotal to the fulfillment of Scripture. Frodsham assented. Quoting from the *Christian Herald*, he foresaw the remaking of Europe.[195] A more devastating war than the first was certain, where Italy and Germany would play decisive roles. On the same page of *PE*, he also contemplated the frequency of earthquakes around the globe, another favorite portent of the end. There was no shortage of ominous news to titillate the apostles of doom.

Oswald Smith's dire prognoses about the antichrist filled advertisements in *PE* after 1925. *Is the Antichrist at Hand?* (1927), *When Antichrist Reigns* (1928), and *Signs of His Coming* (1932) were among his several titles.[196] The apocalyptic fiction of British novelist Sydney Watson were among books "approved" for pentecostal perusal with titles like *In the Twinkling of an Eye* and *The Mark of the Beast*.[197] William Booth-Clibborn recommended Reginald Naish's *The Midnight Hour and After!* (1924) to his audiences, so much so that GPH could barely keep them in stock.[198] In Naish's estimation, the eleventh hour of prophecy started ticking before the ink had dried at the armistice table—autographed at the eleventh hour on the eleventh day of the eleventh month in 1918. Blackstone's *Jesus is Coming* (1878), Torrey's *The Return of the Lord Jesus* (1913), Gray's *Prophecy and the Lord's Return* (1917), Mauro's *Bringing back the King* (1920), and Fred Hagin's *His Appearing and His Kingdom* (1922) assured that the premillennial message would be ever before them.[199] Imbibing from dispensational wells, it was inevitable that the fundamentalist mentality would drip over into other areas as well.

Summary and Conclusion

The move to retain constituents through the Sunday school began to occupy headquarters at both AG and CG. The AG in particular greatly expanded its Sunday school literature to train the "young ones" in the paths of righteousness. Attention to this vital ministry would continue to develop into the next decade and forge an important venue through which pentecostals and fundamentalists would cooperate. While always important at a local level, the Sunday school was gaining importance as an institutional organism to inculcate children effectively in the doctrines of their parents and ensure a future for the movement.

Critical to their juncture with fundamentalism, the teachings of evolution even at the grammar school level alarmed parents and motivated the denomination to action. The Sunday school literature reflected these concerns, reprinting articles from fundamentalist periodicals that championed creationism and the divine origin of humanity. Gouthey's

---

195. Frodsham, "The Outlook and the Uplook," *PE* (14 January 1928) 2.

196. "Is the Antichrist at Hand?" *PE* (16 April 1927) 16; "When Antichrist Reigns," *PE* (18 February 1928) 15; "Change and Decay," *PE* (2 May 1936) 15.

197. "Approved Books," *PE* (13 February 1926) 9.

198. Booth-Clibborn, "A Book All Should Read," *PE* (20 February 1926) 6–7.

199. "More Books on More Subjects," *PE* (20 November 1926) 15.

presentation of evolution was widely popular in Springfield and would help steer the denomination towards finding its own expositions against it. The voice of fundamentalism was becoming the voice of pentecostalism, transitioning from the "content" to the "rhetoric" of fundamentalism.

This was evident in AG attitudes towards the Bible. Early pentecostals had simply assumed that the Word was the authoritative representation of God. Fundamentalists in their struggle against modernism had labored diligently for decades to defend the veracity of the Word. Now those defenses became the prerogatives of pentecostals. A "scientific" approach to the Bible crept into their methodology. The elevation of the Bible was also indicated in the prevalence of Bible conferences now filling the pentecostal schedule. The raw emotionalism of the camp meeting was giving way to the cerebral study of the Word. While this transition can be explained in part by the drift towards institutionalism in the denomination, a similar shift was not manifested in the CG at this time. The AG was attracted to fundamentalist modes of thought as a subconscious ingratiation towards the more dominant fundamentalists. The content of these conferences were often "prophetic" in nature.

The transition from fundamentalist "content" to "rhetoric" was most evident again in the realm of eschatology. Dispensational charts and their presenters crisscrossed the nation in order to inform curious church-goers of future events, attracting large crowds across the denominational spectrum to pentecostal doors. The output of books along dispensational lines at this period shifted pentecostalism from the act of borrowing fundamentalist ideas to that of propagating them as their own. To be sure, this was done in a uniquely pentecostal way, with greater emphasis on the "spiritual" application of the text than on more literalist interpretations, but it allowed them to assume a fundamentalist mentality towards the world which would be completed in the AG in the early 1930s.

Meanwhile, fundamentalists felt pressure from their modernist foes to distance themselves from pentecostalism. Grouped together with a form of worship they did not adhere to, the WCFA publicly rebuked pentecostals in 1928. Other fundamentalists were no less vociferous (e.g., Gaebelein, Shuler, Panton). However, some fundamentalists found cooperation with pentecostals advantageous. Straton courted the assistance of Uldine Utley into a successful partnership in 1927. Pentecostal and fundamentalist interests aligned in the arena of evangelism and revivalism. A chink in the spiritual armor of fundamentalists was beginning to appear at the end of the 1920s and became more apparent as depression gripped the nation. However small, these were important harbingers of future cooperation by the end of the next decade.

Adopting a Fundamentalist Rhetoric (1930–1934)

Introduction

THROUGHOUT THIS PERIOD PENTECOSTALS INCREASINGLY APPROPRIATED THE POSTURE of their fundamentalist peers—further consolidating the grip that fundamentalism had on them. Whereas in the 1920s the AG was content to copy fundamentalist articles in *PE*, in the 1930s they would write books along fundamentalist lines, a trend which first sprang up in their apocalyptic literature as noted in the previous chapter. The dispensationalist mentality occupied AG thinking to such an extent that they sharpened their repudiation of modernism, and it even infiltrated CG eschatology to cause noticeable change in their outlook. But it was the growth of the Sunday schools which intensified efforts to retain the future generation.

Growth, Retention, and the Sunday School

Pentecostalism experienced explosive growth as the depression deepened in the first half of the 1930s. At the outset of Black Tuesday in October 1929, the AG numbered some 92,000 adherents. By 1933 they had gained 45,000 members or 48 percent growth. In 1935 they leapfrogged another 20,000 to 166,000, an increase of 22 percent. Although growth slowed in the second half of the decade, they still catapulted to 184,000 by 1939 and to 210,000 in 1941.[1] The refreshing spirit of revival caused many to reminisce over the initial 1906 outpouring. In a fit of nostalgia, missionary George Kelley reported of a ten-day revival in Shanghai where "the singing, praying, and testifying sounded like the OLD-TIME Pentecostal meetings we used to enjoy years ago."[2] God gave evangelist Maud Adams "a real old-time revival" in Midway, Texas[3] and Pastor A. F. Carr an "old-time Bible revival" in Iraan, Texas in July 1931.[4] Though such professions cannot be directly tied to the depression, anxiety and uncertainty certainly contributed to this longing for the past.[5]

---

1. Statistics compiled from Kendrick, *The Promise Fulfilled*, 98, and Menzies, *Anointed to Serve*, 146.

2. Kelley, "Times of Refreshing in Shanghai," *PE* (14 February 1931) 10.

3. Adams, "Two Texas Revivals," *PE* (5 September 1931) 16.

4. Carr, "Old Time Bible Revival," *PE* (15 August 1931) 13.

5. The earliest post-WWI reference to "old-time power" I found was from T. S. Miles in Collinsville, Oklahoma in August 1928 ("Old-Time Power Falls," *PE* [11 August 1928] 12). These pronouncements only increased after the depression set in.

Meanwhile, Sunday schools shattered attendance records across the country. AG pastors who had once been afraid to number parishioners for fear of committing the "sin of David" were suddenly counting noses in the classroom. To augment this ministry, *PE* featured Sunday school supplements for April 2, 1932, July 8, 1933, April 7 and November 10, 1934, and March 23 and September 14, 1935.[6] The Sunday School Promotion Department formed in 1935 under Marcus Grable to further expand their reach.[7] The investment returned dividends by the end of the decade when Sunday schools multiplied exponentially.

The Sunday school ministry in Okmulgee, Oklahoma spurted from 176 to 237 in the sixteen months prior to May 1931 under pastor Fred Eiting.[8] In the spring of 1933 at Everett, Massachusetts attendance more than doubled from 135 to 275 following Loren Staat's evangelistic campaign there.[9] The Sunday school at Puyallup, Washington soared to a record of 364 at Easter and became the second largest in the city.[10] J. N. Hoover's touch was Midas when it came to ameliorating the Sunday school enrollment. During his visit to Arthur Grave's church in Dallas, numbers jumped from 831 to 1133 and remained above the thousand-level thereafter.[11] Houston's Magnolia Park Assembly set new standards in April 1933 under his month-long tutelage and increased in the summer under Pastor Albert Ott's direction to 635.[12] It was Hoover's conviction that there was "no better institution for the evangelization of the world than the Sunday school."[13] If the church was to retain her constituency, the battle would be fought in the hearts and minds of the "little scholars."

In June 1933 Myer Pearlman tallied 695 students at the headquarters church, where a teachers' training course and a Vacation Bible School were implemented during the summer.[14] Its pastor, Ralph Riggs, had pronounced in 1931, "Next to the church services and the care of the adults of the congregation, without doubt the most important of all phases of church life is the Sunday school"[15] and carried out his convictions rigorously through Central Assembly. An anonymous 1932 article championing the venue echoed, "Surely the Sunday school is one of the greatest channels through which our children and younger folk can have implanted in their hearts the precious Word of God."[16] William Menzies

---

6. "Sunday School Supplement," *PE* (2 April 1932) 9–12; "Sunday School Supplement," *PE* (8 July 1933) 9-19; "Sunday School Supplement," *PE* (7 April 1934) 9–16; "Sunday School Supplement," *PE* (10 November 1934) 9–17; "Sunday School Supplement," *PE* (23 March 1935) 9–16; "Sunday School Supplement," *PE* (14 September 1935) 9–16.

7. McGee, *People of the Spirit*, 286–87. Grable first met Ralph Riggs at an inter-denominational revival in Springfield in 1933. Both were passionate about Sunday school work.

8. J. Zimmerman, "Ministry Mightily Magnetic," *PE* (10 September 1932) 13.

9. K. Pyne, "'There—When the Fire Fell,'" *PE* (15 April 1933) 12.

10. T. Sandall, "Revival Fires at Puyallup," *PE* (10 June 1933) 13.

11. A. Graves, "From 'Old Camp Meetin' Station," *PE* (13 May 1933) 13.

12. E. Yeats, "Houston, Tex.," *PE* (24 February 1934) 12.

13. Hoover, "Evangelism in the Sunday School," *PE* (4 May 1929) 7.

14. Pearlman, "Headquarters Church Growing," *PE* (24 June 1933) 12.

15. Riggs, *A Successful Pastor*, 96.

16. "Happy Sunday School Workers," *PE* (2 July 1932) 10.

believes that AG pastors overcame their fear of education in the early 1930s when they realized that the Sunday school was an effective tool for evangelism.[17] But even deeper than that was the church's resistance to the encroachment of culture. Riggs, citing Professor Clarence Benson of MBI, noted that children spent 12,000 hours in the secular education system for every 170 in the religious.[18] Furthermore, 90 percent of adult churchgoers and 95 percent of ministers attended Sunday school as children, but only 10 percent of church resources were earmarked for that program. He predicted enormous growth in two years if they would allocate more funds to it.

Manuals addressing this need were published in the early 1930s, moving beyond the 1920s storytelling of Frodsham. Riggs penned *A Successful Sunday School* in 1933, which complemented his *A Successful Pastor* from 1931. He geared his advice toward its administration and role in the church. Bringing teacher development to a broader sphere, Pearlman produced *Successful Sunday School Teaching* in 1935. His goal was to make his manual user-friendly and immensely practical. Jettisoning technical jargon while focusing novices on the "art of teaching," he incorporated lessons from D. L. Moody, F. B. Meyer, George Müller, and motivational speaker Dale Carnegie, among others. One fundamentalist source Pearlman used was Philip Howard's *A Little Kit of Teacher's Tools* (1919), published by the Sunday School Times Company of Philadelphia.[19] He also quoted from Benson and nationally recognized curriculum writer Amos Wells's *The Successful Sunday School Superintendent* (1915).[20] But he also appealed to Lutheran theorists Theodore Schmauk and Luther Weigle, whose *The Pupil and the Teacher* (1911) he deemed "masterful."[21]

An institution popular with fundamentalist churches, Vacation Bible School, also came into prominence in AG churches at this time. Its roots stretched back to Epiphany Baptist Church of New York in 1898. Moody Memorial gravitated toward its agenda as means for discipling inner-city children, hosting some 147 students in the summer of 1916.[22] One of the earliest VBSs in the AG was at Long Beach in 1927, which Pastor George Jeffrey implemented shortly after his induction.[23] In the spring of 1933, under the discriminating eye of Eleanor Bowie, CBI tutored its "Religious Education" undergraduates on how to conduct a thriving VBS, applying their skills at Central Assembly that summer. Some 343 children gathered under the banner of "Jesus is Real," opening with worship and salutes to the American and Christian flags before shuffling off to their lessons. Upon its triumph, Riggs announced that VBS was "here to stay."[24] They had discovered what other denominations had known for some time, viz. that it was "so valuable a means of conveying religious truth

---

17. Menzies, *Anointed to Serve*, 266.

18. Riggs, "Development of our Sunday School," *PE* (14 December 1935) 1, 9.

19. Pearlman, *Successful Sunday School Teaching*, 34.

20. Benson's book may have been *The Sunday School in Action*, which was advertised in *PE*.

21. Pearlman, *Sunday School*, 38.

22. "The Daily Vacation Bible School," *GN* (15 July 1916) 71.

23. Jeffrey, "A Prospering Pastorate," *PE* (25 June 1927) 12; Jeffrey, "Prosperous Long Beach," *PE* (6 August 1927) 17.

24. Riggs and Bowie, "Daily Vacation Bible School is Here to Stay," *PE* (22 July 1933) 1, 5.

to their children."[25] Two years later the Full Gospel Tabernacle in Granite City, Illinois launched its first VBS with Bowie as director, attracting more than 200 pupils.[26] Endorsed by the General Council, VBS comprised an important component in recruiting families who would not ordinarily have stepped inside a pentecostal church.

This is hardly to suggest that pentecostals were uninterested in Sunday schools before the 1930s, which had played an important role in the movement since its inception. Not long after organizing on Marietta Street, the Atlanta Pentecostal Mission commenced a Sunday school in April 1908 for children and adults.[27] Clark Eckert's fellowship in Coconut Grove, Florida organized one with a view toward raising missionary support in January 1908.[28] The CG General Assembly encouraged every congregation to host a Sunday school in 1906, the year before Pentecost came to them.[29] Pentecostal material had been desired by them since 1910 but had not been published until *Lighted Pathway* appeared in the autumn of 1928.[30] The 1928 Assembly mandated that every state select a Sunday school superintendent and operate an annual convention.[31] However, the Sunday School and Youth Literature Board was only established in 1944, influenced by models in the NAE and its American Sunday School Committee.[32] In other words, the early movement left education to local initiatives until centralization could allow for a more concerted effort. The later attempts at national organization represent this process of retention to safeguard the future.

J. N. Hoover as ex-Fundamentalist

Nobody exemplified the shift toward fundamentalist thought better than Hoover, a first cousin of the belittled U.S. president. Hoover entered the ministry in 1897 and garnered a national reputation as a writer and conference speaker among his colleagues. "I was a proud and haughty Baptist preacher," he bewailed, staying aloof from holiness and pentecostal clergy.[33] Severe illness in 1920 forced his resignation from the pastorate at Lindsay, California. Relocating to a more salubrious climate at Santa Cruz, health problems from what doctors described as "incurable stomach and intestinal trouble" still plagued him at his next church.[34] Five years later, broken in body and spirit, his board suggested he convalesce at a spa for several weeks, though they did not expect him to return.

Hoover was at a loss as to where he should rest, but with promises that the church would paint his house and pay his salary, he and his wife packed their bags and headed

---

25. Ibid., 1.
26. E. Chamberlain, "Vacation Bible School Here to Stay," *PE* (14 September 1935) 14.
27. "Pentecostal Mission, 136 Marietta Street," *BM* (1 May 1908) 2.
28. Eckert, "Cocoanut Grove, Fla.," *BM* (1 June 1908) 3.
29. Conn, *Like a Mighty Army*, 67, citing *Minutes* for 1906, 16.
30. "[Untitled]," *ELCOGE* (1 May 1910) 4.
31. Conn, *Like a Mighty Army*, 204–5.
32. Ibid., 260.
33. Hoover, "Baptism and Ministry of the Holy Spirit," *LRE* (July 1930) 7.
34. Ibid., 7.

Adopting a Fundamentalist Rhetoric (1930–1934)

over the hills to San Jose. On that November evening in 1925, probably Sunday the 8th, they secured a hotel just a half block from Towner's church, where Charles Shreve was embarking on a campaign. He found the situation intriguing: "A Methodist, Pentecostal evangelist, preaching in a Baptist church was something new to us."[35] On Monday night Shreve invited those anxious to receive the baptism to approach the platform.[36] The altar quickly filled, and Shreve directed Hoover to the pulpit chair, mistakenly thinking he was volunteering assistance. Though called upon by Shreve to pray for the church, he could not and slumped alongside the chair under the guidance of the Spirit, though he did not speak in tongues on this occasion.

At the evening crusade on the twelfth, Shreve intimated that all his listeners' needs would be fulfilled at Calvary. Hoover plodded forward again for prayer, and again the altar brimmed with supplicants. Directed once more to the pulpit chair by Shreve, Hoover begged the Lord to satisfy on Thursday what had been stirred in him on Monday night. In his 1926 account, he lay prostrate on the floor, surrounded by Shreve and "Baur and Eliot."[37] In the 1930 version he knelt in prayer, encircled by Towner, Shreve, a Fred Hart "and others"—changing the personnel and omitting his falling over onto the floor.[38] Likely, he recalled different people at different times. In either case, the outcome was the same. The glories of heaven precipitated upon Hoover, and the praises of God ascended from his lips in cryptic speech. He had been rejuvenated in the Spirit.

Over the course of the next fifteen years, Hoover's sermons were reproduced 55 times in *PE*, *LRE*, *W&Wk*, and *COGE*, although the bulk of the issues from 1926 to 1934 are missing in the *W&Wk* collection. To gain a sense of his interests (and that of his audience), they can be classified into the following topics and number of times preached: evangelism/salvation (11), second advent (6), church/ecclesiology (5), modernism (5), apostasy and the antichrist (4), Jews in prophecy (3), communism and politics (3), divine healing (3), resurrection (3), morals (3), devil/hell (2), Scripture (2), evolution (2), Thanksgiving holiday (1), grace (1), person of Christ (1), Spirit-baptism (1).[39] Some of these were repeated in print and/or slightly altered in presentation. For instance, his two disseminations on evolution were nearly identical in material, as were many of his presentations on the importance of evangelism.

Additionally, his pamphlets reflected themes dear to the fundamentalist heart, such as "When Jesus Comes," "Gigantic Mergers and their Portent," "World Conditions in the Light of Prophecy, or What is the Mark of the Beast?," "Evolution and the Holy Scriptures," "National and Bible Bolsheviks, or, What is Communism?," and "Our Country and Christian Soldiers."[40] Others were less palatable to their tastes, such as "The Holy Ghost Baptism," "The Holy Spirit on the Day of Pentecost," and "Is Scriptural Healing Fanaticism?"

---

35. Ibid., 7.
36. Hoover, "A Baptist Preacher's Testimony," *PE* (13 March 1926) 5.
37. Ibid., 5.
38. Hoover, "Baptism and Ministry of the Holy Spirit," 7.
39. See Appendix H.
40. Pamphlet titles listed on the back cover of Hoover's *World Conditions in the Light of Prophecy* (FPHC).

Still others like "Devotional Use of the Bible" and "The Redemption of Man" would have enhanced any evangelical pew. His eschatological views were similar to Scofield, only substituting "Holy Spirit Dispensation" for the "Dispensation of Grace" on his own chart.[41] He also placed two resurrections before the millennium, although a 1933 radio sermon from Kansas City parroted Scofield by juxtaposing one resurrection before Christ's triumph and the other after.[42]

A typical week-long revival is instructive of how these themes interplayed. At the State Fair Grounds in Pueblo, Colorado in July 1933, Hoover railed against atheists, modern theology, evolution, communists and Mussolini.[43] He also propounded on Hitler's treatment of Jews and on the path to divine healing.[44] In "World Conditions," delivered July 31, he divulged that history was ripe for Christ's return, comparing the modern world to the "days of Noah" which would precede the event (Matt 24:37). Auguries of imminent doom consisted of corporate mergers in the oil, shipping, railroad, banking, retail, and food industries, the rise of political dictators like Mussolini (he neglected Hitler here), a rise in crime (murder and theft), vice (gambling, smoking, and divorce) and the diffusion of evolution and atheism—succored by modernist pundits.[45] Leaflets distributed prior to his engagement invited the desperate and searching to hear solutions to the world's problems. In the uncertainties of the depression such a jeremiad played well upon the popular ear.

The threat of corporate merger had been lighted upon by Hoover earlier in 1932 at Lake Geneva in Alexandria, Minnesota for the North Central District camp.[46] The list of businesses varied slightly from that of 1933, though J. P. Morgan retained the greediest spot.[47] The antichrist would not surface through guns or swords but through "a clever political, financial and religious federation," Hoover maintained, referring to the Federal Council of Churches.[48] His address at General Council in 1927 focused on Mussolini as the harbinger of the antichrist, which he repeated to the Stone Church in 1930.[49] Citing *Jewish Missionary Magazine*, he predicted that the actual antichrist would hail from Greece when

---

41. Hoover, *World Conditions*, inset. The position was not so different from Scofield. In his correspondence course, Scofield commented that it "would not be inappropriate" to call the "dispensation of grace" as the "dispensation of the Spirit," although he preferred to call it the "dispensation of the Son" (*Scofield Correspondence Course: New Testament*, 209–10).

42. Hoover, "After Death: The Two Resurrections," *LRE* (April 1935) 10. "The Two Resurrections" was the title to the fourth chapter of Scofield's *Rightly Dividing the Word of Truth* (pp. 1581–82 in *FSRB*).

43. "Today is Opening Day at the Hoover Revival," *The Pueblo Chieftain* (16 July 1933) n.p. (FPHC).

44. "Divine Healing is Discussed at Hoover Revival," *The Pueblo Chieftain* (21 July 1933) 5; "Hitler and Jews Revival Subject of Dr. J. N. Hoover," *The Pueblo Chieftain* (31 July 1933) n.p. (FPHC).

45. Hoover, *World Conditions*, 1–16. Hoover names Kraft, General Motors, Colgate-Palmolive, J. P. Morgan, Hershey's Chocolate and Standard Oil among the corporate culprits.

46. Hoover, "Giant Mergers Forerunners of the Antichrist," *LRE* (September 1932) 3–6.

47. Hoover included Goodrich Rubber, The Creek Light & Power Co. of California, and U.S. Steel, among others.

48. Hoover, "Giant Mergers," 4.

49. Hoover, "Mussolini: Is the World Preparing for Antichrist?" *PE* (26 November 1927) 1, 6–7; "Mussolini and the Antichrist," *LRE* (August 1930) 3–5.

Adopting a Fundamentalist Rhetoric (1930–1934)

the time was ideal.[50] Much of Hoover's Pueblo sermon "World Conditions" was revisited at the Shrine Mosque in St. Louis in 1934, although he included Hitler this time along with Stalin as omens of the end.[51]

Anti-communism had been rampant within fundamentalism ever since Lenin's revolution in 1917. Gerald Winrod practically made his career out of regaling it, though Gaebelein lagged not far behind. In a 1935 article Hoover alerted readers to the communist infiltration of the U.S. government and its educational system. "The average person in our country does not realize the extent of the propaganda that emanates from Moscow."[52] Stalin banned public worship in Russia, and if Americans did not rally behind the Constitution, he feared that freedom would be curtailed here as well. His message at the end of 1935 in Memphis was even more urgent. Like a pernicious guest undermining the home, foreigners welcomed by Lady Liberty had undermined the Constitution and ought to be deported.[53] He chastised the administration for recognizing Russia and uttered warnings of impending peril unless loyal Americans woke up.[54]

Hoover's most prized sermon slandered theological modernism, first appearing under the title "Bible Bolshevists" in 1928. Drawing on Oswald Smith's *Is the Antichrist at Hand?*, he found the communist sweep of the political world analogous to the modernist sweep of the religious.[55] He charged modernism with promoting evolution and atheism through its skepticism and gauged it to be more insidious than motion pictures, submitting that "the Bible is not the production of a mortal mind. Christ is not a myth. Satan is not unreal. Heaven is not imaginary, nor is hell a dream."[56] He challenged Christians to "take your place, and contend for the fundamental doctrines of salvation through Jesus Christ."[57] Quotations were also provided from Winrod's mouthpiece *The Defender* and the widely consumed *Literary Digest*. The sermon would perch elsewhere as "The Tragedy of Modern Theology" and "Bible Bolsheviks: The Tragedy of Modern Theology" and even cropped up in *COGE* in 1934, copied from *LRE*.[58] While pentecostals were generally wary of modernism, it was Hoover more than any other who waved the standard by warning his audiences of its nefarious effects. In a sense, he spearheaded the battle against modernism, stimulating more and more pentecostals against it in the early 1930s.

---

50. Hoover, "Mussolini: Is the World Preparing for Antichrist?" 6.
51. Hoover, "Days of Noah Then and Now, Mark of the Beast," *PE* (20 January 1934) 1, 8–9.
52. Hoover, "Threshold of Catastrophe," *W&Wk* (April 1935) 5.
53. Hoover, "Communism or Liberty," *W&Wk* (January 1936) 8.
54. Ibid., 8, 10.
55. Hoover, "The Bible Bolshevists," *PE* (3 March 1928) 1.
56. Ibid., 5.
57. Ibid.
58. Hoover, "Tragedy of Modern Theology," *PE* (7 December 1929) 7; Hoover, "Bible Bolsheviks: The Tragedy of Modern Theology," *LRE* (June 1930) 3–5, 9; Hoover, "Tragedy of Modern Theology," *LRE* (January 1933) 6–8; Hoover, "Tragedy of Modern Theology," *COGE* (28 January 1933) 2, 28.

Pentecostal Responses to Modernism

Aside from the occasional rant, pentecostals rarely censured modernism so directly. In CG, vilification was primarily aimed at the formal rituals in modern churches in contrast with their lively style of worship. Homer Tomlinson, for example, ridiculed the fictitious "Dr. Gush's" ornate edifice in two articles in 1915.[59] The next article to tackle modernism came in 1931 with J. H. Walker's "Some College Shipwrecks," in which he documented the loss of faith of three students.[60] In this way, as superintendent of their Bible school, Walker could promote it as a safe haven from the ravages of infidelity in the state universities. A year later, L. A. Webb likened "dead Christianity" to Mary Magdalene's wish to embalm the Lord.[61] But just as the resurrected Christ shook off the grave clothes, so the church would shake off its modernist etiquette. *COGE* of the 1920s is notable for its silence regarding modernism. In fact, the inclusion of Hoover's article in 1933 was about the only attempt to redress this. For the most part, their exuberant worship was insulation enough against malignant theologies.

Similar expressions were at times evident in the AG. L. M. Anglin, a Baptist missionary in China, was ousted from his church when he received the baptism with speaking in tongues.[62] In return, the Lord shed upon him a greater love for the Chinese and inspired him to open an orphanage. Anglin informed his Stone Church audience that though he had never drunk deeply from the waters of modernism, enough incredulity had contaminated his mind for him to question the verity of Scripture. One evening during a pentecostal service a Chinese boy under the sway of the Spirit shouted distinctly in English, "The Bible is the Word of God."[63] As a result, all his doubts dissipated.

Edward Hugh identified his seminary education as the source of his lapsed faith. A Swiss Methodist by birth, Hugh had been trained at Heidelberg, Germany, served as YMCA secretary in Austria, and migrated to Chicago for further study.[64] One of his classmates who had descended from modernism into atheism committed suicide. Though Hugh had determined earlier to abandon the ministry, he now considered rekindling his faith. One night at a prayer conclave his sister was instantly healed of a lingering illness, waking him up to the resources of the supernatural.[65] On April 26, 1926, he received the baptism of the Holy Spirit at the Stone Church and testified to a wondrous transformation.

The Stone Church was more sensitive to modernism than most because of its proximity to the University of Chicago. In 1920, its periodical complained of Chicago's treatment of Isaiah 53, defending the virgin birth just as the fundamentalist controversy was erupting.[66] "We deplore Higher Criticism and hold conferences to combat the rationalistic

---

59. H. Tomlinson, "Financial System of Dr. Gush's Church," *COGE* (9 October 1915) 3; H. Tomlinson, "Dr. Gush's Church," *COGE* (16 October 1915) 3.

60. Walker, "Some College Shipwrecks" *COGE* (29 August 1931) 2.

61. Webb, "A Dead Christianity Embalmed in Worldly Respectability," *COGE* (30 January 1932) 1.

62. Anglin, "Baptism of the Spirit Transforms a Baptist Missionary," *LRE* (April 1921) 2.

63. Ibid., 4.

64. Hugh, "Lost and Found—A Minister's Faith," *LRE* (June 1926) 6–7.

65. Ibid., 7–8.

66. "Here and There," *LRE* (July 1920) 11.

teaching that is filling our pulpits and colleges," the writer said confidently, "but the manifestation of the supernatural in the lives of men and women will do more to confound the teaching of the higher critic than a score of conferences."[67] The shovels of archaeologists might buttress the reliability of Scripture, they added, but divine healing established its unassailable power. In 1926, Pastor Philip Wittich, a superb docent, gave what is probably the first systematic attempt by a pentecostal to authenticate the Jonah story against modernist objections. He pointed out to critics that the word translated "prepare" in Jonah 1:17 meant that God appointed and had not created the fish for its task; that the Hebrew word *dag* indicated "a big fish" and not a whale; and that a man can survive three days in a fish as one Scottish fisherman discovered quite unintentionally.[68] Thus, *LRE* entered into the modernist fray in the early '20s before other pentecostal periodicals took it as a serious threat to their faith.

The official AG organ also was aware of modernism, but much of the pre-1925 material was drawn from fundamentalist sources. One of the earliest articles from 1916, "The End of Higher Criticism," was selected from an unnamed periodical with the attributes of fundamentalism.[69] In 1919, Frodsham identified an apostate church that embraced a "mutilated Bible" alongside Bolshevism as signposts of the rapture.[70] Like *COGE*, *PE* elevated pentecostal effervescence above the carnality of impious, somber worship. Contemporary churchmen would undoubtedly have expelled the tongue-screeching apostles if they had suddenly materialized in their midst.[71] Modernists greeted holy ardor in the despising way that Michal gazed upon her husband David when he danced before the Lord.

The first full-page article to exclusively address modernism ran in 1924—though it was unsigned.[72] It indicted the higher critics for rejecting their Creator by rejecting the Mosaic account of creation. In questioning the book of Isaiah, they questioned the character of God. Learned in the letter, they were ignorant in the Spirit. "Their punishment will be all the greater," the writer warned, "because they have misled others by their torches and . . . obscured the light from heaven by the smoke they have created."[73] An editorial in October accused modernists of being false prophets and "wolves in sheep's clothing."[74] Reminiscent of an earlier debate that year between fundamentalist John Roach Straton and modernist Charles Francis Potter on Christ's divine nature, the article reasoned that "you cannot have His humanity without His deity."[75] Worshipping Christ as an "ideal man" was preparatory to worshipping the antichrist as the "superman" when he should appear. The only aegis against this errant doctrine was God's Word.

67. "Remedy for Higher Criticism," *LRE* (December 1921) 14.
68. Wittich, "Answering the Objections in the Book of Jonah," *LRE* (March 1926) 5.
69. "End of Higher Criticism," *WE* (4 November 1916) 5.
70. Frodsham, "Here and There," *PE* (29 November 1919) 6.
71. "Letting down and Letting out: A Warning to Pentecostal People," *PE* (23 July 1921) 1.
72. "Smoke Screen of Modern Criticism," *PE* (23 February 1924) 1.
73. Ibid., 1.
74. Frodsham, "Modernism, the Harbinger of the Antichrist," *PE* (25 October 1924) 5.
75. Ibid., 5. The last of four public debates between Straton and Potter was on the deity of Christ, held at Carnegie Hall (April 28) 1924.

It is not surprising then that four months later an article—again unsigned—arraigned the modernists of perjury in their objection to the Bible. "They call some things in the Scriptures of truth mistakes, discrepancies, and other highsounding [sic] names."[76] By doing so, "they question Him who is truth, under the pretext of trying to find truth."[77] The editorial by "F.L.H." for that same issue defined modernism simply as "infidelity." Modernists may worship gods of their own minds rather than of their hands, but it was "paganism revived" nonetheless. As we have seen, pentecostals had consciously aligned themselves with fundamentalism by 1924. The unsigned articles may have derived from fundamentalist sources, and if not, are indication of how closely the AG identified themselves with the cause.

The antimodernist articles that are traceable to pentecostals leaked from the pens of Charles Robinson, J. N. Hoover, and Stanley Frodsham, and these largely after 1928. Others contributed as well after 1930. For instance, former Methodist minister John Narver Gortner equated modernism with infidelity in 1931. He observed, "in these days of the great apostasy we find men occupying professedly Christian pulpits in all parts of the country who do not hesitate to preach against what we regard as the fundamentals of the faith."[78] A university play portraying Judas as a misunderstood, tragic figure Gortner considered the ultimate betrayal by "ultramodernists," prompting him to opine, "Surely we are living in the last days . . . Surely it will not be long until we shall see Jesus." Surely fundamentalists would have concurred.

In a lengthy article in May 1931, modernism suffered the disapproval of another ex-Methodist, William E. Moody.[79] Of his eight points as to what was wrong with "present-day" Christianity, the first five singled out modernists: they denied the verbal inspiration of the Bible, the substitutionary atonement of Christ, the necessity of new birth, the effect of sin, and the reality of hell. The next three could equally have been applied to certain fundamentalists: they denied divine healing, the possibility of modern miracles, and the manifestation of tongues. However, on the denial of miracles, Moody waggled his finger at the modernists, who associated miracles with natural phenomenon: "Such is the apostasy and wholesale rejection of the supernatural."[80] By the early 1930s, pentecostal squabbles with the fundamentalists were receding before the greater threat of modernism.

For Warren Allen, human nature had not changed, and neither should the message of the church. He surmised that our minds were not more intelligent than those of the ancients, nor our hearts more pure.[81] In speaking with a local Congregational minister whose faith had withered and contemplated giving up, Allen remarked, "I wish he would." In contrast to the modern, the early church was "dogmatic, doctrinal, and practical."[82] Christ attested to the authority of Scripture, but many in the pulpit denigrated it today and

76. "Penalty of Rejecting God's Word," *PE* (28 February 1925) 1.
77. Ibid., 1.
78. Gortner, "Climax of Modern Infidelity," *PE* (21 February 1931) 3.
79. Moody, "What's Wrong with Present Day Christianity?" *PE* (23 May 1931) 2–3.
80. Ibid., 3.
81. Allen, "Church for the World Today," *PE* (22 July 1933) 2.
82. Ibid., 3.

Adopting a Fundamentalist Rhetoric (1930–1934)

thus failed the Pauline commission to "preach the Word."[83] Like fundamentalists, Allen advocated weighing one's religious experience by Holy Writ and not vice versa—otherwise we could construct our own Bible. The object of his decrial was modernism and not over-exuberant fellow pentecostals. His remedy was to restore precepts like the virgin birth, the atonement, and the baptism of the Spirit.[84] Thus the shift in pentecostalism towards fundamentalist thought was nearing its completion.

A further token of this sea-change in the early '30s was the pentecostal defense of the validity of Scripture from the realms of science and archaeology. Short blurbs like "The Bible Scientifically Accurate" and "Is the Bible Unscientific?" relied on fundamentalist spokesman Harry Rimmer in the first and *Revelation*, edited by Donald Barnhouse, in the second.[85] Rimmer's *Harmony of Bible and Science* (1927) was recommended reading material in *PE* in 1936.[86] Meanwhile, an article by fundamentalist L.W. Munhall also titled "Is the Bible Unscientific?" appeared in *Gospel Gleaners* in 1935.[87] Frodsham took up this theme in a November 1930 editorial. During a convention hosted by fundamentalist firebrand Gerald Winrod, he learned that Dr. Gouthey and *The Defender* had offered a thousand-dollar reward to anyone who could prove the Bible to be "unscientific."[88] So far, they had retained their cash. In June 1931 *PE* advertised *Scientific Christian Thinking for Young People* by Howard Johnson, which "vindicates the fundamental positions of Christianity as being in harmony with present-day scientific thought."[89] In fact, the only article title with the word "scientific" or "science" (excluding "Christian Science") in *PE* prior to 1930 came from the Russian numericist Ivan Panin.[90]

Likewise, though fundamentalists had long referred to archaeological digs to validate the historicity of the Good Book, pentecostals only took a keen interest in the early '30s. The earliest article in *PE* appeared in 1930, with five articles thereafter up to 1936, after which the theme became scarcer.[91] "The Bible Confirmed by Excavators" demonstrated that Jericho had been destroyed sometime between 1600 and 1200 B.C., and "Spade Confirms Bible" revealed that Ahab's palace had extensive ivory work as mentioned in 1 Kings.[92] The only reference of similar purport in *COGE* came in 1936, which reported that

---

83. Allen, "The Church for the World Today," *PE* (29 July 1933) 2.

84. Ibid., 2–3.

85. "Bible Scientifically Accurate," *PE* (3 December 1932) 3; "Is the Bible Unscientific?" *PE* (18 February 1933) 7.

86. "Recommended Books," *PE* (10 October 1936) 11.

87. Munhall, "Is the Bible Unscientific?" *GGl* (6 October 1935) 3.

88. Frodsham, "Editor's Notebook," *PE* (1 November 1930) 4.

89. "Books for Vacation Reading," *PE* (6 June 1931) 16. The excerpt indicated that the book was "specially prepared to meet a definite need among young people today."

90. Panin, "Inspiration of Scripture Scientifically Demonstrated," *PE* (26 May 1928) 6–7. "Science" did appear in *COGE* in Franklin Bowles, "God, Science, Evolution, and the Bible" in two parts (*COGE* [24 July 1926] 1; *COGE* [31 July 1926] 1). See chapter 5.

91. See "The Bible and the Spade," *PE* (10 September 1932) 10; Frodsham, "Passing and the Permanent," *PE* (16 June 1934) 5; "Confirming Bible History," *PE* (30 March 1935) 6; E. Bowman, "The Lost City," *PE* (29 February 1936) 2–3, and the following footnote.

92. "Bible Confirmed by Excavators," *PE* (14 June 1930) 9; "Spade Confirms Bible," *PE* (9 July 1932) 5.

cuneiform tablets attested to the rulership of Belshazzar in Daniel and of Darius's troubles in Haggai.[93] Once again, the CG had not been infected by fundamentalism as early or to the same degree as the AG.

Pentecostal Conversions of Modernists

The number of modernist divines captured into the pentecostal fold is small but not insignificant. Charles Price was a notable example, as previously mentioned. Once more, as a pentecostal Price was largely uninterested in fundamentalist treatises, extemporizing instead upon divine healing and the power of the gospel. Likewise, the testimony of Anglin above shows that he had only mild leanings toward modernism, which was dispelled through his contact with pentecostalism. Another modernist, "art evangelist" and Methodist pastor Dr. Benjamin Titus Duncan of Chicago, underwent pentecostal immersion in 1928.[94] His *modus operandi* was to sketch a drawing on an easel and base his homily from the picture.[95] It is not clear from available sources just how involved he was in modernism.

Harry Stemme admitted to being a modernist, but here too we see a definite fundamentalist stage earlier in his life. Stemme was born into the Chicago slums on July 13, 1890. Reluctantly, he attended Sunday school at a mission, but his heart rebelled. By the time he was sixteen he had been arrested three times and aspired to a career in boxing, forsaking the church altogether.[96] A year later his mother begged him to return to the mission, but he slammed the door on her and departed for a gambling house instead. Conviction seized him on the way, so he relented. The superintendent of the mission was A. H. Leaman, an instructor at MBI. During prayer, Stemme envisioned himself as an old, decrepit man bearing the marks of his sin.[97] On November 10, 1907 Stemme made confession of his reprobate status and received Christ into his heart.

Stemme was deeply impressed with Charles Meeker, minister at Ewing Street Congregational Church, near Hull House. He became passionate for prayer and revival and participated in the church's campaigns, crediting his time there as a preparation for his pentecostal experience: "Fundamentalism in its highest form as expressed in those early days of my life, even more than I probably now realize, has had much to do with helping me to recognize in the Pentecostal movement that Apostolic power which moved the first disciples of the Lord."[98] Meeker encouraged Stemme to enter the ministry and introduced him to Wheaton College president Charles Blanchard. Stemme was a mediocre but persistent student, and, after running out of money, took up residence with a devotee of "ultra-dispensational" Anglican clergyman E. W. Bullinger.[99] William Evans pastored

93. "Ancient Tablets Bear Witness to Bible History," *COGE* (13 June 1936) 4.
94. M. L. Smith, "Gospel in Picture and Power," *PE* (1 October 1932) 12.
95. J. Kellner, "An Inspirational Triumph," *PE* (14 January 1933) 15.
96. Stemme, *Pentecostal Christian*, 5–6 (Carter-ATS).
97. Ibid., 6–7.
98. Ibid., 9.
99. Ibid., 9–10.

the college church at the time, but soon moved on to MBI. His replacement was another Bullinger disciple, Count Vladimir von Gelesnoff. Stemme devoured Bullinger's works.

President Blanchard frequently stressed to students the baptism of the Spirit from a Keswick perspective, which contradicted the ultra-dispensationalist view of Acts and the cessation of gifts. Stemme also gleaned his understanding of Spirit-baptism from the writings of South African divine Andrew Murray. Nonetheless, modernism beckoned to him through his involvement with the YMCA and with older, more progressive pastors.[100] He was attracted to their more liberal attitudes compared to Blanchard's criticisms of the YMCA. "I never intended to be a Modernist, but I began to feel that one could have a more modern approach and yet remain conservative in his theology," he reminisced.[101] Before long, he contemplated seminary and chose Biblical Seminary of New York over Yale and Union, where he had lunched with Harry Fosdick. Biblical was the most conservative of these, and Stemme confessed to goading his professors during his time there.

Ten years of Congregational posts in Illinois followed his graduation. During that time he felt increasingly vacuous and veered back towards fundamentalism, but could not square its beliefs with the operation of the Spirit.[102] Ever thirsty for spiritual guidance, he haunted F. F. Bosworth's campaign in Joliet, where an old-time revival had broken out. The meetings lasted from August 1930 to May 1931.[103] Stemme had received healing once while at Wheaton and now obtained it again after poring over *Christ the Healer*, adding, "I thank God for Brother Bosworth . . . though I do not agree with all this man of God teaches."[104] However, it was not enough to persuade him to join the pentecostals, and he even seemed unaware like Oswald Smith that Bosworth spoke in tongues.

Stemme persevered as a Congregationalist and the next year vigorously opposed the incursion in his town of pentecostals, whom he considered "religious hoodlums outside the pale of religious respectability."[105] Despite his protestations, the proprietors of a local meeting hall refused to padlock the doors against them. As Stemme walked away, he stumbled across a destitute woman whom he had been trying to convert. Her face shone with the glory of God upon it, touched through the power of Pentecost.[106] Like Paul kicking against the goads, Stemme conceded that he had been fighting against God. That night he reflected upon the meaning of consecration through "Deeper Life Conferences" and the writings of S. D. Gordon, R. A. Torrey, and especially in Jonathan Goforth's *By My Spirit*. In prayer, the Lord stripped him of everything he held precious until at last he cried out, "Oh God, Thou art enough."[107] The next evening, slipping into the back of the pentecostal service, he was "mightily baptized" in the Spirit.

100. Ibid., 12–14.

101. Ibid., 15.

102. Ibid., 18–19.

103. See C. C. Fitch, "More 'Good News' from Joliet, Illinois, Meetings," *EF* (October 1930) 13–18; Fitch, "Bosworth Campaign at Joliet, Illinois, Closes," *EF* (May 1931) 8–9.

104. Stemme, *Pentecostal Christian*, 20.

105. Ibid., 20.

106. Ibid., 21.

107. Ibid., 23–24.

In the last quarter of his narrative, Stemme strained to demonstrate the affinity that existed between pentecostals and fundamentalists. Writing in 1938, he cited such examples as Oswald Smith's trip to Sweden and the fundamentalist relationship to the Russian and Eastern European Mission in Chicago, both related in earlier chapters. The secretary of the latter organization was Vaughn Shoemaker, staff cartoonist for *The Daily News* in Chicago.[108] Shoemaker had been a member of the "Christian Business Men's Committee" when he received his pentecostal experience. Fundamentalist luminaries like Dr. French Oliver and William McCarrell happily addressed the Russian and Eastern European Mission. Swedish evangelist Aaron Anderson proclaimed his pentecostal credentials over the radio under the auspices of the "Christian Business Men's Committee" and again at Moody Church during a Swedish Baptist Convention.[109] Furthermore, Stemme knew of at least two prominent Chicago fundamentalists who spoke in tongues, although he withheld their names for privacy's sake.[110] Such links indicate that the divide between the two forms of spirituality was not as distant as many fundamentalists would have liked.

Nor was Stemme uncomfortable with the fundamentalist position, stating baldly that he would rather send his wife and children to a spiritual fundamentalist church than some "so-called" pentecostal churches where the Holy Spirit was aggrieved by the leader's actions. "I am as unalterably opposed to certain exhibitions of so-called Pentecost, as any Fundamentalist who shall read this book," he declared.[111] He also pointed out that pentecostals used Torrey's *What the Bible Teaches* (1898) and William Evans's *Great Doctrines of the Bible* (1912) in their colleges[112] and supported mission work in Chicago without raising disputable tenets.[113] An anonymous mission convert would later agree that pentecostals were among their most enthusiastic and successful workers.[114] The key for Stemme was that God rescued sinners through fundamentalists and pentecostals alike, and the bond of their fellowship was "saving faith in the Lord Jesus Christ."

Fundamentalists and the Holy Spirit

By 1930 fundamentalists had lost their battles for control of the denominations. But far from dying, as J. Carpenter has ably demonstrated, fundamentalism became resurgent away from the public spotlight during the depression.[115] MBI for instance expanded its services despite the shrinking economy.[116] Millions of the despondent tuned their radios to evangelists like Charles Fuller, Paul Rader and scores of others on local and national networks. The aggressive edge of the 1920s toned down in the 1930s. This was evidenced

---

108. Ibid., 36–37.
109. Ibid., 32.
110. Ibid., 30–31.
111. Ibid., 28.
112. Ibid., 42–43.
113. Ibid., 45.
114. Letter quoted in Bauman, *Modern Tongues*, 30–31.
115. Carpenter, *Revive Us Again*, passim.
116. A detailed account of MBI can be found in Runyan, ed., *Dr. Gray at Moody Bible Institute* (1935).

in two letters in *SST* in 1930 which called upon fundamentalists to win over foes rather than antagonize them.[117] Also, fewer articles directly pummeled pentecostalism. Instead, the focus turned towards a rejuvenation of fundamentalism, though the old enemies of Catholicism, communism and modernism continued to occupy their periodicals.

One of the earliest to describe the role of the Spirit to a new generation of fundamentalists was Harry Ironside, now pastor of Moody Church. Ironside authored seven articles on the Holy Spirit for Riley's *Northwestern Pilot* in the late 1920s, explicating the Spirit's function of "filling," "sealing," and "baptizing" the believer.[118] He displayed a classically fundamentalist model with baptism concomitant with conversion and refilled through self-surrender. However, caustic words bled through the page when he remembered a pentecostal incident in Oakland from his original investigation into the movement. Some practitioners at the holiness mission said they could simulate Chinese. Turning to some Chinese Christians for interpretation, he discovered that the tongue-folk were uttering gibberish except a few intelligible syllables fit for the gutter.[119] Ironside claimed to know "a little Chinese" and concluded that since the mission was located in a "thickly settled" district of immigrants, the worshippers must have subconsciously imitated the dialect they had heard on the streets. He was unimpressed to say the least.

Leonard L. Legters, field secretary for the Pioneer Mission Agency, pondered the Holy Ghost with a seven-part series which ran in *SST* from May to July 1930, celebrating the nineteen-hundredth birthday of the church. In light of the momentous occasion, denominations clambering for spiritual revival included Baptists, Methodists, Presbyterians and Disciples of Christ.[120] Legters labored to show that the Holy Spirit could be appropriated through faith and not toil, for God desired to fill every Christian with His Spirit.[121] He removed emotionalism as far from the equation as possible. God primarily touched the intellect to affect the heart.[122] Throughout he discounted the necessity of the redeemed to entice the Spirit into their lives because "the Bible distinctly informs us that we as believers *have been baptized.*"[123] As charismata were sovereignly dispersed by the Spirit, 1 Corinthians 12 obviated any need for specific manifestations like "tongues" or "prophecy."[124] Pentecostal techniques like "tarrying" and "laying on of hands" were to be discouraged[125]

---

117. "What is True Fundamentalism?" *SST* (12 June 1930) 410. C. G. Trumbull added his comments that "true fundamentalism" was based on 1 Corinthians 13, the "love" chapter.

118. Ironside, "Personality of the Holy Spirit," *NW Pilot* (November 1927) 8–9, 15; Ironside, "Holy Spirit in the Old Testament," *NW Pilot* (January 1928) 8–10; Ironside, "Sanctification by the Spirit," *NW Pilot* (February 1928) 6–7, 9–10; Ironside, "Baptism of the Holy Spirit," *NW Pilot* (March 1928) 8–10; Ironside, "Sealing by the Holy Spirit," *NW Pilot* (April 1928) 8–10; Ironside, "Filling with the Holy Spirit," *NW Pilot* (May 1928) 6–7, 10, 15; Ironside, "Power of the Holy Spirit in the Christian Life," *NW Pilot* (June 1928) 8–9, 13.

119. Ironside, "Sealing by the Holy Spirit," *NW Pilot* (April 1928) 8.

120. "Pentecost's 1900th Anniversary," *SST* (24 May 1930) 318.

121. Legters, "Simplicity of the Spirit-Filled Life," *SST* (24 May 1930) 317–18.

122. Legters, "Seven Words about the Holy Spirit," *SST* (31 May 1930) 329.

123. Ibid., 330, italics in original.

124. Legters, "Gift of the Holy Spirit, and His Gifts," *SST* (14 June 1930) 361.

125. Legters, "Witness and the Fullness of the Spirit," *SST* (21 June 1930) 374.

since Pentecost could never be repeated.[126] Yieldedness was essential to the process, with the result that one would be more sensitive to sin and sweeter in speech.[127] In the end, Legters spilled less ink on how to be filled with the Spirit as a Torrey might have done and more persuading how not do it—i.e., like the pentecostals.

Robert McQuilkin's *SST* articles from 1929 on Pentecost were published in a booklet for supernal edification in March 1931 because of a substantial demand. Everywhere fundamentalists were confronted with "pernicious" tongues, amounting to what the advertisement described as "a good deal of confusion."[128] Saints needed tools with which to counter false theology. Attention was also drawn to the subject because the ISSL covered Acts early in 1931. In June 1931 McQuilkin continued his exposition on the Holy Spirit. The first installment provided tips for studying the book of Acts. Here he ignored tongues, asserting that the purpose of pneumatobaptism was to unite the church as a body.[129] In part two, he iterated that Pentecost was a singular experience in the church that could not be repeated.[130] Nevertheless, many Christians were spiritually impoverished and agitating for the Spirit's power. His suggested medicament was to relent to the Spirit's presence in daily surrender to Christ.[131] This summed up well the Keswick position on baptism of which McQuilkin was such an ardent spokesman.

Gaebelein's associate F. C. Jennings wrote a six-part series in *Our Hope* from August 1933 to July 1934. Much of it encapsulated his 1919 article titled "The Holy Spirit."[132] However, this earlier version was more deprecatory towards pentecostals, accusing them of seeking the "lesser gifts" and of currying "power" rather than humility, the true stamp of the Spirit.[133] In both he lambasted Torrey's seven-step theory on baptism as confusing and superfluous.[134] Jennings illustrated the "filling" of the Spirit through well-digging. Abraham excavated a well (the pure gospel) which the Philistines had stopped up with mud and debris (worldliness and works-righteousness) and Isaac had unplugged (rededication).[135] Tarrying meetings were unnecessary to appropriate the Spirit, for He was already resident within every believer.[136] Ultimately, the Spirit was manifest in the meekness of the faithful who exalted Christ and were sweetly disposed toward others.[137] In Jennings's mind pentecostals lacked such virtues.

MBIM printed several calls for the Holy Spirit. In one, Vance Havner complained that the modern church resembled the modern world. In yearning for an infusion of the Spirit,

---

126. Legters, "Condition of the Spirit's Fullness," *SST* (5 July 1930) 397.
127. Legters, "Always Filled with the Spirit," *SST* (19 July 1930) 421–22.
128. "Study of Pentecost," *SST* (28 March 1931) 191.
129. McQuilkin, "How to Study the Acts and Know its Power," *SST* (13 June 1931) 335, 342.
130. McQuilkin, "The Holy Spirit: God's Great Gift of Victory," *SST* (20 June 1931) 347.
131. Ibid., 348.
132. Jennings, "The Holy Spirit," *Hope* (December 1919) 313–24.
133. Ibid., 318–21.
134. Ibid., 315; Jennings, "The Holy Spirit," *Hope* (February 1934) 483.
135. Jennings, "The Holy Spirit," (1919), 322–24; Jennings, "The Holy Spirit," (1934), 487–89.
136. Jennings, "Holy Spirit in the Individual Believer as Unction," *Hope* (March 1934) 538.
137. Jennings, "Holy Spirit in the Individual Believer as Unction (cont'd)," *Hope* (April 1934) 620–28.

"We are not contending for a fantastic emotional experience."[138] He invoked a more sedate infilling as an antidote to spiritual lethargy and spiritual exuberance. Lecturing at MBI, Charles Trumbull considered the surrendered life as the panacea for "defeated Christians," baptized by the Spirit in the manner of Keswick.[139] For Marguerite Russell, the Spirit was the agent of conversion, transformation and empowerment. The disciples received power after Pentecost, and "without this power of the Holy Spirit, the Christian would be helpless."[140] T. T. Shields warned against grieving the Holy Spirit through untruthfulness, unkindness and unforgiveness, potentially robbing oneself of the presence of God.[141]

AG pastor Howard Cotton of Westbrook, Maine, noticed these trends in April 1934, remarking, "Recently it has become quite popular for many Protestant denominations to teach and preach considerably about the Holy Spirit, hoping thereby to receive some semblance of Pentecostal power."[142] Those in the pew quested after spiritual enduement, but obscurantists in the pulpits beguiled them, much like the Pharisees of old who criticized Christ and prevented others from following Him. They taught that there should be nothing "indecorous" about the baptism, but God's Word and pentecostal experience suggested otherwise.[143] In his article, Cotton did not mention "fundamentalism" directly, though he showed no inhibitions in condemning "modern theology" and "formalism." Even so, a battle between pentecostalism and fundamentalism was being waged by the leaders for the hearts of laypeople.

Pentecostal Responses to Fundamentalism

Though the assaults in fundamentalist journals were less vitriolic, rampant opposition to pentecostalism still thundered from pulpit and pew. Certainly tongues as a sign remained a hotly contested issue. Gortner succinctly summarized the dispensational argument in 1932.[144] Under this scenario, the apostles proclaimed the gospel to Israel following the Lord's resurrection. If the Jews had accepted the offer of salvation through Christ, proclaiming him as their king on a national scale, the kingdom of God would have been inaugurated through them. Their rejection of the gospel necessitated that God extend salvation to the Gentiles, beginning with Cornelius and his household, and substantially withdrew the sign gifts from the church. Therefore, the charismata should not be manifest today, and where they are, must to be of satanic origin. In his apology, Gortner appealed to the Montanists and Tertullian to demonstrate that the gifts were in operation at least into the third century.[145] As a good Methodist, he culled Wesley's testimony that the Montanists

---

138. Havner, "Church without the Holy Spirit," *MBIM* (May 1932) 430–31.
139. Trumbull, "Message to Defeated Christians," *MBIM* (May 1932) 431–32.
140. Russell, "Holy Spirit in the Christian Life," *MBIM* (June 1933) 438.
141. Shields, "Grieving the Holy Spirit," *MBIM* (May 1934) 398–99.
142. Cotton, "Revealed Ways of God," *PE* (14 April 1934) 2.
143. Ibid., 2.
144. Gortner, "Are the Sign Gifts in Evidence Today?" *PE* (19 March 1932) 1.
145. Ibid., 9.

were indeed "real Scriptural Christians."[146] Fundamentalists of course would have summarily dismissed the Montanists as heretics, but for Gortner it was sufficient ground on which fundamentalists erred on apostolic gifts and the church.

Along similar lines, Donald Gee encountered the argument from a Baptist pastor, who claimed that the gifts were not found in the epistles (a point also made by McQuilkin).[147] For such opponents the absence of witness to the gifts in the epistles as compared to Acts could only be explained through God revoking them. The issue as Gee saw it between him and the cleric was not belief in a spiritual baptism but whether or not the event should be accompanied by tongues.[148] Gee denied that pentecostals lived strictly in the book of Acts while ignoring the epistles. After all, some fundamentalists took their dispensational theory to ridiculous lengths by assigning some segments of the gospels to the Old Covenant, such as the Lord's prayer. Therefore, they error in imposing a supposed "progress" of doctrine upon Acts.[149] Gee reminded them that most of the Pauline epistles were contemporaneous with Luke's writings and that the two were at one point traveling companions.

Even Scofield admitted that Cornelius's experience in Acts 10 was the "normal" pattern for the NT church, which Gee interpreted as "a manifestation of the Spirit's power."[150] (However, Gee equivocated in that Scofield's comments pertained only to the "normal" mode of reception of the Spirit as "without delay, mediation, or other condition than simple faith in Jesus Christ" without mentioning any necessary manifestations.)[151] Gee maintained that not only did the epistles not contradict the record of Acts, but also that passages like Galatians 3:2 and Ephesians 1:13 (not to mention 1 Corinthians 14) made more sense in the light of a pentecostal experience.[152] To Gee, this made better sense than holding that the "baptism" came upon the disciples "unconsciously" with manifestations occurring at a later time, as some detractors postulated. In short, the epistles ought be interpreted in the light of Acts rather than apart from it as dispensationalists tended to do.

The cessationist argument resurfaced in April 1930, which was refuted in an unsigned article in *PE*. It was actually a reprint of the twenty-second chapter of Frodsham's *With Signs Following* (1926), where he articulated the usual litany of pentecostal outpourings throughout church history, beginning with Chrysostom.[153] The book itself, originally allotted by the presbyters to E. N. Bell, was in many ways an apologia for the pentecostal

---

146. Gortner quotes from *The Journals of John Wesley*, vol. 2, concerning the Montanists (p. 169).

147. McQuilkin, "The Holy Spirit," 347.

148. Gee, "Is 'Pentecost' in the Epistles?" *PE* (7 November 1931) 2.

149. Fundamentalists, particularly ultra-dispensationalists, regarded the Sermon on the Mount as belonging to a previous age and not addressed to Christians but Jews under the OT dispensation. Scofield applies the sermon morally to believers but its "primary" import dispensationally to Jews (see Matt 5:2).

150. Gee, "Is 'Pentecost' in the Epistles?" 2.

151. *OSRB*, Acts 11:44 n. 1.

152. Gee, "Is 'Pentecost' in the Epistles?" 2–3.

153. Frodsham, "Pentecostal Outpouring throughout this Age," *PE* (26 April 1930) 8. See Frodsham, *With Signs Following*, 327–29. Frodsham left out the Irvingites and American manifestations along with select paragraphs from the chapter titled "Pentecostal Outpourings in History." E. N. Bell had originally been assigned to write this volume in 1921, but busyness and ultimately death prevented him from making much progress on the work.

movement, the gist being that no movement could have expanded so quickly if it had not been blessed by God. In 1932, Charles Robinson complained of how pentecostals felt shunned by the denominations. Pastors shut pentecostals out of local ministerial alliances and warned their members to disregard pentecostal meetings.[154] (The AG initiated local fellowship meetings of their own by 1927.)[155] Robinson himself had been removed from his Methodist pulpit for preaching on divine healing, and now many who received the baptism were being ejected from their churches.[156] The trouble as he saw it was that they did not investigate the Scriptures. As it happened with Luther and the Protestants among Catholics, so it was happening to pentecostals.

Pentecostal Assemblies of Canada leader R. E. McAlister aided pentecostalism in a series in 1932, countering an unnamed Canadian preacher's accusations that they did not revere the title "Lord Jesus Christ," denied the trinity (which was true of oneness pentecostalism), and valued the "lesser" gifts above the "greater." His address set out to correct fundamentalism's false impressions about pentecostal theology, focusing his remarks on the person of Christ and on the authority of Scripture, points on which his enemy would doubtless have shouted "amen."[157] In several places he also refuted modernist notions such as that the Bible was a literary product and that Christ endured a natural birth.[158] McAlister also added a "new dispensation" to the fundamentals, viz. the outpouring of the Spirit at Pentecost.[159] Contra Scofield, he deemed the apostolic experience to be the "normal" pattern for today's proselytes, resulting in "equipment for an efficient full-Gospel ministry." Thus, not only did pentecostalism concur with fundamentalism, but it also put the NT into practice in a way that fundamentalism could not.

Otto Klink rebutted the ubiquitous fundamentalist grumbling that pentecostals were too "noisy." Political conventions in Chicago, fanatics at baseball outings, lawyers at the dog tracks in south Florida where he lived; all were just as boisterous.[160] The Psalmists exhorted saints to "make a joyful noise" and "clap our hands," but the church was peopled by amnesiacs; they had forgotten how to praise God. As to tongues, he related the story of how his wife had sung in "Bohemian" at a gathering in Humboldt, Kansas without ever having studied the language.[161] The supposed "lost" conclusion to Mark was attested to in the *Freer Codex*, discovered in the same year as Azusa Street, surely not a coincidence.

---

154. Robinson, "Is Pentecost a New Religion?" *PE* (30 January 1932) 6.

155. Southern Missouri organized one under district superintendent A. A. Wilson in January ("District Fellowship Meeting," *PE* [29 January 1927] 14). Southern California held monthly meetings about this same time ("Southern California Fellowship Meeting," *PE* [5 March 1927, 1]. These were the earliest announcements I could find, though others may have been held earlier.

156. Robinson, "Is Pentecost a New Religion?" 9.

157. McAlister, "What the Pentecostal People Believe and Teach," *PE* (6 February 1932) 2–3.

158. McAlister, "What the Pentecostal People Believe and Teach," *PE* (13 February 1932) 2–3.

159. McAlister, "Pentecostalism Today," *PE* (20 February 1932) 6.

160. Klink, "Is the Pentecostal Movement Scriptural?" *PE* (15 July 1933) 1.

161. Ibid., 9. Her singing in tongues was understood by a man in the audience who identified the song as "Jesus Lover of my Soul."

DISFELLOWSHIPED

Also, contrary to cessationists, a surfeit of charismata had enthralled ecclesial chroniclers of the past, which Klink was only too happy to supply.[162]

This last item ignited the synapses of Carl O'Guin and Guy Renfrow. O'Guin, speaking to the Illinois District Council, challenged the argument of some "well-known" Bible schools and teachers that the pentecostal blessing was given to the Jews only, whom God slighted during the church dispensation.[163] Citing Methodist theologian Adam Clark [sic] and Anglican Dean Henry Alford, O'Guin believed that Pentecost did not complete the Jewish dispensation but sparked the Christian. Jews and Gentiles were heirs together of this blessing (Eph 3:5). To the question "Has the Day of Miracles Passed?," Renfrow responded the way many a pentecostal did; he simply proffered his testimony. A poorly educated Baptist preacher, Renfrow received healing from "tuberculosis of the bone" in one of his legs at a pentecostal rally.[164] As these snippets indicate, pentecostals confronted the cessationist position more in the 1930s than they had in the 1920s.

As a subscriber to *Revelation*, a fundamentalist magazine edited by Presbyterian minister Donald Barnhouse, Frodsham took umbrage with a March 1933 editorial titled "The Devil's Religion."[165] Barnhouse provided an unflattering description of pentecostal worship, accusing them of avoiding the full-title "Lord Jesus Christ" and of devaluing the blood of Christ. Frodsham wrote Barnhouse a letter saying that he had investigated these same claims in 1908 after someone had handed him anti-pentecostal literature. Putting the scriptural test of 1 Corinthians 12:3 to the case, "[I] saw at once that everywhere Jesus was acknowledged as Lord."[166] At his first pentecostal vigil, an unnamed preacher delineated "the precious blood of Christ" from Genesis to Revelation. Furthermore, pentecostals consented to the "verbal inspiration" of Scripture and "all the fundamentals of the faith" but denied that a person was baptized in the Spirit at regeneration as Barnhouse promulgated.

In a second missive, Frodsham waylaid this last point by quoting extensively from Winona Lake director William Biederwolf and from Andrew Murray.[167] As a final rebuttal, he referenced a letter he had scribbled to Charles Trumbull some years before in which he informed Trumbull that unlike the major denominations, pentecostals had not been infected with modernism.[168] In other words, perhaps Barnhouse should consider pentecostals as allies since they had a common adversary and stood with fundamentalists "one hundred per cent true to God's infallible Word." Frodsham's sentiments betokened a plausible alliance that materialized in the next decade.

---

162. Klink, "Are the Gifts of the Spirit for Today?" *PE* (16 June 1934) 2–3.

163. O'Guin, "Are Pentecost Blessings for Today?" *PE* (16 May 1931) 2–3.

164. Renfrow, "Has the Day of Miracles Passed?" *PE* (26 May 1934) 1, 7–8.

165. Frodsham, "Editor's Notebook," *PE* (1 April 1933) 4–5.

166. Ibid., 4.

167. Frodsham, "Editor's Notebook," *PE* (27 May 1933) 4.

168. Ibid., 5. Upon Trumbull's death in 1941, Frodsham commented, "As we have read his writings for many years, have met personally and corresponded with him, we have always been struck by his Christ-like spirit and deep humility" (Frodsham, "Dying World and the Living Word," *PE* [15 February 1941] 10).

Adopting a Fundamentalist Rhetoric (1930–1934)

The AG also switched from defensive to offensive tactics with four specially designed copies of *PE* between 1930 and 1934. The first "Pentecostal Number" premiered during Whitsuntide in 1930, containing testimonials to Spirit-baptism and advice on how to obtain it by E. S. Williams, P. C. Nelson, Lilian Yeomans, Donald Gee, and brothers Stanley and Arthur Frodsham. Stanley supplied an historical defense as well.[169] The second and least polemical "Pentecostal Number" (May 2, 1932) explained their intention, "Argument intensifies hostility . . . But place in their hands some Pentecostal literature and it will work silently, steadily and surely."[170] These special 8-page issues, four in total, bought and distributed through local parishioners, targeted hostile hearts and minds on a cheaper, depression-friendly budget.

The May 14, 1932 "Special Pentecostal Number" was spearheaded by an article from British AG chair Howard Carter, "A Timely Word to Opponents." Carter opened with a brief synopsis of the pentecostal message: "[they] are scriptural in teaching, united in the great fundamentals, missionary in outlook, and claim the old-time power of Pentecost."[171] He stressed the essential similarities between them and other Christians without denying their testimony to God's power to heal and baptize with tongues. Otto Klink proclaimed like Peter that "This is That"; in particular, we were living in the "Holy Ghost dispensation" which commenced at Pentecost and continued today.[172] For Stanley Frodsham, tongues had been foreshadowed in Isaiah's description of "stammering lips" (28.11).[173] Gee was appalled at Methodist evangelist E. Stanley Jones's remark that "Pentecost" needed rescue from the pentecostal movement.[174] He assented that there were excesses within the movement, but he challenged prospective seekers to keep an open mind and examine if personal prejudices had not hindered their attitude toward tongues, for one must separate any overindulgence from the experience itself.[175]

The lead article for the 1934 "Pentecostal Number" was an 1895 address on baptism by Baptist stalwart F. L. Chapell.[176] Canadian Methodist pastor F. M. Bellsmith vouched for his baptism under Harvey McAlister in Toronto in 1928. His training at MBI under

---

169. Yeomans, "This is THE Rest . . . and this is THE Refreshing," *PE* (26 April 1930) 1; Williams, "How Shall We Celebrate Pentecost?" 2–3; S. Frodsham, "Have Ye Received the Holy Ghost?" 3; Gee, "Letter to an Inquirer," *PE* (26 April 1930) 4–5; A. Frodsham, "Receiving the Latter Rain," 5; Nelson, "My Baptism in the Holy Spirit," 6–7; S. Frodsham, "Pentecostal Outpouring throughout this Age," 8.

170. "Witnessing to Thousands," *PE* (2 May 1931) 9.

171. Carter, "A Timely Word to Opponents," *PE* (14 May 1932) 1. The British AG is not formally affiliated with the American group.

172. Klink, "This is That," *PE* (14 May 1932) 2–3.

173. Frodsham, "Rest and Refreshing," *PE* (14 May 1932) 4.

174. Gee, "Pentecost and 'Pentecostalism,'" *PE* (14 May 1932) 6. The reference is to *The Christ of every Road: A Study in Pentecost* (1930). On pp. 46–47 Jones rebukes the present church for its overreaction to pentecostalism's overt emotionalism. Pentecostals had made Pentecost "queer," but Christians still needed the Spirit to live in Christ's presence and power. Just as Christ walked with the disciples on the Emmaus Road, so he walks with all disciples on "every road" (p. 51).

175. Gee, "Pentecost and 'Pentecostalism,'" 6–7. Gee was not so concerned with defending the movement ("Pentecostalism") as he was with the experience ("Pentecost").

176. Chapell, "Baptism in the Holy Spirit," *PE* (19 May 1934) 1, 7–8.

Torrey grounded him in the "fundamentals," immunizing him from modernism.[177] An anonymous article reprinted from 1922 chastised fundamentalists for rejecting the Holy Spirit just as the Pharisees had rejected Christ: "They pride themselves on knowing and holding the Fundamentals, and overlook THE FUNDAMENTAL OF SERVICE—...tarry ye in the city of Jerusalem, until ye be endued with power from on high."[178] These periodicals were crucial to improving pentecostal influence, with some even reporting their own baptism while reading the paper.

Denominational sheep kept coming to pentecostal meetings, despite pastoral prohibition. In Troup, Texas in 1932, Baptists, Methodists, Presbyterians, holiness and Church of God folk gathered to hear G. R. Edwards, where thirty were immersed in the Spirit.[179] "Walls of Prejudice" tumbled in places like Chattanooga, Oklahoma; Ashtabula, Ohio; and Little Rock, Arkansas.[180] Seven Baptists received Pentecost under the direction of S. A. Eversole in Green Forest, Arkansas, and revival invaded the Baptist church in Oldham, South Dakota under Clarence Jensen's admonition.[181] T. C. Long formed the First Pentecostal Baptist Church in San Antonio out of his Spirit-renewed congregation.[182] J. A. McCambridge conducted a revival at First Baptist in Butler, New Jersey early in 1930, where thirteen professed salvation and nine spoke in tongues.[183] Baptist pastor T. J. Logan imported the pentecostal message to his own denomination in St. Petersburg, Florida.[184] MBI graduate and Baptist minister H. T. Gruver inherited pentecostal blessings at a meeting in Lebanon, Missouri.[185] Bereft of material comfort, Methodists, Congregationalists, Nazarenes and scores of others sought spiritual comfort through baptism in healing campaigns and Holy Ghost revivals across the nation. While certainly not all were fundamentalists, there is sufficient evidence that many were at least sympathetic to the movement if not members, grieving their fundamentalist pastors.

Eschatology and the Church of God

CG remained less speculative about the denouement than the AG up to the late 1920s. In an eight-part series on apocalyptic themes, F. J. Lee voiced concern for the first time in September 1927 that Bolshevism embodied the spirit of the antichrist, a spirit which

---

177. Bellsmith, "Testimony of a Methodist Minister," *PE* (19 May 1934) 2–3.

178. "Have any of the Rulers Believed on Him?" *PE* (19 May 1934) 5; reprint of "Have many of the Rulers Believed on Him?" *PE* (2 September 1922) 8. In an undated sermon, Riley feared that fundamentalists might be Pharisees, bigoted and narrow, but the modernists were equally so in their denunciations of them (Riley, "Are the Fundamentalists Pharisees?" 1 [NWC Arch]).

179. Edwards, "As in Days Sweet and Golden," *PE* (8 October 1932) 11.

180. E. Medley, "Walls of Prejudice Crumble," *PE* (8 October 1932) 12; L. Frank, "Convinced Pentecost is Real," *PE* (10 September 1932) 12; R. Gilliam, "Crowds Attend, Prejudice Falls," *PE* (7 October 1933) 20.

181. Eversole, "Outpouring on Baptists," *PE* (9 January 1932) 21; Jensen, "Baptists Receive Full Gospel," *PE* (12 March 1932) 13.

182. T. P. Anthony, "Six Baptists Baptized," *PE* (19 November 1932) 16.

183. C. D. Peters, "Broadcasting His Name," *PE* (8 March 1930) 12.

184. W. H. Couch, "Baptist Minister Affiliates," *PE* (31 January 1931) 12.

185. J. R. Lewis, "Minister's Search Requited," *PE* (9 January 1932) 20.

Adopting a Fundamentalist Rhetoric (1930–1934)

his Scofield Bible defined as the "mystery of lawlessness."[186] Three weeks later he inferred from the popularity of Catholicism, spiritism, atheism and pantheism that the current age would usher in the antichrist.[187] A week later he added business conglomerations and labor unions to the mix of portents.[188] One-world government, earthquakes and the Jewish settlement of Palestine were also subjects of interest.[189] The first association of Mussolini with the antichrist in *COGE* came in March 1929. "Can this man be a forerunner of the Man of Sin, or is He altogether Him?" asked Robert Seyda.[190] Seyda indicted Sir Arthur Conan Doyle's dabbling into spiritism as another post-sign of the coming pseudo-religion. In June 1931 E. C. Clark interpreted Daniel's Beast to be both a kingdom and an individual, Rome and Mussolini.[191] Ancient Rome was symbolized by the "fasces," and Mussolini was not coincidently a "Fascist" reviving the empire.[192] These articles hint at the shift in CG towards fundamentalist modes of thought which had already occurred in the AG in the early 1920s. In other words, they moved from a general description of the apocalypse to a speculative approach typical of dispensationalists.

This trend continued into the 1930s, culminating in a wholesale adoption of dispensational theology by the end of the decade. Modernism posed as great a risk to faith inside the church as atheism outside of it, according to Bessie Thomas.[193] The "spirit of rationalism" was "enthroning" [sic] itself in the pulpits and religious education, reducing belief to a system of ethics. I. H. Marks went a step further and equated modernism with "the great apostasy" in 1931, occasioned by a statement by the liberal president of Southern Methodist Episcopal College, Charles Selecman.[194] Much of the article defended the tale of "Jonah and the whale," which Selecman had derided. Marks bugled, "In these last days of apostasy and falling away let's cling to the Word of God and defend its literal interpretation."[195] S. W. Latimer furnished a scathing assessment of modernism and missions in May 1933 entitled "The Apostasy of the Day." Liberal ministers had embedded themselves inside the ecclesiastical structures of major denominations while undermining the very faith they professed.[196] Prior to 1930 *COGE* condemned modernism and the denominations, especially the Methodists, in terms of their formality in worship. After 1930

---

186. Lee, "Spirit of the Antichrist," *COGE* (10 September 1927) 1.

187. Lee, "Man of Sin," *COGE* (1 October 1927) 1–2.

188. Lee, "His Coming Draweth Nigh," *COGE* (8 October 1927) 1.

189. Lee, "Terrible Beast: The Antichrist and the Government," *COGE* (17 September 1927) 1; Lee, "More about Earthquakes," *COGE* (24 September 1927) 3; Lee, "Israel's Return a Last Day Sign," *COGE* (22 October 1927) 1.

190. Seyda, "Approaching of Devils—Doctrines," *COGE* (16 March 1929) 2.

191. Clark, "Mark of the Beast," *COGE* (20 June 1931) 1.

192. Clark explains, "[A fasces] is a bundle of seven rods, bound around with a leather strap and in the middle of which is a battle axe."

193. Thomas, "The Present Challenge," *COGE* (30 August 1930) 1.

194. Marks, "Great Apostasy," *COGE* (16 May 1931) 1.

195. Ibid., 2.

196. Latimer, "Apostasy of the Day," *COGE* (6 May 1933) 3–4.

modernism acquired eschatological significance in representing an apostate Christianity, confirming CG's enamor with fundamentalism.

Missions secretary Zeno Tharp took a keen interest in signs of Christ's nearing advent in 1931, citing for his sources two secular magazines (*Literary Digest* and *National Republic*), two fundamentalist (*Wonderful Word* and *SST*), and two pentecostal (*PE* and *Pentecostal World*). He dismissed the theory that the antichrist would hail from the Catholic church, for that body acknowledged Christ as incarnate deity.[197] Tharp quoted at length from an article by Nathan Cohen Beskin which appeared in *PE*, which itself had been reprinted from *LRE*.[198] Beskin, extrapolating on the Federal Council of Churches, predicted the uniting of the world's religions. Subsequent articles by Tharp bashed communism, using Frodsham, *Pentecostal World*, *SST*, and *National Republic* as his sources.[199] Other "signs" included earthquakes in diverse places, a mice plague in Australia, and hailstones in Greece.[200] Tharp turned his attention to Russia for the ultimate two articles, chronicling the desperate situation of practicing believers there.[201]

J. L. Goins was equally alarmed at the rise of communism and also at the failure of the League of Nations to prevent war.[202] For Willie Rogers, presages of doom included the League, modernism, armament, Jewish immigration and the speed of travel (an aeroplane could transverse the nation in nineteen hours!).[203] Russia's muscle worried R. H. Bell in March 1933. Quoting Oswald Smith, Russia was a godless nation preparing for battle and world domination.[204] Armageddon couldn't be dawdling far behind. E. C. Clark foresaw a clash between fascist Italy and communist Russia, but he was uncertain as to which side would prevail.[205] Brethren pastor Louis Bauman made an appearance in 1933 via *SST*, pitting the Soviet "bear" against the "Lion of Judah," whose outcome was much more assured.[206] A topic which had made little impression during the heydays of the Red Peril in the early 1920s became something of an obsession by the early 1930s. No article was dedicated to socialism prior to Lee in 1927 while in *PE* it had been a source of consternation since 1919.[207]

Again, the cultivation of homegrown atheism disturbed fundamentalists and excited them as a symptom of Christ's return. In *COGE*, "infidelity" showed up twice in the title of

---

197. Tharp, "Antichrist, Signs and Sorrow, Happenings in Russia," *COGE* (18 July 1931) 1.

198. Beskin, "Mark of the Beast," *PE* (4 July 1931) 1, 8–9 (quote from p. 9); Beskin, "Mark of the Beast," *LRE* (March 1931) 3–7.

199. Tharp, "Communist [sic] against all Religion and Government," *COGE* (25 July 1931) 3; Tharp, "Antichrist, Signs, Sorrows," *COGE* (1 August 1931) 4.

200. Tharp, "Antichrist, Signs, Sorrows (cont'd)," *COGE* (8 August 1931) 4.

201. Tharp, "Antichrist, Signs, Sorrows (cont'd)," *COGE* (15 August 1931) 4; Tharp, "Antichrist, Signs, Sorrows (cont'd)," *COGE* (22 August 1931) 4.

202. Goins, "Distress of Nations with Perplexity," *COGE* (28 November 1931) 1, 3.

203. Rogers, "Some Signs that are to Precede Christ's Coming," *COGE* (29 August 1931) 1.

204. Bell, "The Day of the Lord," *COGE* (4 March 1933) 4–5.

205. Clark, "Growth of Fascism and Communism," *COGE* (3 June 1933) 5.

206. Bauman, "When Russia's Bear meets Judah's Lion," *COGE* (10 June 1933) 3–4, 6.

207. Frodsham, "The Bolshevist Menace," *PE* (29 November 1919) 6.

articles in the 1920s and "atheism" not at all.²⁰⁸ Between 1930 and 1935 *COGE* sustained a steady barrage with fourteen articles on the subject, at least five of which were from fundamentalist sources (*SST*, *MBIM*, *KB*, *The Defender*, and *King's Herald* [Winnipeg Bible College]).²⁰⁹ Additionally, Franklin Bowles, a former manager of a chemical laboratory, penned a series in 1930 that questioned the limits of "reason," for a little reason tended to atheism while much tended to God.²¹⁰ *COGE* editor E. C. Clark connected atheism to eschatology in 1933, seeing its increase as prelude to the antichrist.²¹¹ While it would be unfair to characterize CG theology as fully dispensational at this point, it had certainly sidled further along that route, drawn by the leavening dominance of fundamentalism on the evangelical churches.

Howard Juillerat had described the seven ages utilizing Scofield's terminology in 1918, but *COGE* did not revisit this until editor S. W. Latimer's dispensational articles in 1937, the same year that F. J. Dake joined the denomination.²¹² Latimer authored the series in reply to numerous requests from readers.²¹³ However, Latimer was hardly a slave to Scofield's notes. He differed with him on the meaning of the word "age." Where Scofield equated "age" with "dispensation," Latimer separated their senses.²¹⁴ He also interpolated that the earth had been populous before Adam and Eve's creation since the Lord decreed that they "replenish" it.²¹⁵ In other places he followed Scofield closely, such as his description of the "dispensation of conscience" as the time when Adam "came to a personal experimental knowledge of good and evil," nearly verbatim.²¹⁶ *COGE* first advertised the Scofield Bible in 1936, while J. A. Seiss's *Lectures on the Apocalypse* was advertised in 1934.²¹⁷ Latimer's articles secured the last piece of the dispensational puzzle. The First War had

---

208. "Infidel Credulity," *COGE* (4 April 1925) 2; W. Haslam, "The Infidel and his Dream," *COGE* (30 July 1927) 4.

209. "Our Family of Ten Atheists—and God," *COGE* (25 March 1933) 12, 24. [*SST*]; "Last Days of Charles Darwin," *COGE* (20 January 1934) 3, 12 [*MBIM*]; "Statistics on Atheism," *COGE* (3 February 1934) 1 [*KB*]; "Athiest [sic] Program," *COGE* (20 April 1935) 4 [*The Defender*]; H. Wilson, "God is not Mocked," *COGE* (18 February 1933) 4 [*King's Herald*]. A sixth article from *Gospel Herald* could not positively by identified as fundamentalist (M. Charles, "From Militant Atheism to the Militant Church," *COGE* [16 December 1933] 6–7, 10).

210. Bowles, "Age of Pure Reason," *COGE* (8 March 1930) 1; Bowles, "Age of Pure Reason," *COGE* (15 March 1930) 1, 3; Bowles, "Age of Pure Reason," *COGE* (22 March 1930) 1, 3. The second of these is by far the most interesting and informative.

211. Clark, "Atheism and God," *COGE* (28 January 1933) 7.

212. Juillerat, "The Ages," *COGE* (16 March 1918) 4; Latimer, "Dispensation of Innocence," *COGE* (13 March 1937) 1, 14–15; Latimer, "Dispensation of Conscience," *COGE* (20 March 1937) 3, 15; Latimer, "Dispensation of Human Government," *COGE* (3 April 1937) 3, 13; Latimer, "Dispensation of Promise," *COGE* (10 April 1937) 1, 14–15; Latimer, "Dispensation of Law," *COGE* (17 April 1937) 3, 14; Latimer, "Dispensation of Grace," *COGE* (24 April 1937) 3, 10.

213. Latimer, "Dispensation of Innocence," 1.

214. Ibid., 1.

215. Ibid., 14.

216. Latimer, "Dispensation of Conscience," 3. The phrase is lifted from *OSRB* (p. 10 n. 2).

217. "Scofield Reference Bible," *COGE* (18 April 1936) 16; "Lectures on the Apocalypse," *COGE* (26 May 1934) 16.

heightened interest in apocalyptic themes, if only temporarily; the looming Second War solidified dispensationalism's hold on the denomination.

Summary and Conclusion

The onset of depression increased pentecostal gains as the out-of-work and distressed sought refuge in primitive forms of faith. The ecstatic emotionalism of pentecostal worship provided a cathartic release for the anxieties of the age. Sunday schools assumed a more prominent role in both the AG and CG as they sought to transfer pentecostal values to the rising generation. This concern for children coincided with parental worry over the drift of youth towards atheism. The seeds of doubt planted by higher criticism and theistic evolution in modernism bore fruit in the outright atheism of denominational schools and secular campuses.

The "content" of fundamentalism exposed pentecostals to the dangers of modernism and the larger society against which fundamentalists had barricaded themselves. Pentecostals now assimilated the fundamentalist arguments with alacrity. The transition was exemplified in the ministry of J. N. Hoover, a card-carrying fundamentalist who neatly substituted the "Holy Spirit" for the "church age" on his dispensational chart, preaching fundamentalist themes with conviction. The 1920s featured fundamentalist conversions like Frey, Shreve, Towner, and Hoover. The 1930s highlighted the conversion of Harry Stemme, although just how indebted he was to modernism was questionable. At any rate, this change shifted the focus from fundamentalism to modernism as pentecostals' primary enemy. Their rhetoric mirrored that of fundamentalism, and even the CG, which had largely been silent about fundamentalist issues in the 1920s, now adopted its perspective.

While the attacks of fundamentalism were overt and continued into the 1930s, modernism posed a more devious, surreptitious threat if not unearthed and treated. In the early 1930s fundamentalism had retreated from the victorious outlook of the 1920s. One bulwark which came to prominence against pentecostalism was cessationism. In the 1920s fundamentalists had also steered towards dryer, less demonstrative forms of worship, in part a reaction to pentecostal enthusiasm. The 1930s exposed its more tepid spirituality compared to pentecostal vitality. Both were concerned with revivalism, and the most effective way to revitalize a flagging evangelicalism and oppose modernism was through cooperation, as would be demonstrated by radio evangelist Charles Fuller and his chief supporter, J. Elwin Wright, whose vision for a united evangelical voice would culminate in the NAE.

Battling a Common Foe (1935–1943)

Introduction

MAINSTREAM AMERICAN RELIGION IN THE 1930S ENGINEERED SEVERAL MERGERS THAT changed the face of denominationalism, while fundamentalists suffered separation which left them more fractured than ever. The formation of the National Association of Evangelicals (NAE) followed the first trend while the formation of the American Council of Christian Churches (ACCC) followed the second. Pentecostals, ever desiring recognition from other evangelicals, finally gained it in the NAE, although not without controversy. The first evidences of cooperation with fundamentalists at a national level came in 1936 in the realm of Sunday School education. The effort was occasioned by their mutual distrust of modernism. These trends foreshadowed the NAE as a response to modernism and the Federal Council of Churches (FCC) on the one hand and the stridently sectarian policies of the ACCC on the other. One future ACCC supporter battered pentecostalism, as the next section details.

Frank Norris and Fundamentalist Baptists

1936 renewed J. Frank Norris's effort at undermining pentecostal faith. His barrage of articles pounded John Rice for harboring "pentecostal positions," viz. about present-day miracles and divine healing. Though Rice had closely associated with Norris Norris's church as an evangelist for ten years, Norris admitted that he had never scanned through any of Rice's myriad of pamphlets and sermons, nor his paper *The Sword of the Lord*, launched in 1934.[1] Unflattering accusations by fellow Baptists Louis Entzminger, C. P. Stealey and Harold Strathearn, however, caused him to take a microscopic look.[2] The founding of a rival church in Dallas in 1932 by Rice, which he would pastor for seven years, had already created a strain in their relationship.[3] Even more intolerable was the miasmic waft of Rice's doctrine on healing in several Texas fundamentalist Baptist churches that Rice had spawned but which fell under Norris's auspices.

---

1. Norris, "Western Union Telegram," *Fund* (24 January 1936) 1.
2. Norris, "A Sad Letter Concerning a Friend," *Fund* (24 January 1936) 3.
3. Moore, "Moderate Fundamentalism," 99–100.

DISFELLOWSHIPED

During a revival in Lubbock, Texas in December 1935, a "pentecostal" member from Rice's Dallas congregation "tore the Fundamentalist church all to pieces."[4] Norris was relieved to hear from Pastor George Pemberton that the church had righted itself by standing up to the "oily crowd."[5] At a meeting in Amarillo, Norris explained to visiting pentecostals that they had occupied the "wrong pew." He assured readers that he did not oppose prayer for the sick, "a beautiful and happy thing to do," but drew the line at anointing them with bottles of oil.[6] At Decatur, Texas, Rice proceeded with a healing service despite protests from several deacons in the church and without much effect.[7] Rice's "loose" membership requirements when he had started that church some years earlier had allowed a "Brother House" to stir up trouble along pentecostal lines, though House was soon shown the door, according to deacon J. E. Boyd.[8]

Norris adamantly denounced "this cult [as] the most dangerous enemy of the truth, far more dangerous than out and out rationalistic modernism."[9] They preyed upon "orthodox" churches, whose adherents were susceptible to error if not properly instructed. Norris had recently corrected the theology of several in his flock who had become infected with pentecostal tenets. Nor was it the first time he had encountered their ilk. He had run across these "deluded dear friends" in the "inquiry room" in the basement of his Fort Worth church some time in the late 1910s (when exactly is not clear). These seekers after the Holy Spirit were rolling around the floor and frothing at the mouth like "a dying calf" [sic].[10] He challenged one of them to bring sinners to Christ before making an "asinine, braying" spectacle of himself in their presence.[11] The individual vacated the premises, and the "explosions" terminated. The incident tainted Norris with a poor impression and no doubt led to his conclusion that pentecostals were "anti-missionary" and "anti-evangelistic." Had he bothered, a glance through PE in 1936 would have dissuaded him from that opinion.

Entzminger, a staunch advocate of the Sunday school, worried that "spiritual" and "independent" Baptist churches were particularly vulnerable to pentecostal infiltration.[12] The Taylor Tabernacle in San Antonio for instance had sided with Rice and "caused constant embarrassment" to Entzminger's work there.[13] He blamed a "Pentecostal Baptist" church, undoubtedly T. C. Long's, for causing him much harm. Modernist churches were far less

---

4. Norris, "A Sad Letter Concerning a Friend," *Fund* (24 January 1936) 3.

5. "Fine News from George Pemberton," *Fund* (24 January 1936) 3.

6. Ibid., 3. "Anointing Vials" were regularly advertised in the *PE* and commonly used in healing services.

7. "Fundamentalist Baptist Church, Decatur, Split over Healing Service," *Fund* (31 January 1936) 3.

8. Ibid., 3. It is likely that House was the pastor of the church, who tried to rule the church like a "Methodist Bishop," "but we [Boyd and the church board] soon gave him to understand that we knew no such animal in our Baptist churches."

9. Norris, "A Sad Letter Concerning a Friend," 7.

10. Norris, "'You are of the Devil in Opposing the Baptism of the Holy Ghost,'" *Fund* (7 February 1936) 1. Norris records the event as happening "twenty years ago," which, if accurate, would date the incident to 1916.

11. Ibid., 6.

12. Entzminger, "Four Notable Victories among Fundamentalist Baptists," *Fund* (28 February 1936) 4.

13. Norris, "A Sad Letter Concerning a Friend," 3.

exposed to the menace of pentecostalism, he alleged. Norris concurred, "The tragedy is that these 'Holier-i-than-thou-nuts' always undertake to carry on their propaganda not among dead cold, lifeless modernistic churches, but among Spiritually minded churches."[14] Fundamentalism had swept across the Baptists of 1930s Texas, but the "holy rollers" threatened to destabilize their advance (not to mention Norris's empire).

Norris laid much of the blame at Rice's feet. "As wool in the teeth of the dog shows where he has been, so there are certain earmarks of the modern cult of Pentecostalism," he allegorized in a provocative spur titled "Can True Fundamentalist Baptists Fellowship the Snake-Poison-Oily Crowd?"[15] Despite pleas of innocence, Rice was culpable on two accounts under Norris's glare: he advocated divine healing and modern-day miracles, both positions endorsed by pentecostals. Norris grossly misrepresented pentecostalists at several points, insinuating that they labeled "great soul winners" as "heathens" if they did not perform miracles and that they were uninterested in missions and evangelism.[16] Norris feared that those who were persuaded to join them would succumb to the same lethargy.

By the 1930s the cessationist argument had become a standard arsenal in the fundamentalist war against tongues, and Norris employed it to full effect against Rice. Norris's own transition is telling. He had once advocated present-day miracles in his ministry, but the "perversion that the Pentecostals and Holy Rollers [made] of [miracles]" forced him to scurry back to his Bible and reassess his views.[17] Under his new dogma, he repelled their claims to possess the same miraculous powers that Elijah and the apostles had enjoyed. He saw it as a perversion of Scripture which "makes the perpetrator a candidate for the insane asylum."[18] Norris's dramatic reversal on the issue was instigated through his contact with pentecostalism, indicative of a broader entrenchment in fundamentalism against pentecostals during the 1920s. Though he had golfed with Rice for ten years, more than "all others combined," he regretfully withdrew his stamp of approval on the man.[19] Several of those loyal to Norris quickly retracted their approvals of Rice as well.[20]

Norris considered the fact that Rice never advocated tongues to be irrelevant. He instead focused on Rice's pursuit of "power" through the Holy Spirit, conveniently forgetting that he himself had preached on the enduement in 1923.[21] Rice was receptive to the Keswick position that there were many "infillings" of the Spirit. Comparing Acts 2:4 to 4:21, Rice purported that the disciples were twice filled with the Spirit, a pattern that

---

14. Norris, "'You Are of the Devil,'" 1.

15. Norris, "Can True Fundamentalist Baptists Fellowship the Snake-Poison-Oily Crowd?" *Fund* (24 January 1936) 1.

16. Ibid., 5.

17. Norris, "A Sad Letter Concerning a Friend," 7.

18. Norris, "Can True Fundamentalist Baptists Fellowship?" 5.

19. Ibid., 5.

20. Norris printed the retractions of Earle Griffith, J. W. Harper, P. T. Stanford, Marion Been, and other prominent Fundamentalist Baptists in "Fundamentalist Baptists should have no Part or Lot with Pentecostal 'Holy Ghost Baptism,' Present Day 'Bible-Miracles,' 'Speaking-Chinese,' Talking-New-Languages as-at-Pentecost,' 'Taking Serpents,' and 'Drinking Deadly Poisons,'" *Fund* (14 February 1936) 2, 6.

21. Norris, "Power from on High our Supreme Need," *Search* (28 September 1923) 1–2. In fact, in this sermon on baptism Norris talked about little else except "power."

should be expected in every believer.[22] Like Torrey, he maintained that spiritual baptism occurred subsequent to regeneration. In tackling the issue of evidential tongues, Rice mistakenly attributed the pentecostal teaching to the holiness movement, indicating that he did not sufficiently grasp the differences between the two.[23] He denied that the Spirit had given the disciples the power to speak in "unknown" languages on the Day of Pentecost. Rather, they "were given power to preach the gospel to the people assembled, in their own languages."[24] For Rice, the Bible evidence for the baptism was "soul winning power"—for "God will put power on his testimony."[25] That Norris glossed over the criticisms Rice made against pentecostalism is testament to the rancorous division that had developed between them.

Louis Entzminger was even more virulent in his attitude toward pentecostals. The first issue he paraded was the cessation of miracles, giving one of the clearest delineations on that topic in the eyes of Dr. Earle Griffith, pastor of First Baptist in Johnson City, New York (a judgment to which I concur).[26] Entzminger's triadic argument insisted that biblical miracles were limited to special times (generally when transitioning from one dispensation to another), limited by the number of characters who performed them (Moses, Elijah, Jesus, disciples, etc.), and limited in purpose (generally to denote the authority of the miracle worker).[27] The second issue he tackled was the "baptism of the Holy Ghost," which, in splitting theological hairs, he posited was not mentioned in the NT. The phrase should have been translated "baptism in the Spirit."[28]

Nonetheless, he pronounced Rice guilty of confusing "baptism" with "filling," "sealing," and "gift."[29] Only two baptisms actually happened, said Entzminger, one at Pentecost and the other at Cornelius's house, and in neither case were the recipients commanded to pray for the Spirit. By "tarry in Jerusalem," Jesus meant only that they were to wait for the power to come, although undoubtedly they did pray and worship in the interim.[30] Entzminger rejected the teaching that Jesus was the same "today" as "yesterday" (Heb 13:8), a fallacy perpetuated by pentecostals. Christ's methodology had changed since his terrestrial ministry, though not His character.[31] He also disagreed with fellow Baptists who equated regeneration with pneumatobaptism, though he accepted them as orthodox

---

22. Rice, *The Baptism of the Holy Spirit for Us Today*, 3 (FPHC). Rice wrote this tract from Fort Worth, indicating that he was still identified with Norris at the time, though it was published by Paul Rader, most likely in the early 1930s before his move to Dallas. Norris cites this tract as "Speaking with Tongues" in his articles.

23. Ibid., 2.

24. Ibid., 3.

25. Ibid., 5.

26. Letter quoted by Norris in "Fundamentalist Baptists should have no Part or Lot," 2.

27. Entzminger, "Are Miracles to be Performed Today as in the Bible Times?" *Fund* (24 January 1936) 1, 4, 6–7.

28. Entzminger, "Unscriptural Heresy of 'the Baptism of the Holy Ghost,' and its Evil Consequences," *Fund* (31 January 1936) 1, 4.

29. Ibid., 4. In fact, Rice never used "sealing" as a synonym for "baptism."

30. Ibid., 4.

31. Ibid., 5.

Christians.³² There was only "one baptism" (two, actually, contradicting himself) in partial fulfillment of Joel 2 but many "fillings" for which every believer could petition in order to extend the kingdom. Entzminger's third article asserted that "power for witnessing" was the true intention of the Spirit's advent.³³ The series was published as a 100-page pamphlet together with a message on James 5 by Norris; ten thousand copies went out in the first edition.³⁴

Dallas minister Roy Blackwood mustered a defense in February 1936, the first in CG against fundamentalist attacks since Tomlinson's departure.³⁵ He defied Entzminger's contention that Jesus had altered his methodology. "We are yet living in the church age," he averred, and nothing between the covers of the Bible suggested otherwise.³⁶ Tongues and knowledge would cease only when "perfection" came, which he interpreted as the future heavenly kingdom and not the written word of the NT as his opponent implied. He ridiculed Entzminger's notion that the application of oil in healing was merely medicinal in purpose. Like water for baptism, oil was a symbol, and James would not have required the elders to pray for the sick if it weren't so; otherwise, the local doctor would have done just as well. Were the vessels sick which Moses anointed with oil for worship in the tabernacle? he asked rhetorically.³⁷ He deemed it uncharitable of foes to slight them as "Holy Rollers" and use extreme cases like snake handling to paint the movement in dark hues. Baptists were, like John the Baptist, on the decrease both spiritually and numerically, he hinted in a parting shot.³⁸

Blackwood revisited the cessationist argument in April, emphasizing once again that "charity never failed" where tongues and prophecy would—that is, in the next kingdom.³⁹ In October he rebutted an unnamed Baptist who presided over a local station (KTAT); it was Norris stirring up controversies again in Fort Worth.⁴⁰ However, instead of refuting Norris, he lifted his pen against Entzminger, specifically on the point that NT believers were baptized "in" and not "with" or "of" the Holy Ghost. He employed Rice's distinction that the terms "gift," "filled," and "baptized" were synonymous, and he did not include "seal-

32. Ibid., 6.
33. Entzminger, "Filled with the Holy Spirit for Witnessing," *Fund* (14 February 1936) 1, 4–7.
34. "'Should be Published in Pamphlet Form—I have not seen an Equal,'" *Fund* (14 February 1936) 8.
35. F. Lemons did respond to Asbury Seminary professor George Ridout's attack in the *Pentecostal Herald* in 1933 (Lemons, "A Reply to Unjust Criticism," *COGE* [11 March 1933] 3-4). Ridout's article, "Wresting the Scriptures and Perverting the Word of God," appeared January 18, 1933. Ridout also assaulted pentecostals in "Satan's Devices Deceiving the very Elect" (*PH* [1 September 1920] 4–5). Most of *COGE*'s responses to critics were against holiness and/or Methodist periodicals. F. J. Lee challenged a Methodist minister in four articles in 1925 ("The Unruly Member" [June 6] 13, 20, and 27); J. A. Tarpley against the *Christian Triumph* on 2 October 1926, Blackwood against a "Mr. Bryers" on 1 April 1933, and H. Miller against Godbey, Ridout and E. E. Shelhammer, a Free Methodist minister in Atlanta, on 24 June and 1 July 1933.
36. Blackwood, "Reply to Articles and Arguments," *COGE* (22 February 1936) 3.
37. Ibid., 14.
38. Ibid., 14–15.
39. Blackwood, "Prophecy, Tongues, and Knowledge, Appointed for the Good of the Church," *COGE* (4 April 1936) 3, 15–16. Blackwood quoted much from Adam Clarke's commentaries.
40. Blackwood, "Inconsistency of Holy Ghost Baptism Fighters," *COGE* (1 August 1936) 3, 16. KTAT was bought by FDR's son, Elliot Roosevelt, in 1939.

ing" as Rice had not. It seems that Blackwood was familiar with Rice's thinking. He also distinguished between the "gift" of the Spirit (the Person) and the "gifts" of the Spirit (for ministry) in 1 Corinthians 12, which Entzminger had failed to separate.[41] If detractors truly believed in the verbal inspiration of Scripture, then why did they not accept that Jesus baptized in the Spirit today?

Blackwood's attention to fundamentalism was a sign of the shift taking place in CG. The shift was predicated on their turn in eschatology towards dispensationalism as outlined in the previous chapter, opening the pathways into other fundamentalist concerns. With the increase of radio purchases in the 1930s, CG laypeople could listen to fundamentalist programs (and read their literature) to a degree not experienced in the 1920s. Furthermore, Blackwood was in an urban locale where fundamentalist centers like Norris's were strong, while the CG in general had a rural composite.

Jonathan Perkins' Repudiation of Pentecostals

Through much of the 1920s, Jonathan Perkins pastored a prominent AG church in Tulsa and contributed infrequently to *PE*. In the late '30s he switched allegiances to the Fundamentalist Baptists, turning on his former acquaintances in a scathing booklet, *Pentecostalism on the Washboard* (1939). He had known Norris since 1922 and once introduced the "Texas Tornado" to a divided auditorium in Amarillo on the issue of bootlegging.[42] "From that day to this I have been his outspoken friend at all times and places without apology," Perkins confessed.[43] He had even contemplated uniting with Norris's Fort Worth congregation when J. W. Welch lured him into heading up the literature department for the AG in 1924.[44] At Perkins's request, Entzminger quizzed a number of pentecostal leaders as to Perkins's character. He received favorable replies from them all, including one by J. Roswell Flower, now serving as General Secretary. "If the Pentecostal movement had more men in it of the type of [Flower], this publication would never have been produced," Entzminger commented.[45]

Perkins addressed his volume to AG General Superintendent Ernest Williams, whom he accused of supporting "free lovism" by not stamping it out in the denomination. Specifically, Williams was part of a junta along with Robert Brown, Goertner [sic], Frodsham, Joseph Tunmore (superintendent of Pennsylvania) and Carl O'Guin that ousted Welch (whom Perkins fervently admired) as General Superintendent in 1926 and replaced him with W. T. Gaston, who later admitted to an illicit affair (or "spiritual marriage") with a Mrs. Keel.[46] Furthermore, Stanley Frodsham was unabashedly in love with his assistant,

---

41. Blackwood, "Inconsistency of Holy Ghost Baptism Fighters," *COGE* (8 August 1936) 6, 16.

42. Perkins, *Pentecostalism on the Washboard*, 6. Perkins noted that he had been friends with Norris for 17 years and introduced him in Amarillo just before meeting with Welch.

43. Ibid., 6.

44. Ibid., 6. Perkins claimed to have ghost-written several early books printed by GPH. He joined the AG in March 1924 (J. R. Flower to Louis Entzminger, letter dated 12 October 1939 [FPHC]).

45. Entzminger, "Introduction" to Perkins, *Washboard*, 2.

46. Perkins, *Washboard*, 8–12. In an interview, C. O'Guin conceded that he had helped engineer Welch's downfall at Eureka Springs in favor of someone with broader appeal ("Notes from telephone call Tuesday, April 17, 1984, Wayne Warner with Carl O'Guin, Madison, Illinois" [FPHC]).

Marjorie Head, while his first wife was still alive.[47] Charles Price was a philanderer and hypnotist,[48] his lackey Everett Parrot an effeminate charlatan,[49] Raymond Richey an unscrupulous hustler,[50] and Sister Aimee a chronic drunk.[51] The last half of the work Perkins devoted to the unsoundness of pentecostal and holiness fanatics who based faith on feeling rather than the Word of God as both Quakers and spiritualists had.[52] The AG as the leading pentecostal church was responsible for all the wrongness of the "healing racket," and Williams was a "moral coward" for not opposing it.[53] Perkins also incorporated the Fundamentalist Baptist condemnation of pulpiteering women into the fracas. Like most revivalists, subtlety was not a strong trait in Perkins.

Not surprisingly, AG officials were furious upon its publication. Gortner mailed Perkins a lengthy rejoinder, pointing out the errors in both his judgment and personal conduct.[54] He reminded Perkins that he (Perkins) had already apologized to Price for his allegations and then rescinded his apology when Price was forced by external circumstances to cancel a campaign in connection with Perkins's church in Los Angeles. When Price removed his campaign to Bethel Temple, the leading AG church in the Los Angeles area, Perkins then abused its pastor, Louis Turnbull. Furthermore, Perkins had passed a week in jail for libel. Even Paul Rader (a most congenial fundamentalist if there ever was one) had broken with Perkins on account of his irascibility. In other words, Perkins was a perfidious troublemaker whose could not be trusted.

Perkins belatedly demanded payment from the AG in 1949 for the 3,000 copies of his book that had been burned under Fred Vogler's supervision in Fort Worth in 1939.[55] (According to a conflicting witness, Perkins repented of his diatribe and voluntarily turned the books over to Vogler, who allegedly destroyed them.)[56] Perkins further threatened to publish more tracts if his demand to meet with the executive council at the upcoming convention in Seattle was not met. He then accused Flower of being the "greatest traitor" to pentecostalism by "selling out" to the NAE, particularly after Donald Barnhouse jeered pentecostal beliefs at an NAE meeting in Columbus, Ohio. He also accused Flower of "gambling" with AG money by risking missionary funds on the stock market.

In the opinion of Gerald Winrod, under whom Perkins later labored, Perkins was quick to play Quisling with his employers and offered dirt in print for monetary com-

---

47. Perkins, *Washboard*, 13–16. Frodsham and Head married with his daughter Faith's blessing in 1930 (F. Campbell, *Stanley Frodsham*, 97).

48. Perkins, *Washboard*, 16–18.

49. Ibid., 19.

50. Ibid., 21–22.

51. Ibid., 22–26.

52. Ibid., 28–47.

53. Ibid., 11, 47.

54. Gortner to J. E. Perkins, letter dated 10 November 1939 (FPHC).

55. Perkins to J. R. Flower, letter dated 27 June 1949.

56. "Wayne Warner's telephone conversation with Mrs. Carl Stewart, Fort Worth, Texas, Friday, August 19, 1988" (FPHC).

pensation.[57] In 1949, another former fundamentalist employer, Gerald K. L. Smith, felt the brunt of Perkins's ire after four years of servitude under Smith's anti-Communist organization, the Christian Nationalists. Perkins had been his chief fundraiser but revealed Smith to be the "biggest hypocrite in America" in a scintillating exposé.[58] In short, Perkins had a history of lodging grievances that he had difficulty proving. Needless to say, the AG did not pay for Perkins's lost books nor meet with him in Seattle. It is also telling that Perkins's defection from pentecostalism in the 1930s steered him toward Norris and the Texas fundamentalists. Pentecostals viewed fundamentalists as natural allies in the battle to save souls, but the feeling was rarely mutual.

E. C. Miller's Rebuttal of Louis Bauman

Louis Bauman was the long-time pastor of First Brethren Church in Long Beach, California and prolific augmenter to fundamentalist periodicals. In 1931, he authored a pamphlet implicating pentecostalism as a Satan-inspired perversion of true Christianity.[59] Though admitting there were some splendid members in the "Tongues Movement," it made no difference at its source, "for Satan himself is transformed into an angel of light."[60] Bauman focused his critique on 1 Corinthians 14, which placed tongues last on Paul's list of gifts.[61] Conceding that Paul "forbade not tongues," still it was better to speak a few words intelligibly in church. Bauman argued that "signs" were intended for Jews only since they were God's instrument for ushering in new dispensations like the "Church Age" and the impending "Millennial Age."[62] Tongues had become superfluous once the NT record was obtained; indeed, pentecostals "set their babbling 'experiences' above the Word of God itself."[63] He included a number of damning testimonies, including one by a woman from his church that had appeared in *SST* in 1927.[64] He also denied that women had ever spoken in tongues in the NT, honoring them instead with "prophesying," which he defined as "expounding" the divine word that God had revealed to men only.[65] McPherson and her

---

57. In Roy, *Apostles of Discord*, 114 (FPHC).

58. Perkins, *Biggest Hypocrite*, 23–24. On the front cover, Perkins promoted it as "the most sensational book that has been written in our day."

59. Gaebelein, "Pernicious Tongue-Movement," *Hope* (July 1931) 16–17. Gaebelein commented of Bauman's work, "Surely the influence of demons can be seen in these cults of Tongues and Pentecostalism."

60. Bauman, *Modern Tongues*, 1.

61. Ibid., 2–4.

62. Ibid., 5–6.

63. Ibid., 4, 6.

64. Ibid., 12–14, 34–35. Frodsham's opinion of this article was covered in a previous chapter, see "From the Pentecostal Viewpoint," *PE* (9 July 1927) 4. Other testimonies came from Sir Robert Anderson's "Spirit Manifestations" on India (Bauman, *Modern Tongues*, 8–10) and H. J. Prince (ibid., 23–24), R. A. Torrey's condemnation of Parham and Lupton (ibid., 24–25), a personal acquaintance of his whose relative thought she could speak Hebrew but failed to convince Jewish neighbours (ibid., 32–33) and a letter written in response to the first edition in which the writer noted that he simultaneously had sexual urges while receiving his baptism (ibid., 30–31).

65. Ibid., 15–17.

two divorces also fell into rude censorship.⁶⁶ In many ways, Bauman's critique was typical of 1930s fundamentalism with its bans on extra-biblical miracles and women commandeering the pulpit.

His critique did not go unanswered. In 1936, the AG published a series of letters written by a Baptist lawyer, Elmer C. Miller. Miller had been seeking the baptism of the Spirit for about two years at Bethel Pentecostal Assembly in Newark, New Jersey. Most likely, it was the same E. C. Miller who attended a 1923 meeting of the Bible Baptist Union in Toronto under Norris and T. T. Shields. The report described Miller as a New York businessman who proposed to the floor that "we give first place in all our thinking to the bringing about, the bringing down from above, of a great spiritual revival," which met with a hearty "amen."⁶⁷ It would not at all be unusual to identify a New York lawyer as a businessman since the two professions often intertwined in the metropolis. Thus, even from the early 1920s Miller demonstrated Pastor Philpot's assertion that the most spiritual fundamentalists were attracted to pentecostalism. At his local Baptist church in Caldwell, New Jersey, a visiting preacher, LeRoy Lincoln, berated charismatic devices.⁶⁸ Miller responded to Lincoln with a letter, written November 8, 1933. This led to an exchange of letters between Miller, Lincoln, Rev. Edward Drew, and a "Sister D" between 1933 and 1934, three of which were reprinted in the booklet. As Miller challenged Bauman's pamphlet in the last of these letters, I will deal with it first.

Miller built his polemic against cessationism on the plank of history. Tongues had appeared in many religious movements like the Huguenots, and even F. B. Meyer corroborated the existence of tongues in modern-day Estonia.⁶⁹ Miller inserted a lengthy section from A. J. Gordon's *The Ministry of Healing* (1882) in which the author admitted that the charismatic gifts belonged to the present age.⁷⁰ From his personal observation, Miller estimated that only one percent of the pentecostal sermons he had heard actually advocated tongues while the others promoted salvation, healing, the second coming, and other themes friendly to fundamentalism.⁷¹ From Bauman's accusation to the contrary, he deduced that Bauman had little first-hand knowledge of the movement. Speaking as a lawyer, he believed that the majority of testimonials Bauman submitted as evidence would have been dismissed by the law courts as mere "hearsay."⁷² To pilfer a few samples of immorality and project them onto the whole was exceedingly unfair. Miller could think of countless Baptist ministers who had disgraced their profession, including a prominent clergyman who had killed a man in his own study [viz., Norris in 1926].⁷³ And yet none of these incidents impugned Baptists as a whole.

66. Ibid., 25–29. The first in 1921 to Harold McPherson, the second in 1931 to David Hutton, whose remarks on McPherson's drinking formed the nucleus of Perkins's attack on her.

67. "Bible Baptist Bible Union Conference," *Search* (16 November 1923) 2.

68. Miller, *Pentecost Examined*, 9–10.

69. Ibid., 101–2.

70. Ibid., 102–6.

71. Ibid., 109–10.

72. Ibid., 123–24.

73. Ibid., 124. Norris shot a layman of a rival congregation in 1926, pulling out the pistol of the night-

He called attention to Bauman's egregious handling of Scripture. There were for instance many lists concerning "gifts" in the NT while Bauman highlighted only the one in Ephesians, which omitted tongues.[74] In purporting that "signs" were for Jews only, Bauman had neglected to quote all of 1 Corinthians 14:22 where Paul stated that tongues were a "sign for unbelievers." "The devil is accused of using the same method in quoting Scripture," he noted.[75] In assigning tongues to men only, had Bauman not read where Deborah and Huldah were described as prophetesses of God?[76] Further, Bauman was guilty of limiting the definition of "prophecy" in *Young's Analytical Concordance* to "publicly expound" while failing to supply *Young's* first definition of "prophecy" as foretelling.[77] Bauman's translation of Acts 2:13 as "*men* drunk on new wine" rather than the more inclusive pronoun "they" as in the original Greek was puzzling to Miller.[78] How *Moody Monthly* or anyone else could recommend Bauman's study as "one of the best" on pentecostalism was beyond him.[79]

Bauman was not the sole fundamentalist quarry of Miller. A Reverend Edward Drew had written to Miller waving the dispensationalist flag. In response, Miller doubted that the supposed "transition" from a Jewish to a Gentile church in Acts had much merit.[80] True, Paul always toted the gospel to the Jews first, but nothing indicated that he ignored them after the Gentile church had been formed. Nor was there satisfactory evidence that "Israel" rejected "Pentecost" as Drew intimated, for many Jews were enfolded into the church after the event.[81] As rebuttal, he set his sights on I. M. Haldeman, demonstrating the preposterous lengths to which ultra-dispensationalists could sometimes go. Haldeman, mimicking Bullinger, had radically separated Jew from Gentile, declaring that the Lord's Prayer in Matthew had been prescribed under the old dispensation (i.e., prior to the crucifixion) and therefore should only be repeated by Jews (despite its use throughout church history).[82] Even *MBIM* had rejected such extremes in theology.[83] Furthermore, dispensationalists abused the phrase "rightly dividing the Word," which correctly rendered should have read "handling aright the word of truth" or "holding a straight course in the word," not dissecting it into component parts.[84] As a seeker, Miller could point to the genuine manifesta-

---

watchman from his drawer when the man approached him in a threatening manner. He pleaded self-defence and was acquitted by jury in 1927.

74. Miller, *Pentecost Examined*, 109; Bauman, *Modern Tongues*, 4.

75. Miller, *Pentecost Examined*, 110–11; Bauman, *Modern Tongues*, 5.

76. Miller, *Pentecost Examined*, 113; Bauman, *Modern Tongues*, 15–17.

77. Miller, *Pentecost Examined*, 114–15; Bauman, *Modern Tongues*, 4. In *Young's Analytical Concordance to the Holy Bible*, the first definition of "prophecy" is "to lift up, a burden, a message" (p. 779). The verb "prophesy" Young defines as "publicly expound" in the case of 1 Cor 14 (definition 7, p. 779). I did not find "foretell" as one of the definitions in the 8th edition (1939).

78. Miller, *Pentecost Examined*, 114; Bauman, *Modern Tongues*, 16.

79. Miller, *Pentecost Examined*, 126.

80. Ibid., 92–93.

81. Ibid., 90–92.

82. Ibid., 94–95.

83. Ibid., 95–97. Miller quotes from James Gray's article "Dispensationalism Running Wild" (*MBIM*, February 1933, 253–54).

84. Ibid., 98–99. Scofield's "rightly divided" Scripture into prophecies dealing with Jews or Gentile, seven

tion of tongues as authentication of pentecostal truth. In his view, pentecostal experience trumped hermeneutical gymnastics, and reason succored pentecostal interpretation.

In his initial letter to Reverend Lincoln above, Miller dealt more adequately with the cessationist argument. According to Miller, tongues had occurred after Pentecost in both Acts and the Corinthian church.[85] Jesus' promises to the disciples encompassed miraculous signs as much as they did salvation, according to Gordon,[86] which Miller illustrated by an historical apologetic from Iraeneus to Parham.[87] Miller rejected the view that Spirit-baptism was concomitant with new birth, summoning aid from Torrey's *The Holy Spirit*.[88] He also appealed to Finney, Goforth, Goode, Gordon, Meyer, Moody and Murray to show that the baptism empowered the evangel and was to be expected in the present age.[89] He felt however that J. M. Gray erred in preventing believers from supplicating God for the Spirit since both the Samaritans and the Ephesian elders had done just that.[90] Scofield's fault lay in dividing the baptism of the Spirit into three cases: "with," "in," and "upon." Scofield's notes on Acts 2:4 had failed to elaborate on the "upon," which would surely have contradicted his belief that baptism was contiguous with the new birth.[91] Furthermore, Moody, Gray, and Haldeman all disagreed as to their doctrines on the baptism of the Spirit, so at least two of them wrongly interpreted the Word.

If fundamentalists had accepted Holy Writ at face value as they professed to do, their opinion would have accorded with those of Finney, Moody and Torrey, great soul-winners all, that baptism followed conversion.[92] To Miller, the world consisted of three types of preachers: pentecostal, fundamentalist, and modernist. Modernism posed the greatest danger to the church, and pentecostalism its greatest cure.[93] Fundamentalists stood somewhere in between, but even *SST* and Gray could admit the need for present-day miracles, which could be found in abundance in pentecostal meetings. Miller was simply not intimidated by fundamentalists like Bauman and Lincoln, for he knew their writings well and raided them to his advantage.

---

dispensations, two advents, two resurrections, five judgments, two natures of the believer, law versus grace, and salvation versus reward (Scofield, "Rightly Dividing the Word of Truth," *FSRB*, 1567–1608).

85. Ibid., 14–15.

86. Ibid., 16–18. Miller included Gordon's quotations from Albrecht Bengel, Theodore Christlieb's *Modern Doubt and Christian Belief*, and Rudolph Stier (probably from his *Commentary on St. James*).

87. Ibid., 18–20.

88. Ibid., 26–29.

89. Ibid., 34–45.

90. Ibid., 53.

91. Ibid., 63–65. Scofield commented that "with" indicated God's approach to the soul, "in" described the Spirit's abiding presence, but made no comment on "upon" (Acts 2:4, *OSRB*, 1149–50 n. 1[7]). However, Scofield did define "upon" in his correspondence course as "having to do with believer's outward activities, imparting gifts for service, clothing the believer with Himself in power, guiding him in his service, and uniting him to the living body of Christ" (*Scofield Correspondence Course: New Testament*, 209). Baptism initiates the believer in the power, and the filling of the Spirit renews him or her in it. The difference between Scofield and pentecostals on baptism was when it took place and the results it produced.

92. Miller, *Pentecost Examined*, 66–68.

93. Ibid., 46, 78–83.

Pentecostal Rejection of Modernism

In the latter half of the 1930s pentecostal repudiation of modernism became more vituperative and sustained. The need to retain the loyalties of the next generation lay at its heart, wherein modernism constituted a viable threat to the movement. Curious minds were open to new modes of thought available through secular education and textbooks. Nearly half the teen population graduated from high school in 1930 compared to less than ten percent in their parents' generation; the numbers would have been even lower for pentecostals.[94] Many of these schools now used science textbooks that were favorably disposed to evolution.[95] Modernism did not creep in through pentecostal pulpits but rather through the broader culture. The children of pentecostals could not be insulated forever if the movement was to expand, and therefore the potential havoc to faith could not entertain their silence.

Five books of the late 1930s illuminate this reaction toward modernism. First, Otto Klink penned *Why I am not a Modernist* in 1938, published by Frank Lindquist in Minneapolis. Klink had been tempted to title it *Why I am not an Infidel* but decided he had already covered that topic in an earlier work.[96] He had once studied under Adolph von Harnack at the University of Berlin and was thus well acquainted with modernist tactics.[97] For Klink there were only two approaches to Scripture: the fundamentalist, which cherished its literalness, and the modernist, which relished in "deheart"-ing it.[98] The latter robbed the Bible of supernaturalism while the former guarded it. (A similar sentiment had been expressed by T. T. Shields fifteen years earlier.)[99] Much of the work consisted of a proof on the authenticity of both testaments in which Klink explained how each was recorded and passed on to succeeding generations.[100] In the remaining portion, he provided four reasons why he accepted the sacred text as true: it fulfilled its prophecies, it kept its promises, its moral influence proved efficacious, and it withstood all attempts historically to eradicate it.[101] In the conclusion, he quoted Noah Webster's prediction concerning the demise of the country if she ignored biblical principles, adding, "the Modernist and his teaching [sic] can never take the place of the Bible."[102] Klink's approach can be contrasted with Myer Pearlman's biblical surveys in the early 1930s. Pearlman's purpose had

---

94. See Draney, *When Streams Diverge*, 92. Increasing literacy also forced Bible schools to upgrade the quality of their curriculum. Also, Boorstin, *Americans*, 53.

95. Numbers, *Creationists*, 39.

96. Klink, *Why I am not a Modernist*, 3, referring to *Why I am not an Atheist* (1931).

97. Ibid., 27.

98. Ibid., 3. Klink does not separate here pentecostal and fundamentalist into two distinct groups. Likely he conceived pentecostalism as a sub-set within fundamentalism.

99. Shields wrote in 1923 of the BBU, "This union is made up of those who believe that the Modernism which denies the supernatural is an enemy of Christian religion" ("The Bible Baptist Union," *KB* [October 1923] 11). Here again is a sample of how fundamentalists and pentecostals were united in their opposition to modernism, even if they could not agree on what form supernaturalism should take.

100. Klink, *Why I am not a Modernist*, 5–51.

101. Ibid., 51–66.

102. Ibid., 65.

been to familiarize pentecostals with the Bible through a broad overview of its contents.[103] Klink on the other hand buttressed the authority of the Bible through fundamentalist assumptions.

Charles Elmo Robinson adopted a similar strategy in 1939 with *God and His Bible*, although it was not directed so much at modernists as skeptics of all stripes. Still, he charged higher criticism with introducing skepticism into the church by suspecting the Bible's veracity.[104] Like Uzzah, the servant who laid his hand on the ark to steady it, modernists had laid their hands on Holy Writ in an unholy manner. Many conservatives made little distinction between outright atheism and dubious modernism. Robinson was not as systematic as Klink in defending the Bible, covering a number of issues such as the reliability of the synoptic gospels, the fulfillment of Scripture through specific prophecies, the authenticity of Moses' law, the inadequacy of evolution to account for design in nature, and the authorship of the Pauline epistles via William Paley's *Horae Paulinae* (1790).[105] He also quoted extendedly from Ivan Panin's numerics in two sections to prove the uniqueness of its inspiration.[106] Both he and Klink made rationalistic defenses of Scripture characteristic of fundamentalism.

Also in 1939, Kenneth G. Olsen found in evangelism *The Cure for Empty Pews*. "The dry root of Modernism has spread to an alarming extent among the great Protestant denominations," he assailed, taking as example the Northern Baptist Convention, where less than half the members participated on a regular basis.[107] His model for the cure was the Korean Presbyterian Church, which had effectively evangelized its nation through leadership training and vigorous proclamation. People needed to get out of the pews and into the streets if the church was to grow. The bulk of the book detailed various methods of door-to-door outreach into the community. Curiously, there was nothing specifically "pentecostal" about the volume. It could have been enjoyed by any evangelical without offence. (This was true as well of Robinson's *The Winning of Ailene* (1939), perhaps the first pentecostal to publish with an evangelical press.)[108]

A fourth antimodernist work, *The Minister* (1939), spilled from the quill of Mae Eleanor Frey in what amounts to the first pentecostal novel of its type. Frey had begun her career as a society reporter before her conversion in her late teens. In 1937, aged seventy-two, the itinerant evangelist finally settled into a pastorate in upstate New York and engaged in her first calling as a writer.[109] Her story opened at Easter at Hempstead Memorial, a prosperous denominational church in California presided over by the thirty-five year-old and highly marriageable Rev. Dr. James Stillwell.[110] In the congregation that morning sang

---

103. Pearlman, *Seeing the Story of the Bible* (1930); *Through the Bible Book by Book*, 4 vols. (1935).

104. Robinson, *God and His Bible*, 15, 32.

105. Robinson's cosmological argument for design by an "intelligent" watchmaker was reminiscent of Paley's arguments in *Natural Theology*.

106. Robinson, *God and His Bible*, 18–30, and Appendix, 131–60.

107. Olsen, *Cure for Empty Pews*, 9.

108. *The Winning of Ailene* was published by Eerdmans.

109. "Watertown, N.Y.," *PE* (11 December 1937) 18.

110. Frey, *The Minister*, 5–7.

blue-eyed, curly-red Mildred Curryman, warbling lyrically from the front row. Stillwell was struck by Cupid, but Mildred, so it turned out, was a pentecostal transplant from the East, residing with her uncle after her parents died. Stillwell was a progressive evolutionist with membership in the Freemasons. Nonetheless, they were engaged within the month.

Not long afterwards, Floyd Graham, an outsider to the city, pitched a revival tent, replete with divine healing and tongues speech. Stillwell and the local ministerial associate wished to shut Graham down, but the Baptist fundamentalist in town came to his aid. (This was based on an actual incident Frey had witnessed.)[111] And no wonder the association was upset; they were losing members to an upstart preacher, a recent Bible school graduate at that. Stillwell had attended the University of Chicago for his degree! One of his more spiritually-minded laymen, Mr. Lambert, offered to construct a tabernacle for Graham, and Mildred joined the opening ceremony, which placed a strain on their looming marriage just two months away. Milred's baptism in the Spirit, which Stillwell regarded as a "mild form of insanity," further distanced their relationship. On a drive to San Francisco, he to hear a lecture on Benjamin Disraeli, she to attend Glad Tidings Temple, they discussed their divergent theologies.[112] Learning that her aunt was planning to commit her to an asylum, Mildred escaped to New York and returned the engagement ring to Stillwell. To keep matters short, all providentially works out for good in the end, with Mildred leaving for the mission fields of India, and a repentant Stillwell following in her wake.

Frey followed her success with a second adventure—*Altars of Brick* (1943).[113] In contrast to her first opus, this was published by Eerdmans and stripped of any pentecostal references. The modernist minister in this case was Rev. Marshland at Center Church someplace near the metropolis of New York, calling to mind the mushy theology of a mainline denomination. The rival minister was Dr. Townsend of Calvary Tabernacle, reminiscent of Dr. Towner of San Jose (where she had preached) and Straton's Calvary Baptist (to whose NBC she once belonged)—solid theology for the redeemed. Frey's career demonstrates the shift in the AG poignantly—a Baptist curious about the Spirit in 1907 at a CMA convention in Chicago, she transferred to pentecostalism in 1919 and reported on the NBC fundamentalist pre-convention in Buffalo in 1920, preached to Baptists and Methodists alike, and wrote a pentecostal, anti-modernist novel in 1939 and an evangelical, anti-modernist one just as the NAE formed in 1943.

These books betray how seriously the specter of modernism addled pentecostals. Thus, a church in Bolivar, Missouri would view its 1937 revival as insulation against modernism and apostasy.[114] Excerpts confirming the historicity of the Bible through archaeological digs continued, such as a lengthy piece on the "lost city" of Petra and another chronicling recent discoveries under the spade.[115] More importantly, a 1938 fundamentalist excerpt in *PE*, "When Intolerance is a Virtue," typified attitudes toward modernists in an imaginary

111. Ibid., 4.
112. It was at Glad Tidings that Frey led Myer Pearlman through the sinner's prayer in 1923.
113. Frey, *Altars of Brick* (1943).
114. J. L. Whittaker, "Bolivar, Mo.," *PE* (6 November 1937) 10.
115. E. Bowman, "The Lost City," *PE* (29 February 1936) 2–3; R. Cunningham, "Confirming the Scriptures with the Spade," *PE* (21 January 1939) 3, 13.

dialogue about biblical truth. For the fundamentalist the eternal destiny of the soul was at stake, but for the modernist only a few inconsequential opinions.[116] Again, there was no question as to where pentecostal loyalties lay along this religious spectrum. By the end of the decade, pentecostal antagonism toward modernism had aligned them concretely with the interests of fundamentalism.

Pentecostal and Fundamentalist Cooperation within the Sunday School

The earliest example of cooperation on a national level between fundamentalists and pentecostals entered in the realm of the Sunday school. The AG worried over the seemingly modernistic bent of the International Sunday School Lessons, developed by the Religious Education Council and used by most denominations of the day. MBI professor Clarence Benson estimated that two-thirds of the Bible had not been covered by the latest seven-year curriculum, but editors of the AG thought the fraction was nearer to three-fourths.[117] In the midst of preparing a new plan, headquarters was approached by Standard Publishing Company, a fundamentalist Sunday school purveyor in Cincinnati.[118] The editor at Standard was equally alarmed at the modernist leanings of ISSL and hesitated at printing the next cycle. He had uncovered a previous three-year curriculum "by very godly men." Likely he was referring to "The Whole Bible Course" of the WCFA, published in 1923.[119] The program was repeated by the Bible Baptist Union in 1927 under the same title.[120]

The resurrected version of "The Whole Bible Course," envisioned and executed cooperatively through Standard and the AG, began where else but at "the beginning"—Genesis. The AG supplemented this material with its teachers' quarterlies and its children's literature.[121] Each side agreed to tailor their notes to the wants of their constituency, but the outlines would be identical. What prompted Standard's solicitation is not recorded, but I believe it was the aggressive manner in which the AG had distributed its curriculum to fundamentalist churches mentioned earlier (Chapter 6).

Contiguous with this angst over modernism was AG apprehension over evolution being taught in the public schools. As seen earlier, pentecostals were less anxious about evolution's effect on adults than on children. Tempers broiled over at AG headquarters

---

116. "When Intolerance is a Virtue," *PE* (15 January 1938) 12–13.

117. "The 'Whole Bible' Course for our Sunday School," *PE* (11 April 1936) 8.

118. Standard had printed the first "uniform lesson" in 1873 when it originated.

119. "The Whole Bible Sunday School Lesson Series," *Search* (7 September 1923) 1; "'Christian Fundamentals' Sunday-School Lessons," *SST* (18 August 1923) 485; "The Whole Bible Sunday School Course," *CFSC* (October–December 1923) 4–6. The WCFA only ran the series once and discontinued its use.

120. Cf. Dollar, *History of Fundamentalism*, 169. However, Dollar also wrongly dates the BBU beginnings to 1927 rather than 1923.

121. "Creation," *The Adult and Young People's Teachers' Quarterly* (January–March 1937) 3–7; the January issue of the youth magazine *The Christ's Ambassadors Herald* is non-extant and evolution only gets brief mention in February and March (Y. Olson "'God's Foolishness'" [*CAH* (February 1937) 7] and G. Horst, "The Church on Fire" [*CAH* (March 1937) 8]; "The Wasp Surgeon," *GGl* [January 1937] 8 [likely written by Charles Robinson]).

in 1935 when they ascertained that Darwinism had infiltrated the lower grades of the local schools.[122] As the sapling needed more care than the fully developed tree, so children needed godly guidance before error could whisk their hearts away, they reasoned.[123] To offset the "awful tide of evil," the editors at *PE* developed a fresh periodical in 1936 for the consumption of the youngsters at home, the *Primary Story Paper*. "The first issues contain the story of creation, told in a simple way, emphasizing the truth that God created man in His own image," they informed.[124] The publication was intended as a supplement to Sunday school instruction. The fight against modernism and evolution coalesced around the children's curriculum and brought fundamentalists and pentecostals together under one roof, uniting against rampant infidelity.

Additionally, Sunday schools underwent a substantial expansion. In 1935, Ralph Riggs reported that 66,000 were attending Sunday schools in AG churches, slightly less than one-third of its membership.[125] Proportional to other Protestant denominations in the U.S., Riggs calculated that the AG had a responsibility to mould 200,000 children for the gospel. According to one survey, ninety percent of adult churchgoers had attended Sunday school as a child.[126] If the typical church spent ten percent of its budget on children's education, then the investment in the future was woefully inadequate. Riggs was keen on correcting this discrepancy.

In 1938 the push to expand the Sunday schools gained momentum. By the end of the year 1,089 programs had been added to the 3,000 already existing across the country.[127] In January 1939 *PE* called upon the AG faithful to pray for an enlargement of 1,250 Sunday school programs for the year. By November they had scaled 1,180, lifting the denomination well above the 5,000 barrier.[128] Aside from Riggs, GPH appointed Marcus Grable to promote its literature in 1935.[129] Grable had attended the International Sunday School Convention in Kansas City in 1924, where he first met Riggs, and brought the convention format to the AG in 1940. 1935 also saw the creation of the first district Sunday school office in Oklahoma, further evidence of the pentecostal desire to train children more systematically.

The antimodernist campaign was also waged in the cartoons that accompanied the Sunday school lessons in *PE*, particularly after 1936. In one, a collared cleric walks down the road of "compromise" away from a flock of sheep while a wolf lathers its lips nearby, ready to pounce. The subtext reads, "Impotent wordiness in the pulpit means subtle

---

122. "Does Your Heart Respond to this?" *PE* (9 November 1935) 5.
123. "To Help the Little Ones," *PE* (14 March 1936) 3.
124. "Does Your Heart Respond to this?" 5.
125. Riggs, "Development of Our Sunday Schools," *PE* (14 December 1935) 1.
126. Ibid., 9.
127. "Pray! Our Goal for 1939—1250 New Sunday Schools," *PE* (14 January 1939) 13. Some of the churches added to the AG list had existing schools that hadn't been using "The Whole Bible Lesson," but the vast majority according to Riggs were new programs.
128. "1180 New Sunday Schools," *PE* (4 November 1939) 18.
129. Menzies, *Anointed to Serve*, 266–67.

worldliness in the pew."[130] In another, a professor and a parson stand before Christ's tomb ("the church"), unable to roll the stone away because of their "unbelief" in the cardinal doctrines.[131] A 1940 illustration featured "Rev. Dr. Dryasdust" at his desk, propped over a Bible, tearing out pages labeled "Miracles," "Baptism in the Spirit," and "Second Coming" into a rubbish bin under the caption, "He wants a shorter Bible."[132] Not all the drawings were against modernism. One in particular depicted a pentecostal preacher surrounded by dignified figures instructing him to not mention "tongues" and stop holding tarrying meetings which lead to "fanaticism." "Don't Compromise with Aaron" said the header with a reminder underneath from Hebrews 10:23 to "hold fast" to the faith.[133] Another featured a "spirit-filled" David fighting the "good fight" against Goliath, who bore his shield of "disbelief in the supernatural."[134] No doubt the cartoonist had the giant of fundamentalism in mind when he drew it.

William Menzies postulates that many AG pastors had been reluctant to bring education into their churches until they realized the inherent advantages it held for child evangelism by the early 1930s.[135] However, the concern to pass on the faith should not be overlooked, what sociologists of religion have termed "traditioning." The AG had reached this stage in the growth of the denomination, the point at which the lessons of the first generation are passed along to the second. Sunday schools were the ideal institution to pass pentecostal traits to future leaders. The move towards their amelioration at a national level amply demonstrates this.

The AG's contribution to evangelical causes led to other forms of cooperation. In 1939, the American Bible Society in New York invited AG superintendent Ernest Williams as an observer to its annual advisory board meeting.[136] Unable to attend, Williams sent Frodsham in his stead. Frodsham toured the vaunted organization, which housed original Bibles of Tyndale, Coverdale and the Authorized Version. Frodsham was impressed by the hospitality he received. Enthusiastic supporters of Bible distribution, pentecostals were now gaining acceptance into evangelical enterprises.

A Word on Women, Morals, and Culture

Janet Evers Powers has observed a decline in the number of ordained women in the AG after 1920.[137] Could this have been, at least in part, the result of fundamentalist influences upon the AG? While the issues are complex, any analysis should bear in mind that fundamentalism itself had changed over the years. For instance, William Trollinger has shown that Riley championed women pastors from the inception of Northwestern in 1902 and

---

130. "The Sunday School Lesson," *PE* (15 May 1937) 6, bold in original. See Appendix I.
131. "The Sunday School Lesson," *PE* (22 May 1937) 1.
132. "The Sunday School Lesson," *PE* (8 June 1940) 4. See Appendix J.
133. "The Sunday School Lesson," *PE* (14 August 1937) 6. See Appendix K.
134. "The Sunday School Lesson," *PE* (31 December 1938) 8.
135. Menzies, *Anointed to Serve*, 266.
136. Frodsham, "A Visit to the Bible House in New York City," *PE* (21 January 1939) 1, 8–9.
137. Powers, "'Your Daughters Shall Prophesym,'" 313.

only limited their role in the 1930s.[138] Early in his career, Riley commissioned females to fill empty Baptist posts throughout the Upper Midwest in order to extend his influence. Also, two of Northwestern's most active evangelists up through the 1920s were the tandem of Alma Reiber and Irene Murray. At the college, Jessie Van Booskirk taught Hebrew and OT courses and was an efficient administrator until her untimely death in 1917. At the pre-conference of the NBC in 1920, Frey praised Riley and fellow fundamentals for encouraging the development of female preachers.[139] Active support for women in ministry by Northwestern administrators like C. W. Foley declined after 1930.[140] By 1935 Riley had reversed his position, discovering an absence of women pastors in the NT.[141] This suggests that some fundamentalists at least were far more open to female clergy than is often alleged, particularly in the early stages of the movement when attitudes were less entrenched and the paucity of preachers more apparent.

This "institutionalizing" effect was concurrently taking place within pentecostalism. In 1931, for instance, the AG restricted the role of women in licensed ministry to evangelism and barred them from performing marriages and funerals.[142] However, in 1935 they did allow women to be ordained as pastors. Scholars Charles Barfoot and Gerald Shepherd have noted the transition from the prophetic-type ministry characteristic of the early fluidity of the movement and the priestly-type ministry characteristic of the later congregational basis of the movement.[143] This is not to deny any influence from fundamentalism nor to deny that elements within fundamentalism were more misogynistic than others (sometimes in response to "McPhersonism"—as with Gaebelein), but any analysis of the effect of fundamentalism must consider the institutional alterations that accompanied both movements.

Another reason not hitherto considered for this change was a restriction on females mandated by the U.S. Clergy Bureau in 1922. The pretext had to do with discounted railroad rates to which active clergy were entitled. These privileges cut into railroad profits, and one way to curb the loss was to reduce the number of recipients. As many pentecostal women worked closely with their husbands and traveled with them in ministry, their licenses became a target. Sometime in 1922 the AG sent out a letter to all ministers explaining the new rules, "They [the Bureau] say a minister's wife, even though fully ordained, must also actually preach the Gospel, and have appointments to preach separate from her husband, and receive separate collections, in order to secure rates."[144] This posed a problem. William Moody for one struggled whether or not to renew his wife's credentials. In August he wrote to headquarters, "In view of the strict regulations that are now

---

138. Trollinger, *God's Empire*, 104–7.

139. See chapter 4.

140. Trollinger, *God's Empire*, 105–6.

141. Ibid., 104.

142. Noll, *An Introduction*, 93.

143. Barfoot and Shepherd, "Prophetic vs. Priestly Religion," 2–17, cited in Holmes, "The 'Place' of Women," 303–4.

144. "Dear Brother Minister in the Lord," AG letter sent 7 [July?] 1922 (FPHC—the handwritten date is obscure—it was sent on the 7th of a month in 1922 which appears to be July).

in force by the Clergy Bureau, she would be willing to have her name dropped from the Ministerial List, as she would not seek for reduced railway rates."[145] In July 1923 the couple had changed their minds and applied for her re-ordination along with a six-dollar donation to headquarters.

Similarly, attitudes concerning dress codes also changed. As Carpenter comments, "By the 1930s there were a number of signs that fundamentalists were making their behavioral expectations, which had been largely a matter of community consensus and taken-for-granted practice, into an explicit and energetically enforced code."[146] In 1931, for example, Wheaton College introduced a pledge by which the student promised to live by the school's "standards of life."[147] In 1939, the pledge had to be signed yearly. One reason for this change in V. L. Brereton's opinion is that the pre-1930 students at Bible schools tended to be highly motivated and more mature than their peers who came later.[148] Randall Balmer attributes this phenomenon to parental concern over their children's education. First generation evangelicals readily subscribe to taboos after their conversion, but the process is often reversed in the second generation. The children grow up with the "trappings of godliness" without the requisite conviction.[149]

A similar process transpired in pentecostalism. For example, in 1939 Narver Gortner and Robert Brown proposed that a dress code for female students be adopted at all AG schools. It was, as Blumhofer has stated, evidence of the "institutionalizing" process at work.[150] Early pentecostals applied such standards naturally, having inherited many of the strictures from their holiness roots. All three branches of the evangelical movement shared moral codes against dancing, attending theaters and "moving pictures," playing cards, drinking, and smoking—all in sharp contrast to modernism's liberality. Former dance instructor T. A. Faulkner's ominous volume *From the Ball Room to Hell* could be found advertised in pentecostal, holiness and fundamentalist periodicals.[151] Faulkner himself converted from fundamentalism to pentecostalism in 1919 under Gortner's preaching.[152]

For many pentecostals, Spirit-baptism was the ultimate panacea for worldliness. Charles Robinson put his thumb on the matter in 1928, likening the inner life to a Ford that did not "hit on" all cylinders properly.[153] The problem was that it had lost its fire. Many had written the *PE* asking them to condemn short skirts and narrow blouses and movies and ballgames. But these were only symptoms of the selfishness within, Robinson

---

145. Moody to J. W. Welch, letter dated August 3, 1922 (FPHC).

146. Carpenter, *Revive us Again*, 59.

147. Ibid., 60.

148. Brereton, "Bible Schools and Conservative Evangelical Higher Education," 125–27; cf. Carpenter, *Revive Us Again*, 59–60.

149. Balmer, *Mine Eyes*, 106.

150. Blumhofer, *Restoring*, 153.

151. "Our Book List," *WE* (17 February 1917) 15–16; "From the Ball Room to Hell," *PH* (27 August 1919) 15; Gaebelein, "From the Dance Hall into Eternity," *Hope* (September 1925) 162–63.

152. Gortner, "Ex-Dancing Master Receives his Pentecost," *CE* (22 February 1919) 7.

153. Robinson, "Treating Symptoms," *PE* (8 December 1928) 8.

contended, and the born-again, Spirit-filled soul was its cure.[154] Nonetheless, as an ex-holiness Methodist pastor, Robinson was as vocal as anyone in condemning movie-going and bobby cuts.[155] Rising hemlines and descending necklines deserved severe censure from fundamentalists and pentecostals alike.

Pentecostals implored fundamentalists to deepen their spirituality, but on the subject of grace, they often dipped their buckets into fundamentalist wells. A lengthy article on "The Grace of our Lord Jesus Christ" by D. M. Panton appeared in 1922, defining the subject as "God's saving love, self-prompted, reaching far beyond the bounds of sinful humanity."[156] Cecilia Barton's article from 1929 contrasting law and grace contained two-thirds quotation from Scripture and one-third quotation from Scofield.[157] She in fact contributed nothing original of her own. In 1932 Harry Steil linked grace to the seven dispensations in the Bible, likening them to a business cycle, which was presently at a downturn.[158] Even so, pentecostals felt they had a spiritual edge over fundamentalists. An anonymous correspondent upbraided fundamentalists in 1925 for appropriating the gift of salvation in Romans but not the gifts of the Spirit in Corinthians. They lived in grace but not in the fullness of their salvation, "and if you have more grace, you will let go of your preconceived notions and will launch out to receive what you have not."[159] The Spirit lifted pentecostals onto a higher plain.

Elwin Wright and the Formation of the NAE

The First Fruit Harvesters had been founded with an ecumenical vision. Joel Wright eschewed all patterns of religious organization, which he considered symbolic of lifeless Babylon, whether it be Catholic, Protestant or holiness. "The only church which Jesus is building is here set forth [in Matt 16:18], not an organization, but a living organism," he stated.[160] While disparaging organizations that killed the spirit on the one hand, Wright built one based on a spirit of cooperation on the other. It was the paradox of many holiness groups. In the desire to unite a "pure" Christianity through the bonds of charity, they distanced themselves from the taint of the world through sectarianism. Wright opened his crusades to all ministers regardless of creed and yet steered none of his converts to their churches, banding them together instead under what they believed to be the Spirit's direc-

---

154. Ibid., 8–9.

155. Robinson, "The Movies," *PE* (2 June 1928) 3; Robinson "Conforming to the World," *PE* (3 December 1927) 6–7. Robinson received sanctification after reading holiness minister S. A. Keen's *Pentecostal Papers* about 1895. His Spirit-baptism came in 1914 in Memphis (Robinson, "How the Baptism Came to Me," *PE* [1 August 1931] 7).

156. Panton, "Grace of Our Lord Jesus Christ," *PE* (19 August 1922) 1.

157. Barton, "Grace vs. Law," *PE* (12 January 1929) 6–7. The Scofield commentary was taken from the notes to Gal 3:19, 24 (*OSRB*, 1244–45).

158. Steil, "Cycles of God's Grace," *PE* (5 March 1932) 1, 10–11; Steil, "Cycles of God's Grace," *PE* (12 March 1932) 6–7.

159. "What Paul Teaches," *PE* (15 August 1925) 5.

160. J. Wright, *To What Church Do You Belong?* 1 (BGC).

tion.[161] Inspired by Old Orchard, Wright dubbed his property at Rumney, New Hampshire, the "World's Missionary Campground." Pentecost became an added tool to the evangelical push in 1908, though Wright never endorsed the "evidential tongues" doctrine.[162]

When the latter rain showers fell upon Rumney, Joel's son Elwin exulted, "where formerly was contention and self seeking now the Spirit has brought oneness to His people and with oneness has come power over all power of the enemy."[163] The quest for unity remained central to the FFH message, yet as a pentecostal organization, doctrinally and geographically isolated, the leaders made little headway towards its completion. Despite protestations to the contrary, FFH had become as sectarian as any other pentecostal entity. Leadership passed from father to son in 1924, and Elwin determined to invigorate evangelicalism along his father's original vision. In 1923 FFH sponsored a crusade in Tampa, Florida with R. A. Torrey and Will Houghton, then pastor of the Baptist Tabernacle in Atlanta.[164] In 1929 Wright invited Riley to be its keynote speaker for their annual summer conference at Rumney. The response of pastors across New England was enormous, inspiring Elwin to even greater heights.

In 1930 he settled in Boston and joined historic Park Street Church. Its longtime pastor, A. Z. Conrad, was succeeded by the young, urbane Harold John Ockenga in 1936. Ockenga was a member of the WCFA after Paul Rood took over from Riley.[165] Wright rechristened the FFH as the New England Fellowship with headquarters in Boston. Within a year over five hundred pastors had affixed their names to his rosters. In 1937 Wright and his Fellowship Radio Ensemble embarked on a coast-to-coast tour and predicted that "in the next decade a united effort among the more irenic and cooperative evangelicals would bring a national revival."[166] His great success in 1939 was to host Charles Fuller and his Old Fashioned Revival Hour at Mechanics Hall in Boston. Fuller returned two years later to Boston Gardens. The FFH had thus transitioned from holiness to pentecostal to more mainstream evangelical beliefs.

Fuller and his wife Grace teamed up as a weekly fixture on the radio for millions of listeners during the depression. From his humble stint as pastor of Calvary Church in Long Beach, Fuller broadcasted sermons over station KGER in 1928.[167] Resigning from his pastorate in March 1933, he launched an independent ministry the same week a major earthquake shook the city. In 1935 he reached most of the western states over the airwaves and published a newsletter called "Heart-to-Heart Talks," resembling a spiritual version of FDR's Fireside Chats.[168] With money tight and reliant on cash-strapped partisans, a switch to the Mutual Broadcast Network in 1937 tripled his expenses and quadrupled his audi-

---

161. Berends, "Social Variables," 70.

162. Ibid., 71.

163. E. Wright, "Rumney, N.H." *W&Wk* (November 1908) 342.

164. Carpenter, *Revive Us Again*, 143. A more detailed account of Ockenga's role in neo-evangelicalism can be found in Rosell, *Surprising Work of God* (2008).

165. Ockenga interview with James Hedstrom, cassette recording, Nashville, TN, 1979 (BGC).

166. Carpenter, *Revive Us Again*, 144. The quote is Carpenter's paraphrase of Elwin's sentiments.

167. E. Wright, *Old Fashioned Revival Hour*, 86.

168. Ibid., 89–94.

ence. In his first national program, Fuller cleared five dollars over the financial hurdle and soon hosted the most popular religious program on the radio.[169] By March 1940 he had reached South America, Asia, and the South Seas.

A significant rift developed within fundamentalism in the meantime between irenic leaders like Ockenga and Fuller and the more strident Presbyterian Carl McIntire and Baptist Robert Ketcham. The first group would in time style themselves "neo-evangelicals" and include pentecostals in their ranks under the umbrella of the NAE. The second group barricaded themselves in opposition to both modernism and pentecostalism as the American Council of Christian Churches (ACCC). The NAE in Ockenga's opinion mirrored the ACCC in all its doctrines except that they had grown tired of the rancor.[170] The second group carried on the militant spirit of the first generation. The face of fundamentalism itself had changed since the 1920s.

By the late 1930s many of the old-guard fundamentalists had passed away. A. T. Pierson died in 1911; Simpson in 1919; Scofield in 1921; Dixon and Bryan in 1925; Torrey in 1928; Straton in 1929; Haldeman in 1933; Gray in 1935. Others had reached their twilight years—Trumbull died in 1941; Gaebelein in 1945; Riley in 1947; Bauman in 1950; Ironside in 1951; Chafer and Norris in 1952; Barnhouse in 1960. Of these, Ironside, Chafer and Barnhouse joined the NAE, and Riley showed himself sympathetic but cautious.[171] In their place came younger visionaries like Fuller (d. 1980), Ockenga (d. 1985), and perhaps most importantly, Billy Graham (still living). The fight that typified 1920s fundamentalism had been exhausted through defeat and retreat in the 1930s. Others were not so willing to give up the ghost. McIntire (d. 2002) and Ketcham (d. 1978) led the strand that followed in the footsteps of their predecessors.

Ockenga recalled in a 1979 interview that the ACCC formed in response to the NAE. Records show that it was the other way around.[172] McIntire and other representatives of the Bible Presbyterian Church met with officials from the Protestant Bible Church on September 27, 1940 in Westerville, New Jersey.[173] Their aim was to counter the FCC as the voice of Christianity in America. A constitution was adopted a year later in New York. Their problem, as Carpenter explains, was that their membership was too limited to represent the Christian faith on a national scale.[174] They also refused cooperation with moderate evangelicals like Ockenga and Barnhouse, who also shunned the FCC but remained within their denominations (Congregational and Presbyterian, respectively).

---

169. Ibid., 95–96. In one incident, after Fuller had gone off-air at a radio rally in Los Angeles, someone in the audience stood up and spoke in tongues and another gave a "beautiful interpretation." Reportedly, Fuller told his audience to not be afraid of the Spirit's workings. The date of this episode is not recorded [Melon, *We've Been Robbed*, 43].

170. Ockenga interview with J. Hedstrom, cassette, 1979.

171. William Pettingill (d. 1950), president of Philadelphia School of the Bible (founded by Scofield), also supported the NAE.

172. Ockenga interview with J. Hedstrom, cassette, 1979.

173. Gasper, *The Fundamentalist Movement*, 81.

174. Carpenter, *Revive Us Again*, 145.

The main personalities behind the NAE were Wright and William Ayer, who succeeded Will Houghton at Straton's pulpit at Calvary Baptist. Ockenga however credited Wright with playing the major role.[175] Ockenga identified radio broadcasting as the main impetus behind the NAE's formation. The FCC restricted airtime, which it received gratis, to only those ministers approved by their council. Many evangelicals paid for the honor and would have been shut out altogether if the FCC had had its way. It was imperative that they band together to protect their rights to broadcast the gospel. Another area of contention was over chaplaincy appointments as WWII loomed closer. The FCC excluded evangelicals from serving as chaplains in the U.S. military. Behind all this lay Wright's hope for a nationwide revival through evangelical cooperation. The 1939, 1940 and 1941 NEF conferences at Rumney passed resolutions calling for such an organization.[176]

An initial meeting between McIntire, Wright, and Ralph Davis (president of Africa Inland Mission) convened at MBI in October 1941, with President Will Houghton and a trustee, Henry Crowell, presiding.[177] Fuller, Ironside, Stephen Paine (president of Houghton College), and Raymond Edman (president of Wheaton College) were also present along with a dozen others.[178] McIntire would not bend on his principle that only separatists could participate in the ACCC, so the two groups went their separate ways. The "Committee for United Action among Evangelicals" explored cooperation at Ayer's New York study in November 10, 1941 along with Wright, Barnhouse, Davis, John Bradbury (editor of the *Watchman-Examiner*), and Howard Ferrin (of Providence Bible Institute).[179] The gentlemen rejected Barnhouse's proposal that they start big with the Southern Baptists and Presbyterians and then draft smaller denominations into their ranks. Instead, a letter was distributed to potential partners to gather in St. Louis in April 1942 with three objectives in mind: to create a "front" for evangelicals in governmental matters, to be "a clearing house for all matters of common interest," and to present a united stand against apostasy and unbelief "which threaten our liberties and our very civilization."[180] Several more meetings in early 1942 prepared for St. Louis, with Wright traveling extensively to drum up interest amongst potential participants.

That pentecostals were summoned to the occasion is significant to the history of evangelicalism. Officials from the AG (Ernest Williams, J. Roswell Flower, Ralph Riggs and Noel Perkins), CG (J. H. Walker, Earl Paulk, E. L. Simmons, M. P. Cross, and Earl Clark) and PHC were invited.[181] Significantly, no representative from the Foursquare Gospel was

---

175. Ockenga interview with J. Hedstrom, cassette, 1979. Wright did much of the organizing but Ayers helped bridge the gap with fundamentalists from his New York office. Houghton pastored Calvary Baptist from 1930 to 1934 before moving to MBI, succeeding Gray as president.

176. Menzies, *Anointed to Serve*, 185, cite Shelley, *Evangelicalism in America*, 73.

177. They met on the 27th and 28th, though Houghton and Crowell left early to attend to a business meeting for the institute. Crowell's father founded the Quaker Oats company.

178. Carpenter, *Revive Us Again*, 146; Menzies, *Anointed to Serve*, 185.

179. "Minutes of the Committee for United Action among Evangelicals," n.p. (BGC).

180. Ibid., n.p.

181. Blumhofer, *Assemblies of God*, 2:13. Menzies does not include Riggs in his list but does have Thomas Zimmerman as an unofficial observer (*Anointed to Serve*, 185–86).

invited until 1945, the year after Sister Aimee died. As a woman and a divorcée, she had two strikes against. She had also long been a divisive figure among pentecostals and fundamentalists alike because of her on- and off-stage antics. She did not fit the image of propriety that evangelicals wished to portray. The other pentecostal denominations embraced the opportunity to be recognized as authentic evangelical believers at last.

McIntire was incensed at the inclusion of pentecostals. He invited himself to the Coronado Hotel in St. Louis and demanded that the new organization condemn the FCC and break with the pentecostals before the ACCC would join it. Ockenga and others leaders deplored this type of negativity as the basis of their fellowship and rejected McIntire's proposal.[182] McIntire walked out with fifteen others in tow, repeatedly lampooning Ockenga and the NAE thereafter in the *Christian Beacon*. For him, pentecostalism was an expression of the great apostasy, a demonic movement designed to derail true Christianity from its course and every bit as evil as modernism. It was not surprising that Norris joined his chorus, and for a time, so did John Rice, who withdrew from the ACCC in 1960.

Relationships between pentecostals and neo-evangelicals were not always docile. Controversy flared at the 1944 session in Columbus, Ohio when Barnhouse objected to the chants of a pentecostal singing trio on stage. Flower even offered on behalf of pentecostals to withdraw from the NAE and participate only as observers if it should preserve harmony, for which he was later roundly chastised by Jonathan Perkins. Ockenga stood firmly in favor of their participation.[183] Nevertheless, Ockenga viewed pentecostals as sincere but mistaken believers, ortho- in their doxology though not in their praxis.[184]

Pentecostal Participation in the NAE

What accounts for this new alliance? Revivalism lay at the heart of Wright's vision. Pentecostals were growing enormously throughout the depression and demonstrated a passionate commitment to evangelism and missions. They sponsored revivals in local communities, attracted large numbers of seekers through their healing crusades, and dispatched missionaries around the globe. Fundamentalists had lost some of their confidence from the heady battles of the 1920s. Their retreat from culture gave them opportunity to restructure their faith around the gospel in spiritual rather than intellectual terms. They needed rejuvenation and saw it modeled in the exuberance of pentecostalism.

For their part, pentecostals craved respect from their fundamentalist peers. They did not expect admiration from the world, with whom they were at odds morally, but they did hope to find it from evangelical leaders of the day. Fundamentalism represented an intellectual validity and enjoyed a broad cultural appeal which they lacked. Pentecostals had long felt inferior to fundamentalists in these two areas despite their conviction that

---

182. Ockenga interview with J. Hedstrom, cassette, 1979.

183. Menzies, *Anointed to Serve*, 187. It was this incident over which J. E. Perkins complained to Flower.

184. Ockenga wrote in 1959, "For an individual or a church to seek for and wait for certain gifts from the Holy Spirit in order to prove that they have been filled with the Spirit is error. We are not to look for supernatural attestation in our personal experience today" (*Power through Pentecost*, 21).

they had a superior gift to offer. They devoured fundamentalist literature and adopted its theology as a framework for their own beliefs.

Conflict plays as much a role in dividing movements as it does in uniting them. According to sociologist David Moberg, "The struggle for power in society often leads to cooperation for limited purposes by organizations otherwise in conflict with each other."[185] This process can be seen throughout history, say for example in the Crusades. Far from being solely a Muslim-Christian conflict, changing alliances within the Holy Land brought Muslim-Christian factions together against greater threats from without, such as the Mongol invasion.[186] For fundamentalists, those who saw modernism as the greater menace were willing to partner with pentecostals to ward off its evil. Those who abhorred pentecostalism as an aberrant form of Christianity rallied to McIntire's ACCC in an attempt to combat both. Beginning in conflict against one another, pentecostals and fundamentalists found partnership through conflict from without.

One expression of Christianity tends to "leaven" the others in any given era, as Carpenter reminds us.[187] During much of the twentieth century, holiness permeated the evangelical movement, while for much of the twentieth fundamentalism enjoyed center stage, particularly during the first half. The "leavening" of the Nazarene Church by fundamentalism during this period has been well documented by Paul Basset.[188] Frodsham had warned pentecostals against the leaven of the Pharisees, and no doubt some today would wish they had heeded his advice. David du Plessis lamented a distinct lack of influence of pentecostals in the NAE, which was dominated then by fundamentalist leaders. He mused that by wedding itself to fundamentalism pentecostals had missed opportunities in the charismatic movement of the 1960s.[189] Certainly it may be argued that by joining the NAE pentecostalism lost the vitality of its witness. By catering to fundamentalism, its unique testimony to the Spirit's work in the believer weakened.

Conversely, it may be argued that the process towards "fundamentalization" among pentecostals began long before the NAE coalesced. In other words, the NAE was a culmination of this leavening effect rather than its beginnings. As we have seen, pentecostals had been drifting into the fundamentalist camp by bits and pieces since the 1910s. The NAE only solidified this relationship. Paradoxically, Russell Spittler has remarked on a dual effect within evangelicalism since the 1940s. By his reckoning, from roughly then until the 1970s pentecostalism experienced its "evangelicalization."[190] In the next quarter century, the reverse happened whereby evangelicalism has experienced its "pentecostalization." I would even expand these dates. The evangelicalization of pentecostalism came from 1920 to 1980 and the pentecostalization of evangelicalism from 1980 to the present.

185. Moberg, *Social Institution*, 242

186. Read in *The Templars* gives a fascinating account of the order in its political context in "Outremer" (the Holy Land).

187. Carpenter, "The Fundamentalist Leaven," 275. Carpenter limits the "leavening" effect of fundamentalism to the 1930s and 1940s, but it had begun much earlier.

188. Bassett, "Fundamentalist Leavening," 65–91.

189. Howard, "David du Plessis," 285.

190. Spittler, "Are Pentecostals and Charismatics Fundamentalists?" 112–13.

More precisely, I would divide this earlier period as "fundamentalization" (1920–1940) and "evangelicalization" (1940–1980). Since then, pentecostalism has made it fashionable to raise one's hands in praise in fundamentalist churches today where it would have been anathema twenty years ago. Much of the credit belongs to John Wimber and the Third Wave. Synan has dubbed the twentieth century as the "Century of the Holy Spirit."[191] That may well belong to the twenty-first.

Summary and Conclusion

The Sunday school played a catalytic role in the development of pentecostalism in the late 1930s. First, there was the ongoing need to retain the existing generation and also to attract young converts and their families, thus guaranteeing a future for the movement. Organization of Sunday schools had moved from the local level in the *genesis* stage to a regional level at the beginnings of the *retention* stage and to a national level by the end of the *retention* stage. Second, the Sunday school formed the nucleus around which pentecostals and fundamentalists could cooperate. Inculcation in evangelical mores secured the vitality of future leaders and was essential to the emergence of the later neo-evangelical alliance. They could agree on a curriculum which reflected their values without impinging upon each other's peculiarities. While the American Sunday School Association (1945) was less visible than other branches of the NAE, it nevertheless was crucial to future cooperation where differences could be set aside in view of the secularization of the mainline churches.

Meanwhile, the "rhetoric" of fundamentalism overwhelmed AG views of the Bible and the world. Articles by pentecostals had shifted from defining themselves against fundamentalism to defining themselves against modernism. Pentecostals became champions of the defense of God's Word against the incursion of higher criticism and evolution. Early pentecostals assumed the Word to be infallible but had no compelling reason to prove it. By the early 1930s the movement had become preoccupied with the "scientific" reliability of Scripture in fundamentalist terms. Additionally, pentecostal children who were attending public schools in larger numbers than the first generation were exposed to opinions contrary to those of their parents. Fundamentalism provided the template for them to engage with and counter the barrage from culture.

The most visible means for evangelicals to redeem the public sector and influence American culture was through revivalism. Popular radio preachers like Charles and Grace Fuller and Paul Rader reached a broad constituency of the American lower and middle classes, supported by pentecostals and fundamentalists alike. A resurgent evangelicalism was gaining momentum by the end of the 1930s, but it was not the staid, intellectual fervor of their fundamentalist forefathers of the 1920s. Having lost that battle, the new evangelicalism shaped itself around revivalism, appealing to the heart rather than the head. It was this vision of unity around the revivalist tradition that brought fundamentalists, pentecostals and holiness leaders together in St. Louis against the *bête noire* of modernism.

---

191. Synan, ed., *Century of the Holy Spirit* (2001).

Personal squabbles would continue and theological differences accentuated. But these would melt into the background as pentecostals enjoyed a heightened profile through the NAE. Having finally gained the recognition from fellow evangelicals they had always desired, they were determined to see the NAE function healthfully at any cost. In order not to give offence to fellow evangelicals, the pentecostal witness was muted at NAE functions as du Plessis and others noted. Though still committed to their distinctive theology and eager to share it with others, it was done in an evangelical context. AG pastor Carl Brumback's *What Meaneth This* (1947) was just such a tactical defense, born out of a radio program in south Florida. Pentecostalism had entered into a larger arena and a new stage in its dealings with the wider culture. No longer a "backwoods" religion of ignorant enthusiasts, the next generation of pentecostals could anticipate advanced leadership and educational opportunities that their parents could scarcely have imagined.

PART FIVE

Conclusion

9

Conclusion

Summary

PENTECOSTALISM WAS BORN INTO AN EVANGELICAL ENVIRONMENT THAT HAD BEEN shaped in the nineteenth century by the holiness movement in both its Wesleyan and Keswick expressions. Keswick theology had been espoused by protofundamentalists such as D. L. Moody and A. T. Pierson from about 1890, but several of them had previously been transformed through "sanctification"-like experiences in the early 1870s. Those who had done so frequently turned to premillennialism, and increasingly to dispensationalism as the century progressed. Several like A. B. Simpson and A. J. Gordon also advocated divine healing, which, together with premillennialism, infiltrated holiness teachers like M. W. Knapp and W. B. Godbey in the late nineteenth century. Meanwhile, radical holiness teachers like R. C. Horner in Ontario and B. H. Irwin in Iowa taught a "three-blessing" doctrine that separated holiness and sanctification from the baptism of the Holy Spirit, thus setting the stage for "tongues" to appear at the turn of the century.

During its *genesis*, pentecostalism grew at the expense of the holiness movement, as has been traced through mission halls and camp meetings from 1906–1909. Fundamentalists were also affected, although to a lesser extent and at a later date then holiness counterparts. Fundamentalists were further theologically from pentecostals, but their congregations were not immune to its effect. A. B. Simpson was the first to regard tongues in his typically irenic manner. A. T. Pierson, familiar with the outpouring at Pune, India, responded later in 1907, which permitted others like W. B. Riley and A. C. Gaebelein to join the fray. Moody Church in Chicago felt its impact through Andrew Urshan, prompting A. C. Dixon to criticize the movement in print in 1908.

The takeover of holiness institutions was complete by 1910, after which internal discord forced pentecostals to *adapt* their conquered space into the semblances of denominations, divided along theological, regional, and ecclesiastical lines. W. H. Durham and the "finished work" caused much of the havoc in pentecostal ranks, ultimately forming into "Wesleyan" (CG, PHC, COGIC) and "Keswick" (AG, Foursquare) branches. Further agitation created a rupture within the AG as "oneness" groups revolted over the water baptismal formula. Meanwhile, fundamentalists like R. A. Torrey and I. M. Haldeman launched attacks on pentecostals on both doctrinal and moral grounds, which obligated pentecostals like A. J. Tomlinson and Robert Brown to respond. The publication of the Scofield

Reference Bible in 1909 also made an immediate impact in the area where pentecostals and fundamentalists were most alike: premillennialism. The "vocabulary" of dispensationalism and of fundamentalism wove their way into pentecostal terminology, though their concepts were still divergent. It was not so much a disagreement as to the content but as to where the emphasis lay: fundamentalists on the inerrant Word and on the person of Christ; pentecostals on the charismata and the person of the Holy Spirit.

In the early 1920s, pentecostal denominations stabilized, establishing permanent Bible schools while adjusting themselves to the muscle of fundamentalism. AG leadership in particular gravitated toward fundamentalism and adopted the "content" of dispensational thought, which had made steady inroads during the previous decade. This challenged them to maintain a "pentecostal" identity without becoming overwhelmed by fundamentalist strength. Meanwhile, healing evangelists like A. S. McPherson, F. F. Bosworth, and Ray Richey gained a wide following, causing a reaction from fundamentalists like A. C. Gaebelein and R. A. Torrey among others. Fundamentalist leaders preached against the dangers of "tongues" but were unable to prevent their flock from attending pentecostal services at night.

The *retention* of pentecostalism was evident in the attention given to Sunday school literature from 1925 onwards, ensuring that pentecostal "DNA" would be transferred to the next generation. The pentecostal and fundamentalist conflict reached a climax in 1928 when the WCFA, under pressure from modernists, distanced itself from tongue-speakers. Pentecostals like S. H. Frodsham responded with chagrin while W. E. Booth-Clibborn responded with bravado. In the late 1920s, fundamentalism waned while pentecostalism waxed. Pockets of cooperation existed through evangelists like Uldine Utley with J. R. Straton and F. F. Bosworth with Paul Rader, among other examples.

The AG adopted the "rhetoric" of fundamentalism as it transitioned into the 1930s. Baptists like J. N. Hoover had already joined the movement and carried their doctrine with them. References to a "scientific" approach to Scripture appeared, and advocacy for the reliability of the Bible and the divine origins of humankind poured from pentecostal pens like that of C. E. Robinson. By this period cessationism, though never absent in the discussion, had taken a more prominent role in the fundamentalist arsenal against pentecostalism. But cessationism was not indispensable to a dispensational theology, as several fundamentalists demonstrated, and pentecostals nimbly substituted the "age of the Spirit" for that of the church. Dispensationalism seized CG in the early 1930s, which culminated in its wholesale adoption by S. W. Latimer in 1937. CG had thus acquired the "content" of fundamentalism in the 1930s though it had not yet adopted its "rhetoric."

It was their common evangelical ethos, radiating from nineteenth-century holiness precedents, which provided grounds for cooperation by the mid-twentieth century. Leavened by influential fundamentalist writers and speakers, pentecostals donned the fundamentalist mantel that increasingly repudiated modernism by the late 1930s. At the potential threat of an apostate Christianity dominating American religious policies, evangelicals banded together to form a united voice to advance their interests in radio, the military, Sunday school curriculum, and all matters relating to government agencies in order to reach an unsaved culture. Fundamentalists, having lost prestige in their failure to sway either their denominations or American culture, turned their resources inward to recover a lost sense of spirituality. Pentecostals, striving for prestige and recognition, turned their resources outward to their intellectual heroes to gain credence and acceptance. Having begun in division, they were able to discard differences in lieu of mutual interests.

Retrospect

Faupel has identified four motifs of pentecostalism: "apostolic faith," "latter rain," "pentecostal," and "full gospel."[1] Each theme, I propose, was ascendant at different times. "Apostolic faith" encapsulated the restorationist mantra and was ensconced in early periodical and church names.[2] This was eclipsed by the "latter rain," which established pentecostalism upon a biblical, covenantal foundation. The precipitous imagery served a dual purpose: restoration both recovered original Christianity and realized earlier showers initiated at the Reformation. "Pentecostal" did not enjoy currency until the 1910s, as Wacker observes.[3] Pentecostals had not formed a sufficient identity to distinguish them from their holiness brethren until well into the 1910s. Indeed, the Church of the Nazarene did not drop "pentecostal" from its nomenclature until 1919.

As Blumhofer has noted, the "full gospel" added new meaning in the 1920s as a response to fundamentalism, which had a comparatively incomplete salvation.[4] A number of churches in this period attached "Full Gospel" to their names so that by the 1930s it had become quite common. One of the earliest to do so was the "Full Gospel Assembly, Persian Mission" in 1919. This church, formed from the remnants of Urshan's "Persian boys," established their mission directly across the street from Moody Church.[5] Pentecostals differed with fundamentalists as to processes and results on healing and baptism but varied little on redemption and the Second Advent. It was in this last point that fundamentalism had its greatest impact on pentecostals. Thus, it is not surprising that fundamentalist literature became indispensable to pentecostal education. Torrey, Evans, Gray, et. al., penned commentaries and theological guides pentecostals could respect, sharing an evangelical commitment to the veracity of God's Word and the necessity of redemption through faith in a personal savior. Ian Randall has applied Bebbington's fourfold rubric to British pentecostalism during the same time period as this study in *Evangelical Experiences* (1999).[6] Much of what Randall has said can be applied to their American cousins.

Literalism was central to the pentecostal understanding of the Word, and evangelism and missions were as core to their agenda as to that of the most zealous fundamental-

---

1. Faupel, *Everlasting Gospel*, 28–43.

2. Crawford and Clara Lum absconded with Seymour's mailing list in 1908, effectively shutting him up as the voice of pentecostalism. They kept the title but moved offices to Portland, Oregon.

3. Wacker, *Heaven Below*, 16–17.

4. Blumhofer, *Restoring*, 5–6.

5. "Full Gospel Assembly, Persian Mission," *CE* (29 June 1918) 14. The church was now pastored by Jeremiah Werda and sat opposite to Moody Church at Chicago Ave. and La Salle St. Urshan had by this point identified himself with oneness doctrine.

6. Randall, *Evangelical Experiences*, 206–37. Bebbington defined evangelicalism through its biblicism, conversionism, crucicentrism, and activism (see chapter 1).

ist, perhaps even more so with the added unction of the Holy Spirit. Fundamentalists like Riley and Norris grumbled that pentecostals neglected to spread the good news in their passion to spread tongues. But, as we have seen, only one of J. N. Hoover's fifty-five sermons in print advocated tongues; and E. C. Miller estimated that only 1 percent of the approximately 200 pentecostal sermons he had heard were dedicated to the topic.[7] Even if Miller exaggerated, any statistical study of pentecostal growth in the past hundred years would not support the supposed lack of interest in missions.

By the 1930s, AG pentecostals had adopted the fundamentalist "rhetoric" as their own. The critical year was 1928, which saw pivotal contributions by Hoover along fundamentalist themes, writing as he did on the threat of modernism, communism, and other issues dear to fundamentalists. For his audiences, he combined the edginess of a fundamentalist discourse with the credibility of a pentecostal immersion. McPherson tried to be a fundamentalist, but her own demeanor made the fit uncomfortable. Price, though he turned from modernism, never made fundamentalism his platform. Hoover, on the other hand, simply replaced "the church age" with "the Holy Spirit age" in his dispensational chart and transformed himself into an instant pentecostal-fundamentalist.

It is in 1928 that A. P. Gouthey toted antievolutionary arguments to Springfield to so much acclaim. Before that Darwinism was of secondary interest, a battle with which they could side with fundamentalism as bystanders. Now the battle had entered through their own doors. Thus, new primary school periodicals featured antievolutionary arguments from fundamentalist sources. Another 1928 milestone is that "modernism" was used for the first time in the title of an article by Charles Robinson. References to modernism as an opprobrium only increased from there until it became the archenemy of pentecostalism. The shape and trajectory of pentecostal denominations had heavy influence from the fundamentalists.

1928 was also important to fundamentalism. Here Riley and the WCFA officially ostracized pentecostalism from their movement. At the same time, cracks appeared in the fundamentalist armor. Philip Mauro dropped a bombshell on fundamentalism when he openly criticized dispensationalism in *The Gospel of the Kingdom*, which Campbell Morgan, who had himself written a dispensational volume, recommended.[8] Ironside and McQuilkin both struggled to reassert the Keswick interpretation of the baptism of the Holy Ghost upon the movement.[9] Merely rejecting the pentecostal message was insufficient to stave off potential losses. The conservative Princeton NT scholar Charles Erdman's remarks on pentecostalism that year gave notice: "There may be too much religious fervor and excitement in some religious gatherings, but surely not in many; and most churches need to pray earnestly for a new moving and inspiration of the Holy Spirit in order that the

---

7. Miller, *Pentecost Examined*, 109–10.

8. Mauro, *Gospel of the Kingdom* (1928). Trumbull called the book "regrettable" ("Philip Mauro's Regrettable Book," *SST* [22 December 1928] 766). Morgan wrote *God's Methods with Man* (1898) along a dispensational theme but abandoned this position after reading Mauro (see Rutgers, *Premillennialism in America*, 172ff.). Rutgers called dispensationalism as "Coccejianism" run riot—after Dutch covenantal theologian Johannes Cocceius (d. 1669).

9. Ironside wrote a seven-part series on the Holy Spirit from November 1927 to June 1928 in *The Pilot* and McQuilkin wrote two articles on Pentecost in January 1929 for *SST* (chapter 6).

hearts of the worshipers may know something of the passion, the joy, the rapture, the exaltation, the triumphant hope, which was the common experience of the early Christians even in Corinth."[10] Fundamentalists would have done well to heed his advice.

The "leavening" of CG bread by fundamentalist yeast lagged the AG by approximately five to ten years. Their shift also began in the late 1920s when articles appeared with fundamentalist interest denouncing Mussolini and communism. The eschatological focus intensified in *COGE* in the early 1930s with employment of fundamentalist sources like *SST* and increased attacks on modernism, resulting in the first advertisement for Scofield in 1936 and a demand from readers for dispensational truths, satisfied by Latimer in 1937.[11] To be sure, CG's adoption of dispensationalism was never as congruent with the fundamentalist mentality as that of the AG. There were both geographic and theological reasons for this.

First, the AG had a greater presence in the North and the Far West. Their centers were in fundamentalist strongholds like New York, Chicago, Minneapolis, and Los Angeles. CG, except for a few pockets like the Dakotas, was almost exclusively Southern. Meanwhile, fundamentalism did not have an appreciable impact on the South until after the Scopes trial. Neither Norris nor Riley could persuade the Southern Baptist Convention to support their efforts to ban evolution in Tennessee in 1925, despite the convention meeting in Memphis. CG was more bucolic in composition. According to a 1926 government survey, three-fourths of its churches were in rural communities while in the AG the percentage was half.[12] Unlike *LRE* and the Stone Church in Chicago, CG's rural character insulated it from big city squabbles. It required a Dallas pastor (Blackwood) to tune into a fundamentalist radio station (Norris's) for them to take note.

The second reason was theological. CG had deeper Methodist-holiness roots than AG ministers. The fundamentalist controversies occurred largely among northern Baptists and Presbyterians in the 1910s and 1920s, although the antecedents went back decades further. A fundamentalist response to modernism among Methodists did not emerge until the 1920s. H. C. Morrison, for example, established Asbury Seminary in 1923 in order to confront modernism among Southern Methodists. Methodists in general resisted the confessional formulae of Reformed-minded denominations. CG likewise disdained theological fineries, retaining Wesley's experiential approach to Scripture that was less conducive to higher critical interference or resistance. The AG had a stronger implant from the CMA and unofficially recognized a Reformed definition of sanctification, though it was still Arminian in its view of human agency.

---

10. Erdman, *First Epistle of Paul to the Corinthians*, 147.

11. 1933 saw increased attacks on modernism, e.g., Hoover, "Tragedy of Modern Theology," *COGE* (28 January 1933) 2, 28; Latimer, "Apostasy of the Day," *COGE* (6 May 1933) 3–4; and the anonymous article "Demand for a New Religion," *COGE* (27 May 1933) 28.

12. *Religious Bodies, 1926: Separate Denominations* (1929), vol. 2, 60 (AG), 358 (CG).

Fundamentalist Arguments and Pentecostal Responses

Adversarial complaints fell broadly into three categories: biblical (e.g., least of the gifts), theological (e.g., cessationism), and moral (e.g., it was disruptive [schismatic], unseemly [neither decent nor in order], or undisciplined [adulterous leaders]). They attributed tongues to two causes: demons mimicking genuine revival in an attempt to destroy the real and deceive the many, or a form of hysteria either mild (through "hypnotic" techniques of leaders) or nearing dementia (as a result of unstable personalities in the recipients). Holiness opponents utilized the first approach almost exclusively, while fundamentalists referred to both. Those who favored the first argument tended towards a more ultra-dispensational interpretation of Scripture (Panton, Gaebelein); those who favored the second were less dogmatic and in some ways more sympathetic (Gray, Riley). Some were willing to allow for the possibility of tongues, at least initially, like Pierson and Riley, though Riley retracted his endorsement later. Modernists attributed tongues exclusively to unstable, fanatical sorts as Blosser had, likening the experience to something akin to hypnotism induced in an atmosphere of "suggestibility."

Pentecostals did not attack fundamentalists in kind, nor were they in a position to do so. Many longed for acceptance from fellow evangelicals and had no desire to antagonize them further, though they were unwilling to sacrifice their experience for the sake of harmony. The cathartic release of tongues made too indelible an impression to deny. While this study has neglected matters of exegesis, pentecostals showed themselves equal to the task when it came to handling NT passages, frequently upbraiding fundamentalists for misquoting Scripture through omission. They also appealed to their own adherence to the "fundamentals" of the faith as values which they shared with their detractors. They saw themselves not as the enemy but as fulfillers of a "full gospel" that accepted the entire Bible as their rule, which they believed fundamentalists professed to do in theory but failed to do in practice.

While tension continued throughout the period, some fundamentalists were willing to work directly with pentecostal evangelists, but these were typically the "least pentecostal" of the pentecostals. Aimee Semple McPherson distanced herself from the pentecostal movement and downplayed her manifestation of tongues during the early 1920s in order to attract a broader audience. Both Richey and Bosworth were licensed with the CMA (though Richey did return to the AG in the late 1930s). Bosworth in particular left the AG over his disagreement with "evidential" tongues, and there is little evidence that either Oswald Smith or Harry Stemme knew he was a tongues-speaker. Uldine Utley, though converted through McPherson and having a pentecostal background, did not emphasize the charismata in her ministry. It would hardly be accurate to say that any of them ever denied tongues as a gift of the Holy Spirit or discontinued the practice of tongues either in private or public, but none of them made tongues their central platform or insisted that it was indispensable to the Christian life.

What accounts for the rancor between fundamentalists and pentecostals? Wacker tentatively suggests five possibilities. The first is that of religious proximity.[13] This is the

---

13. Wacker, "Travail of a Broken Family," 38.

most obvious and satisfactory explanation, fitting well with the Wuthnow-Lawson ecological model of religious movements. The two movements were so alike in theology and temperament that conflict was inevitable. Holiness saints responded first because the initial outbreak of tongues occurred within their precincts. Fundamentalists were by no means immune, but their delayed reaction suggests that it affected them later and in smaller doses. Competition for parishioners' hearts and minds (not to mention wallets and time) lay at the center of this fracas.

Wacker's third suggestion (I will handle number two below) articulates Melvin Dieter's observation that holiness advocates had only recently been reprimanded by their Methodist forebearers that their worship was prone to demonstrative excess.[14] Perhaps the pentecostal movement reminded them of their own excesses and therefore encouraged them to distance themselves from pentecostals in order to ingratiate themselves with the mother church. This does not account for the fundamentalist reaction, which did not share in the holiness movement's ties to Methodism, and therefore can only partially explain the rivalry between pentecostals and other evangelicals.

A fourth suggestion is the need for religious movements to define themselves against others, or what we have already seen in McGrath's terms as the "social" function of doctrine (chapter 4). But whereas I applied the principle to the internal disputes of pentecostals, here Wacker means between near kin—i.e., pentecostal and holiness. As Wacker states, "An unresisted movement soon becomes an unknown one."[15] Here the difference was not so much theological as experiential. Pentecostals had a demarcation that was clear and precise. Wacker suggests that if pentecostals had been less insistent on tongues that relations may have been more placid.[16] The problem was that pentecostals were ill-content to be quiet. The experience itself encouraged shouting and ebullience. Demarcation played a role in their need to set boundaries, but it was a result of their closeness that such need existed.

Wacker's second suggestion implicates evangelicals for ornery dispositions. They were "accomplished mudslingers" accustomed to theological brawls on seemingly minuscule issues.[17] I think there is something deeper at work here and therefore subsume this under point five of Wacker's, which is that they engaged in "a life-and-death struggle over premises and goals."[18] Certainly both sides viewed the stakes as eternal and loyalty as absolute. Hell (or heavily scorched heavenly rewards) awaited those who disobeyed God, whether in resisting the Holy Spirit if they opposed tongues or in falling under the sway of the devil if they didn't. Such a mentality afforded no middle ground, and, for me, constitutes the second most important factor for their bickering. Each side was convinced that Scripture and the angels supported their presuppositions. One of the grosser sins one could be accused of was to be a "compromiser," which accounts for the bitter "mudslinging" that preoccupied participants.

14. Ibid., 39–40, cite Dieter, "Wesleyan/Holiness and Pentecostal Movements," 10–11.
15. Ibid., 40. Anderson makes a similar point (*Vision*, 149).
16. Ibid., 40.
17. Ibid., 38–39.
18. Ibid., 41.

A sixth possibility not considered by Wacker is class division. R. Anderson has attributed holiness opposition to this type of struggle. Holiness leaders by the time of Azusa Street had graduated into the middle classes and looked down upon the lower ranks of society, rendering pentecostals as misfits in their midst.[19] As a counterpunch, Wacker has elsewhere attempted to rescue pentecostal adherents from the impression that they were more poorly educated and impecunious than most Americans.[20] What emerges from his study is that pentecostals were not so different from the average American, and that the average American was in a rather sorry state.[21] That many pentecostals came from a deprived social background should not be surprising. But Anderson's class division fails to account for why modernists, who occupied the higher echelons of society, virtually ignored pentecostalism except as a strategy to demean fundamentalists. Perhaps they felt pentecostals to be so far beneath them that the movement was not worthy of mention.

Here again proximity played the greater role. Pentecostals had so little contact with modernist churches and so little threat to their well-being that it scarcely deserved mention. Also, their holiness brethren were not much above pentecostals on the social scale, but their resistance came quicker and more vociferously than fundamentalists because the threat was more immediate. In his celebrated study *Millhands and Preachers*, Liston Pope argues that "sects" do attract members of higher classes to which they aspire once they show promise of stability and growth.[22] In his observation, pentecostal millhands did not become managers despite being more industrious. Rather, managers became pentecostals because they could exert more influence in the growing sectarian churches than they could in the more well-heeled denominational churches dominated by mill owners. Something like this happened between pentecostals and fundamentalists in the 1920s. Fundamentalists found something attractive in the pentecostal movement to which they could subscribe. Those who joined it in the early 1920s like Towner, Hoover, and Frey were in distress at the time of their conversion. Whatever they lacked pentecostalism supplied.

Desmond Cartwright has grouped the most intense opposition to pentecostalism in Britain into four periods: 1907–1908, 1913, 1921–1922 and 1930.[23] The 1921–1922 period undoubtedly refers to the pentecostal revival under George and Stephen Jeffreys during the Prophetic Society annual conferences.[24] Other than an initial period from 1907–1909 and the healing controversy which reached its apex in 1924–1925, I do not believe a similar assessment can be applied to the American scene. Rather, fundamentalist attacks varied

---

19. Anderson, *Vision*, 150–52.

20. Wacker, *Heaven Below*, 205–12.

21. Wacker depicts American society circa 1910 as a comparable to a pear in its shape, with relatively few people on top and a vast majority filling the middle with only a handful at the very bottom. Far more pentecostals hailed from somewhere in the middle of the pear than the bottom.

22. Pope, *Millhands and Preachers*, 118–19.

23. Cartwright, "Everywhere Spoken against," 4. He has labeled each period respectively as "the curious, the cautious, the critical and the caustic."

24. A number of articles covering this revival appeared in *PE*. Ernest Goode, the Presbyterian secretary of the society, praised pentecostalism as the best hope for world revival ("A Message to the Churches," *PE* [2 September 1922] 3). Cecil Polhill, a wealthy and prominent British pentecostal who financed the meetings, was one of the "Cambridge Seven" with C. T. Studd, whose brother George also became a pentecostal.

according to local circumstances. A. B. Simpson worried over church property in 1914, assuming a stance against evidential tongues that pentecostals did not appreciate. Torrey replied to a specific question about tongues in 1913 in *KB*. Shuler and Torrey attacked pentecostals in *KB* after the moratorium was lifted off Biola following Stewart's death. Riley refreshed his attack in 1926 when modernists tried to discredit fundamentalism by associating it with pentecostalism. Gaebelein, who severed his ties to Methodism in 1899, viewed himself as a sort of pastor-at-large over the fundamentalist movement and capitalized on every opportunity to malign pentecostals. To apply an Old West analogy, he was like a gunslinger entering a saloon and plugging away at everything before him. I can only speculate as to why Bauman attacked pentecostalism in 1930. Perhaps it had something to do with the woman in his congregation who had a negative experience in 1927, together with local conditions in Long Beach. Norris's attack on pentecostals resulted from Rice's healing activities in Texas in 1936.

In short, these were specific occasions that aroused fundamentalist ire, much of which had to do with territorialism within fundamentalism. Martyn Percy has critiqued fundamentalism for its emphasis on power and the desire for control.[25] While Percy's lens is too narrow, I do think power was a factor here. Fundamentalists often built up regional bases from which to operate, Norris in Fort Worth, Riley in Minneapolis, Winrod in Kansas, Torrey in Los Angeles, Gray, Ironside, and Rader in Chicago, Shields in Toronto, Gaebelein in New York (and at-large). Pentecostals were not yet in a position to claim earthly power, but they did infringe upon these territories and brought fundamentalists into their fold.

Theology merely supplied window dressing to a deeper divide: according with an opponent's position was itself an admission of wrong. If pentecostals were right, then fundamentalists would be forced to join them. Their leaders were too entrenched in their own power bases to risk loss by switching allegiances. They had everything to lose and nothing to gain by doing so. Pentecostals, who had no established base, had by contrast nothing to lose and everything to gain. Their leaders were younger, more rural, and more rudimentarily educated than fundamentalists, and thus the new movement gave ample opportunity for the "disinherited" to attain leadership and respect.

Areas for further Research

Several areas deserve more attention than I have been able to give here, such as the role of dispensationalism in pentecostalism, particularly at its sources. Pentecostals borrowed subconsciously from a number of antecedents. One of the difficulties in studying pentecostals is their reluctance to credit sources. Why? For one, truth seemed to descend from above. A sign of spirituality was the ability to discern new insight into Scripture without reference to mundane authority. Secondly, many of the ideas which pentecostals did glean from others could conceivably percolate about the head for years before pouring out in speech and print, information that could masquerade as epiphany. As an example from the

---

25. Percy, *Words, Wonders, and Power* (1996). Percy's study is on John Wimber, whom he calls a "preeminent fundamentalist." His category, as A. Anderson points out, is too broad in that he subsumes almost anything that is conservative under the fundamentalist label (*Introduction*, 258–59).

holiness movement, when Godbey dictated his commentary on Revelation, his amanuensis (probably Byron Rees) described the event as though he were listening to an oracle from the Holy Spirit.[26] And yet, in examining Godbey's exposition on the seven letters to the Asian churches, one can readily detect the influence of John Wesley's *Notes on the New Testament*.[27]

I suspect that the influence of A. B. Simpson runs much deeper in pentecostalism of both Reformed and Wesleyan orientations than is often recognized. It was after all his fourfold gospel, recognized by Dayton, that formed the pentecostal *gestalt*. Meesaeng Lee Choi has demonstrated how Simpson's fourfold gospel has influenced the Korean holiness movement, surely connections exist elsewhere in the United States between Simpson and holiness-pentecostals.[28] There are of course other sources to pentecostalism as well. A. J. Gordon was significant to Martin Knapp, though Gordon belonged to the historicist premillennialist school, which put him at odds with dispensationalists like Brookes and Scofield. Gaebelein enjoyed wide circulation among pentecostals as a respected commentator despite his virulence.

Also, further attention needs to be paid to the development of pentecostal dispensationalism from the 1910s to the 1930s. I have here only given the briefest of outlines, showing its piecemeal adoption by pentecostals. This however transpired more quickly among Keswick pentecostals than Wesleyan ones. And even in the Keswick camp it betrays varying degrees of loyalty. A. S. Copley, who leaned towards Calvinism, I suspect to be reliant in places upon David Myland. Kerr and Peirce did not adopt a full-blown dispensational theology, but neither were they far away. Riggs altered his dispensationalism to fit pentecostal tastes. F. J. Lee touches dispensational eschatology, but there is little evidence that he accepted its historicism. Larry McQueen's current research into CG eschatology promises to solve some of these issues, at least for one half of the equation.[29]

Another area of interest is pentecostal involvement in the Ku Klux Klan. There have been a number of articles addressing racism and pentecostalism which are well nuanced of this complicated issue, but little specifically on the Klan. My suspicion is that many of the fundamentalists and pentecostals who joined it did so under a false impression that the organization was anti-communist and pro-democracy.[30] The founder, William Simmons, disguised the more nefarious intentions of the Klan by capitalizing on the Red Scare following the Bolshevist revolution and the end of WWI. "Foreign" elements, like Italian-born (and Catholic) anarchists Ferdinando Nicola Sacco and Bartolomeo Vanzetti, fuelled a certain xenophobia that catapulted KKK's membership into the millions in a brief period, only to plummet again by the end of the 1920s.[31] We know the KKK contributed to

26. Seth Rees, "Books," *TRev* (20 July 1899) 11.
27. Godbey, *Revelation* (1896); Greathouse, "John Wesley's View of the Last Things," 139–41.
28. Choi, *Korean Holiness*, passim.
29. McQueen, "Opposing Visions," passim.
30. I have written briefly on pentecostal involvement in the Klan in "Mae Eleanor Frey," 57–62.
31. Sacco and Vanzetti, members of an Italian anarchist group, robbed and murdered two payroll masters in Braintree, Massachusetts in May 1920. They were executed in 1927. KKK membership reached 4.2 million by 1924 and fell to 30,000 by 1930.

pentecostal pockets, but aside from Parham and very briefly McPherson (she apparently was duped), how involved were pentecostals?

A comparison of pentecostal and fundamentalist hermeneutics could bear more scrutiny, particularly forms of discourse in which they engaged and how that changed over time through fundamentalist influence upon pentecostals. How and when did more rationalistic forms of thought alter pentecostal approaches to Scripture? Did that affect their expression of worship? What in fact was a pentecostal hermeneutic in 1910? How did dispensationalism affect pentecostal hermeneutics? Did it become more literalistic? Kenneth Archer assumes that holiness teachers resorted to the "Bible Reading Method" of protofundamentalism, but I am not convinced.[32] My hunch is that early pentecostalism emphasized an allegorical ("spiritual") interpretation and only became more literalist in the 1930s.

There were a number of pentecostals that came into the movement with fundamentalist sympathies in the 1920s, but just how many is difficult to determine. A more detailed study of a particular locale may shed light on the transfer rate from fundamentalist to pentecostal during this time. However, there are a number of difficulties with this. Identifying just who was a fundamentalist in the denominational pew is a precarious adventure. Methodists could be fundamentalists, and Baptists could be modernists, and many people fluctuated between the two extremes. Membership rolls may give some idea of how pentecostalism grew, but that also is subject to local conditions that would be difficult to extrapolate upon the whole.

Riley estimated that there were about 20 million fundamentalists in the U.S. in the 1920s and '30s. Some of the growth rate in pentecostal churches can be attributed to the siphoning off of these members. As we have seen, leaders could not prevent parishioners from occupying pentecostal seats. E. C. Miller attended a fundamentalist church even while seeking the baptism in the evenings with his wife (who did receive tongues) at Bethel Pentecostal Assembly. It was not unusual for pentecostal churches to have higher attendance on Sunday evening than on Sunday morning.[33] How many fundamentalists were merely curious about healing services compared to active seekers of tongues?

I suspect the overall percentage of fundamentalists who became pentecostal to be rather low. If twenty million Americans did call themselves fundamentalists (or sympathetic to fundamentalism), and AG and CG increased together by roughly 120,000 from 1930 to 1940, if one-quarter of these converts were fundamentalists, we would be talking about a very small portion indeed. Riley's numbers may well be exaggerated, and this too depends on whom one considers to be a fundamentalist. The number of fundamentalist sympathizers who became pentecostal could also be higher than my estimate. In the event, the number was certainly enough to cause concern for the fundamentalist hierarchy.

The role of Bible schools in pentecostal education would also be of interest. Could someone do for pentecostal education what Virginia Lieson Brereton has done for Bible

---

32. Archer, "Pentecostal Hermeneutics," 63–81.

33. Frank Lindquist's Gospel Tabernacle in Minneapolis for instance registered 400 regular members in the morning but over 600 attendees in the typical Sunday evening (W. Argue with F. J. Lindquist, "The Get Acquainted Page," *LRE* [January 1934] 8).

schools in general?[34] Did they develop along fundamentalist lines? Could a study be conducted between Keswick-pentecostal and Wesleyan-pentecostal institutions as Kimberly Alexander has done in the area of faith healing?[35] What about pentecostals and the radio, another venue dominated by fundamentalists? Several pentecostal churches operated their own radio stations, most notably McPherson, and others bought airtime on local stations. How did pentecostals employ new technologies to spread their message? How did this affect their views of the FCC and liberals? Was it the crucial factor that led to the formation of the NAE as Ockenga has suggested?

Conclusion

Surveying the literature concerning the relationship between fundamentalists and pentecostals, it largely amounts to several pages by Robert Anderson, two chapters by Edith Blumhofer, one article by Russell Spittler, one by Matthew Sutton and a smattering of paragraphs or sentences by observers of evangelicalism.[36] This study has attempted to map the landscape in greater detail, explore the boundaries that historically existed between them and document their influences upon each other up to the NAE. Some subsume pentecostalism under a fundamentalist pall, others see them as entirely separate entities; as in many cases, the truth lies somewhere in between.

This study has traced pentecostalism's roots in the nineteenth-century holiness movement. But the holiness movement also informed fundamentalist spirituality through the Keswick movement. While there was a rationalist strain in fundamentalism, it should not dwarf the pietistic dynamic which ran through all forms of evangelicalism into the twentieth century. Piety also informed modernism but did not share in pentecostalism's or fundamentalism's commitment to revivalism and conversion of the heart. And proto-fundamentalism contributed to the shape of pentecostal theology through the fourfold gospel, providing an additional structural link between the two movements. Pentecostals and fundamentalists shared ancestors, but pentecostalism was the direct descendent of a radical holiness movement.

This study has also recorded the shifts in both pentecostalism and fundamentalism. Neither movement should be treated monolithically. There was a great variety of opinion in both camps, and views altered over time. Pentecostalism grew into fundamentalism through the leavening process described in this thesis. Thus, I concur with Spittler that pentecostals were "fundamentalistic," but they were not fundamentalists.[37] I have traced here how the "leaven" of fundamentalism shaped pentecostalism through "vocabulary," "content," and "rhetoric." In future, I hope that this can serve as a model for other studies on the transference of value from one religious group to another.

---

34. Brereton, *Training God's Army* (1990).

35. Alexander analyzes faith healing from both Finished Work and holiness views in *Pentecostal Healing*.

36. Blumhofer has given the most attention to fundamentalism in the conclusion to her dissertation (Waldvogel, "The Overcoming Life") and in chapter 8 of *Restoring the Faith*. Anderson has several insightful passages scattered throughout *Vision of the Disinherited*.

37. Spittler, "Are Pentecostals and Charismatics Fundamentalists?" 113.

Conclusion

While a sect-to-denomination model could have been used as a framework for this study, the Wuthnow-Lawson ecological model has had the particular advantage in incorporating the dynamic relationship of new religious groups against other groups of like "species," thus explaining the competition which often exists between them. Many previous studies of pentecostalism have been written from a denominational perspective and thus have lacked an account for changes within denominations according to outside pressures, both religious and cultural. By using this model, pentecostalism can be viewed organically in its broader religious context as it developed and matured through the stages of *genesis*, *adaptation* and *retention*. The hostility exhibited between the two movements should not obscure their essential similarity.

Appendix A

Articles by A. J. Gordon on Healing in *The Revivalist* in 1899:

Gordon, A. J. "Jesus is Victor." *TRev*, 27 April 1899, 10.
———. "A Miracle." *TRev*, 1 June 1899, 10.
———. "Gems from Gordon." *TRev*, 1 June 1899, 10.
———. "Healing of Jennie Smith." *TRev*, 13 July 1899, 10.
———. "Gold from Gordon." *TRev*, 20 July 1899, 10.
———. "George Fox and Divine Healing." *TRev*, 10 August 1899, 10.
———. "Practice of the Waldenses." *TRev*, 10 August 1899, 10.
———. "Hints on Healing." *TRev*, 24 August 1899, 10.
———. "Gems from Gordon." *TRev*, 7 September 1899, 3.
———. "Luther and Melancthon." *TRev*, 7 September 1899, 10.
———. "Gordon on Healing." *TRev*, 7 September 1899, 10.
———. "Gems from Godbey's Commentary." *TRev*, 14 September 1899, 15.
———. "Gold from Gordon." *TRev*, 28 September 1899, 10.
———. "Healed by Prayer." *TRev*, 7 December 1899, 10.

Articles by A. J. Gordon on Premillennialism in *The Revivalist* in 1899:

Gordon, A. J. "The Uplifted Gaze." *TRev*, 2 March 1899, 6.
———. "A Flaming-Up." *TRev*, 23 March 1899, 6.
———. "Embracing the World." *TRev*, 6 April 1899, 8.
———. "Gold from Gordon." *TRev*, 13 April 1899, 13.
———. "The Mock Millennium." *TRev*, 25 May 1899, 7.
———. "The End of the Age." *TRev*, 1 June 1899, 7.
———. "Adjusted." *TRev*, 15 June 1899, 7.
———. "Lukewarm." *TRev*, 22 June 1899, 7.
———. "Fire and Frost." *TRev*, 20 July 1899, 7.
———. "'As the Angels.'" *TRev*, 27 July 1899, 7.
———. "Probation Not Closed." *TRev*, 27 July 1899, 7.
———. "At His Coming." *TRev*, 10 August 1899, 7.
———. "Translated." *TRev*, 17 August 1899, 2.
———. "Heavenly Citizenship." *TRev*, 24 August 1899, 7.
———. "Agents." *TRev*, 31 August 1899, 7.
———. "The Sun of Israel." *TRev*, 14 September 1899, 7.
———. "From Beyond the Veil." *TRev*, 21 September 1899, 7.
———. "Eyes Best Forward." *TRev*, 21 September 1899, 7.
———. "The Awakening." *TRev*, 5 October 1899, 7.
———. "Christ, the Light." *TRev*, 2 November 1899, 7.
———. "Glorified." *TRev*, 23 November 1899, 7.
———. "Two Resurrections." *TRev*, 30 November 1899, 7.
———. "Antichrist." *TRev*, 14 December 1899, 7.

Appendix B

Bibliography of Anti-Pentecostal Articles in Holiness Periodicals (1906–1910)[*]

Averill, R. L. "The Apostolic Faith Movement." *The Holiness Evangel* (1 January 1907) 1(?).
———. "The 'Tongues' People as I Saw them." *Pentecostal Advocate* (10 January 1907) 2.
Bresee, P. F. "Editorial." *Nazarene Messenger* (8 August 1907) 6.
———. "Fanaticism and Humbugs." *Nazarene Messenger* (27 June 1907) 6.
———. "The Gift of Tongues." *Nazarene Messenger* (13 December 1906) 6.
———. "Pentecostal Power." *Nazarene Messenger* (1 October 1908) 6–7.
———. "The Primary Purpose of the Holy Ghost Baptism." *Nazarene Messenger* (4 February 1909) 1–2.
Campbell, P. B. "The Gift of Tongues." *Beulah Christian* (6 April 1907) n.p.
Chambers, Oswald. "Gift of Tongues." *God's Revivalist and Bible Advocate* (11 July 1907) 3–4.
Cowman, C. E. "Tongues and Foreign Missions." *Nazarene Messenger* (4 March 1909) 2–3.
Coulson, Amanda. "The Tongues Meeting as I Saw it." *Pentecostal Advocate* (18 May 1911) 7.
"A Craze for Tongues." *The Gospel Trumpet* (17 January 1907) 1, 8, 9.
Detwiler, George. "The Gift of Tongues." *Evangelical Visitor* (15 April 1907) 2.
"The Drift of the Times." *The Gospel Message* (October 1910) 12–14.
Eddings, S. H. "Some more Foxfire." *The Gospel Trumpet* (9 May 1907) 7.
Ellyson, E. P. "The Texas Holiness University." *Pentecostal Advocate* (25 November 1909) 5.
Goodwin, J. W. "'The Tongue Movement.'" *Nazarene Messenger* (15 August 1907) 3.
Haynes, B. F. "Fanaticism and its Progeny." *Pentecostal Advocate* (10 February 1910) 2.
Henricks, A. O. "Beware of Fanaticism." *Nazarene Messenger* (16 January 1908) 2.
Hinchman, E. D. "Signs Following." *Nazarene Messenger* (12 March 1908) 2–3.
Huckabee, B. W. "The 'Gift of Tongues,' and other Gifts." *Pentecostal Advocate* (21 February 1907) 8–9.
———. "The Gift of Tongues, Again." *Pentecostal Advocate* (14 March 1907) 8–9, 13.
Humphrey, L. H. "Don't Serve the Devil." *Nazarene Messenger* (19 March 1908) 2–3.
Jernigan, C. B. "Steadfast." *The Holiness Advocate* (2 September 1908) 4.
Kelley, William V. "The Gift of Tongues." *Methodist Review*, vol. 90—sixth series, vol. 24, 757–64. Cincinnati: Jennings and Graham; New York: Eaton and Mains, September 1908.
Kumarakulasinghe, Kittie Wood. "The Tongues Earthquake Scare in Ceylon." *The Free Methodist* (17 December 1907) 11.
LaFontaine, C. V. "The More Excellent Way." *Nazarene Messenger* (19 July 1906) 10–12.
"Letters of Warning." *The Gospel Trumpet* (14 February 1907) 1.
Martin, I. G. "Los Angeles Letter." *The Pentecostal Messenger* (December 1906) 2–3.
"Miraculous Gifts of the Spirit." *The Gospel Message* (November 1906) 11–12.
"The Mystery of Iniquity." *The Gospel Message* (October 1906) 10–11.
Neal, G. T. "Unknown Tongues." *The Gospel Trumpet* (31 January 1907) n.p.
Nelson, T. H. "Sermon: Tongues Bogus and Genuine." *The Herald of Light* (23 February 1907) 7, 10, 16.
Roberts, C. E. "Abiline District." *Pentecostal Advocate* (19 May 1910) 10.
"Satan Transformed." *Beulah Christian* (12 January 1907) 5.
St. Claire. "Milton, Cal." *Nazarene Messenger* (17 January 1907) 5.
"Seeking Pentecost." *The Gospel Trumpet* (27 December 1906) n.p.

* List compiled with permission from photocopied items at FPHC

Appendix B

Speakes, Josiah N. "The Bible Evidence." *The Holiness Evangel* (24 March 1909) 1.
Stuckey, Wallace M. "Where Miracles Belong." *Christian Standard* (25 April 1908) 8, 9.
"Their Common Denominator." *Christian Standard* (14 March 1908) 14, 15.
"The 'Tongues' Movement." *The Gospel Message* (June 1907) 15.
"Unknown Tongues." *The Gospel Message* (December 1906) 11–12.
"Varieties of the Gift of 'Tongues.'" *Evangelical Visitor* (2 September 1907) 6–7.
Wilson, G. W. "... Feeling in Relation to Truth ..." *Nazarene Messenger* (3 September 1908) 1.
Winchester, Olive M. "The Gift of Tongues." *Beulah Christian* (19 June 1909) 4.
Woodrow, O. C. "The Gift of Tongues." *Pentecostal Advocate* (10 January 1907) 13.
Zook, J. R. "Gifts of the Spirit." *Evangelical Visitor* (15 August 1907) 8.

Appendix C

Book Advertisements in the *Christian Evangel* in 1915*

Pentecostal: [4 titles, 23x]
Arthur Booth-Clibborn, *Blood against Blood* [5x]
Alice Flower, *Blossoms from the King's Garden* [7x]
Maria B. Woodworth-Etter, *Acts of the Holy Ghost* [9x]
William G. Schell, *Primitive Church Government* [2x]

Protofundamentalist: [1 title, 12x]
Charles Finney, *Lectures on Revivals* [12x]

Fundamentalist: [2 titles, 4x]
Scofield Reference Bible [3x]
R. A. Torrey, *Gist of the Lesson, 1916* [1x]

Holiness: [0 titles, 0x]

Evangelical: [1 title, 1x]
Tarbell's Teachers' Guide [1x]

---

* I have used 1920 as a demarcating line between "protofundamentalists" and "fundamentalists." Those who died before 1920 fell under the former and those after 1920 fell under the latter. For "evangelical." I have assigned those who cannot readily be identified as fundamentalist either by name, material, or publisher. Devotional works, Bible study aides and Sunday school guides also came under this category. I have excluded from the list Bibles (other than Scofield), hymnals, and "evangelical" children's literature. [These designations will also apply for Appendix D and Appendix G.]

Appendix D

Book Advertisements in the *Pentecostal Evangel* in 1920

Pentecostal: [14 titles, 60x]

Arthur S. Booth-Clibborn, *Blood against Blood* [1x]
A. P. Collins, *The Sign of the Son of Man* [6x]
Alice Flower, *Blossoms from the King's Garden* [1x]
Maria Gerber, *Past Experiences, Present Conditions and Plans for the Future* [3x]
The Gift of Tongues and the Pentecostal Movement [5x]
B. F. Lawrence, *The Apostolic Faith Restored* [5x]
Alice Luce, *Pictures of Pentecost* [5x]
Aimee Semple McPherson, *This is That* [1x]
Carrie Judd Montgomery, *The Prayer of Faith* [7x]
Sammy Morris—A Spirit-filled Life [6x]
David W. Myland, *The Book of Revelation* [4x]
Maria B. Woodworth-Etter, *Holy Ghost Sermons* [5x]
———, *Questions and Answers on Divine Healing* [6x]
———, *Signs and Wonders* [5x]

Protofundamentalist: [33 titles, 117x]

W. E. Blackstone, *Jesus is Coming* [5x]
James Brookes, *I am Coming* [1x]
———, *Maranatha, or The Lord Cometh* [1x]
Charles Finney, *Autobiography* [3x]
———, *Gospel Themes* [3x]
———, *Lectures to Professing Christians* [4x]
———, *Lectures on Revival* [3x]
A. J. Gordon, *The Ministry of Healing* [5x]
David Gregg, *Things of Northfield and other Things* [3x]
C. H. McIntosh, *Notes of the Pentateuch* (6 vols.) [2x]
F. B. Meyer, *Christian Living* [1x]
———, *Christ in Isaiah* [4x]
———, *The Directory of the Devout Life* [1x]
———, *Paul, a Servant of Christ* [6x]
———, *The Shepherd Psalm* [4x]
George Müller, *How God Answers Prayer* [3x]
Andrew Murray, *The Holiest of All* [1x]
———, *Like Christ* [5x]
———, *Waiting on God* [2x]
———, *With Christ in the School of Prayer* [5x]
John G. Paton, *An Autobiography* [1x]
A. T. Pierson, *George Müller of Bristol* [4x]
———, *Many Infallible Proofs* [3x]

Appendix D

J. A. Seiss, *Lectures on the Apocalypse* (3 vols.) [2x]
———, *Voices from Babylon* [2x]
A. B. Simpson, *All in All, Christ in Colossians* [5x]
———, *The Christ Life* [6x]
———, *Epistles of the Advent* [5x]
———, *The Gospel of Healing* [5x]
———, *The Life of Prayer* [5x]
Hannah Whitall Smith, *The Christian's Secret of a Happy Life* [3x]
C. H. Spurgeon, *The Soul Winner* [3x]
Henry Clay Trumbull, *Personal Prayer* [1x]

Fundamentalist: [38 titles, 140x]

Len Broughton, *The Prayers of Jesus* [1x]
The Brown God and His White Imps [6x]
Dan Canright, *Seventh Day Adventism Renounced* [1x]
J. Wilbur Chapman, *Another Mile and other Sermons* [1x]
———, *Hadley, A Miracle of Grace* [1x]
———, *The Personal Touch* [2x]
———, *Revival Sermons* [1x]
William Evans, *How to Prepare Sermons* [5x]
Expectation, Short Paper on the Second Coming [1x]
W. Faulkner, *From the Ballroom to Hell* [6x]
———, *The Lure of the Dance* [4x]
A. C. Gaebelein, *Ezekiel* [5x]
James Gray, *Antidote to Christian Science* [1x]
———, *Christian Worker's Commentary on the Old and New Testament* [9x]
———, *Prophecy and the Lord's Return* [8x]
———, *Synthetic Bible Studies* [1x]
———, *A Text-book on Prophecy* [7x]
Stuart Holden, *Will the Christ Return?* [5x]
Philip Mauro, *After This—The Church, the Kingdom and the Glory* [1x]
———, *The Number of Man* [1x]
———, *The World and its God* [3x]
S. W. Pratt, *The Deity of Jesus Christ* [2x]
Paul Rader, *Beating Baal and other Sermons* [7x]
———, *The Empty Cottage at Silver Falls* [7x]
———, *Hell, and How to Escape* [7x]
———, *How to Win and other Victory Messages* [7x]
———, *Signs of the Times* [7x]
———, *Straight from the Shoulder Messages* [7x]
Scofield Reference Bible [4x]
C. I. Scofield, *What do the Prophets Say?* [6x]
Gipsy Smith, *As Jesus Passed by and other Sermons* [1x]
W. C. Stevens, *The Book of Daniel* [4x]
R. A. Torrey, *Gist of the Lesson for 1920* [2x]
———, *Topical Text Book* [3x]
Leon Tucker, *Rader's Redemption* [3x]
C. W. M. Turner, *Outline Studies in the Book of Revelation* [5x]
———, *Book of the Revelation and Key to Chart of the Ages* [1x]
Sydney Watson, *In the Twinkling of an Eye* [3x]
———, *The Mark of the Beast* [3x]

Appendix D

Holiness: [0 titles, 0x]

Evangelical: [33 titles, 108x]

Arnold's Practical Commentary on the Sunday School Lesson for 1920 [2x]
Harold Begbie, *Other Sheep* [3x]
C. H. V. Bogatzky, *The Golden Treasury* [4x]
Elijah Brown, *Point and Purpose in Preaching* [5x]
Francis E. Clark, *Similes and Figures from Alexander Maclaren* [2x]
Sydney Collett, *All about the Bible* [7x]
C. C. Cook, *Fourfold Sonship of Jesus* [5x]
Daily Light on the Daily Path [1x]
Charles R. Erdman, *The Gospel of John* [2x]
John T. Faris, *Reapers of His Harvest* [3x]
Frances Havergal, *Evening Thoughts* [5x]
———, *Kept for the Master's Use* [4x]
———, *My King and His Service* [1x]
"I Cried, He Answered" [7x]
J. Kilia, *Outlines and Instructions for Preachers and Teachers* [1x]
A. E. Knight, *Concise History of the Church* [3x]
G. Lawson, *Deeper Experiences of Famous Christians* [4x]
William Lincoln, *Lectures on Revelation* [5x]
A. H. McKinney, *Guiding Boys* [1x]
Pastor Hsi, One of China's Millions [5x]
Peloubet's Select Notes on the Sunday School Lessons for 1920 [2x]
C. Perren, *Evangelistic Sermons in Outline* [7x]
———, *Revival Sermons in Outline* [2x]
———, *Seed Corn for the Sower* [3x]
H. T. Sell, *Studies in Early Church History* [5x]
Sermon Outlines of the New Testament [4x]
James Stalker, *Life of Christ* [2x]
Tarbell's Teachers' Guide for 1920 [1x]
Twentieth Century Story of the Christ [1x]
John Urquhart, *The Wonders of Prophecy* [4x]
L. Wooten, *Holiness* [1x]
A. S. Worrell, *Didactic and Devotional Poems* [5x]

Appendix E

A. C. Gaebelein's Anti-Pentecostal and Anti-Healing Articles from *Our Hope*

29 Anti-Pentecostal Articles by Gaebelein from *Our Hope*, 1920–1925 (listed by date):

Gaebelein, A. C. "Is it that?" *Hope* (November 1920) 258–63.
———. "'Pentecostal' Mis-interpretation." *Hope* (December 1920) 321–23.
———. "Demon Possession." *Hope* (January 1921) 403–10.
———. "The Irvingite Delusion." *Hope* (March 1921) 520–22.
———. "Why Is It Thus?" *Hope* (March 1921) 522–23.
———. "The Pentecostal Movement." *Hope* (April 1921) 590.
———. "The Holy Spirit in Romans." *Hope* (May 1921) 641–47.
———. "Spirit Manifestations." *Hope* (May 1921) 653.
———. "A Warning." *Hope* (June 1921) 725–30.
———. "Sir Conan Doyle." *Hope* (July 1922) 45–48.
———. "Another Tragedy." *Hope* (December 1922) 335–36.
———. "Concerning Feet Washing." *Hope* (September 1923) 175–77.
———. "Perplexed Christians." *Hope* (October 1923) 208–11.
———. "The Gamaliel Route." *Hope* (November 1923) 266–70.
———. "Light on 'Dr. Price.'" *Hope* (November 1923) 271–73.
———. "The Gospel of John: Chapter XVI." *Hope* (November 1923) 276–82.
———. "What Power." *Hope* (February 1924) 465–66.
———. "The Gospel of John: Chapter XVI." *Hope* (March 1924) 535–40.
———. "Montanus." *Hope* (April 1924) 590–91.
———. "More Dangerous than Mrs. Mary Baker Eddy." *Hope* (April 1924) 591–93.
———. "Beware!" *Hope* (May 1924) 650–52.
———. "The Frightful Increase of Religious Insanity." *Hope* (June 1924) 746–47.
———. "Leaders of Deception and Delusion." *Hope* (September 1924) 176–77.
———. "McPhersonism Repudiated." *Hope* (January 1925) 401–3.
———. "False Prophetess." *Hope* (April 1925) 595–97.
———. "Horrible Demonism." *Hope* (April 1925) 625–26.
———. "Mrs. McPherson's Expensive Float." *Hope* (April 1925) 626–27.
———. "Pentecostalism in India." *Hope* (May 1925) 657.
———. "Sowing the Seed of Disruption." *Hope* (October 1925) 243–44.

16 Anti-Healing Articles by Gaebelein from *Our Hope*, 1921–1925 (listed by date):

Gaebelein, A. C. "Camouflage." *Hope* (March 1921) 519–20.
———. "A Trail of Hopelessness." *Hope* (July 1922) 14–17.
———. "Faith Cure." *Hope* (August 1922) 75–76.

———. "Sad Results." *Hope* (September 1922) 208.
———. "Faith Healers Everywhere." *Hope* (December 1922) 354–55.
———. "Another Healer." *Hope* (August 1923) 81–83.
———. "Untruths." *Hope* (August 1923) 83–84.
———. "The Healing Craze in a New Form." *Hope* (September 1923) 167–68.
———. "Some Find Out." *Hope* (September 1924) 145.
———. "Anointing with Oil." *Hope* (February 1925) 471–72.
———. "Divine Healing." *Hope* (March 1925) 548–53.
———. "A Perverted Text." *Hope* (April 1925) 597–99.
———. "A Divine Healing Suicide." *Hope* (August 1925) 81–82.
———. "Disastrous Praying." *Hope* (September 1925) 137–38.
———. "A False Report." *Hope* (September 1925) 138–39.
———. "Superstitions and Fanaticism." *Hope* (October 1925) 201–3.

Appendix F

D. M. Panton's Articles in *Pentecostal Evangel* from 1920–1925 (listed by date)

Panton, D. M. "Israel's Peril." *PE* (7 August 1920) 2–3.
———. "The Return of Miracles." *PE* (7 February 1920) 1.
———. "Earnestly Contend for the Faith." *PE* (3 April 1920) 1–2.
———. "At any Moment." PE (26 June 1920) 3.
———. "Last Preparations for the Anti-Christ." *PE* (4 September 1920) 6–7.
———. "Watchman, What of the Night." *PE* (7 January 1922) 1, 7.
———. "Our Attitude to Laodicea." *PE* (1 April 1922) 2–3.
———. "Another War in 1927?" *PE* (1 April 1922) 7.
———. "The Grace of our Lord Jesus Christ." *PE* (19 August 1922) 1, 3.
———. "Coming Again of the Lord Jesus." *PE* (28 October 1922) 1.
———. "Coming War." *PE* (25 November 1922) 10.
———. "God's Challenge of Intercession." *PE* (21 July 1923) 4.
———. "Christ Risen a Fact." *PE* (12 April 1924) 2–3.
———. "[Untitled]." *PE* (4 April 1925) 3.
———. "The Fact of Christ's Resurrection." *PE* (11 April 1925) 2–3, 14.
———. "The Coming Collapse." *PE* (12 September 1925) 6–7.

Appendix G

Book Advertisements in the *Pentecostal Evangel* in 1925

Pentecostal: [23 titles, 122x]

E. N. Bell, *Questions and Answers* [4x]
Helen Dyer, *Pandita Ramabai* [2x]
Stanley Frodsham, *The Boomerang Boy* [4x]
———, *Happy Hours with Little Folks* [12x]
———, *Little Folk's Story-Hour* [8x]
Joshua Calvert Jaeys, *The Cave of Adullam* [6x]
S. A. Jamieson, *The Great Shepherd* [7x]
Clarence Jenson, *Back to the Old Time Religion* [1x]
D. W. Kerr, *Waters in the Desert* [9x]
Life and Testimony of Mrs. Woodworth-Etter [1x]
Alice Luce, *The Messenger and his Message* [14x]
Carrie J. Montgomery, *Prayer of Faith* [2x]
———, *Secrets of Victory* [3x]
Samuel Morris [1x]
J. E. Perkins, *The Brooding Presence* [6x]
Redemption through Christ Jesus [5x]
Charles Robinson, *Praying to Change Things* [1x]
A. G. Ward, *Soul-Food for Hungry Saints* [9x]
Smith Wigglesworth, *Ever-Increasing Faith* [13x]
Maria B. Woodworth-Etter, *Holy Ghost Sermons* [2x]
———, *Marvels and Miracles* [2x]
———, *Spirit-Filled Sermons* [1x]
Amy Yeomans, *The Golden Bird* [9x]

Protofundamentalist: [32 titles, 50x]

W. E. Blackstone, *Jesus is Coming* [1x]
James Brookes, *An Outline of the Books of the Bible* [1x]
Charles Finney, *Gospel Themes* [1x]
———, *Lectures to Professing Christians* [1x]
———, *Revival Lectures* [1x]
A. J. Gordon, *The Ministry of Healing* [3x]
David Gregg, *Things of Northfield* [2x]
Francis McGraw, *Praying Hyde* [1x]
Andrew Murray, *Abide in Christ* [1x]
———, *Holiest of All* [1x]
———, *Like Christ* [1x]
———, *Ministry of Intercession* [2x]
———, *Prayer Life* [4x]

Appendix G

———, *Waiting on God* [2x]
Pastor Blumhardt [1x]
G. H. Pember, *Earth's Earliest Ages* [1x]
A. T. Pierson, *The Bible and Spiritual Life* [2x]
———, *George Müller of Bristol* [3x]
———, *Knowing the Scriptures* [1x]
———, *Many Infallible Proofs* [1x]
———, *The New Acts of the Apostles* [2x]
Joseph Seiss, *Holy Types* [3x]
A. B. Simpson, *Christ in the Tabernacle* [2x]
———, *The Christ Life* [1x]
———, *Epistles of the Advent* [1x]
———, *The Gospel of Healing* [2x]
———, *Practical Christianity* [1x]
Hannah Whitall Smith, *Living in the Sunshine* [3x]
Spurgeon's Sermon Notes [1x]
C. H. Spurgeon, *The Treasury of David* [1x]
Charles Spurgeon, Jr., ed., *The Letters of C. H. Spurgeon* [1x]
H. Clay Trumbull, *Hints on Child Training* [1x]

Fundamentalist: [84 titles, 131x]

Samuel Andrews, *Christianity and Anti-Christianity* [1x]
William Biederwolf, *The Unvarnished Facts about Christian Science* [1x]
Mrs. Cyril Bird, *Little is Much when God is in It* [2x]
Keith Brooks, *The Summarized Bible* [3x]
W. J. Bryan, *The Bible and its Enemies* [2x]
———, *Christ and his Companions* [1x]
———, *Famous Figures of the Old Testament* [2x]
———, *In His Image* [2x]
———, *The Last Message of William Jennings Bryan* [3x]
———, *Seven Questions in Dispute* [3x]
J. Wilbur Chapman, *Evangelistic Sermons* [2x]
J. E. Conant, *The Church, the Schools and Evolution* [1x]
———, *Divine Dynamite* [4x]
George Davis, *China's Christian Army* [1x]
———, *The Patmos Vision* [1x]
A. C. Dixon, *The Glories of the Cross* [1x]
Mildred Edwards, *Elocile, or The King's Return* [1x]
William Evans, *The Book Method of Bible Study* [2x]
———, *The Book of Books* [2x]
———, *The Great Doctrines of the Bible* [3x]
———, *How to Prepare Sermons and Gospel Addresses* [2x]
———, *Outline Study of the Bible* [2x]
———, *Personal Soul Winning* [1x]
———, *The Shepherd Psalm* [1x]
Henry Frost, *Men who Pray* [1x]
———, *What Should Determine our Christian Fellowship?* [1x]
Rosiland Goforth, *How I Know God Answers Prayer* [2x]
F. W. Grant, *Facts and Theories as to a Future State* [1x]
James Gray, *Christ in the Sacrificial Offerings* [2x]
———, *How to Master the English Bible* [2x]
———, *Prophecy and the Lord's Return* [2x]
———, *Synthetic Bible Studies* [1x]

Appendix G

———, *A Text-Book on Prophecy* [2x]
W. H. Griffith-Thomas, *"Let us Go on"* [2x]
Ada Habershon, *The Study of the Types* [1x]
Fred E. Hagin, *His Appearing and His Kingdom* [1x]
I. M. Haldeman, *Morality or Immortality?* [2x]
Norman Harrison, *His Salvation* [1x]
John Horsch, *Modern Religious Liberalism* [1x]
Howard Kelly, *A Scientific Man and the Bible* [2x]
J. C. Massee, *Eternal Life in Action* [1x]
Philip Mauro, *After This* [1x]
———, *Bringing back the King* [1x]
———, *God's Present Kingdom* [3x]
———, *The Kingdom of Heaven* [1x]
———, *Never Man Spake like this Man* [1x]
Robert Middleton, *The Coming Great World Changes* [1x]
H. S. Miller, *The Christian Workers' Manual* [2x]
R. T. Naish, *The Midnight Hour and After* [3x]
J. Frank Norris, *To Die is Gain* [1x]
———, *The Virgin Birth* [1x]
Ford Ottman, *The Coming Day* [2x]
———, *The Psalm of the Pilgrim* [1x]
Outline Studies in Christian Doctrine [2x]
C. Pankhurst, *Some Modern Problems* [1x]
George Pardington, *Outlines of Christian Doctrine* [1x]
George M. Price, *The Phantom of Organic Evolution* [1x]
C. E. Putnam, *The Power of Jesus' Blood and its Relation to Sin* [1x]
Paul Rader, *The Signs of the Times* [2x]
———, *"Hell" and "How Shall We Escape"* [1x]
W. B. Riley, *Ephesians—The Threefold Epistle* [3x]
———, *The Seven Churches of Asia* [1x]
The Scarlet Woman, or the Revival of Romanism [1x]
C. I. Scofield, *What do the Prophets Say?* [1x]
William Smith, *A Primer of Prophecy* [1x]
Spiritualism: Spiritism Exposed [1x]
W. C. Stevens, *Book of Daniel* [2x]
———, *Why I Reject Millennial Dawn* [1x]
Grant Stroh, *The Next World-Crisis* [2x]
B. B. Sutcliffe, *The Bible through a Telescope* [1x]
Richard Swain, *The Real Key to Christian Science* [1x]
R. A. Torrey, *The Bible, The Peerless Book* [1x]
———, *Getting the Gold out of the Word of God, or, How to Study the Bible* [1x]
———, *The Gist of the Sunday School Lesson for 1925* [2x]
———, *The Gist of the Sunday School Lesson for 1926* [1x]
———, ed., *The New Topical Text-Book* [3x]
———, *The Return of the Lord Jesus* [4x]
———, *What the Bible Teaches* [1x]
Leon Tucker, *Studies in Romans* [2x]
———, *Studies in the Second Book of Luke* [1x]
Sydney Watson, *In the Twinkling of an Eye* [1x]
———, *The Mark of the Beast* [1x]
———, *Scarlet and Purple* [1x]
John Weaver Weddell, *Your Study Bible* [1x]
C. F. Wimberly, *The Seven Seals of the Apocalypse* [1x]

Appendix G

Holiness: *[3 titles, 6x]*
Herbert Booth, *The Saint and the Sword* [3x]
D. O. Teasley, *The Bible and How to Interpret It* [2x]
Arthur C. Zepp, *Demon Activity in the Latter Times* [1x]

Evangelical: [54 titles, 79x]
Arnold's Practical Commentary on the International Sunday School Lesson [4x]
Harriet Bainbridge, *Life for Body and Soul* [1x]
J. G. Bellett, *The Minor Prophets* [1x]
Helen Bingham, *An Irish Saint* [1x]
W. G. Blaikie, *Manual of Bible History in Connection with the History of the World* [1x]
———, *Personal Life of David Livingstone* [1x]
A. Douglas Brown, *The Great Harvester* [1x]
Book of Points for Christians and Personal Workers [1x]
Eleanor Boyd, *The Gospel in Exodus* [1x]
———, *The Gospel in Genesis* [2x]
———, *The Gospel in Leviticus* [1x]
———, *The Meaning of the Cross* [2x]
Consider Him [1x]
Conybeare and Howson, *Life and Epistles of Paul* [1x]
J. M. Coon, *Bible Readers and Christian Workers' Selfhelp Hand Book* [1x]
Daily Light [1x]
R. Diterich, *Protestantism* [1x]
Kate Drew, *The Revival at Broad Lane* [1x]
Charles Edwards, *For Heavenly Warfare* [1x]
Charles R. Erdman, *The Lord We Love* [1x]
Charles Foster, *Story of the Bible* [1x]
E. E. Helms, *Forgotten Stories* [1x]
———, *The Gate to the Gospel* [1x]
———, *God in History* [1x]
E. A. Hewitt, *Handfuls of Help* [1x]
Hurlbut's Story of the Bible [1x]
I Cried, He Answered [1x]
Julia Johnson, *Fifty Missionary Heroes every Boy and Girl should Know about* [2x]
Joseph Kemp, *Outline Studies in the Book of Revelation* [1x]
A. E. Knight, *A Concise History of the Church* [4x]
Robert Lee, *Outlined Romans* [2x]
W. P. Livingstone, *Mary Slessor of Calabar* [2x]
———, *Of Okoyong White Queen* [1x]
J. Kennedy Maclean, *The Answer Came* [1x]
Robert Nichols, *The Growth of the Christian Church* [1x]
E. J. Pace, *Christian Cartoons* [2x]
P. L. Parker, *The Heart of Wesley's Journal* [1x]
Thomas Payne, *The Greatest Force on Earth* [1x]
C. Perren, *Revival Sermons in Outline* [4x]
A. T. Robertson, *Studies in Mark's Gospel* [1x]
L. R. Scarborough, *Holy Places and Precious Promises* [1x]
Jesse Silver, *Will Hell be Vacated?* [2x]
James Smith, *Handfuls on Purpose* [1x]
———, *Trips and Adventures, Handfuls on Purpose* [1x]
Talks to Candidates for Divine Healing [1x]
"An Unknown Christian." *The Happy Christian Life* [2x]

Appendix G

"An Unknown Christian." *He Shall Come Again* [5x]
"An Unknown Christian." *How to Live the Victorious Life* [4x]
John Urquhart, *The Wonders of Prophecy* [1x]
Gordon Watt, *The Cross in Faith and Conduct* [1x]
———, *The Meaning of the Cross* [1x]
———, *The Strategic Value of Prayer* [1x]
W. Pakenham Walsh, *Early Heroes of the Mission Field* [2x]
Ann Wright, *Burton Street Folks* [2x]

Appendix H

Sermons of J. N. Hoover

Evangelism/Salvation (11): *(listed by publication and date)**

Hoover, J. N. "God's Master-Piece." *LRE* (September 1930) 15–17.
———. "Our Heavenly Home." *LRE* (January 1932) 15–17, 22.
———. "How to Reach the Unsaved." *LRE* (February 1934) 20–22.
———. "Evangelism." *PE* (22 October 1927) 7.
———. "Evangelism in the Sunday School." *PE* (4 May 1929) 7–8.
———. "Christian Efficiency." *PE* (10 December 1932) 8.
———. "Soul-Winning Evangelism." *PE* (15 April 1933) 1, 7.
———. "How to Reach the Unsaved." *PE* (8 September 1934) 6.
———. "What is the Soul?" *W&Wk* (December 1936) 9.
———. "A Soul in Distress." *W&Wk* (January 1937) 4.
———. "How to Reach the Unsaved." *W&Wk* (February 1937) 8.

Premillennial advent (6):

Hoover, J. N. "When Jesus Comes." *LRE* (November 1930) 18–20.
———. "When Jesus Comes." *LRE* (December 1930) 19–21.
———. "Christ's Coming: First and Second." *LRE* (December 1937) 6–7, 23.
———. "The Second Coming of Christ." *PE* (26 January 1929) 8–9.
———. "Does the World Need a Saviour?" *PE* (15 March 1930) 1–2.
———. "Signs of His Coming." *W&Wk* (September 1936) 5–6.

Church/ecclesiology (5):

Hoover, J. N. "Women Preachers—Is it Scriptural?" *LRE* (August 1932) 7–9.
———. "Financing the Local Church." *PE* (10 November 1928) 7.
———. "Stewardship." *PE* (22 October 1932) 2–3.
———. "Water Baptism." *W&Wk* (March 1936) 7, 14.
———. "Is the Church Failing?" *W&Wk* (November 1936) 4–5.

Modernism (5):

Hoover, J. N. "The Tragedy of Modern Theology." *COGE* (28 January 1933) 2, 28.
———. "Bible Bolsheviks: The Tragedy of Modern Theology." *LRE* (June 1930) 3–5, 9.
———. "The Tragedy of Modern Theology." *LRE* (January 1933) 6–8.
———. "The Bible Bolshevists." *PE* (3 March 1928) 1, 5.
———. "The Tragedy of Modern Theology." *PE* (7 December 1929) 7.

* Some of the sermons printed are duplications or variations, as would be expected of a travelling evangelist. Others were printed in parts and others still excerpted. This list does not include his personal testimony, which was printed in *PE* and *W&Wk*.

Apostasy and the Antichrist (4):

Hoover, J. N. "Mussolini and the Antichrist." *LRE* (August 1930) 3–5.
———. "Giant Mergers Forerunners of the Antichrist." *LRE* (September 1932) 3–6.
———. "The Seven Churches." *PE* (12 December 1931) 3.
———. "Days of Noah Then and Now, Mark of the Beast." *PE* (20 January 1934) 1, 8–9.

Jews in Prophecy (3):

Hoover, J. N. "The Return of the Jews." *LRE* (May 1931) 14–15, 23.
———. "The Jews." *PE* (31 January 1931) 6–7.
———. "Hitler and the Indigestible Jews." *PE* (24 February 1934) 2–3.

Communism and Politics (3):

Hoover, J. N. "Is National Defense Biblical?" *LRE* (November 1935) 22–23.
———. "Threshold of Catastrophe." *W&Wk* (April 1935) 5.
———. "Communism or Liberty." *W&Wk* (January 1936) 8–10.

Divine Healing (3):

Hoover, J. N. "Is Scriptural Healing Fanaticism?" *LRE* (January 1931) 7–10.
———. "Divine Healing—Is it Practical or Fanactical." *LRE* (November 1934) 9–11.
———. "Divine Healing." *PE* (8 February 1930) 5.

Resurrection (3):

Hoover, J. N. "After Death: The Two Resurrections." *LRE* (April 1935) 10–11, 21.
———. "After the Resurrection." *PE* (24 March 1934) 1, 7.
———. "The Resurrection of Christ." *PE* (13 April 1935) 1.

Morals (3):

Hoover, J. N. "Trifling with the Soul." *PE* (29 July 1933) 1, 5.
———. "Cigarette Smoking." *PE* (24 October 1936) 16.
———. "Trifling with the Soul." *W&Wk* (March 1937) 8.
———. "The Tragedy of Intemperance." *W&Wk* (June 1938) 3, 14.

Devil/hell (2):

Hoover, J. N. "Where are the Dead?" *PE* (15 July 1933) 9.
———. "Satan the Devil." *PE* (12 August 1933) 3.

Scripture (2):

Hoover, J. N. "Holy Scriptures." *PE* (5 August 1933) 10.
———. "The Holy Scriptures." *W&Wk* (December 1934) 5, 15.

Evolution (2):

Hoover, J. N. "The Origin of Life." *LRE* (May 1936) 20–22.
———. "The Origin of Man." *W&Wk* (March 1935) 7–8.

Appendix H

Thanksgiving Holiday (1):
Hoover, J. N. "Thanksgiving." *PE* (25 November 1933) 1, 15.

Grace (1):
Hoover, J. N. "God and His Gifts." *W&Wk* (May 1937) 9–10.

Person of Christ (1):
Hoover, J. N. "What Think Ye of Christ?" *PE* (27 May 1933) 1, 7.

Spirit-baptism (1):
Hoover, J. N. "The Baptism and Ministry of the Holy Spirit." *LRE* (July 1930) 5–7, 21.

Appendix I

From *Pentecostal Evangel* (15 May 1937, p. 6); reprinted with permission from Gospel Publishing House.

Appendix J

From *Pentecostal Evangel* (8 June 1940, p. 4); reprinted with permission from Gospel Publishing House.

Appendix K

From *Pentecostal Evangel* (14 August 1937, p. 6); reprinted with permission from Gospel Publishing House.

Bibliography

Primary Sources
Books and Pamphlets

Anderson, Sir Robert. *Spirit Manifestations and "the Gift of Tongues."* New York: Loizeaux Bros., n.d.
Bartleman, Frank. *Azusa Street.* Plainfield, NJ: Logos, 1980.
Baxter, Robert. *Narrative of Facts.* London: Nisbet, 1833.
Bishop, A. E. *Tongues, Signs and Visions, not God's Order for Today.* Chicago: Moody, 1920.
Bettex, Jean Frederick. "The Bible and Modern Criticism." In *Back to the Bible: The Triumphs of Truth*, edited by A. C. Dixon, translated by David Heagle, 103–23. London: Partridge, n.d.
Blosser, J. W. *Emotional Delusions.* New York: The Congregational Home Missionary Society, n.d.
Bosworth, F. F. *Christ the Healer.* Author, 1924.
———. *Do all Speak with Tongues?* Dayton, Ohio: Scruby, 1918.
Boyd, Frank M. *The Budding Fig Tree.* Springfield, MO: Gospel Publishing House, 1926.
Bryan, W. J. *Is the Bible True?* Chicago: Bible Institute Colportage Association, 1924.
———. *The Last Message of William Jennings Bryan.* New York: Revell, 1925.
Campbell, John. *The Bible under Fire.* New York: Harper & Brothers, 1928.
Dake, Finis J. *Revelation Expounded.* Tulsa, OK: author, 1931.
Dixon, A. C. *Speaking with Tongues.* Chicago: n.p.; n.d.
Dixon, Helen C. A. *A Romance of Preaching.* 1931. Reprint, New York: Garland, 1988.
Eerdman, Charles R. *The First Epistle of Paul to the Corinthians: An Exposition.* 1928. Reprint Philadelphia: Westminster, 1966.
First Annual Catalog, Central Bible Institute, 1922–1923. Springfield, MO: Assemblies of God, 1922.
Fosdick, Harry Emerson. *The Living of these Days: An Autobiography.* London: SCM, 1957.
Frey, Mae Eleanor. *Altars of Brick.* Grand Rapids: Eerdmans, 1943.
———. *The Minister.* Springfield, MO: Gospel Publishing House, 1939.
Frodsham, Stanley H. *Things which must shortly come to Pass.* Springfield, MO: Gospel Publishing House, 1928.
———. *Wholly for God: A Call to Complete Consecration Illustrated by the Story of Paul Bettex, a truly consecrated Soul.* Springfield, MO: Gospel Publishing House, 1934.
———. *With Signs Following: The Story of the Latter-Day Pentecostal Revival.* Springfield, MO: Gospel Publishing House, 1926.
Gaebelein, Arno C. *Half a Century: The Autobiography of a Servant.* New York: Publication Office of "Our Hope," 1930.
———. *The Healing Question.* New York: Offices of "Our Hope," 1925.
Godbey, William B. *Autobiography.* Cincinnati: God's Revivalist Office, 1909.
———. *Commentary on the New Testament: Revelation*, vol. 1. 2nd ed. Cincinnati: Revivalist Office, 1896.
———. *Current Heresies.* Cincinnati: God's Revivalist Office, 1908.
———. *Spiritualism, Devil-worship and Tongues.* N.p., n.d.
———. *Tongue Movement, Satanic.* Zarepath, NJ: Pillar of Fire, 1918. In *William B. Godbey: Six Tracts*, edited by D. W. Dayton. Higher Christian Life Series 6. New York: Garland, 1985.
Godbey, William B., and Seth C. Rees. *The Return of Jesus.* Cincinnati: God's Revivalist Press, 1898.
Gortner, John Narver. *Studies in Daniel.* Springfield, MO: Gospel Publishing House, 1948.
———. *Studies in Revelation.* Springfield, MO: Gospel Publishing House, 1948.

Bibliography

Haldeman, Isaac M. *An Address on the Holy Spirit.* New York: Francis Emory Fitch, n.d.
———. *Holy Ghost Baptism and Speaking with Tongues.* New York: author, c. 1925.
Hills, A. M. *A Hero of Faith and Prayer; or, Life of Rev. Martin Wells Knapp.* Cincinnati: God's Revivalist Office, 1902.
Horner, Ralph C. *Evangelist: Reminiscences from his own Pen.* Brockville, Canada: Standard Church Book Room, n.d.
Hoover, J. N. *World Conditions in the Light of Prophecy, or What is the Mark of the Beast?* Santa Cruz: author, 1933.
Ironside, H. A. *Apostolic Faith Missions and the so-called Pentecost.* New York: Loizeaux, c. 1913.
———. *Divine Priorities and other Messages.* New York: Revell, 1945.
———. *Holiness, The Fake and the True.* New York: Loizeaux, 1912.
Jones, E. Stanley. *The Christ of Every Road: A Study in Pentecost.* London: Hodder & Stoughton, 1930.
Klink, Otto J. *Why I am not an Atheist.* Springfield, MO: Gospel Publishing House, 1931.
———. *Why I am not an Evolutionist.* Springfield, MO: Gospel Publishing House, 1931.
———. *Why I am not a Modernist: An Attempt to Prove the Divineness of the Bible.* Minneapolis, MN: Northern Gospel, 1938.
Larkin, Clarence. *The Book of Revelation: A Study of the Last Prophetic Book of Holy Scripture.* Philadelphia: Edwin W. Moyer, 1919.
Lee, F. J. *Book of Prophecy: Question and Answers on the entire Book of Revelation.* Cleveland, TN: Church of God, 1923.
———. *Divine Healing.* Cleveland, TN: Church of God, 1925.
Luce, Alice E. *The Little Flock in the Last Days.* Springfield, MO: Gospel Publishing House, 1927.
McCrossan, T. J. *Bodily Healing and the Atonement.* N.p., 1930. Reprint, Tulsa, OK: Faith Library, 1982.
———. *Speaking with other Tongues: Sign or Gift—Which?* Harrisburg, PA: Christian, 1970.
MacKenzie, Kenneth. *Our Physical Heritage in Christ.* Chicago: Revell, 1923.
Mauro, Philip. *Evolution at the Bar.* N.p., 1922. Reprint Swengel, PA: Reiner, 1976.
———. *The Gospel of the Kingdom: An Examination of Modern Dispensationalism.* 1928. Reprint, Sterling, VA: Grace Abounding Ministries, 1988.
Miller, Elmer C. *Pentecost Examined by a Baptist Lawyer.* Springfield, MO: Gospel Publishing House, 1936.
"Minutes of the Committee for United Action among Evangelicals, 10 November 1941," typed manuscript.
Ockenga, Harold John. *Power through Pentecost.* Grand Rapids: Eerdmans, 1959.
Pearlman, Myer. *Seeing the Story of the Bible.* Springfield, MO: Gospel Publishing House, 1930.
———. *Successful Sunday School Teaching.* Springfield, MO: Gospel Publishing House, 1935.
———. *Through the Bible Book by Book,* 4 vols. Springfield, MO: Gospel Publishing House, 1935.
Perkins, Jonathan E. *The Biggest Hypocrite in America: Gerald L. K. Smith Unmasked.* Los Angeles: American Foundation, 1949.
———. *Pentecostalism on the Washboard.* Fort Worth, TX: author, 1939.
Pierson, Arthur Tappan. *Forward Movements of the Last Half Century.* New York: Funk & Wagnalls, 1900.
———. *The New Acts of the Apostles; or, the Marvels of Modern Missions.* New York: Baker & Taylor, 1894.
Pohle, Ella E., comp. *Dr. C. I. Scofield's Question Box.* Chicago: Bible Institute Colportage Association, 1917.
Religious Bodies, 1926: Separate Denominations, vol. 2. Washington, DC: United States Government Printing Office, 1929.
Rice, John R. *The Baptism of the Holy Spirit for Us Today: The Bible Evidence.* Chicago: Chicago Gospel Tabernacle, n.d.
Riggs, Ralph M. *A Successful Pastor.* Springfield, MO: Gospel Publishing House, 1931.
———. *A Successful Sunday School.* Springfield, MO: Gospel Publishing House, 1933.
Riley, William B. "A. C. Dixon: America's Fundamentalist Minister," typed manuscript, 1925.
———. "Are the Fundamentalists Pharisees?" typed manuscript, n.d.
———. "The Christian Fundamentals Movement—Its Battles, its Achievements, its certain Victory," address to 4th annual WCFA meeting, Los Angeles, June 25—July 2, 1922, typed manuscript.
———. *The Conflict of Christianity with its Counterfeits.* Minneapolis: author, 1940.
———. "Speaking with Tongues." Minneapolis: Hall & Black, 1907.
Robinson, Charles E. *The Adventures of Blacky the Wasp.* Springfield, MO: Gospel Publishing House, 1936.

———. *God and His Bible.* Springfield, MO: Gospel Publishing House, 1939.
Scofield, C. I. *Scofield Correspondence Course: New Testament.* New York: author, 1907.
Smith, Oswald J. *The Great Physician.* New York: Christian Alliance, 1927.
Stemme, Harry A. *The Faith of a Pentecostal Christian.* Milwaukee: Word & Witness, 1938.
Straton, John R. *Divine Healing in Scripture and Life.* New York: Christian Alliance, 1927.
Torrey, R. A. *Divine Healing.* 1924. Reprint, Grand Rapids: Baker, 1974.
———. *The Holy Spirit.* Westwood, NJ: Revell, 1927.
———. *Is the Present "Tongues Movement of God?"* Los Angeles: Biola Book Room, c. 1913.
———. *The Person and Work of the Holy Spirit.* New York: Revell, 1910.
Urshan, Andrew. *The Life Story of Andrew Bar David Urshan: An Autobiography of the Author's first Forty Years.* Portland, OR: Apostolic, 1967.
Warfield, B.B. *Counterfeit Miracles.* 1918. Reprint, London: Banner of Truth, 1972.
———. *Perfectionism.* New York: Oxford University Press, 1931.
White, Alma. *Demons and Tongues.* Bound Brook, NJ: Pentecostal Union, 1910.
Wright, Joel A. *To What Church Do You Belong?* Rumney, NH: author, 1897.
Wright, J. Elwin. *The Old Fashioned Revival Hour.* Boston: Fellowship Press, 1940.

Periodicals:

The Apostolic Faith (Los Angeles, CA), 1906–1908
Bridal Call (Los Angeles, CA), 1918–1929
The Bridegroom's Messenger (Atlanta, GA), 1907–1916
The Christ's Ambassadors Herald (Springfield, MO), 1926–1942
The Christian Evangel (Plainfield, IN), 1913–1915
Christian Fundamentals in School and Church (Minneapolis, MN), 1920–1942
The Christian Worker's Magazine (Chicago, IL), 1910–1920
Confidence (Sunderland, UK), 1908–1926
The Churchman (New York, NY), 1924–1927
Church of God Evangel (Cleveland, TN), 1914–1942
The Dawn (Panton), 1925–1938
The Evening Light and Church of God Evangel (Cleveland, TN), 1910
Exploits of Faith (Bosworth), 1927–1931
The Faithful Standard (Cleveland, TN), 1922
The Fundamentalist (Fort Worth, TX), 1927–1936
Glad Tidings Herald (New York, NY), 1927–1939
God's Revivalist (Cincinnati, OH), 1901–1907
Golden Grain (Price), 1926
Good News (Chicago, IL), 1916
Gospel Gleaners (Springfield, MO), 1928–1939
The Institute Tie (Chicago, IL), 1900–1910
Intercessory Missionary (Fort Wayne, IN), 1910
The King's Business (Los Angeles, CA), 1909–1928
Latter Rain Evangel (Chicago, IL), 1908–1939
Life of Faith (London, UK), 1907
The Lighted Pathway (Cleveland, TN), 1931–1932
Missionary Review of the World (New York, NY), 1907–1908
Midnight Cry (New York, NY), 1911–1925
Moody Bible Institute Monthly (Chicago, IL), 1920–1938
Northwestern Pilot (Minneapolis, MN), 1920–1942
Our Hope (New York, NY), 1907–1942
The Pentecost (Indianapolis, IN; Kansas City, MO), 1908–1910
The Pentecostal Evangel (Springfield, MO), 1919–1942
Pentecostal Herald (Louisville and Wilmore, KY), 1906–1925
Pentecostal Testimony (Chicago, IL), 1909–1911

Bibliography

Petals from the Rose of Sharon (Utley), 1927
Record of Christian Work (Northfield, MA), 1900–1925
Revelation (Philadelphia, PA), 1931–1936
The Revivalist (Albion, MI; Cincinnati, OH), 1890–1900
School and Church (Minneapolis, MN), 1916–1920
The Searchlight (Fort Worth, TX), 1923
The Shiloh Scroll (Zion, IL), 1935–1937
Sunday School Times (Philadelphia, PA), 1906–1942
Triumphs of Faith (Buffalo, NY; Oakland, CA), 1907–1910
The Way (Cleveland, TN), 1904
Way of Faith (Columbia, SC), 1906–1908
The Weekly Evangel (St. Louis and Springfield, MO), 1915–1919
Word and Witness (Malvern, AR), 1912–1915
Word and Work (Framingham, MA), 1899–1940

Letters

AG to Clergy, "Dear Brother Minister in the Lord," 7 July[?] 1922 [FPHC].
J. R. Flower to L. Entzminger, 12 October 1939 [FPHC].
J. N. Gortner to J. E. Perkins, 10 November 1939 [FPHC].
W. E. Moody to J. W. Welch, 5 December 1916 [FPHC].
W. E. Moody to J. W. Welch, 3 August 1922 [FPHC].
J. E. Perkins to J. R. Flower, 27 June 1949 [FPHC].

Interviews

Ockenga, Harold John. Interview by James Hedstrom, cassette recording, Nashville, TN, 1979.
Straton, George Douglas. Interview by Wayne Warner, digital recording, 1990.
"Wayne Warner's telephone conversation with Mrs. Carl Stewart, Fort Worth, Texas, Friday, August 19, 1988," typed manuscript, n.p.

Secondary Sources

Ahlstrom, Sydney E. *A Religious History of the American People*. New Haven: Yale University Press, 1972.
Alexander, Kimberly Ervin. *Pentecostal Healing: Models in Theology and Practice*. JPTSup 29. Dorset, UK: Deo, 2007.
Ammerman, Nancy T. "North American Protestant Fundamentalism." In *Fundamentalisms Observed*, edited by Martin E. Marty and R. Scott Appleby, 1–65. Chicago: University of Chicago Press, 1991.
Anderson, Allan. *An Introduction to Pentecostalism: Global Charismatic Christianity*. Cambridge: Cambridge University Press, 2004.
———. "Revising Pentecostal History in Global Perspective." In *Asian and Pentecostal*, edited by Allan Anderson and Edmond Tang, 147–73. Kuala Lumpur, Malaysia: Regnum, 2005.
———. "Revival and the Global Expansion of Pentecostalism after Azusa Street." In *The Azusa Street Revival and its Legacy*, edited by Harold D. Hunter and Cecil M. Robeck Jr., 175–91. Cleveland, TN: Pathway, 2006.
———. *Spreading Fires: The Missionary Nature of Early Pentecostalism*. London: SCM, 2007.
———. *Zion and Pentecost: The Spirituality and Experience of Pentecostal and Zionist/Apostolic Churches in South Africa*. Pretoria: University of South Africa Press, 2000.
Anderson, Allan, and Edmond Tang, editors. *Asian and Pentecostal: The Charismatic Face of Christianity in Asia*. Kuala Lumpur, Malaysia: Regnum, 2005.
Anderson, Robert M. *Vision of the Disinherited: The Making of American Pentecostalism*. Peabody, MA: Hendrickson, 1979.
Armstrong, Karen. *The Battle for God: Fundamentalism in Judaism, Christianity and Islam*. New York: Knopf, 2000.

Bibliography

Balmer, Randall. *Encyclopedia of Evangelicalism*. Louisville, KY: Westminster John Knox, 2001.

———. *Mine Eyes Have Seen the Glory: A Journey into the Evangelical Subculture in America*. Oxford: Oxford University Press, 1993.

Barfoot, Charles H., and Gerald T. Shepherd. "Prophetic vs. Priestly Religion: The Changing Role of Women Clergy in Classical Pentecostal Churches," *Review of Religious Research* 22 (September 1980) 2–17.

Barr, James. *Fundamentalism*. London: SCM, 1981.

Bassett, Paul. "The Fundamentalist Leavening of the Holiness Movement: 1914–1940," *Wesleyan Theological Journal* 13 (Spring 1978) 65–91.

Beale, David O. *In Pursuit of Purity: American Fundamentalism since 1850*. Greenville, SC: Unusual, 1986.

Bebbington, David. *Evangelicalism in Modern Britain: A History from the 1730s to the 1980s*. London: Routledge, 1989.

———. *Holiness in Nineteenth-Century England: The 1998 Didsbury Lectures*. Carlisle, UK: Paternoster, 2000.

Berends, Kurt O. "Social Variables and Community Response." In *Pentecostal Currents in American Protestantism*, edited by Edith L. Blumhofer, Russell P. Spittler, and Grant A. Wacker, 68–89. Urbana: University of Illinois Press, 1999.

Bergunder, Michael. "Constructing Indian Pentecostalism: On Issues of Methodology and Representation." In *Asian and Pentecostal*, edited by Allan Anderson and Edmond Tang, 117–213. Kuala Lumpur, Malaysia: Regnum, 2005.

Bloch-Hoell, Nils. *The Pentecostal Movement: Its Origin, Development, and Distinctive Character*. Oslo: Universitetsforlaget; London: Allen & Unwin, 1964.

Blumhofer, Edith L. *Aimee Semple McPherson: Everybody's Sister*. Grand Rapids: Eerdmans, 1993.

———. *The Assemblies of God: A Chapter in the Story of American Pentecostalism*. 2 vols. Springfield, MO: Gospel Publishing House, 1989.

———. "'A Little Child shall Lead them': Child Evangelist Uldine Utley." In *The Contentious Triangle: Church, State and University*, edited by Rodney L. Peterson and Calvin A. Pater, 301–17. Kirksville, MO: Thomas Jefferson University Press, 1999.

———. "Restoration as Revival: Early American Pentecostalism." In *Modern Christian Revivals*, edited by Edith L. Blumhofer and Randall Balmer, 145–60. Urbana and Chicago: University of Illinois Press, 1993.

———. *Restoring the Faith: The Assemblies of God, Pentecostalism, and American Culture*. Urbana and Chicago: University of Illinois Press, 1993.

———. "William H. Durham: Years of Creativity, Years of Dissent." In *Portraits of a Generation: Early Pentecostal Leaders*, edited by James Goff Jr. and Grant Wacker, 123–42. Fayetteville: University of Arkansas Press, 2002.

Boller, Paul F. "The New Science and American Thought." In *The Gilded Age: Revised and Enlarged Edition*, edited by H. Wayne Morgan, 239–57. Syracuse, NY: Syracuse University Press, 1970.

Boorstin, Daniel J. *The Americans: The Democratic Experience*. Vol. 3. New York: Vintage, 1973.

Brereton, Virginia Lieson. *Training God's Army: The American Bible School, 1880–1940*. Bloomington and Indianapolis: Indiana University Press, 1990.

Brumback, Carl. *Suddenly . . . from Heaven: A History of the Assemblies of God*. Springfield, MO: Gospel Publishing House, 1961.

Bruner, Frederick Dale. *A Theology of the Holy Spirit: The Pentecostal Experience and the New Testament Witness*. Grand Rapids: Eerdmans, 1970.

Bundy, David. "G. T. Haywood: Religion for Urban Realities." In *Portraits of a Generation: Early Pentecostal Leaders*, edited by James Goff Jr. and Grant Wacker, 237–53. Fayetteville: University of Arkansas Press, 2002.

Campbell, Faith Frodsham. *Stanley Frodsham: Prophet with a Pen*. Springfield, MO: Gospel Publishing House, 1974.

Carpenter, Joel A. "Contending for the Faith once Delivered: Primitivist Impulses in American Fundamentalism." In *The American Quest for the Primitive Church*, edited by Richard T. Hughes, 99–119. Urbana and Chicago: University of Illinois Press, 1988.

———. "The Fundamentalist Leaven and the Rise of an Evangelical United Front." In *The Evangelical Tradition in America*, edited by Leonard I. Sweet, 257–88. Macon, GA: Mercer University Press, 1984.

Bibliography

———. *Revive Us Again: The Reawakening of American Fundamentalism.* Oxford: Oxford University Press, 1997.

Cartwright, Desmond. "Everywhere Spoken against: Opposition to Pentecostalism, 1907–1930," 1–7. Online: http://www.smithwigglesworth.com/pensketches/everywhere.htm.

Chan, Simon. *Pentecostal Theology and the Christian Spiritual Tradition.* Sheffield, UK: Sheffield Academic, 2000.

———. "Whither Pentecostalism?" In *Asian and Pentecostal*, edited by Allan Anderson and Edmond Tang, 575–86. Kuala Lumpur, Malaysia: Regnum, 2005.

Choi, Meesaeng Lee. *The Rise of the Korean Holiness Church in Relation to the American Holiness Movement: Wesley's "Scriptural Holiness" and the "Fourfold Gospel."* Pietist and Wesleyan Studies 28. Lanham, MD: Scarecrow, 2008.

Clayton, Allen. "The Significance of William H. Durham for Pentecostal Historiography," *Pneuma* 1 (1979) 27–42.

Cole, Stewart G. *The History of Fundamentalism.* New York: Smith, 1931.

Collier, Peter and David Horowitz. *The Rockefellers: An American Dynasty.* London: Jonathan Cape, 1976.

Conn, Charles W. *Like a Mighty Army: A History of the Church of God.* Cleveland, TN: Pathway, 1977.

Cox, Harvey G. *Fire from Heaven: The Rise of Pentecostal Spirituality and the Reshaping of Religion in the Twenty-first Century.* Cambridge, MA: Da Capo, 1995.

Dayton, Donald W. "From 'Christian Perfection' to the 'Baptism of the Holy Ghost.'" In *Aspects of Pentecostal-Charismatic Origins*, edited by Vinson Synan, 39–54. Plainfield, NJ: Logos, 1975.

———. *Theological Roots of Pentecostalism.* Peabody, MA: Hendrickson, 1987.

Dempster, Murray W., Byron D. Klaus, and Douglas Peterson, eds. *The Globalization of Pentecostalism: A Religion Made to Travel.* Irvine, CA: Regnum, 1999.

Dieter, Melvin Easterday. *The Holiness Revival of the Nineteenth Century.* Metuchen, NJ: Scarecrow, 1980.

Dollar, George W. *A History of Fundamentalism in America.* Greenville, SC: Bob Jones University Press, 1973.

Dorrien, Gary J. *The Making of American Liberal Theology: Idealism, Realism, and Modernity, 1900–1950.* Louisville, KY: Westminster John Knox, 2003.

———. *The Making of American Liberal Theology: Imagining Progressive Religion, 1805–1900.* Louisville, KY: Westminster John Knox, 2001.

Draney, Daniel W. *When Streams Diverge: John Murdoch MacInnis and the Origins of Protestant Fundamentalism in Los Angeles.* Studies in Evangelical History and Thought. Milton Keynes, UK: Paternoster, 2008.

Epstein, Mark. *Sister Aimee: The Life of Aimee Semple McPherson.* New York: Harcourt Brace Jovanovich, 1993.

Fankhauser, Craig C. "The Heritage of Faith: An Historical Evaluation of the Holiness Movement in America." MA thesis, Pittsburgh State University, 1983.

Faupel, D. William. *The Everlasting Gospel: The Significance of Eschatology in the Development of Pentecostal Thought.* JPTSup 10. Sheffield, UK: Sheffield Academic Press, 1996.

———. "Whither Pentecostalism? 22nd Presidential Address, Society for Pentecostal Studies, November 7, 1992," *Pneuma* 15 (Spring 1993) 9–27.

Franklin, W. J. *Biography of A. S. Copley.* Author, 1969.

Furniss, Norman F. *The Fundamentalist Controversy, 1918–1931.* New Haven: Yale University Press, 1954.

Gasper, Louis. *The Fundamentalist Movement, 1930–1956.* Grand Rapids: Baker, 1963.

Gibson, Scott M. *A. J. Gordon: American Premillennialist.* Lanham, MD: University Press of America, 2001.

Goff, James R., Jr. *Fields White unto Harvest: Charles F. Parham and the Missionary Origins of Pentecostalism.* Fayetteville: University of Arkansas Press, 1988.

Graf, Jonathan L., ed. *Healing: Three Classics on Divine Healing.* Eugene, OR: Wipf & Stock, 1992.

Greathouse, William H. "John Wesley's View of the Last Things." In *The Second Coming: A Wesleyan Approach to the Doctrine of Last Things*, edited by H. Ray Dunning, 139–60. Kansas City: Beacon Hill Press of Kansas City, 1995.

Hall, J. L. "Urshan, Andrew David." In *DPCM*, 866.

Bibliography

Hambrick-Stowe, Charles E. *Charles G. Finney and the Spirit of American Evangelicalism.* Grand Rapids: Eerdmans, 1996.

Handy, Robert T. *A History of the Churches in the United States and Canada.* New York: Oxford University Press, 1976.

Harris, John W. *Tears and Triumphs: The Life Story of a Pastor-Evangelist.* Louisville: Pentecost, 1948.

Haught, John F. *God after Darwin: A Theology of Evolution.* Boulder, CO: Westview, 2000.

Hindmarsh, D. Bruce. "The Winnipeg Fundamentalist Network, 1910-1940: The Roots of Transdenominational Evangelicalism in Manitoba and Saskatchewan." In *Aspects of the Canadian Evangelical Experience*, edited by George A. Rawlyk, 303-19. Montreal: McGill-Queen's University Press, 1997.

Hollenweger, Walter J. *Pentecostalism: Origins and Developments Worldwide.* Peabody MA: Hendrickson, 1997.

———. *The Pentecostals.* Translated by R. A. Wilson. London: SCM, 1972.

Holmes, Pamela. "The 'Place' of Women in Pentecostal/Charismatic Ministry since the Azusa Street Revival." In *The Azusa Street Revival and its Legacy*, edited by Harold D. Hunter and Cecil M. Robeck Jr., 297-315. Cleveland, TN: Pathway, 2007.

Howard, Rick. "David du Plessis: Pentecost's 'Ambassador-at-Large.'" In *The Spirit and Spirituality: Essays in Honour of Russell P. Spittler,* edited by Wonsuk Ma and Robert P. Menzies, 271-97, JPTSup 24. London: T. & T. Clark, 2004.

Hutchison, William R. *The Modernist Impulse in American Protestantism.* Cambridge: Harvard University Press, 1976.

Ingersol, Stanley. "Strange Bedfellows: The Nazarenes and Fundamentalism." *Wesleyan Journal of Theology* 40 (2005) 123-41.

Irvin, Dale T. "Pentecostal Historiography and Global Christianity: Rethinking the Question of Origins." *Pneuma* 27 (2005) 35-50.

Jacobsen, Douglas. "Knowing the Doctrines of Pentecostals: The Scholastic Theology of the Assemblies of God, 1930-55." In *Pentecostal Currents in American Protestantism*, edited by Edith L. Blumhofer, Russell P. Spittler, and Grant A. Wacker, 90-107. Urbana: University of Illinois Press, 1999.

———. *Thinking in the Spirit: Theologies of the Early Pentecostal Movement.* Bloomington, IN: Indiana University Press, 2003.

Kendrick, Klaude. *The Promise Fulfilled: A History of the Modern Pentecostal Movement.* Springfield, MO: Gospel Publishing House, 1961.

King, Gerald W. "Evolving Paradigms: Creationism as Pentecostal Variation on a Fundamentalist Theme." In *The Spirit Renews the Face of the Earth: Pentecostal Forays in Science and Theology of Creation*, edited by Amos Yong, 93-114. Eugene, OR: Wipf & Stock, 2009.

———. "Mae Eleanor Frey: Pentecostal Evangelist and Novelist." *Assemblies of God Heritage* 29 (2009) 57-62.

———. "When the Holiness Preacher Came to Town: Re-dating W. B. Godbey's Visit to Azusa Street," *Cyberjournal of Pentecostal-Charismatic Research* 18 (January 2009) n.p.

———. "Streams of Convergence: The Pentecostal-Fundamentalist Response to Modernism," *PentecoStudies* 7 (2008) 64-84.

King, Paul L. *Genuine Gold: The Cautiously Charismatic Story of the Early Christian and Missionary Alliance.* Tulsa, OK: Word & Spirit, 2006.

Kostlevy, William. "Nor Silver, nor Gold: The Burning Bush Movement and the Communitarian Holiness Vision." PhD diss., University of Notre Dame, 1996.

Land, Stephen J. *Pentecostal Spirituality: A Passion for the Kingdom.* JPTSup 1. Sheffield, UK: Sheffield Academic, 2001.

Lavigne, T. J., ed. *Uldine Utley: Why I am a Preacher.* Kissemmee, FL: Cloud of Witnesses, 2007.

Lawrence, Bruce B. *Defenders of God: The Fundamentalist Revolt against the Modern Age.* Columbia: University of South Carolina Press, 1989.

Lovelace, Richard. "Baptism in the Holy Spirit and the Evangelical Tradition," *Pneuma* 7 (1985) 101-23.

McGee, Gary B. "Minnie F. Abrams: Another Context, another Founder." In *Portraits of a Generation*, edited by James Goff Jr., and Grant Wacker, 87-104. Fayetteville: University of Arkansas Press, 2002.

———. *People of the Spirit: The Assemblies of God.* Springfield, MO: Gospel Publishing House, 2004.

Bibliography

———. "Working Together: The Assemblies of God—Russian and Eastern European Mission Cooperation, 1927–40," *Assemblies of God Heritage* 9 (Winter 1988–1989) 12.

McGrath, Alister E. *The Genesis of Doctrine: A Study in the Foundations of Doctrinal Criticism.* Oxford and Cambridge, MA: Blackwell, 1990.

McGraw, Gerald E. "The Doctrine of Sanctification in the Published Writings of Albert Benjamin Simpson." PhD diss., New York University, 1986.

McLoughlin, William G. *Modern Revivalism: Charles Grandison Finney to Billy Graham.* New York: Ronald, 1959.

McQueen, Larry. "Opposing Visions: Early Eschatologies in the Church of God (Evangel), 1910–1923 (Tomlinson vs. Lee)." Paper presented to the 39th Annual Meeting of the Society of Pentecostal Studies, Minneapolis, MN, March 4–6, 2010.

Marsden, George M. *Fundamentalism and American Culture: The Shaping of Twentieth Century Evangelicalism, 1870–1925.* Oxford: Oxford University Press, 1980.

———. *Understanding Fundamentalism and Evangelicalism.* Grand Rapids: Eerdmans, 1991.

Marty, Martin E. *A Nation of Behavors.* Chicago: University of Chicago Press, 1976.

———. *Pilgrims in their own Land: 500 Years of Religion in America.* New York: Penguin, 1984.

Masserano, Frank C. "A Study of the Worship Forms of the Assemblies of God Denomination." ThM thesis, Princeton Theological Seminary, 1966.

Melon, Mildred. *We've Been Robbed.* Plainfield, NJ: Logos, 1971.

Menzies, William W. *Anointed to Serve: The Story of the Assemblies of God.* Springfield, MO: Gospel Publishing House, 1971.

———. "The Non-Wesleyan Origins of the Pentecostal Movement." In *Aspects of Pentecostal-Charismatic Origins*, edited by Vinson Synan, 81–98. Plainfield, NJ: Logos, 1975.

Moberg, David O. *The Church as a Social Institution: The Sociology of American Religion.* Englewood Cliffs, NJ: Prentice-Hall, 1962.

Moore, Howard. "The Emergence of Moderate Fundamentalism: John R. Rice and *The Sword of the Lord*." PhD diss., George Washington University, 1990.

Murray, Iain H. *The Puritan Hope: A Study in Revival and the Interpretation of Prophecy.* London: Banner of Truth, 1971.

Neinkirchen, Charles W. *A. B. Simpson and the Pentecostal Movement: A Study in Continuity, Crisis, and Change.* Peabody, MA: Hendrickson, 1992.

———. "Conflicting Visions of the Past: The Prophetic Use of History in the Early American Pentecostal-Charismatic Movements." In *Charismatic Christianity as a Global Culture*, edited by Karla Poewe, 119–33. Columbia: University of South Carolina Press, 1994.

Nelson, Douglas J. "For Such a Time as This: The Story of Bishop William J. Seymour and the Azusa Street Revival, a Search for Pentecostal/Charismatic Roots." PhD diss., University of Birmingham (UK), 1981.

Nichol, John Thomas. "Pentecostalism: A Descriptive History of the Origin, Growth, and Message of a Twentieth Century Religious Movement." PhD diss., Boston University, 1965.

———. *Pentecostalism: The Story of the Growth and Development of a Vital New Force in American Protestantism.* New York: Harper & Row, 1966.

Noll, Mark A. *American Evangelical Christianity: An Introduction.* Malden, MA: Blackwell, 2001.

———. *America's God: From Jonathan Edwards to Abraham Lincoln.* New York: Oxford University Press, 2002.

———. *Between Faith and Criticism: Evangelicals, Scholarship, and the Bible.* 2nd ed. Leicester, UK: Apollos, 1991.

———. *The Scandal of the Evangelical Mind.* Grand Rapids: Eerdmans, 1994.

Noll, Mark A., David W. Bebbington, and George A. Rawlyk, eds. *Evangelicalism: Comparative Studies of Popular Protestantism in North America and the British Isles, and Beyond, 1700–1990.* Oxford: Oxford University Press, 1994.

Numbers, Ronald L. "Creation, Evolution, and Holy Ghost Religion: Holiness and Pentecostal Responses to Darwinism," *Religion and American Culture* 2 (1992) 127–58.

———. *The Creationists: The Evolution of Scientific Creationism.* Berkeley, CA: University of California Press, 1992.

———. *Darwinism Comes to America*. Cambridge, MA: Harvard University Press, 1998.
Olson, Roger E. *Arminian Theology: Myths and Realities*. Downers Grove, IL: InterVarsity, 2006.
Percy, Martyn. *Words, Wonders, and Power: Understanding Contemporary Christian Fundamentalism and Revivalism*. London: SPCK, 1996.
Pope, Liston. *Millhands and Preachers: A Study of Gastonia*. 1942. Reprint, New Haven: Yale University Press, 1964.
Powers, Janet Everts. "'Your Daughters shall Prophecy': Pentecostal Hermeneutics and the Empowerment of Women." In *The Globalization of Pentecostalism: A Religion Made to Travel*, edited by Murray W. Dempster, Byron D. Klaus, and Douglas Peterson, 313–37. Irvine, CA: Regnum, 1999.
Randall, Ian M. *Evangelical Experiences: A Study in the Spirituality of English Evangelicalism, 1918-1939*. Studies in Evangelical History and Thought. Carlisle, UK: Paternoster, 1999.
Rausch, David A. *Arno C. Gaebelein, 1861-1945: Irenic Fundamentalist and Scholar*. New York: Mellen, 1983.
Reed, David A. *"In Jesus' Name": The History and Beliefs of Oneness Pentecostals*, JPTSup 31. Blandford Forum, UK: Deo, 2008.
Robeck, Cecil M., Jr. *The Azusa Street Mission and Revival: The Birth of the Global Pentecostal Movement*. Nashville, TN: Nelson, 2006.
———. "Florence Crawford: Apostolic Faith Pioneer." In *Portraits of a Generation: Early Pentecostal Leaders*, edited by James Goff Jr. and Grant Wacker, 219–35. Fayetteville: University of Arkansas Press, 2002.
Robert, Dana L. *Occupy until I Come: A. T. Pierson and the Evangelization of the World*. Grand Rapids: Eerdmans, 2003.
Robinson, E. B. "Myland, David Wesley." In *DPCM*, 632–33.
Rose, Susan. "Christian Fundamentalism and Education in the United States." In *Fundamentalisms and Society: Reclaiming the Sciences, the Family, and Education*, edited by Martin E. Marty and R. Scott Appleby, 452–89. Chicago: University of Chicago Press, 1993.
Rosell, Garth. *The Surprising Work of God: Harold John Ockenga, Billy Graham, and the Rebirth of Evangelicalism*. Grand Rapids: Baker Academic, 2008.
Roy, Ralph Lord. *Apostles of Discord*. Boston: Beacon, 1953.
Runyan, William M., editor. *Dr. Gray at Moody Bible Institute*. New York: Oxford University Press, 1935.
Rutgers, William H. *Premillennialism in America*. Goes, Holland: Oosterbaan & Le Cointre, 1930.
Ruthven, Jon. *On the Cessation of the Charismata: The Protestant Polemic on Postbiblical Miracles*. JPTSup 3. Sheffield: Sheffield Academic, 2003.
Sandeen, Ernest R. *The Roots of Fundamentalism: British and American Millenarianism, 1800-1930*. Chicago: University of Chicago Press, 1970.
Sanders, Carl E., II. *The Premillennial Faith of James Brookes: Reexaming the Roots of American Dispensationalism*. Lanham, MD: University Press of America, 2001.
Salzer, Tom. "The Danzig Gdanska Institute of the Bible." *Assemblies of God Heritage* 9 (1988) 9–11, 18–19.
Schlesinger, Arthur M. *The Rise of Modern America, 1865-1951*. New York: Macmillan, 1951.
Sheppard, Gerald T. "Word and Spirit: Scripture in the Pentecostal Tradition: Part One." *Agora* (1978) 4–5, 17–22.
Sinclair, Upton. *The Jungle*. New York: Doubleday, 1906.
Smith, Timothy L. "The Evangelical Kaleidoscope and the Call to Christian Unity." *Christian Scholar's Review* 15 (1986) 125–40.
———. *Revivalism and Social Reform: American Protestantism on the Eve of the Civil War*. Baltimore: Johns Hopkins University Press, 1980.
Spittler, Russell P. "Are Pentecostals and Charismatics Fundamentalists?: A Review of American Uses of these Categories." In *Charismatic Christianity as a Global Culture*, edited by Karla Poewe, 103–16. Columbia: University of South Carolina Press, 1994.
———. "Suggested Areas for further Research in Pentecostal Studies." *Pneuma* 5 (1983) 39–56.
Stanley, Susie C. "Alma White: The Politics of Dissent." In *Portraits of a Generation: Early Pentecostal Leaders*, edited by James Goff Jr. and Grant Wacker, 71–83. Fayetteville: University of Arkansas Press, 2002.
Stephens, Randall J. *The Fire Spreads: Holiness and Pentecostalism in the American South*. Cambridge, MA: Harvard University Press, 2008.

Bibliography

Storms, Jeanette. "Carrie Judd Montgomery: The Little General." In *Portraits of a Generation: Early Pentecostal Leaders*, edited by James Goff Jr. and Grant Wacker, 271–88. Fayetteville: University of Arkansas Press, 2002.

Sumrall, Lester. *Pioneers of Faith*. Tulsa: Harrison, 1995.

Sung, Kee Ho. "Doctrine of the Second Coming in the Writings of Albert B. Simpson." PhD diss., Drew University, 1990.

Sutton, Matthew A. *Aimee Semple McPherson and the Resurrection of Christian America*. Cambridge, MA: Harvard University Press, 2007.

———. "'Between the Refrigerator and the Wildfire': Aimee Semple McPherson, Pentecostalism, and the Fundamentalist-Modernist Controversy." *Church History* 72 (March 2003) 159–88.

Sweet, Leonard I., ed. *The Evangelical Tradition in America*. Macon, GA: Mercer University Press, 1984.

Sweet, William Warren. *The Story of Religion in America*. New York: Harper & Sons, 1950.

Synan, Vinson, ed. *Aspects of Pentecostal-Charismatic Origins*. Plainfield, NJ: Logos, 1975.

———, ed. *The Century of the Holy Spirit: 100 Years of Pentecostal and Charismatic Renewal, 1901–2001*. Nashville: Nelson, 2001.

———. *The Holiness-Pentecostal Movement in the United States*. Grand Rapids: Eerdmans, 1971.

———. "Holmes, Nickels John." In *DPCM*, 410.

———. *The Old-Time Power*. Franklin Springs, GA: Advocate, 1973.

Thompson, A. E. *The Life of A. B. Simpson*. Harrisburg, PA: Christian, 1920.

Tipple, John. "Big Businessmen and a new Economy." In *The Gilded Age: Revised and Enlarged Edition*, edited by H. Wayne Morgan, 13–30. Syracuse, NY: Syracuse University Press, 1970.

Trollinger, William Vance, Jr. *God's Empire: William Bell Riley and Midwestern Fundamentalism*. Madison: University of Wisconsin Press, 1990.

Wacker, Grant A. *Heaven Below: Early Pentecostals and American Culture*. Cambridge, MA: Harvard University Press, 2001.

———. "Playing for Keeps: The Primitivist Impulse in Early Pentecostalism." In *The American Quest for the Primitivist Church*, edited by Richard T. Hughes, 196–219. Urbana and Chicago: University of Illinois Press, 1988.

———. "Travail of a Broken Family: Radical Evangelical Responses to the Emergence of Pentecostalism in America, 1906–1916," In *Pentecostal Currents in American Protestantism*, edited by Edith L. Blumhofer, Russell P. Spittler, and Grant A. Wacker, 23–49. Urbana: University of Illinois Press, 1999.

Waldvogel, Edith L. "The 'Overcoming Life': A Study in the Reformed Evangelical Origins of Pentecostalism." PhD diss., Harvard University, 1977.

Wakefield, Gavin. *Alexander Boddy: Pentecostal Anglican Pioneer*. Milton Keynes, UK: Paternoster, 2007.

Ware, Steven L. "Restoring the New Testament Church: Varieties of Restorationism in the Radical Holiness Movement of the Late Nineteenth and Early Twentieth Centuries." *Pneuma* 21 (1999) 233–50.

Warner, Wayne E. "Worrell, Adolphus Spalding." In *DPCM*, 903.

Weber, Darryl H. "Portrait of a Premillennialist: Arno C. Gaebelein (1861–1945)." MA thesis, Queen's University, Kingston, Ont., 1992.

Weber, Timothy P. *Living in the Shadow of the Second Coming: American Premillennialism, 1875–1925*. New York: Oxford University Press, 1979.

Wilson, Everett A. "They Crossed the Red Sea, Didn't They?: Critical History and Pentecostal Beginnings." In *The Globalization of Pentecostalism: A Religion Made to Travel*, edited by Murray W. Dempster, Byron D. Klaus, and Douglas Peterson, 85–115. Irvine, CA: Regnum, 1999.

Wilson, Everett A., and Ruth Marshall Wilson. "Alice E. Luce: A Visionary Victorian." In *Portraits of a Generation: Early Pentecostal Leaders,* edited by James Goff Jr. and Grant Wacker, 159–76. Fayetteville: University of Arkansas Press, 2002.

Wilson, Lewis. "Book Review: *Restoring the Faith*." *Pneuma* 17 (1995) 119–22.

Wuthnow, Robert, and Matthew P. Lawson. "Sources of Christian Fundamentalism in the United States." In *Accounting for Fundamentalism: The Dynamic Character of Movements*, edited by Martin E. Marty and R. Scott Appleby, 18–56. Chicago: University of Chicago Press, 1994.

Index

Abbot, Lyman, 24
Abrams, Minnie F., 44, 62
Adams, Maud, 151
Ahlstrom, Sydney, 19
Alexander, Charles, 94, 113n160
Alexander, Kimberly, 218
Alford, Henry, 170
Alford, Roxie, 137
Allen, Warren, 160–61
Altamont Bible Institute, 40
"Ambassadors of Christ," 147
American Bible Society, 193
American Council of Christian Churches, 177, 198–201
American Sunday School Committee, 154, 202
Ammerman, Nancy, 15
Anderson, Aaron, 164
Anderson, Allan, 4, 7, 28, 215n25
Anderson, Robert Mapes, 3, 8, 11, 20, 28, 59, 66, 68, 70, 213n15, 214, 218
Anderson, Sir Robert, 47, 100, 184n64
Angel, Luema, 41
Anglin, L. M., 158
Antichrist, 88–90, 117, 119, 155–56, 172–74
Apostasy, 87–88, 102, 127, 130, 160, 173, 190, 208
"Apostolic Faith," 48, 209
Appleby, Scott, 10
Archer, Kenneth, 217
Argue, A. H., 107
Argue, Watson, 107
Armageddon, 87, 90–91, 174
Arminianism, 12, 20, 26–27, 33, 211
Armstrong, Karen, 11–12
Arroyo Seco Camp Meeting, 70, 75, 83
Ashcroft, J. J., 107
Assemblies of God, 6, 8, 68–71, 85–86, 91–96, 98, 106–8, 110, 113, 115–16, 120–21, 125, 127, 130, 145, 149–53, 158–60, 162, 176, 182–83, 191–94, 199–200, 202–3, 207–8, 210, formation of, 69
Ayer, William, 199
Azusa Street Revival, 37–39, 43, 68, 115, 169

Ballard, Hudson, 58
Balmer, Randall, 16
Barfoot, Charles, 194
Barnhouse, Donald, 161, 170, 183, 198–200
Barr, James, 9, 16
Barratt, Thomas B., 144–45
Barth, Hattie, 80
Bartleman, Frank, 55, 57, 117n184
Barton, Cecilia, 196
Bassett, Paul, 201
Baulin, Otto, 48
Bauman, Louis, 142, 174, 184–85, 187, 198, 215
Baxter, Richard, 45, 84
Beale, David, 9, 21, 94n1
Bebbington, David, 12n54, 15, 209
Beck, James, 148
Beecher, Henry Ward, 24, 26
Beecher, Lyman, 24, 26
Been, Marion, 179n20
Bell, E. N., 69–70, 82, 98, 110–11, 113, 119, 148, 168
Bell, R. H., 174
Bellsmith, F. M., 171–72
Benson, Clarence, 153, 191
Bergunder, Michael, 6
Beskin, Nathan Cohen, 174
Bettex, Jean Fredrick, 145
Bettex, Paul, 145–46
Bible Baptist Union, 141, 185, 191
Bible conferences, 136–38
Bible Crusaders, 147
Bible Presbyterian Church, 198
Bible Union of China, 110
Biederwolf, William, 106, 138, 170

Index

Biffle, S. K., 107
Biola (University), 51, 98, 120, 215
Bishop, A. E., 144–45
Blackstone, William, 32, 87, 149
Blackwood, Roy, 181–82, 211
Blake, H. L., 66
Blanchard, Charles, 71, 85, 162–63
Blosser, J. W., 50, 67n22, 212
Blumhofer, Edith, 3, 28–30, 31n80, 66, 75n76, 92, 96, 97n20, 113, 132, 195, 209, 218
Boardman, William, 13, 30
Bob Jones University, 9
Boddy, A. A., 55, 57–58
Boddy, J. T., 90, 117–18
Bodie, Mary, 138
Bolsheviks (–ism), 119, 155, 157, 159, 172, 216
Booskirk, Jessie van, 194
Booth, Catherine, 146
Booth, William, 146n170
Booth-Clibborn, Arthur, 146n170
Booth-Clibborn, Eric, 146n170
Booth-Clibborn, William, 143–44, 146n170, 149, 208
Bosworth, Bert, 104, 114
Bosworth, F. F., 7, 99, 104–6, 112n151, 114, 120, 163, 208, 212
Bowie, Eleanor, 153–54
Bowles, Franklin, 128, 175
Boyd, Frank, 96, 110, 111n141, 147–48
Boyd, J. E., 178
Bradbury, John, 199
Brent, Charles, 99n36
Brereton, Virginia L., 3n4, 195, 217–18
Bresee, P. F., 42
Brian-Kellogg Peace Pact, 118
Briggs, Charles, 24n39, 114n166
Brookes, James, 30–31, 216
Brown, Marie Burgess, 77
Brown, Robert, 77–78, 95, 182, 195, 207
Brown, William Adams, 25
Brumback, Carl, 203
Bruner, Dale Frederick, 8, 29
Bryan, William Jennings, 71n48, 98, 106, 121, 125–28, 132, 198
Buddhism, 88
Bullinger, E. W., 162–63, 186
Burnham, Edwin, 53
Burning Bush movement, 59
Bushnell, Horace, 26, 114n166

Butlin, J. T., 99, 145n161
Caldwalder, C. H., 109
Calvinism, 14, 20, 30, 33, 216
Campbell, John, 94, 136
Campbell, Helen, 133
Camp meetings, 40–42, 57, 136
Cane Ridge Revival, 83–84
Carlyle, George, 90
Carnegie, Dale, 153
Carothers, W. F., 41
Carpenter, Joel, 10–11, 21, 28, 127n12, 164, 195, 201
Carr, A. F., 151
Carter, Howard, 171
Cartwright, Desmond, 44n51, 214
Cashwell, G. B., 39–40, 50
Catholicism, 22–23, 87, 173
Central Bible Institute, 3n2, 96, 110, 113, 115, 118n201, 134, 137
Cessationism, 76–77, 80, 84, 110, 113–14, 130–31, 139, 168, 170, 179–81, 184, 186–87, 208, 212
Chafer, Lewis Sperry, 113n160, 140, 198
Chambers, Robert, 26n48
Chambers, Oswald, 138
Chan, Simon, 6, 12
Chapell, F. L., 89, 171
Childe, Frederick, 137
China Inland Mission, 74, 81n120
Choi, Meesaeng Lee, 216
Christian and Missionary Alliance, 56–59, 65–66, 70–71, 85–86, 92–93, 104–6, 190, 211–12
Christian Science, 47, 88, 111, 114, 161
Chrysostum, John, 84, 168
Church Missionary Society, 148
Church of God, 6, 62, 68–69, 78, 84, 91–93, 95–96, 109, 119–20, 125, 149–51, 154, 158, 162, 172–76, 181–82, 199, 207–8, 211
Church of God in Christ, 207
Civil War (U.S.), 13, 19–22, 87
Clark, E. C., 173–75, 199
Clarke, Adam, 113n164, 170, 181n39
Clarke, William Newton, 25
Clayton, Allen, 66
Cole, Stewart, 10, 94n1
Collier, H. L., 118, 137, 147
Collins, A. P., 87, 91, 111
Collins, Warren, 107

Communism, 119, 155–57, 174, 184, 211
Congress of Religions, 88
Conlee, J. R., 48
Conrad, A. Z., 197
Conwell, Russell, 116–17
Cook, Glenn, 56
Cooper, A. H., 104
Copley, A. S., 138, 216
Corry, Percy, 142
Cossum, W. H., 88
Cotton, Howard, 167
Covington, A. J., 116
Cox, Harvey, 12
Cramer, Warren, 56
Crawford, Florence, 38–39, 51, 75, 209n2
Cross, M. P., 199
Crowell, Henry, 199
Culbreth, J. A., 40
Cullis, Charles, 31, 52

Dake, Finis J., 137, 175
Darby, J. N., 30, 31n79, 92
Darwinism. See Evolution.
David, Ira, 85
Davis, J. A., 84
Davis, Ralph, 199
Dayton, Donald, 7, 30, 31n83, 59, 216
Dieter, Melvin, 12n54, 213
Dilts, Lee, 118
Dispensationalism, 17, 30–31, 37, 46, 56, 59, 61–62, 81–82, 86–90, 92, 94, 96, 100, 102n60, 105, 110, 114, 116–21, 137–38, 147–49, 151, 156–57, 168n149, 169, 173–75, 186, 208, 210, 216
Divine Healing, 31, 58, 96–99, 103–8, 120–21, 133, 155–56, 181, fundamentalist critique of, 98–99, 104–5, 114, 179
Dixon, A. C., 49–51, 62, 66, 72, 89, 94–95, 108, 198, 207
Dollar, George, 9, 191n120
Dorrien, Gary, 14
Dowie, John Alexander, 32, 66, 104, 111, 136
Downie, A. H., 54
Doyle, Sir Arthur Conan, 173
Drew, Edward, 185
Drummond, Henry, 19n4
Duncan, Benjamin, 162
Duncan, E. E., 84
Duncan sisters, 7, 55
Durham, William H., 9, 39, 65–68, 75, 80, 207

Eckart, Clark, 154
Edman, Raymond, 199
Edward, G. R., 172
Edwards, Jonathan, 20, 27, 29–30
Edwards, Reginald, 104
Eiting, Fred, 152
Entzminger, Louis, 177–78, 180–81
Erdman, Charles, 210–11
Evangelicalism, definition of, 15–16, demise of, 21–23, "empire" of, 20–21, piety of, 27
Evans, J. R., 111n141, 128
Evans, William, 94, 113, 162, 164, 209
Evans, W. I., 110, 111n141
Eversole, S. A., 172
Evolution, 14–15, 24–26, 71n53, 110, 113, 121, 125–29, 133, 136n84, 149–50, 155–56, 176, 188, 191–92, 210–11
Ewart, Frank, 68, 74n70

Farrow, Lucy, 38
Falcon Camp Meeting, 40
Farrar, F. W., 143
Faulkner, T. A., 195
Faupel, D. William, 3, 12, 20, 26–27, 30, 31n80, 59, 66, 68, 86n163
Faux, William, 111n141
Federal Council of Churches, 156, 174, 177, 198–99, 218
Ferrin, Howard, 199
"Finished Work," 9, 65, 68–69, 71, 75, 207
Fink, G. F., 39, 46
Finney, Charles, 12, 20, 26–27, 29–30, 53, 83–84, 187
Fire-Baptized Holiness Association, 32
First Fruit Harvesters, 41, 57, 196–97
Fish, Milton, 147
Fitch, F. F., 102n60
Fiorenza, Francis Schüssler, 14
Fletcher, Jonathan, 59
Flower, Alice, 138
Flower, J. Roswell, 70, 85, 111n141, 113, 115, 182, 199–200
Foley, C. W., 194
Fosdick, Harry Emerson, 14, 26, 95, 110n136, 163
Fostekew, Ray, 107
Fourfold Gospel, 7–8, 30, 107, 216
Foursquare Gospel, International Church of, 8, 199–200, 207

Index

Fox, George, 84
Frey, Mae Eleanor, 58, 108–9, 175, 189–90, 214
Frodsham, Arthur, 119, 171
Frodsham, Stanley, 83–84, 97, 100, 102–3, 111–13, 115–17, 119, 121, 130–31, 141–42, 145–49, 159–60, 168–71, 182–83, 184n64, 193, 201, 208
Frost, Henry, 74, 81n120
Fuller, Charles, 164, 176, 197–98, 202
Fuller, Grace, 197, 202
Fundamentalism, and premillennialism, 11, 30, 44, 48, 208, and politics 3, critique of divine healing, 98–99, 104–5, 114, critique of pentecostalism, 43–52, 62, 66, 72–76, 99–102, 129–30, 139–41, 165–67, 177–82, 184–85, definition of, 9–12, leavening process of, 5, 201, 208, 211, 218, origin of the name, 95, relationship to pentecostalism, 3–4, 9, 17, 27, 62, 66–67, 70–71, 76, 93–94, 108, 110–16, 121, 125, 130–34, 146, 149–51, 164, 176, 200–202, 207–15, rise of, 94–96
Fundamentalist Baptists, 108–9, 177–82
Fundamentals, The, 70, 93, 98, 113
Furniss, Norman, 10

Gaebelein, A. C., 46–48, 51, 62, 70n44, 73, 76–77, 81n120, 87, 91n205, 93, 97n18, 99–104, 107, 110, 113n164, 114, 136, 139–40, 150, 166, 194, 198, 207–8, 212, 215–16
Galmond, Mary, 61
Garr, A. G. and Lillian, 38, 46, 59
Garrigas, Alice, 57
Gaston, W. T., 111n141, 182
Gee, Donald, 115, 135, 138, 142, 144, 168, 171
Gelesnoff, Count Vladimir von, 163
General Association of Regular Baptists, 141–42
Gibson, Scott, 31n81
"Gift Adventists," 53
Gladden, Washington, 19, 23
Glad Tidings Bible Institute, 138
Godbey, William B., 42–43, 68, 181n35, 207, 216
Goforth, Jonathan, 163, 187
Goins, J. L., 174
Goode, Ernest, 116, 187, 214n24

Gordon, A. J., 13, 31–32, 70n44, 89, 114, 120, 128, 133, 185, 187, 207, 216
Gordon, Ernest, 142
Gordon, George, 19, 25
Gordon, S. D., 99, 163
Gortner, J. N., 111n141, 138, 160, 167–68, 182–83, 195
Goss, Howard, 69
Gouthey, A. P., 127–28, 149, 161, 210
Grable, Marcus, 152, 192
Graham, Billy, 198
Grave, Arthur, 152
Gray, James M., 73, 93, 113n160, 128, 135, 149, 187, 198, 209, 212
Great Awakening, 20
Great Lakes Bible Institute, 138
Great Tribulation, 60–61, 81, 88–90, 102, 119–20, 139, 148
Griffith, Earle, 179n20, 180
Griffith Thomas, W. H., 94, 113n160
Gruver, H. T., 172

Hagin, Fred, 149
Haldeman, Isaac M., 77, 80, 81n120, 102, 113n160, 186, 198, 207
Hall, L. C., 87
Hambrick-Stowe, Charles E., 26n53
Hammond, Hattie, 138
Harnack, Adoph von, 25, 26n54, 188
Harris, Harriet, 8n28, 16
Harris, John, 41–42
Havner, Vance, 166–67
Hawkins, Louis, 68
Head, Marjorie, 183
Hewitt, E. F., 138
Hezmalhalch, Tom, 38
Hicks, Percy, 118
Hickson, James, 99n36, 145n161
Higher Criticism, 14–15, 25–27, 66, 71n53, 110, 118, 128, 134, 136n85, 158–59, 189
Hill, F. E., 39
Hinduism, 88
Hitler, Adolph, 156–57
Hodge, A. A., 10
Hodge, Charles, 24
Holderby, William, 104–6
Holiness movement, 4, 6, 33, and baptism of the Holy Spirit, 32, and premillennialism, 32, 59, critique of pentecostalism, 41–43, definition of, 12–13, rise of,

Holiness movement (*cont.*)
    20–21, relationship to pentecostalism, 27, 29, 33, 37, 39–40, 52, 75–76, 129, 212–13
Hollenweger, Walter, 6, 9
Holmes, N. J., 40, 50, 62, 96
Hoover, J. N., 97, 137, 148–49, 152, 154–58, 160, 176, 208, 210, 214
Horner, Ralph, 32–33, 208
Horr, George, 54
Horton, T. C., 98n31
Hoste, D. E., 81n120
Houghton, Will, 197, 199
Howard, Philip, 153
Huckabee, R. W., 42
Hugh, Edward, 158
Huguenots, 52–53, 185
Hull House (Chicago), 23, 162
Hutchison, William, 14, 26
Hutton, David, 185n66

Immigration, 22–23
Ingersol, Stanley, 112n149
Inglis, James, 31n79
Interchurch World Movement, 108, 117
Iowa Holiness Association, 32
Irenaeus, Bishop of Lyon, 52
Ironside, Harry, 75–76, 114, 165, 198, 210, 215
Irving, Edward (Irvingites), 30, 53, 74, 84, 139, 168n153
Irwin, B. H., 32–33, 208
Islam, 88, 91, 201

Jacobsen, Douglas, 3, 7, 8, 66, 96
Jamieson, S. A., 111n141
Jeffrey, George, 147, 153
Jeffreys, George and Stephen, 214
Jennings, F. C., 101–102, 166
Jensen, Clarence, 172
Jeter, J. J., 39
Jews, 22, 54, 61, 88–89, 148, 155–56, 168n149, 173–74, 184, 186
Johnson, Howard, 161
Jones, E. Stanley, 171
Jones, H. W., 94
Jones, Sam, 68
Jordan, W. A., 107
Juillerat, Howard, 175
Junk, Thomas, 39, 54

Kelley, George, 151
Kennan, George, 139
Kent, C. R., 60
Kenyon, E. W., 66
Kerr, D. W., 96, 113, 116, 118, 135, 216
Keswick (movement), 6, 11–13, 29, 33, 44, 73, 81n120, 93, 166–67, 179, 207, 210, 216, 218
Ketcham, Robert, 198
Keys, L. R., 133
Kinne, S. D., 41–42
King, Henry Churchill, 26
King, J. H., 32
King, Paul, 56–57, 86
Klink, Otto, 169–71, 188–89
Knapp, Martin Wells, 32, 59, 208, 216
Kortkamp, A. W., 107
Kostlevy, William, 59
Kraum, Cecile, 140
Ku Klux Klan, 216–17
Kumarakulasinghe, Kittie Wood, 46

LaFontaine, C. V., 42
Land, Steven, 8–9, 29
Larkin, Clarence, 137
Latimer, S. W., 173, 175, 208, 211
"Latter Rain," 47–48, 53, 56, 72–73, 114, 116, 143, 209
Lawrence, B. F., 85
Lawrence, "Brother," 138
Lawrence, Bruce, 10
Laws, Curtis Lee, 95
Laymen's Missionary Movement, 88
League of Nations, 117–18, 174
Leaman, A. H., 162
Leavitt, G. W., 46
Lee, Flavius J., 79–80, 95, 99, 120, 128, 172, 181n35, 216
Legters, Leonard, 165–66
Lemons, Frank, 120, 181n35
Lincoln, LeRoy, 185, 187
Lindbald, Frank, 107
Lindquist, Frank, 188, 217n33
Llewellyn, J. S., 126
Locke, John, 20
Logan, T. J., 172
Long, T. C., 172, 178
Lord Balfour, 91
Lovelace, Richard, 29
Luce, Alice, 148

Index

Lum, Clara, 209n2
Lupton, Levi, 39, 46, 74, 184n64
Luther, Martin, 52–53, 84, 109n132, 169
Lyell, Charles, 25

MacArthur, William, 85
Machen, J. Gresham, 142
Macintosh, Douglas, 26
Mackenzie, William, 99
Mackinlay, L. M., 111
McAlister, Harvey, 171
McAlister, R. E., 113, 169
McCafferty, William Burton, 118, 134
McCambridge, J. A., 172
McCarrell, William, 164
McConkey, J. H., 135
McCrossan, T. J., 104
McDowell, David, 56, 57n146, 86, 111n141, 113, 130, 146
McGrath, Alister, 65, 213
McGraw, Gerald, 30n77
McGraw, M. M., 144
McIntire, Carl, 198–200
McLoughlin, William, 12n54, 21n10, 31n80
McPherson, Aimee Semple, 97–98, 100–104, 106, 109, 112, 114, 120–21, 127, 132–33, 139–40, 183–85, 200, 208, 210, 212, 217–18
McPherson, Harold, 185n66
McQueen, Larry, 216
McQuilkin, Robert, 140–41, 166, 168, 210
Mahan, Asa, 12, 30
Manley, William, 38
"Mark of the Beast," 92, 119, 155
Markley, Morse, 106
Marks, I. H., 173
Marsden, George, 10–11, 14–15, 19, 21, 26–27, 107
Martin, C. C., 84
Marty, Martin, 4, 8, 15
Marvin Camp Meeting, 41
Massee, J. C., 95
Masserano, Frank, 128
Mathews, Shailer, 14, 26, 95
Mathewson, B. G., 53
Matthews, Mark, 145
Maurice, Frederick, 25
Mauro, Philip, 72–73, 93, 101n52, 126, 149, 210
Meeker, Charles, 162

Meier, Irving, 107
Mencken, H. L., 25, 125
Menzies, William, 29, 152–53, 193, 199n181
Methodists, 12, 19, 24, 31–32, 49, 53, 56, 68, 78, 84, 86, 98, 106–7, 125, 136–37, 165, 172–73, 211, 213, 217
Meyer, F. B., 153, 185, 187
Miles, T. S., 151n5
Miller, B. C., 99
Miller, Elmer C., 185–87, 210, 217
Miller, Jacob, 130
Miller, R.V., 88
Moberg, David, 5, 201
Modernism, and ethics, 29, and missions, 25, 110, definition of, 14–15, relationship to fundamentalism, 11, 17, 33, 129, 178–79, relationship to pentecostalism, 3, 27, 67, 103–4, 135–36, 151, 157–64, 173, 187–91, 210, 211n11, 212, takeover of seminaries, 25
Moeran, J. W. W., 134
Montanism, 29, 139, 167–68
Montgomery, Carrie Judd, 40, 57, 96–97
Montgomery, George, 57
Moody Bible Institute, 49, 73, 105n94, 113, 117n184, 120, 138, 148, 153, 162–64, 167, 171–72, 191
Moody Church, 49–50, 57, 105, 126, 130, 164–65, 207, 209
Moody, D. L., 13, 19, 30–31, 40, 136, 153, 187, 207
Moody, William, 19
Moody, William E., 110, 136, 160, 194–95
Moorhead, Max Wood, 84–85, 113
Morgan, George, 66
Morgan, G. Campbell, 83, 113n164, 136, 210
Morgan, J. P., 22, 156
Mormonism, 7, 29, 74, 84, 111
Morris, Frank, 106–7
Morrison, Henry Clay, 112n149, 211
Moss, Harold, 136, 144
Mott, John, 25
Moule, Handley, 59, 113n164
Muir, Elmer, 107
Müller, George, 31, 147n181, 153
Munhall, L. W., 97, 106, 113n160, 121, 161
Murrah, E. L., 60
Murray, Andrew, 116, 129, 138, 163, 170, 173, 187
Murray, Iain, 30n78

Murray, Irene, 194
Mussolini, Benito, 119–20, 148–49, 156, 211
Muslim. See Islam.
Myland, David Wesley, 56, 73, 89–90, 91n205, 92, 216

Naish, Reginald, 149
National Association of Evangelicals, 5–6, 17, 71, 154, 176–77, 183, 190, 218, formation of, 196–202
National Holiness Association, 13, 31
Nazarene, Church of the, 42, 112n149, 172, 201, 209
Needham, George, 21
Nelson, P. C., 171
New England Fellowship, 197, 199
Niagara Prophecy Conference, 13, 19, 21, 31n81, 31n84, 102n60
Niebuhr, H. Richard, 11n45
Niebuhr, Reinhold, 15
Nienkirchen, Charles, 58, 86
Noll, Mark, 15–16
Norris, Frank, 109–110, 144, 177–182, 184–85, 198, 200, 210–11, 215
North Carolina Holiness Association, 40
Northern Baptist Convention, 11, 27, 94–95, 108, 110n136, 141, 189–90
Northfield Conference, 13, 19
Nichol, John Thomas, 8
Numbers, Ronald, 125

Oberlin College, 12–13, 26, 30
Ockenga, Harold John, 16, 197–200, 218
O'Guinn, Carl, 131, 170, 182
Old Orchard Beach (Maine), 31, 57, 197
Oliver, French, 164
Olson, Kenneth G., 189
Olson, Roger, 27
Opperman, D. C. O., 96
Orthodox Presbyterian Church, 142
Osterberg, A. G., 131
Otis, Addie, 40
Otis, Samuel, 40, 44, 53, 54n122, 57, 92
Ott, Albert, 152
Ozman, Agnes, 33, 37, 39

Paine, Stephen, 199
Paley, William, 103, 189
Palmer, Phoebe, 13, 20–21, 27, 30, 37, 85
Panin, Ivan, 135, 161, 189

Panton, D. M., 106, 117, 119, 139, 142, 148, 150, 196, 212
Parham, Charles, 19, 32–33, 37–38, 74, 184n64, 187, 217
Parker, D. R., 75–76, 78
Parrot, Everett, 183
Paul, Jonathan, 86
Paulk, Earl, 199
Pearlman, Myer, 138, 148, 152–53, 188–89, 190n112
Peckham, Frank, 134
Peirce, Willard, 118
Pember, G. H., 53, 89n191
Pemberton, George, 178
Pentecostal Holiness Church, 32, 71, 199, 207
Pentecostalism, and premillennialism, 17, 56, 59–62, 90–92, 146–50, 172–76, 208, defense of, 52–56, 62, 67, 77–85, 102–3, 111–13, 141–46, 167–72, 181–82, 185–87, definition of, 6–9, Oneness, 8, 66, 75–76, 207, 209n5, relationship to fundamentalism, 3–4, 9, 17, 27, 62, 66–67, 70–71, 76, 93–96, 108, 110–16, 121, 125, 130–34, 146, 149–51, 164, 176, 200–202, 207–15, rise of, 38–41
Percy, Martyn, 215
Perkins, Jonathan, 107, 182–84, 200
Perkins, Noel, 199
Perry, Sam, 84, 91
Peterson, Paul, 145
Pethrus, Lewi, 105
Pettingill, William, 198n171
Philpot, Peter, 113, 185
Pierson, A. T., 13, 19n4, 30–31, 43–46, 58, 62, 93, 113n164, 114, 128, 135, 148, 198, 207, 212
Pierson, Delevan, 31n83, 135
Pike, J. M., 112
Pinson, M. M., 69
Piper, William H., 77n92, 87, 125
Pleasant Grove Camp Meeting, 40
Plessis, David du, 201, 203
Plymouth Brethren, 31n81, 53, 100–101, 102n60
Pohle, Ella, 81n120
Polhill, Cecil, 214n24
Prayer Meeting Revival, 13, 21, 27, 53
Presbyterians, 11, 70, 78, 83, 104–7, 125, 141, 165, 172, 199
Preston, C. E., 53n114, 87

Index

Price, Charles, 103–4, 120, 136–37, 162, 183, 210
Prince, H. J., 47, 184n64
Prohibition, 125, 127
Prophetic Society (London), 116, 214
Pope, Liston, 214
Pope, Willard, 107
Postmillennialism, 30, 31n82, 87
Potter, Charles Francis, 159
Powers, Janet Evers, 193
Proctor, W. C., 113
Purkie, Lida, 40

Quakers, 3, 20, 30, 52–53, 66n9, 85, 93, 183
Quinn, C. J., 61

Rader, Paul, 105–6, 113n160, 121, 164, 180n22, 183, 202, 208, 215
Ramabai, Pandita, 44–46
Randall, Ian, 209
Rapture, 46, 60–61, 81, 90, 118–19, 148, 159, 211
Rausch, David, 101
Rauschenbusch, Walter, 23
Rawlson, A. F., 55
Reed, David, 70n44
Rees, Byron, 216
Rees, Seth, 68
Reformed, 6, 8–9, 11–13, 20, 27, 29–30, 66, 211, 216
Reiber, Alma, 194
Reich, Max, 138
Reid, Isaiah, 32
Reiff, Anna, 126, 130
Renfrow, Guy, 170
Restorationism, 28–29
Rice, John R., 177–82, 200, 215
Richey, Ray, 106–7, 120, 183, 208, 212
Ridout, George, 112
Riggs, Ralph, 152–53, 192, 199, 216
Riley, William B., 48, 62, 71, 94–95, 102, 104, 106, 108, 111, 113n160, 114, 125, 129–31, 136, 138, 141, 144, 172n178, 193–94, 197–98, 208, 210–12, 215, 217
Rimmer, Harry, 161
Ritschl, Albert, 25
"Robber barons," 22
Robeck, Cecil (Mel), 38, 51
Robert, Dana, 31n83, 44
Robertson, Frederick, 25

Robinson, Charles, 128, 135–36, 144, 160, 169, 189, 195–96, 208, 210
Robinson, Elsie, 39
Rockefeller, J. D., 22, 95
Rogers, Willie, 174
Romanticism, 25–26
Rood, Paul, 197
Roosevelt, Elliot, 181n40
Rose, Susan, 15
Rudner, Lewis, 54
Ruff, Ernest, 109n132
Russell, Marguerite, 67
Russell, R. M., 94
Russian and Eastern European Mission, 145, 163
Russian Missionary Society, 145
Rutgers, William, 210n8
Ruthven, Jon, 114n166
Ryan, M. L., 41

Salvation Army, 107, 146
Sandeen, Ernest, 10–11, 31n79, 94n1
Sanders, Carl E. II, 31n79
Sanford, Frank, 32, 111
Sawders, J. E., 41, 56
Schell, William, 85
Schleiermacher, Frederick, 25
Schmidt, Gustav, 145
Schmauk, Theodore, 153
Scopes Trial, 10, 25, 125, 127, 211
Scofield, C. I., 19, 31, 70n44, 81–82, 90, 111, 113n160, 118, 140, 144, 148, 156, 168–69, 175, 187, 198, 216
Scofield Reference Bible, 17, 37, 61–62, 77n91, 81n122, 82, 86, 88, 90, 93, 110–11, 142n139, 175, 186n84, 187, 196, 207–8, 211
Scott, Douglas, 145
Scottish Common Sense Realism, 10, 12n54, 27
Scriptures, defense of, 134–36, 150, 158–62, 188–89, 202, 208
Scroggie, Graham, 58
Scruby, John, 112
Sea Coast Bible Conference, 19
Second Advent, 27, 60, 62, 155, 209
Second Great Awakening, 20, 83–84
Seiss, J. A., 175
Selecman, Charles, 173
Sexton, Elizabeth, 55, 60–61, 84, 86–87, 92

Index

Seyda, Robert, 173
Seymour, William J., 37–38, 43, 52, 59–60, 68–69, 209n2
Shaw, S. B., 57n138
Shelhammer, E. E., 181n20
Sheppard, Gerald, 71, 194
Shields, T. T., 131, 141, 167, 185, 188, 215
Shiloh Bible Institute, 138
Shoemaker, Vaughn, 164
Shreve, Charles, 97, 155, 175
Shuler, Bob, 98, 150, 215
Simmons, Dale, 66
Simmons, E. L., 199
Simmons, V. P., 52–54
Simmons, William, 216
Simpson, A. B., 30–31, 33, 57, 70n44, 71, 81n120, 86, 96, 104, 120, 198, 207, 215
Simpson, W. W., 81, 86
Sinclair, Upton, 23
Sisson, Elizabeth, 117
Smale, Joseph, 58
Smith, Charles, 127
Smith, Gerald K. L., 184
Smith, "Gypsy," 50, 107
Smith, Hannah Whitall, 30, 138
Smith, Oswald, 105–6, 149, 157, 163–64, 174, 212
Smith, Sydney, 101n53
Smith, Timothy, 16, 19
Smith, William Pearsall, 30
Soltau, George, 100, 102
Southern Baptist Convention, 109, 111, 211
Spiritualism (spiritism), 88, 100, 139, 173, 183
Spittler, Russell, 12, 42n33, 96, 129, 201, 218
Spurgeon, Charles, 134
Staat, Loren, 152
Stalin, Josef, 157
Stanford, P. T., 179n20
Stealey, C. P., 177
Steelberg, Wesley R., 147
Steele, Daniel, 68n28
Steil, Harry, 196
Stemme, Harry, 162–64, 176, 212
Stewart, Lyman, 51, 98, 215
Stockton, Amy, 133
Stone Church (Chicago), 56, 65, 85–86, 88, 156, 158–59, 211
Strathearn, Harold, 177
Straton, George, 132n58, 133

Straton, John Roach, 99, 113n160, 131–34, 150, 159, 190, 198–99, 208
Straton, Warren, 132–33
Strong, A. H., 113n164
Studd, C. T. and George, 214n24
Student Volunteer Missions, 25
Stumpf, Louis, 131
Sunday, Billy, 104, 113, 132
Sunday schools, 17, 146–47, 149, 151–54, 162, 191–93, 202, 208
Sung, Kee Ho, 31n82
Sutton, Matthew, 16, 127, 218
Sweet, William Warren, 24
Swanson, C. W., 145
Swing, David, 15, 24, 33
Synan, Vinson, 29, 125, 202

Tarpley, J. A., 181n20
Taylor, Nathaniel, 26
Texico Bible Institute, 138
Tharp, Zeno, 174
Thomas, Bessie, 173
Thompson, A. E., 30n77, 91n204
Todd, S. C., 50, 67n22
Tomlinson, A. J., 78–80, 91, 95–96, 109, 181, 207
Tomlinson, Homer, 158
Torrey, R. A., 13, 19n4, 25n43, 52, 62, 74, 79–80, 83, 93–94, 98, 102, 114, 130, 136, 140, 149, 163–64, 166, 172, 180, 184n64, 187, 197–98, 207–9, 215
Towner, William K., 97–98, 103, 109, 155, 175, 190, 214
Troeltsch, Ernst, 25–26
Trollinger, William, 193
Trotter, William, 51
Trudel, Dorothea, 31
Trumbull, Charles G., 76, 138, 165n117, 167, 170, 198
Tufts, Goram, 43n40
Tunmore, Joseph, 182
Turner, May, 107
Turney, H. M., 39
Twain, Mark, 23

Ulster Revival, 52
United Brethren, 99, 107, 116, 142
Union Rescue Mission (Los Angeles), 51
Urbanization, 23
Urshan, Andrew, 49–50, 80–81, 207, 209

261

Index

Utley, Uldine, 131–34, 150, 208, 212

Vacation Bible School, 147, 153–54
Vogler, Fred, 183
Von, Ora de, 138
Vienna Holiness Association, 41

Wacker, Grant, 28, 42, 209, 212–14
Wakefield, Gavin, 57n144
Waldvogel, Edith. See Blumhofer, Edith.
Walker, J. H., 158, 199
Walle, Bernie van de, 59
Walthall, Jethro, 134, 137n91
Ward, A. G., 103
Ware, Steven, 28
Warfield, B. B., 10–11, 13, 76, 114, 139
Warner, Charles, 23
Watson, Sydney, 149
Weaver, Albert, 88, 90
Webb, Burt, 135
Webb, L. A., 158
Weber, Darryl, 101n56
Weigle, Luther, 153
Welch, J. W., 91n203, 110–11, 182
Wellhausen, Julius, 25
Wells, Amos, 153
Welsh Revival, 21, 44, 83
Wesley, John, 30, 52–53, 84–85, 113n164, 167, 211, 216
Wesleyanism, 30, 68, 92, 207, 216, 218
West, Nathaniel, 148
"Whitbyanism." See Postmillennialism.
White, Alma, 43
Whittle, Daniel, 30n77
Wheatlake, S. K., 79

Wheeler, J. C., 88
Williams, Bert, 116
Williams, Ernest Swing, 111n141, 113n164, 127, 142, 171, 182–83, 193, 199
Wilson, A. A., 169n155
Wilson, Lewis, 28
Wimber, John, 202
Winona Lake Bible Conference, 132, 136, 170
Winrod, Gerald, 157, 161, 183, 215
Wittich, Philip, 159
Woelfkin, Cornelius, 95
Women, controversy over, 76–79, 99–100, 193–94
Woodward, Adelaide, 145
Woodworth-Etter, Maria, 74, 97, 105
World's Christian Fundamentals Association, 71, 94, 101n53, 110, 113n160, 125, 129–31, 144, 150, 191, 197, 208, 210
World's Faith Missionary Association, 66
World War I, 6, 11, 13, 19, 88, 90–92, 95, 117–18, 148, 151n5, 175, 216
World War II, 176, 199
Worrell, A. S., 41, 54
Wright, Elwin, 41, 176, 197–200
Wright, Joel, 41, 196–97
Wuthnow-Lawson Ecological Model, 4–5, 37, 65, 213, 219

Yeomans, Amy, 137, 147
Yeomans, Lilian, 171
Yoakum, F. A., 96
Young, Edward (Eddie), 112, 116
Young Man's Christian Association, 158, 163

Zimmerman, Thomas, 71, 199n181

www.ingramcontent.com/pod-product-compliance
Lightning Source LLC
Chambersburg PA
CBHW081418230426
43668CB00016B/2274